The Whole Mystery of Christ

THE WHOLE MYSTERY
OF CHRIST

CREATION AS INCARNATION
IN MAXIMUS CONFESSOR

JORDAN DANIEL WOOD

foreword by
JOHN BEHR

University of Notre Dame Press
Notre Dame, Indiana

Library of Congress Control Number: 2022935756

ISBN: 978-0-268-20347-4 (Hardback)
ISBN: 978-0-268-20350-4 (WebPDF)
ISBN: 978-0-268-20346-7 (Epub)

Nicht jedwedem ist gegeben, das End zu wissen, wenigen,
die Uranfänge des Lebens zu sehen, noch wenigeren, das Ganze vom
Ersten bis zum Letzten der Dinge zu durchdenken.

—F. W. J. von Schelling, *Die Weltalter*

In hac autem consideratione est perfectio illuminationis mentis,
dum quasi in sexta die videt hominem factum ad imaginem Dei.
Si enim imago est similitudo expressiva, dum mens nostra contemplatur
in Christo Filio Dei, qui est imago Dei invisibilis per naturam,
humanitatem nostram tam mirabiliter exaltatem, tam ineffabiliter unitam,
videndo simul in unum primum et ultimum, summum et imum,
circumferentiam et centrum, *alpha et omega*, causatum et causam,
Creatorem et creaturam, librum sciliet *scriptum intus et extra;* iam
pervenit ad quandam rem perfectam, ut cum Deo ad perfectionem
suarum illuminationum in sexto gradu quasi in sexta die perveniat, nec
aliquid iam amplius restet nisi dies requiei, in qua per mentis excessum
requiescat humanae mentis perspicacitas *ab omni opere, quod patrarat.*

—St. Bonaventure, *Itinerarium mentis in Deum* VI.7

αὐτου γάρ ἐσμεν ποίημα, κτισθέντες ἐν Χριστῷ Ἰησοῦ ἐπὶ ἔργοις
ἀγαθοῖς οἷς προητοίμασεν ὁ θεὸς ἵνα ἐν αὐτοῖς περιπατήσωμεν.

—Ephesians 2:10

Βούλεται γὰρ ἀεὶ καὶ ἐν πᾶσιν ὁ τοῦ Θεοῦ Λόγος καὶ Θεὸς τῆς αὐτοῦ
ἐνσωματώσεως ἐνεργεῖσθαι τὸ μυστήριον.

—St. Maximus Confessor, *Ambigua ad Iohannem* 7.22

CONTENTS

FOREWORD

John Behr

According to *The Martyrology of Jerome*, "On March 25, our Lord Jesus Christ was crucified, conceived, and the world was made." Whatever the original author made of this coincidence of dates and the sequence in which the actions are given, it summarizes well this exceptional and groundbreaking—and provocative—book by Jordan Daniel Wood!

The heart of this present work is not Maximus's "Christology" but rather the "Christo-logic" that undergirds his theology as a whole. As has long been known, Maximus asserts that "the Word of God and God wills eternally and in all to accomplish the mystery of his Incarnation" (*Amb.* 7, and repeatedly in other formulations elsewhere). Such statements have routinely been taken as metaphorical or as extending the work of "the [real] Incarnation" on a cosmic scale. Jordan, however, takes Maximus at his word. He does this by first exploring, with great precision, the metaphysics of Neo-Chalcedonian Christology—Maximus's Christo-logic—in a much more comprehensive manner than is generally done. Doing so shows that it is precisely in Christ, who is both God and human, without confusion, in one hypostasis, that the very distinction between uncreated and created is at once grounded, differentiated, and unified, so that the idea of *creatio ex nihilo* proves to be *creatio ex Deo*. This then provides the basis—the Christo-logic again—for a sophisticated treatment of protology and eschatology, necessarily treated separately though ultimately not to be divided. Here we read a truly profound exposition of Maximus's

ix

otherwise perplexing assertion that Adam turned away from God "to-gether with coming-into-being" (something also never really taken seri-ously in Maximian scholarship), thereby bringing about the phenomenal but illusory (and death-dealing) world, which is nevertheless inscribed, through the juxtaposition of providence and judgment, within the cre-ative work of God. And so God's creation is brought to completion at the end, when the creature, necessarily brought into existence involuntarily (for how could it be otherwise?), now voluntarily gives assent to be born into life in *and as* Christ, entailing that creation is indeed Incarnation.

Jordan's argument is complex and sophisticated yet laid out clearly and comprehensibly. After an initial review of the way in which Maxi-mian scholarship has treated such problematics (largely by avoiding the implications of Maximus's words), the bulk of the work is four tightly argued and structured chapters. The argument running throughout these chapters is presented concisely at the end of the first chapter, in terms of two premises (first, the four elements of Maximus's Christo-logic, and, second, how these four elements likewise define his "cosmo-logic") and the conclusion (that "Incarnation" does in fact mean in cosmology what it also means in Christology), as well as how these four chapters all address different aspects of the statement from *Ambiguum* 7 quoted above. The Preface discusses the hermeneutical issues involved in doing historical theology, and the Conclusion explores the implications that his findings have for more systematic questions about how we understand God, Christ, and creation. Jordan also offers a most useful "Analytic Appen-dix" of the key terms used by Maximus, noting with precision the way in which they are used; reading through the Appendix, one can see, *in nuce*, the grand scheme laid out. In fact, readers might do well to begin there before working through the main text.

There is one particular aspect of Jordan's work that I would like to emphasize. In his Preface, discussing what it means that his work is a piece of historical theology, Jordan comments that "*theology* is the noun that *historical* modifies." He explains this by reference to a point made by Bernard Lonergan, that the task of the historian is to comprehend "texts" rather than the "objects" these texts refer to, in this case the mystery of Christ that Maximus expounds in all its dimensions. He also points to the notion of a "thick retrieval," meaning, first, listening attentively to the author, but then also bringing into the conversation the author's own questions. As Gadamer made so clear, understanding always takes place in a hermeneutical circle. Understanding is always historical (how could it be otherwise?), but understanding is always in the present (again, how could it be otherwise?). One must project a historical horizon, he insists, to hear the distinctive voice of the author one hopes to hear. Yet if understanding is to be achieved, this horizon cannot "become solidified into the self-alienation of a past consciousness"; rather, it "is overtaken by our own present horizon of understanding. In the process of understanding, a real fusing of horizons occurs."[1] In such a "melding of horizons" we will inevitably find more in a text, a surplus of meaning; this is not a claim to "understand the author better than he understood himself" but a further understanding resulting from a conversation. Perhaps one can go further. As Bakhtin asserted: "Works break through the boundaries of their own time, they live in centuries, that is, in *great time* and frequently (with great works, always) their lives there are more intense and fuller than are their lives within their own time. . . . It seems paradoxical that . . . great works continue to live in the distant future. In the process of their posthumous life they are enriched with new meanings, new significance: it is as though these works outgrow what they were in the epoch of their creation."[2] Having read a great interpretation of a great work of art, for instance, one can never see that work in the same way again; text and interpretation have, in Gadamer's terms, fused. Achieving this requires meticulous historical study, careful analysis of the text, and, in this way, hearing the voice of the author. But it also requires great clarity of mind of the scholar, asking the right questions to find meaningful answers and so arrive at a new expression of the reality itself and the vision of a new profundity.

It is just such a vision that we meet in Jordan's book. He has presented us not simply with a picture of one aspect, as it were, of Maximus's theology, to take its place alongside other historical examinations, but rather the whole vision, that which underlies everything else, but seen again, anew. It is indeed a remarkable achievement, a work of theology proper, worked out through rigorous historical study, yet offering a systematic vision grounded in the crucified and risen Lord. It is my hope that, precisely as a work of historical *theology*, this contribution can help reunify not only the increasingly separated fields within theology, as a singular discipline, but also the supposedly distinct "doctrines" that are really nothing other than various aspects of the single and whole mystery that it contemplates.

PREFACE

Perhaps the last serious Western reader of Maximus Confessor (580–662 AD), prior to the twentieth century at least, was the Irish monk, prodigious translator of significant Greek fathers (Maximus among them), and court theologian John Scotus Eriugena (815–77 AD). Eriugena attributes many insights to Maximus. He credits Maximus with special insight into the riddle of the world's procession from God. And so he writes in the preface to his *versio Latina* of Maximus's *Ambigua ad Iohannem*:

> To mention a few of many points, [Maximus most lucidly explains] in what way the Cause of all things, who is God, is both a simple and manifold One: what sort of procession there is—and here I mean the multiplication of divine Goodness through all the things which are—which descends from the summit all the way down, first through the general essence of all things, then through the most general genera, then through less general genera, still further through more specific species right into the most specific species, even into differentia and properties. And again, concerning the same divinity, we see what sort of reversion of Goodness there is—I mean the gathering together, through those same grades, from the things that exist in infinite diversity and multiplicity right up to that simplest unity of all things, which is in God and which God is. So [we see] that God is all things and all things are God. And [we understand] indeed in what way this divine procession into all things is called ἀναλυτικὴ, that is, unraveling, but reversion [is called] θέωσις—deification.[1]

Maximus taught Eriugena how the light of God's ineffable transcendence most glitters when we see that and how God and the created world are "one and the same."[2] And to see this you need the crucial lens Maximus cuts: the "primordial reasons" of all things not only find their eternal ground in the Word of God, they "are the very [Word] Himself."[3] God and world are identical because the one Word is both.

I share Eriugena's conviction that with Maximus dawned what may be the profoundest insight of patristic tradition into the peculiar role the Word plays in God's creative act, the Word who remains consubstantial with Father and Spirit even as he descends into and as the generation of all things. I stand with Eriugena too when he says of the God-world relation—more exactly, how God and world are identical and distinct in the Word—that "there is no more profound question than this that seekers after the truth should investigate."[4] I sympathize still more when Eriugena, dumb before "the manner and reason of the establishment of all things in the Word," yet sighs, "Let the one speak who can; myself, I confess I do not know."[5] In one more way I follow Eriugena: just here, where the trail runs cold, I look to Maximus.

Hence a broad and systematic question animates my study: Does the historical Incarnation of the Word disclose anything about the fundamental God-world relation, and if yes, what? I pose this question to Maximus, who, if the genre of ἐρωταπόκρισεις that much of his oeuvre assumes offers any indication, would not blithely dismiss such a ζήτημα.[6] That this question motivates the study does not mean the study can resolve it, of course. But it might make a start. I take up another of Maximus's practices, though without his ingenuity, in hunt of his answer: I comment on texts in Maximus that are, I think, misread, or at least read shallowly. So the systematic question becomes an exegetical one too. I ask it thus: What is the relation between creation and Incarnation in Maximus?

I argue that Maximus conceives creation as Incarnation. More precisely, creation and Incarnation are identified in Maximus because they bear the same logic and are ultimately the same event or act. To those familiar with Maximus or his modern commentators, this may appear a prosaic if overstated thesis. Many have spoken of the intimate link in Maximus's theology between his Neo-Chalcedonian Christology and his conception of the world.[7] Who among those who have read it could forget that breathtaking declaration, this book's main epigraph: "The Word of God, very God, wills that the mystery of his Incarnation be actualized always and in all things"?[8] Still I contend not only that recent scholarship on Maximus has moved noticeably away from taking this cosmic Incarnation as literal Incarnation—where *literal* means in the technical sense of Christology proper, that is, according to the very logic of the Incarnate Word—but that Maximus's readers have seldom taken him literally here, even his first and greatest reader in the West, Eriugena.[9]

A BRIEF WORD ON METHOD

This is a work of historical theology. *Theology* is the noun that *historical* modifies. Historical theology, if it be anything other than history or systematic (or moral, or fundamental, etc.) theology, cannot forget that *theology* names its substance, *historical* its first quality. My focus on Maximus, one of the brightest luminaries in the patristic era, surely makes this study *historical*. It will therefore traffic in word studies, intertextual connections (patristic and philosophical), liturgical context, the Greek monastic lifestyle, and all the rest as they prove pertinent. The noun *theology* does not justify shoddy analysis of the sources in their intricate settings. But neither does understanding a text historically amount to theology, even when the text speaks theologically.

Bernard Lonergan helpfully frames this approach in the following way. The historian aims to comprehend "texts," not necessarily the "objects" these texts refer to. The objects themselves belong to systematic theology.[10] The difference here, as Lonergan also knows, is not that history merely reports while theology (or philosophy) constructs or comprehends.[11] True, the rise of historical consciousness in the modern era initially induced a decidedly von Rankean, positivist outlook in academic history—"Wie es eigentlich gewesen!"[12] Positivists wanted history to replicate the method of the natural sciences in order to replicate their success too. That view died, and not simply under the knife of postmodern philosophy and critical theory. The hard sciences themselves came to know better than to indulge any simplistic subject-object methodological partition. In his 1957 Gifford lectures, for example, Werner Heisenberg found occasion to ramify quantum theory, which he had formulated thirty years prior, into broader precincts. His ten theses pronounce plainly: "Natural science does not simply describe and explain nature; it is a part of the interplay between nature and ourselves; it describes nature as exposed to our method of questioning."[13] Since "methods and object can no longer be separated from each other," Heisenberg concludes thus: *"The scientific world-view has ceased to be a scientific view in the true sense of the word."*[14] And if so in natural science, certainly in history.[15]

Still more in historical *theology*. I seek more than Maximus's meaning; I seek also the truth he means. Historical theology cannot limit itself to simple repetition or observation. It can suspect an author of inconsistency or even bad faith. It can ask whether an author's view is true or false, and indeed perhaps more or less true than the author herself did or could know. Theology seeks revealed truth. And divine truth, who is the frolicsome Word playing in ten thousand places (to pair Maximus with Gerard Manley Hopkins),[16] can surface in words whose original intent was not the fullness of that infinite Word—for all true words remain preeminently the Word's before any author's.[17]

In fact, permit me another theological justification here. Against certain trends that would commend a strict historicism around scholarly treatments of Maximus's thought, I maintain that those who wish to give Maximus the spiritual and theological authority he merits should expect his words to disclose far more than their apparently plain sense.[18] Observe Maximus's remark in the prologue of the *Ambigua ad Iohannem* regarding one of his greatest authorities, St. Gregory of Nazianzus: "For you are well aware that Saint Gregory the Theologian was a man of profound thoughts but of comparatively few words, and so he compels his interpreters—even those who command extraordinary powers of speech and philosophical brilliance—to go on at great length and touch on a wide range of subjects."[19] Maximus suggests that the mark of a truly illuminating intellect is its ability to generate thought beyond the supposedly intended meaning of its words. And to state perhaps the deepest motive for putting specific questions to Maximus's writings: the more one believes Maximus's words to bear some special authority, even divine inspiration, the more one should anticipate their nearly limitless power to generate fresh speculative insight. That, after all, is just what Maximus claims of divine scripture and Gregory's words alike.[20] I therefore submit that overcautious reticence to ask of Maximus's oeuvre pointed speculative questions, however reverent one's disposition, would amount to denying the divine authority of his words. At the very least it would mean refusing to follow his own example. Yet is he not worthy of imitation?

We must then allow historical theology to ask luminaries a question they might not have asked themselves, or at least not in precisely the same terms. I suspect this is what Cyril O'Regan intimates when he calls Hans Urs von Balthasar's method "thick retrieval."[21] Retrieving requires first listening to the author in his or her own voice. That is good conversation etiquette.[22] But the retrieval, the conversation, is *thick*, inevitably saddled with the questioner's own worries and wonders. It is thick too because what the questioner thinks she hears from her bygone interlocutor she must comprehend, judge, and communicate in today's idiom. There is nothing frivolous or feigned about this enterprise. Nor is it unworthy or impertinent.

Happily Balthasar's method appears to have made a comeback in modern Maximus scholarship. Paul Blowers makes liberal use of Balthasar's "theodramatic" categories in his recent and knowledgeable presentation of Maximus.[23] And some scholars have ventured defenses of the kinds of questions Balthasar asked. Many once worried that Balthasar's method transgresses by anachronism. Can you really put Hegel's questions to Maximus? Élie Ayroulet takes a convincing and optimistic view: "Rather than accusing the Balthasarian reading of anachronism, might we not see therein evidence of the inspiring and creative potency of Maximian thought?"[24] Joshua Lollar (as well as Ayroulet) concedes the predictable perils involved in laying modern concerns at Maximus's feet but also warns us to "be equally cautious with ready dismissals and charges of anachronism lest we miss an essential component of von Balthasar's interpretation of Maximus, namely, his performance of him."[25] I proceed in concert with these commentators. And so I borrow Ayroulet's words to characterize this study's fundamental approach and animating spirit: "Engaging Maximus's texts in a lively manner, letting them inspire us and thereby to progress in our own understanding of the faith—these are the objectives of our method, which seeks to be that of a speculative and systematic theology in the spirit of Maximus the Confessor."[26]

ACKNOWLEDGMENTS

Over the course of this book's genesis and gestation I had the privilege of incurring many debts. I shared the burden of this undertaking most directly with my family. To my wife, Alexis, and to our four daughters, Rayna, Edith, Magdalena, and Fionnuala—I am forever and happily indebted to you. I thank my parents and two brothers (along with their families) for their support, which always comes in many forms.

Since the book began as a dissertation written and defended at Boston College, I wish to thank my committee there. My immense gratitude to Boyd Taylor Coolman, Rev. Brian Dunkle, S.J., Paul M. Blowers, and John R. Betz. Their patient reading, questioning, and guidance made this study far better than it would have been otherwise. Of course they are responsible for none of its errors. Several professors and colleagues encouraged me along the way: Brian Robinette, Andrew L. Prevot, Ty Monroe, Clifton Stringer, and Katie Wrisley-Shelby. Timothy Morgan proved a perspicacious interlocutor. I also received vital encouragement from many masters, particularly when my stamina waned. I am very grateful to Rev. John Behr (particularly for his lovely Foreword), David Bentley Hart, and Aristotle Papanikolaou for their unflagging support. Finally I must acknowledge my very best friends. These possess eversharp intellects, and I am so fortunate to call them theological comrades: Jack Pappas, Taylor Ross, and especially Justin Shaun Coyle. But they too should not be held liable for what follows, except for, of course, what is actually good.

ABBREVIATIONS

MAXIMUS'S WORKS

These are cited without being preceded by Maximus's name as author.

Add.	*Additamenta* (enumerated by Roosen)
Amb.	*Ambigua ad Thomam et Iohannem*
Amb. ad Ioh.	*Ambigua ad Iohannem* (for prologue separately enumerated)
Amb. ad Thom.	*Ambigua ad Thomam* (for prologue separately enumerated)
CC	*Capita de charitate*
CT	*Capita theologiae et oeconomiae*
Ep.	*Epistulae* 1–45
Exp. Orat. Dom.	*Expositio Orationis Dominicae*
In psal.	*Expositio in psalmum 59*
Lib. ascet.	*Liber asceticus*
Myst.	*Mystagogia*
Opusc.	*Opuscula theologica et polemica*
Pyr.	*Disputatio cum Pyrrho*
Q. et dub.	*Quaestiones et dubia*
Q. Thal.	*Quaestiones ad Thalassium*

OTHER

ACO	*Acta conciliorum oecumenicorum.* Edited by Eduard Schwartz and Johannes Straub. Berolini: W. De Gruyter, 1914–.
Aetius, *Plac.*	*Placita*
Alexander of Aphrodisias, *De mixt.*	*De mixtione*
Aquinas, Thomas, *ST*	*Summa theologiae*
Aristotle, *Cat.*	*Categoriae*
———, *De an.*	*De anima*
———, *Metaph.*	*Metaphysica*
———, *Phys.*	*Physica*
———, *Po.*	*Poetica*
Athanasius, *Contra gent.*	*Contra gentes*
———, *De incarn. Verb*	*De incarnatione Verbi Dei*
———, *Ep. ad Afros.*	*Ad Afros epistola synodica*
Augustine, *De div. quaest.*	*De diversis quaestionibus*
Basil the Great, *Ep.*	*Epistulae* 1–366
CAG	Commentaria in Aristotelem Graeca
CCSG	Corpus Christianorum, Series Graeca. Turnhout: Brepols, 1976–.
Clement of Alexandria, *Protr.*	*Protrepticus*
———, *Strom.*	*Stromateis*
CSCO	Corpus Scriptorum Christianorum Orientalium. 1903–.
Cyril of Alexandria, *Ep.*	*Epistulae* 1–110
Cyril of Scythopolis, *Libel*	*Libellus de erroribus Origenianis*

Diodochus of Photice, *De perf.*	*Capita centum de perfectione spirituali*
Dionysius, *DN*	*De divinis nominibus*
———, *EH*	*De ecclesiastica hierarchia*
———, *Ep.*	*Epistulae*
Eulogius of Alexandria, *Frag. dogm.*	*Fragmenta dogmatica*
Evagrius [Ponticus], *De orat.*	*De oratione*
———, *Ep. fid.*	*Epistula fidei*
———, *Gnost.*	*Gnostikos*
———, *In Prov.*	*Scholia in Proverbia*
———, *KG*	*Kephalaia Gnostica*
Evagrius Scholasticus, *HE*	*Historia ecclesiastica*
Galen, *Nat. fac.*	*De naturalibus facultatibus*
Georgius Monachus, *Chron.*	*Chronicon.*
GNO	*Gregorii Nysseni Opera*, 17 vols. (Leiden: Brill, 1960–.
Gregory of Nazianzus, *Carm. Moralia*	*Carmina moralia*
———, *Ep.*	*Epistulae* 1–244
———, *Or.*	*Orationes*
Gregory of Nyssa, *C. Eun.*	*Contra Eunomium*
———. *De anim. et resurr.*	*De anima et resurrectione*
———, *De hom. opif.*	*De hominis opificio*
———, *De mort.*	*De mortuis*
———, *De virg.*	*De virginitate*
———, *Hex.*	*Apologia in Hexaemeron*
———, *Hom. in Cant.*	*In canticum canticorum*

———, *Hom. in Eccl.*	*In Ecclesiasten*
———, *Or. cat.*	*Oratio catechetica*
Iamblichus, *De myst.*	*De mysteriis*
Irenaeus, *Haer.*	*Adversus haereses*
John Grammaticus, *Apol.*	*Apologia Concilii Chalcedonensis*
John of Damascus, *Dialectica fus.*	*Dialectica (recensio fusior)*
John of Scythopolis, *SchDN*	*Scholia in De divinis nominibus*
Justinian, *Adv. Tria Capitula*	*Confessio rectae fidei adversus Tria Capitula*
———, *Ep. ad. conc.*	*Epistula ad patres concilii*
Lampe	*A Patristic Greek Lexicon.* By Geoffrey W. H. Lampe. Oxford: Clarendon Press, 1961.
Leontius of Byzantium, *CNE*	*Libri tres contra Nestorianos et Eutychianos*
———, *Epil.*	*Epilyseis*
Leontius of Jerusalem, *Contra Mon.*	*Contra Monophysitas*
———, *Adv. Nest.*	*Adversus Nestorianos*
LSJ	*The Online Liddell-Scott-Jones Greek-English Lexicon.* By Henry George Liddell, Robert Scott, Henry Stuart Jones and Roderick McKenzie. 9th ed. http://stephanus.tlg.uci.edu/lsj/#eid=1.
Oribasius, *Coll. medic.*	*Collectiones medicae*
Origen, *Cels.*	*Contra Celsum*
———, *Comm. in Jo.*	*Commentaria in Evangelium Joannis*
———, *Princ.*	*De principiis*
———, *Hom. in Gen.*	*Homiliae in Genesim*
———. *Hom. in Jer.*	*Homiliae in Jeremiam*

———. *Hom. in Lev.*	*Homiliae in Leviticum*
———. *Hom. in Luc.*	*Homiliae in Lucam*
———. *Hom. in Num.*	*Homiliae in Numeros*
PG	Patrologia Graeca. Edited by J.-P. Migne. 162 vols. Paris, 1857–86.
Philo, *Dec.*	*De Decalogo*
———, *Quod deus sit immut.*	*Quod deus sit immutabilis*
Plato, *Leg.*	*Leges*
———. *Parm.*	*Parmenides*
———. *Theat.*	*Theatetus*
———, *Tim.*	*Timaeus*
Plotinus, *Enn.*	*Enneades*
Plutarch, *Comm. not*	*De communibus notitiis adversus Stoicos*
———, *St. rep.*	*De Stoicorum repugnatiis*
PO	Patrologia Orientalis. Turnhout: Brepols, 1903–.
Porphyry, *Isag.*	*Isagoge*
Proclus, *El. Theol.*	*Elementatio theologica*
———, *In Parm.*	*In Parmenides*
———, *PT*	*Theologia platonica*
Pseudo-Macarius, *Hom.*	*Homiliae 1–50*
SC	Sources Chrétiennes. Paris: Cerf, 1943–.
Severus of Antioch, *Or. 2 ad Nephalium*	*Orationes ad Nephalium 2*
Socrates, *HE*	*Historia ecclesiastica*
SVF	*Stoicorum veterum fragmenta.* Edited by H. von Arnim. 1903–5. Reprint, Stuttgart: Teubner, 1964.
Syrianus, *In Metaph.*	*In Aristotelis Metaphysica commentaria*

Introduction

*The God-World Relation
in Modern Maximus Scholarship*

THE PERL PHENOMENON

In the preface I asserted that most of Maximus's readers have not taken his bolder statements about the God-world relation seriously. But I begin my survey of the secondary literature on the question with a notable exception that I call the "Perl phenomenon."[1] Eric Perl's 1991 dissertation on Maximus at Yale was never published and yet is still often cited today.[2] A very brief distillation of his argument was published in just the first half of a twenty-five-page essay.[3]

What makes Perl a phenomenon, though, is his actual argument. His study examines the philosophical dimensions of "participation" (μέθεξις) in Maximus. Participation—basically the ancient problem of the One and the Many (hence Perl begins with a meditation on Plato's *Parmenides*)— is the philosophical *locus classicus* of the God-world relation. And yet Perl's avowed self-restriction to matters philosophical does not prevent his careful reading of Maximus to lead where Maximus always leads—to

1

the Incarnate Word. Having surveyed "participation" in thinkers such as Plotinus, Proclus, Gregory of Nyssa, and Dionysius, Perl elucidates Maximus's Neo-Chalcedonian Christology and its conceptual convergence with and transfiguration of the metaphysical doctrine of participation.[4] Perl discerns in Maximus's technical use of *enhypostasia* or "enhypostatization" the Christological equivalent to and warrant for "perfect participation."[5] A provocative upshot: "perfect participation" in God, since this describes the ultimate *telos* of human deification, means that the destiny of created being is to become enhypostasized in the Word:

> This hypostatic union of God and creation, the identity of identity and difference, is the one mystery precisely because, as the uttermost explanation of all reality, it cannot itself be explained in terms of anything else. . . . The distinction between hypostasis and nature enables [Maximus] to accept the perfect identity and perfect difference of God and the world, and the perfect identity of these. Thus in ontology enhypostasization allows him to avoid both the monist and the dualist tendencies of the theory of participation, just as in Christology it allows him to avoid both monophysitism and Nestorianism. Instead of undermining the metaphysical theory in attempting discursively to escape the paradox, Maximus exalts it as the supreme mystery.[6]

Perl's view reaffirms Balthasar's that Maximus makes Neo-Chalcedonian Christology "a fundamental law of metaphysics."[7] But the claim that the Word enhypostasizes the world moves well beyond Balthasar. Perl himself seems not to have seen this, and indeed I sense a certain ambiguity for just this reason. Perl exceeds Balthasar precisely where he thinks himself at one with Balthasar. Enhypostatization or, to drop the barbarism for now, Incarnation, is actually *not* "perfect participation," at least if participation here is conceived Neoplatonically. Christ's human nature did not participate his hypostasis, not even perfectly. The relation between Christ's person and either of his natures surpasses participatory (Perl) and analogical (Balthasar) logic. So Perl does follow Balthasar in two ways: he sees that Neo-Chalcedonianism and its flowering in Maximus open new metaphysical logic—the logic of "person" and "perichoresis" (taken from Trinitarian theology and applied to the God-world relation) rather than that of "essence" or "nature."[8] And, second, he makes of this logic a cosmological principle. "Perfect participation," Perl thinks, codifies Maximus's achievement, first discerned by Balthasar. But Perl also edges toward a more direct application, something like a *formal* one, of Christologic to the whole God-world relation. Only thus can he pronounce what never lights upon Balthasar's tongue: that God and world should enjoy "hypostatic union."

Modern Maximus scholars often cite but never follow Perl's work in its core claim.[9] In fact, modern Maximus scholarship has moved conspicuously away from Perl during the two and a half decades since. Take, for instance, Melchisedec Törönen's opening argument, endorsed by Andrew Louth, that far too much has been made of the "Neochalcedonian logic" of "union" and "distinction" in Maximus, since these were perennial *topoi* in both Greek philosophy and Christian theology long before Chalcedon.[10] And yet the scholarly consensus contra Perl has never to my mind offered a direct engagement and refutation of his principal thesis. How then to explain the phenomenon that Perl's audacious thesis has both commanded the attention of scholars to such a degree that it is still cited in unpublished form while the dominant theme of its melody has apparently fallen on deaf ears? Maximus studies have played four other notes, and these, I think, compose a harmony dissonant with Perl's and my own. Listening to these situates this study among the scholarly literature.

FOUR DISSONANT NOTES

Analogizing Maximus:
Balthasar Recruits Maximus for the Analogy of Being

In its 1941 and 1961 recensions Balthasar's crowning patristic achievement, *Kosmische Liturgie*, dons a double laurel: it remains "a fountainhead and continuing inspiration of modern Maximus scholarship,"[11] and many consider it perhaps the decisive moment of retrieval for Balthasar's own constructive project.[12] In the preface I adumbrated Balthasar's general approach to Maximus and why I share it. Here I want to suggest that Balthasar retrieved Maximus as perhaps the definitive justification or exemplary case of the *analogia entis* between God and world, where *definitive* and *exemplary* mean, to meet Barth's restive concern, "Christological."[13] He also needed to dissipate that great spectral nimbus hovering about so much modern theology, the shade of German idealism, Hegel's above all. It is no accident that Balthasar opens his book on Maximus with reference to Franz Anton Staudenmaier's attempt to recruit elements of Eriugena's thought to resist "the pantheism of Hegel."[14] Balthasar chooses Maximus. And he does so for the same reason that makes Maximus a fitting riposte to Barth: "Maximus looks straight into the eye of Hegel," recognizes a kindred Christological instinct to synthesize created contraries, but outstrips Hegel by insisting that Chalcedon's Definition govern every synthesis. Indeed, any reader of Maximus "recognizes that his ontology and cosmology are extensions of his Christology, in that the synthesis of Christ's concrete person is not only God's final thought for the world, but also his original plan."[15]

And so Maximus's maxim, the watchword that speaks always the final word in Christian metaphysics, is *unconfused* (ἀσύγχυτος).[16] That natures human and divine, created and uncreated, coalesce in the "unconfused union" achieved by and in the person of Christ—this for Balthasar constitutes the dogmatic justification of the God-world *analogia entis*. It justifies, I mean, what is often doubted (particularly when the "Asiatic" religious mood predominates): that the finitude of the world, its infinite difference from God, must forever perdure in all its individuality and diversity, even and especially in its apical union with the one God. In Christ, Creator became creature and yet remained Creator; therefore creature will remain creature when it becomes, in a sense, Creator. Sublation need not spell obliteration. Hypostatic union justifies, indeed valorizes, the analogy of being. And I say "justifies" deliberately. One way I disagree with Balthasar emerges just here. For Balthasar, despite momentary lapses, Maximus derives from Chalcedonian Christology the *epistemic justification* for the true God-world relation, an analogical concinnity of the two natures in Christ. For me Maximus divines in Chalcedon the peculiar *metaphysical form* of creation itself, a (Christo-) logic insisting that an analogy between infinitely incommensurable natures holds only within a deeper identity of those natures in and as a hypostasis or person, in and as Christ the Word.

Balthasar flatly denies that any "higher" or "deeper" identity obtains in the God-world relation and often recruits Maximus's authority for the point.[17] Maximus becomes the most valiant defender of analogy because he found a way to speak of the permanent integrities of God and world in an atmosphere threatening their collapse, beset as it was by Neoplatonism, Origenism, and the ascetic flight from the world. Christ unites without confusion—behold the definitive truth that gives the lie to every illicit elision, every seduction toward the "original sin" of metaphysical identity![18] Incarnation verifies that *analogia entis* is the one inviolable rule of Christian metaphysics.[19] Balthasar's recruitment of Maximus cannot but cast a long shadow over any kind of identity thesis when one is seeking Maximus's deepest insight into the God-world relation.[20]

Platonizing Maximus:
Sherwood Calls for Study of "Participation" in Maximus

Balthasar made substantial revisions to the first edition of his Maximus opus (1941), largely in response to criticisms from the other great Maximus scholar of the era, the Benedictine monk Polycarp Sherwood. The gap between the two lay mostly in method. On essentials they were at one.[21] They also agreed on what required closer scrutiny in Maximus: his reliance on the Cappadocians and Dionysius, the exact nature of sixth-century "Neo-Chalcedonianism" and Maximus's use of it, and so on. Sherwood's important 1964 review essay pled for a more pressing task: "A study on 'participation,'" he wrote, "would serve to clarify what is, perhaps, the acutest problem in Byzantine theology: the relation of the finite to the infinite, of the created to the uncreated, not so much in the moment of creation as in the moment of deification."[22] Here he commended I.-H. Dalmais's concern to investigate "participation" in Maximus with the express aim to define "divinization by grace . . . without falling into pantheism."[23]

This was wise counsel. Notice, though, the parameters fixed from the outset: to grasp the God-world relation in Maximus you should analyze the concept of "participation"—a concept whose lineage reaches deep into times past and extends widely across various thought worlds— and you should focus on eschatological union, and you should do so taking care to avoid "pantheism," a longtime polemical term apparently requiring no exact definition.[24] Sherwood's call, whatever its limitations from my vantage, has certainly borne fruit. An interesting and lively debate about whether "participation" is even a proper concept in Maximus, and if so, what it means, has transpired for the good of all in the Maximus guild. I will not rehearse it here.[25] Rather, I take issue with what appears to be a governing assumption within the debate and without: we must seek the essential contours of the God-world relation in Maximus under the horizon of "participation." At first blush this seems a promising way forward, not only because the relation of God and world restates the classic question of how the Many participates the One—a problem Plato's *Parmenides* articulates in its acutest form, as the Neoplatonists knew[26]— but because participation is of course of biblical vintage as well (2 Pet. 1:4: ἵνα . . . γένησθε θείας κοινωνοὶ φύσεως).[27]

Participation as such is not the problem. The problem arises when we imagine that participation should govern what can be said positively of the God-world relation. More than anyone, Maximus challenges this assumption precisely because he always discovers that the contours of the cosmos are those of Christ. This book tries to follow him in that identification. In other words, Maximus problematizes the *final* adequacy of "participation" for contemplating the God-world relation. If creation itself is Incarnation, then we must find some way to see that Maximus's technical Christology really is his metaphysics or cosmology. Christ, I mean, must be the paradigm of creation, the perfect microcosm of the true world. Prima facie this identification means that the truth of the doctrine of Christ must be the truth of the doctrine of creation.

Hence the question becomes: Does participation describe the peculiar logic of the Incarnate Word? No. Many have appreciated, and appreciate anew today, that the period of Christological debates before and after Chalcedon straight through Maximus's time needed to forge new theological and philosophical concepts.[28] Concepts such as person or hypostasis, the *enhypostatos*, and Maximus's original use of perichoresis in Christology pose significant problems for any facile claim that Christology and cosmology converge in a concept like participation. We have only to ask, as I did before: Do we say that Christ's human nature participated his person? Not with much sense. Not only would that insinuate a species of Nestorianism or adoptionism (since it implies natural separation between Christ's humanity and his hypostasis), but it makes little (Neoplatonic) sense to say a nature participates a *hypostasis*: the latter just is the concrete instance of the former.[29] Or again: Does perichoresis mean participation? Not if it will remain orthodox in any historical and systematic sense. Against a certain (if misguided) reading of Origen, the Son (and the Spirit) does not participate the Father.[30]

And yet the drift of Maximus's thought moves the reader to posit the most direct correspondence between the logic of Neo-Chalcedonian Christology and the logic of creation—the logic of God's relation to the world he spoke into existence. We saw Balthasar do so, and most do. Two more examples, though, nicely illustrate the problem with making participation the regulative concept for the God-world relation and then making Christ the paradigm of that relation.

Torstein Tollefsen's *The Christocentric Cosmology of St. Maximus the Confessor* is the most recent monograph-length treatment of my principal themes. There he agrees with Balthasar and Lars Thunberg (against Törönen and Louth, it seems) that the presence of the four famous Chalcedonian adverbs in Maximian metaphysics, especially *unconfused* (ἀσυγχύτως), flows from Maximus's original insight that "the same ontological logic . . . governs the relation between the uncreated and the created being in incarnation as well as in participation."[31] Recall, though, that these adverbs refer to the relations between Christ's two *natures*: united but unconfused, distinct but inseparable. Chalcedonian adverbs describe an essential or natural logic, a logic that pertains to and among metaphysical natures abstractly considered. This, I think, is why Tollefsen relaxes his initial claim that Christ is the paradigm of creation.[32] The mystery of Christ is not the same as that of creation after all. Hypostatic union is "the mystery *par excellence*" because it is "not a nature-union"— unlike participation, where higher and lower beings share the content of natures in varying degrees of intensity and determination, that is, in different modes. A man, an angel, and the divine Logos are all rational by nature. Just *how* they are is what differs. (And the Son is rational to an infinitely higher degree exactly because he is by nature reason itself.) A telling passage near the end of Tollefsen's chapter on participation in Maximus: "In His historical Incarnation as Jesus Christ, the Logos becomes immanent, but He does not become participated by His human nature, nor does He, as God, participate His own humanity. On the other hand, the Incarnation makes participation possible. Therefore, the human nature of Christ is deified *by participation* in the divine activity."[33]

But how is that divine activity participated by Christ's humanity? Track the sequence here: in the historical Incarnation (Christology proper) the person of the Word becomes immanent in a mode that exceeds participatory logic (creation proper), since here humanity does not participate the divine person, nor does divinity participate humanity; indeed, the deeper identification of both natures in the one hypostasis is the very condition of any participation between the two natures; therefore Christ's human nature is deified by participating the divine activity. But isn't it rather that everything preceding this conclusion together forms the *whole condition* of deification? Would it not be better to say that Christ's human nature is deified given two conditions, (1) by participating the divine activity; yet this very participation is only possible because (2) this same human nature is identical to the divine person? And isn't it precisely this final and deepest condition—hypostatic identity—that makes this participation peculiarly *Christo*-logical? I can see only one way to comprehend Tollefsen's affirmation that for Maximus Christ is "the paradigm" of creation, and it is Balthasar's too: he appears to mean that Christ only verifies or confirms or gives epistemic credence to an idea already articulated in basic Platonic metaphysics. Balthasar calls this idea "analogy of being," Tollefsen calls it "participation." Neither means that Maximus's Neo-Chalcedonian Christology describes the very same logic of the God-world relation.[34]

As a final example I return to Perl. I have already implied that his concept of "perfect participation" retains the parameters set by the classical concept of metaphysical participation. Perl differs from Balthasar, Tollefsen, and others because he emphasizes the identity-pole of participation while they emphasize the difference. Now, he does deny that this results in mere identity, since, for instance, he thinks perfect participation need not entail the obliteration of created nature as such. That constitutes his sole reply to the charge of pantheism.[35] But what happens to created hypostases?[36] Are they preserved in the consummation of perfect participation? Their absence in Perl's account of Maximus's eschatology suggests their final absence too, at least *qua* created hypostases. Perhaps they return to God the Word, are enhypostatized in him, and so persist only as primordial powers or *logoi*. Then the Logos alone (with the other divine persons) would remain *in actu*, a divine hypostasis, which is now also the sole instantiation of a generic created nature—a rather vexing abstraction, and one that rings more Evagrian.[37] But that is to speculate, since Perl says no more. We have only the lingering suspicion that Perl's intuitions might be better served by parting with participation, at least where its Neoplatonic strictures prove too strict: precisely in Christology.

Minimizing Maximus:
The Tendency to Subject Maximus to Thomas Aquinas

A final cacophonous note sounds from the 1970s. Comparison of Maximus to Thomas dates (in the modern period) from the start of the twentieth century,[38] but the seventies saw a concerted effort to bring the two into accord on all essentials. This démarche, led by the Dominican Juan-Miguel Garrigues, had some merit.[39] It became controversial because of the fairly typical, grandiose claims these Dominicans made. Garrigues put it this way: "In fact [Maximus] serves as precursor to [Thomas], especially since the latter took up and systematized the most fundamental views of the former. And indeed the theological intelligence of Thomas's work presupposes the patristic patrimony, Maximus's in particular, which was transmitted through and beyond St. John of Damascus."[40] There is no reason to detail the many contentious points this judgment evokes. Jean-Claude Larchet and Thunberg have done that with dispatch.[41] Important here is how this rapprochement strategy dictates what is possible (or impossible) for Maximus to say about the God-world relation.

An example. In recent years Antoine Lévy undertook the Dominican charge. He is significant both because he carries on the Thomist negotiation with Maximus and because he does so over the heart of the matter: the exact relation between "created" and "uncreated."[42] Lévy's work has much to commend it. He puts Thomas in direct conversation with Maximus rather than, say, with Palamas's Maximus.[43] This allows him to embed Maximus within the Greek patristic and Greek philosophical contexts of his own day, a move that revitalizes the possible exchange between the two estranged luminaries.[44] For Lévy this reveals a Maximus very favorable to Thomism. Maximus and Thomas differ only in perspective, not in substance. Between them there is "perfect doctrinal coincidence,"[45] and "the created-uncreated relation unfolds identically" in each's system. The two systems are "isomorphic."[46] True, Maximus surveys the God-world relation from a "ktizo-centric" lookout, whence he sees only a mysterious energy pouring forth into (and as) creation from an utterly ineffable divine essence; and Thomas takes a "ktisto-centric" vantage, ever attentive to the created intellect's strain to apprehend anything that exceeds its own laws. Different vantages produce different articulations, though the thing seen—God's totally free, utterly supernatural relation to the world—remains the very same.[47]

Lévy claims that Maximus's *logoi*-talk amounts to Neoplatonic talk of *energeia* (activity) and *skhesis* (relation). So when Maximus says God creates the world through the Logos's condescension as and in the world's *logoi*, he repeats the Neoplatonist Simplicius's doctrine that the One (or any higher principle) "proceeds into external realities by means of relation." And so "We understand that even as it remains uncreated, God's *energeia* is grasped *here* as a consequence of the world's being-in-relation, as a consequence of the *skhesis* of all things to a God who remains *there* in view of his simple and absolute *energeia*."[48] Said differently, Maximus conceives the essence-energy distinction in God in terms of Neoplatonic emanation, specifically the doctrine of double activity. On this view causality comprises two distinct, inseparable acts, one interior and the other exterior.[49] A higher principle "first" is what and how it alone is, and only "then," simply by being what it is, does it emanate the creative energy that becomes the causal potency of lower effects. Maximus, Lévy argues, construes God's "essence" as the first act (interior), his energy as the second (exterior).[50] Since therefore Thomas tends to view the God-world relation more in terms of the second act—necessarily so given his starting point "from below"—while Maximus views it in terms of the first act or indeed both, the two merely pronounce the same thing in different registers. And what they say is clear enough: the created and the uncreated are related as effect to cause, as more limited natural power (*esse determinatum*) to the less determinate act of its causal principle, as participating to participated, as at once (graciously) alike and infinitely different—as analogous.

Metaphorizing Maximus: Speculative Perils

The three preceding notes, though different in provenance, compose one melody. They share a bass clef as old as Eriugena's lyrical praise of Maximus. Together they replay the assumption that Maximus cannot mean what he often says. For his part Eriugena never says that Maximus did not, for instance, literally mean that creation is Incarnation. But Eriugena himself makes a point to deny the identification in his own speculative thought.[51] Cyril O'Regan rightly says that Balthasar is forced to interpret all talk of "becoming God" in Maximus as "metaphorical."[52] Tollefsen too insists that when Maximus says creation is "Incarnation" (ἐνσάρκωσις, ἐνσωμάτωσις, etc.) we have a "metaphorical usage of the term."[53] And yet

Maximus himself never makes such qualifications.[54] Our reasons for doing so must therefore lie elsewhere, beyond the realm of simple exegesis. To cite an interested bystander: "Although . . . in an extravagant moment, Maximus does seem to claim that deification causes such a fundamental change of status, the logical and theological problems entailed in such a claim are enormous—unless, of course, it is taken as hyperbolic doxology to the sanctifying power of the Almighty."[55]

Anna Williams here articulates the only two options when faced with Maximus's identification of creation and Incarnation, as well as the deciding factor. Either we take Maximus's "extravagant" moments as nothing more than "hyperbolic doxology," or we take him at his word and see what results. Almost everyone, we have seen, has taken the former road. And the deciding factor has often been exactly "the logical and theological problems entailed." They are indeed "enormous." I myself have already raised some with respect to Perl's view, though I broadly endorse it. If the world is destined to be enhypostasized in the Word, as was Christ's human nature, what becomes of created hypostases as such? Or as Louth once objected to Perl, if we take Maximus's claims of a God-world identity in too straightforward a manner (say, as we do in Christology), would not this number him among the Origenist *isochristoi*?[56] Are we really all Christ?

Even so, this study takes the second path. Yes, the speculative worries must and will be addressed, and this in tandem with a thorough reading of Maximus's entire oeuvre. It is a path Maximus scholarship has in many ways abandoned. Some (Törönen, Louth) openly eschew the relevance of technical Christo-logic in Maximus's cosmology. Some (all the rest) permit it only as epistemic validation and metaphorical expression of some otherwise self-standing participatory metaphysics. I suggest that these are but different forms of evading the seriousness of Maximus's words. Few (if any) today take Maximus at his word that "the Word of God, very God, wills that the mystery of his Incarnation be actualized always and in all things" (*Amb.* 7.22).

Still I ask: Is this not a worthwhile undertaking? Do not Maximus's own pronouncements invite such a risk? Is it really so obvious a metaphor when Maximus says that Adam's original, *natural* vocation was to show that God and man are "one and the same [ἕν καὶ ταὐτὸν δείξειε] by the state of grace, the whole man wholly pervading the whole God [ὅλος ὅλῳ περιχωρήσας ὁλικῶς τῷ Θεῷ], and becoming everything that God is,

without, however, identity in essence [κατ' οὐσίαν ταὐτότητος]"?[57] Or
when Maximus ceaselessly stresses the perfect symmetry between God's
Incarnation and our deification? To the same extent "God by condescension is and is called man,"[58] He makes "humans gods and sons of God."[59]
And this because God wills to be "united with those who become Gods,
and by His goodness makes all things His own."[60] Is Maximus indulging
in metaphor or pious hyperbole when he extols Melchizedek as the paradigm of our final unification with God in the most extravagant terms?
Melchizedek "was deemed worthy to transcend time and nature and to
become like the Son of God," so that "he became by grace what the Giver
of grace is by nature."[61] And he explains what "by grace" entails for
Melchizedek's union: "[Melchizedek] was begotten of God through the
Word in the Spirit by grace, so that he now bears within himself, unblemished and fully realized, the likeness of God [τοῦ . . . Θεοῦ τὴν ὁμοίωσιν],
for birth creates identity between the begetter and the begotten [ἐπεὶ καὶ
πᾶσα γέννησις ταὐτὸν τῷ γεννῶντι πέφυκεν ἀποτελεῖν τὸ γεννώμενον]."[62]
And then: "He becomes without beginning or end [cf. Heb. 7:3] [γέγονε
καὶ ἄναρχος καὶ ἀτελεύτητος] . . . but possesses only the divine and eternal life of the Word dwelling within him [μόνην δὲ τὴν θείαν τοῦ
ἐνοικήσαντος Λόγου], which is in no way bounded by death."[63] So deification "by grace" is supernatural indeed. But here *supernatural* means
that Melchizedek's ascent into God is also the Word's descent into him,
and the Word comes bearing divine properties. No wonder then that
Maximus also says of the deified: "The Word . . . gazes out from within
them."[64] No surprise either that he dares to outstrip the classic image-to-
likeness schema for deification: when we "in reception of the archetype"
become "images of Christ," we further "become one with Him through
grace (rather than being a mere simulacrum), or even, perhaps, become
the Lord Himself, if such an idea is not too onerous for some to bear."[65]
That might well sound "isochrist" tones, but there it is.[66]

Maximus can brave all this about our end because of what he says
about the God-world relation as a whole: creation is Incarnation. Thus creation's final union with God requires both our ascent and God's *descent*.
"For they say that God and man are paradigms of each other, so that as
much as [τοσοῦτον] man, enabled by love, has divinized himself for God,
to that same extent [ὅσον] God is humanized for man by His love for mankind."[67] The same Chalcedonian symmetry or reciprocity that obtains be-

tween Christ's two natures does so between God and the (deified) world. Somehow, it seems, God's act of creation comes about in and through Christ, indeed through the historical Incarnation. Maximus calls this "the whole mystery of Christ" (τὸ κατὰ Χριστὸν μυστήριον), known and willed by God from before the foundation of the world: "All the ages as well as the things in these very same ages have received in Christ their ground and goal of being."[68] He calls this "the principle of condescension" (συγκαταβάσεως λόγῳ) and formulates it thus: "Just to the extent that he contracted us for himself into union with himself, to that same extent he himself expanded his very self for us through the principle of condescension."[69]

This short sampling of passages—a mere handful of many to be scrutinized anon—justifies the suspicion that "Creation is Incarnation" moves beyond mere metaphor.[70] And if more than metaphor, then God's creative act is also an act of self-identification with that creation. In fact his becoming the world is the world's very generation, yet he retains the full integrity of his divinity. And if in the Word God identifies himself with the world, then the God-world relation bears a deeper and different identity than whatever unity obtains between created and uncreated natures (say, analogy or participation or the limitation of act by power). What kind of identity? Just here the "enormous" systematic problems return. But if we take Maximus seriously that creation is Incarnation, even the specter of crude pantheism starts to fade.

Consider one point, which both terminates this survey and commences my attempt to follow the second path mentioned above. Maximus's polemic against Origenism contains a slew of arguments, most of which scholars have long known.[71] I find it extremely significant that none notices just how Maximus describes the Origenist "henad" preexisting in union with God. Perhaps Origenists such as Evagrius misapprehended the metaphysics of creaturely motion, particularly the point that being created necessarily entails being moved. But I think Maximus detects a deeper flaw in the way Origenists conceive the whole God-world relation, beginning to end. He opens his famous refutation of Origenism with a concise description of Origenist protology: we rational beings were once "a unity of rational beings, by virtue of which we were *connatural* with God" (τῶν λογικῶν ἑνάδα καθ' ἣν συμφυεῖς ὄντες Θεῷ).[72]

Maximus's fundamental issue with Origenists cannot simply be that they posit a primordial and illicit God-world identity. We have seen, and this study lays out in further detail, that Maximus too conceives a God-world identity.[73] It is not *that* Origenists conceive an identity but *how* they do so that matters. And I suspect Maximus sees too that Origenism fails to grasp in protology and eschatology what every heresy fails to grasp in Christology. In all cases the essential error is to misconceive the precise sort of identity that underlies all difference. And in all cases the sole antidote becomes that determinate logic disclosed only in a rigorous and faithful apprehension of the Incarnate Logos. Hence Maximus, about thirty paragraphs after his indication that Origenists conceive a natural identity between God and their "henad," announces his own version of the God-world identity (here viewed from its final perfection): "When this happens, *God will be all things in everything* [1 Cor. 15:28], encompassing all things and hypostasizing them in Himself [πάντα περιλαβὼν καὶ ἐνυποστήσας ἑαυτῷ]."[74]

Let us concede no natural or abstract God-world identity. In the Word, though, and in the fullness of God's creative act, Maximus permits "hypostatic" identity. What then? Maybe Maximus's intensely technical Christology is also his intensely technical cosmology. Maybe his idiosyncratic emphasis on how the historical Incarnation, understood by Neo-Chalcedonian lights, reveals an entirely new and previously inconceivable kind of identity of created and uncreated natures—maybe this emphasis opens upon new ways of conceiving a God-world identity as well.[75] What exactly that God-world identity means and what it entails name the themes of this book.

ARGUMENT IN BRIEF

I intend to trace somewhat relentlessly the potential implications of allowing Maximus to mean what he often seems to say. Doing so necessitates facing "enormous" systematic problems but also scintillating systematic possibilities. Or so I'll argue. If creation is Incarnation—if, I mean, Maximus does propose that the world itself comes into being in and through Jesus Christ—what can this possibly mean, and what implications follow from this rather strange speculative vision? This study assays a response as follows.

In chapter 1 I begin my presentation of Maximus's answer to the question of the God-world relation. Maximus calls Christ (not just God, as in Dionysius) "the beginning, the middle, and the end" of the world.[76] We must first go to the middle where that beginning and end have come upon us, to Jesus of Nazareth. This chapter reviews the many important contributions to an understanding of Maximus's Neo-Chalcedonian Christology but does so with an eye to what exactly "Incarnation" means for Maximus and how it comes to describe the metaphysics of creation. Its main question is: Why and how does Maximus stress the copula in the statement that the person of Christ *is* the two natures? A rubric emerges by which we might better perceive Maximus's Incarnation-talk elsewhere, what it means for him to say God *is* the world. My argument could be presented in the form of a basic induction:

> First premise: four distinctive elements of Maximus's "Christo-logic" properly define "Incarnation" (chapter 1);
> Second premise: these four elements define his cosmo-logic too— both his protology (chapter 2) and his eschatology (chapter 3);
> Conclusion: therefore "Incarnation" means in his cosmology what it means in his Christology.

Then comes the beginning. Chapter 2 comprises the first of two treatments of Maximus's famous *logoi* doctrine. Save Perl, no one has tried to read the *logoi* as an application of Neo-Chalcedonian logic to metaphysics proper. Here I do so in regard to protology. I take interest in how Maximus conceives God's emanation or movement of condescension into and as all creatures. I set his own originality in relief by showing how he differs from John of Scythopolis, Neoplatonism generally and Dionysius in particular, and Alexandrian-mediated Stoicism—all while retaining the essentials of each. This chapter concludes that the created world's subsistence is the Word's own hypostasis, the Word kenotically given as the "is" of all things visible and invisible.

My second approach to the *logoi* doctrine advances from the other direction, from eschatology. So chapter 3 treats the role of the *logoi* in Maximian deification. The governing question here is: What does Maximus mean when he says we "become God *by grace*"? Most subject Maximus either to Thomas or to earlier patristic precedents on this point, as even Balthasar did. This would imply that becoming God by grace somehow means we will forever be less divine than Christ is, since he is God by nature. Actually, though, many of Maximus's statements about our final union with God verge far nearer to Origenist than Thomist views. And yet if Maximus holds that our eschatological identity with God is also God's kenotic and personal identity with us, how can he avoid the Origenist error of finally obliterating created hypostases? I attempt a re-tort to this question first and then conclude that Maximus's cosmology follows Pauline ecclesiology; for Maximus Christ's Body is (potentially) both church and world. Here "analogy" assumes altogether jarring senses different from those one often encounters in much modern theology. Here it implies a God-world *symmetry* grounded in their hypostatic iden-tity (as with Christ's natures).

Chapter 4 faces up to an immediate and daunting challenge to this entire way of construing the God-world relation. If creation is nothing but the Word's loving, ecstatic condescension in and as every creature and the whole cosmos, then why did creation fall? Not only did it fall. According to Maximus this world fell at the very moment it appeared in existence. How can he conceive creation as both the Word's sublime In-carnation and as an immediate failure? Answering this objection opens up a most unexpected perspective on creation itself. To wit, this world's condition of devastation does not disprove that creation is Incarnation. Rather, it indicates that this world is not yet God's true creation. The world is not creation until the Word incarnates into every time, place, event, creature—everything.

I organize these chapters around the main epigraph, *Ambiguum* 7.22: "Βούλεται γὰρ ἀεὶ καὶ ἐν πᾶσιν ὁ τοῦ Θεοῦ Λόγος καὶ Θεὸς τῆς αὐτοῦ ἐνσωματώσεως ἐνεργεῖσθαι τὸ μυστήριον." The "mystery" the Word wills to achieve in all things and in all times is not something other than the historical Incarnation, the hypostatic union, where the created and the uncreated become and are concretely "one and the same." Maximus speaks of the "mystery according to Christ" as the goal and the very ground of all creation.[77] Nowhere does he qualify it or make a distinction between different kinds of mystery, as if, when it comes to the Word's presence in and identity with all creatures, we speak of something quali-tatively different from the mystery of the Word's human life. And indeed, as I seek to show in the coming chapters, we have sufficient reason to think the contrary. The mystery God the Word wills to actualize in all creation is just what Maximus says it is: "his Incarnation."

So this whole study can be read as an attempt to interpret a single statement in all its starkness. I schematize it thus, where the italicized portion of the epigraph corresponds to what the respective chapter tries to interpret at length and in detail:

> Chapter 1 seeks what the "mystery" means: "The Word of God, very God, wills that *the mystery of his Incarnation* be actualized always and in all things."
>
> Chapter 2 seeks what the Word's creative procession means: "*The Word of God, very God*, wills that the mystery of his Incarnation be actualized always and *in all things*."
>
> Chapter 3 seeks what sort of "actualization" of the Word characterizes creation's perfection: "The Word of God, very God, wills that the mystery of his Incarnation *be actualized* always and in all things."
>
> Chapter 4 seeks the course of this event given its apparent failure in time: "The Word of God, very God, *wills* that the mystery of his Incarnation be actualized *always* and in all *things*."

I terminate the study with a recapitulation of the argument and various systematic reflections on and responses to potential objections to the Maximian vision. Mostly I can but promise further exploration of what the results presented here might mean for Maximus studies in particular and Christian theology in general. In many ways this book's main success, if it enjoys any success, would be to clear the exegetical ground for Maximus's more arresting insights to emerge for careful scrutiny by modern theologians—many of the very insights that so captivated Eriugena centuries ago. At least in the West, these have fallen on deaf ears or on no ears at all. My contention is that Eriugena long ago and Balthasar more recently were right to perceive in Maximus an especially illuminating contemplative of the God-world relation but that neither adequately realized just how right—and provocative—Maximus's speculative vision truly was and is.

CHAPTER ONE

The Middle

Christo-Logic

This chapter has three goals. The principal one is (1) to define what Maximus means by "Incarnation" in Christology proper. What counts as a divine Incarnation? What are the criteria? Doing so introduces a subordinate goal: (2) I catalog and emphasize three original features of Maximus's Christology that scholars have noticed but have never to my knowledge explicated as a coherent whole. These three signature characteristics, I mean, form and disclose a deep, logical development of the Neo-Chalcedonian doctrine of Christ. Together they form one signature. Tracing and reading this signature does more than clarify Maximus's Christology. It also (3) reveals why and how this Christology assumes relevance for cosmology. Clearer: Maximus's three original accents in Christology constitute a "Christo-logic" (as I call it to distinguish my view from mere "Christo-centrism") that immediately implicates cosmology in general and the doctrine of creation from nothing in particular. His precisions about God's Incarnation in the middle of history elucidate God's creative act at history's beginning, middle, and end—indeed, they disclose the truth of the whole creative act.

Most of this chapter performs (2) in order to achieve (1), with (3) indicated along the way when germane. This chapter merely prepares the soil for the fuller harvest of (3), the exposition of which unfolds in the subsequent three chapters.

1.1. NEO-CHALCEDONIANISM AND ITS DISCONTENTS

It seems fairly certain that Neo-Chalcedonianism names a real and identifiable development in the history of Christology.[1] Also certain is that identifying the exact criteria that distinguished a Neo-Chalcedonian thinker in the late patristic era has required further precision over the past century since the label first surfaced in scholarship. To the term *Neo-Chalcedonian* Joseph Lebon appended two general criteria: first, that a Neo-Chalcedonian interpret Chalcedon through Cyril of Alexandria; second, that he employ a sophisticated "scholastic" conceptual apparatus derived from the philosophical schools in order to construct a coherent science of Christ.[2] These have since been refined.[3] Another certainty: Maximus too merits the title "Neo-Chalcedonian," even if cautiously.[4]

I do not here rehearse the history of Neo-Chalcedonian Christology and its critical players. Such is well-covered terrain, at least for scholarship beyond the Anglophone world.[5] Nor do I chart all the points where Maximus converges with other Neo-Chalcedonians.[6] Instead I focus on what seems the single solid criterion that everyone agrees qualifies Neo-Chalcedonianism, for good or ill: the conscious attempt to define and develop a distinct logic of Chalcedon's "one hypostasis or person."[7] After a brief survey of this development I address key criticisms of Neo-Chalcedonianism. These criticisms, though issuing from concerns perhaps particular to an earlier generation of scholars, remain mostly unacknowledged even as they continue to reverberate in Neo-Chalcedonian and Maximian scholarship today. They exercise notable influence on how Maximus is and has been read, I think, and indeed pose fundamental challenges to this book's argument at its core, that is, in Christology proper. Those criticisms appear still more significant when we realize that their underlying concerns should only intensify with regard to Maximus's own signature contributions to Christology.

1.1.1. Defining Hypostasis

It was far from evident that Cyril's Christology had any chance at concinnity with Chalcedon's. Among several apparent divergences was that while Cyril could sometimes use *physis* and *hypostasis* as synonyms,[8] Chalcedon's Definition demanded their conceptual distinction:

> We all with one voice teach the confession of one and the same Son, our Lord Jesus Christ: the same perfect in divinity and perfect in humanity, the same truly God and truly man, of a rational soul and a body; consubstantial with the Father as regards his divinity, and the same consubstantial with us as regards his humanity; like us in all respects except for sin; begotten before the ages from the Father as regards his divinity, and in the last days the same for us and for our salvation from Mary, the virgin Mother of God, as regards his humanity; one and the same Christ, Son, Lord, only-begotten, acknowledged in two natures which undergo no confusion, no change, no division, no separation; at no point was the difference between the natures taken away through the union, but rather the property of both natures is preserved and comes together into a single person and a single hypostasis.[9]

Hypostasis alone is "one" in Christ, whereas the natures are "two." Nature and hypostasis therefore differ. How? Chalcedon merely intimated the ways. What it did say was enough to identify at least one salient feature of each distinct logic: Cyril's restive insistence on Christ's subjective *singularity* ("one and the same Son, our Lord Jesus Christ") is calibrated to the one person or hypostasis; Christ's perfect and natural *symmetry* ("consubstantial with the Father . . . consubstantial with us"), to the two natures or essences.

This distinction worked well enough in Cappadocian Trinitarian theology, where the divine essence names "the common" or "universal" and the divine hypostasis "the particular" or "proper" characteristics that distinguish an individual.[10] That last constitutes the first definition of hypostasis. But can we really just transfer those conceptual correlations to the Son's economy? Replicating this distinction in Christology became the great burden of pro-Chalcedonians, just as undermining it became the chief concern for anti-Chalcedonians such as Severus of Antioch.[11]

Consider one of Severus's more penetrating attempts.[12] Defenders of Chalcedon claim Christ had two natures, divine and human. But is, say, Christ's human nature "specific" or "individual"?[13] If specific—that is, "universal" in the sense that it appears wholly and equally as the essence of many individuals of the same species—then the reality of Christ's human nature is just the whole of human nature along with every individual human; thus "the Holy Trinity itself is [therefore] incarnate in the whole of humanity, that is the human race."[14] If individual—that is, the "concrete particular" who is *that* human—then that human nature is just its own hypostasis (recall here the Cappadocian correlation of hypostasis to particular): a regress to Nestorianism. Since Neo-Chalcedonians promoted the complete and real integrity of two natures in Christ, Severus here asks about the principle that allows Christ to be at once really two and really one. Doesn't maintaining Chalcedon's strict symmetry of real natures imply that Christ's human nature is itself individuated (since it is concrete—lest we toy with an abstract, merely conceptual human essence)[15]—that is, has its own particular reality that is *not* the one subject, One of the Holy Trinity? After all, every party agrees that "there is no [real] nature without a hypostasis."[16] Two real natures = two hypostases. Whatever the shortcomings of Severus's own Christology,[17] his incisive interrogation here raises a problem not often detected even by those deftly at work on its resolution:[18] How do Christ's two natures attain concrete particularity or individuality if Christ's hypostasis remains one? What is the principle of individuation operative in the Incarnation?

A second definition of hypostasis arose among the Neo-Chalcedonians, and with it some promising ways to resolve Severus's dilemma. Early on they adopted the first (Cappadocian) definition,[19] "the distinguishing properties" characterizing an individual. Now they added another: "that which exists in itself" (τὸ καθ' ἑαυτὸ ὑπάρχον, or other variants). That precision unleashes a fairly seismic metaphysical tremor, not least because it moves manifestly away from a Platonic realism that would claim that more universal species and genera such as "man" and "the intelligible" subsist, in act and mode, prior to their individual instances.[20] The two definitions often appear together. So Leontius of Jerusalem: "And this sort of 'hypostasis' is said more directly and properly than all the previous: as if, with respect to the determinate combination [i.e., bundle of properties], it is also what has been marked off by a *recognized prop-*

erty from all those of the same species and of different species, [what] manifests the individual subject which *is in itself* a certain separation and distinction of indistinct essences in order to [constitute] the number of each person."[21]

The second definition of hypostasis also moves beyond (the Porphyry-mediated) Aristotle. In that tradition it is the "bundle of characteristics," and for many merely the bundle of accidents, that "characterize" or "distinguish" an individual.[22] Again, that is the first definition. That definition was useful because it preserved the universal essence of, say, the shared divinity between Father and Son, or of the Son's shared humanity with us. Accidents particularize but do not modify essences as such.[23] But neither do hypostases *qua* hypostases—the entire burden of the Neo-Chalcedonian articulation of the two logics (of nature and of hypostasis) in Christology. The second definition, I mean, now sees *the hypostasis itself*—here the eternally singular, divine Son—as what alone grounds the concrete existence, and so the particularity or individuality, of the nature assumed. While that nature did not "preexist" (I table for now the exact sense of saying this), *he* did. As the other Leontius put it: "The hypostasis does not simply or even primarily signify that which is complete, but that which *exists for itself*, and secondly that which is complete; while the nature signifies what *never exists for itself*, but most properly that which is [formally] complete." And the second definition includes the first: into this "principle of hypostasis" (τὸν τῆς ὑποστάσεως λόγον) the distinguishing "characteristics" of that hypostasis are assumed.[24] The two definitions of hypostasis indicate the two metaphysical functions that are necessary and proper to it: the hypostasis (1) grounds and (2) individualizes. These are necessary at least in Christo-logic, since Christ's particular human nature only "had its hypostasis in the Logos," was real solely as *his* reality, and his reality is just his very person constituted from eternity by the Father's generation.[25]

So then, Neo-Chalcedonians retained the first definition of hypostasis ("the particular characterizing properties") and appended the second ("what exists in itself"). This latter differs from Platonic and Aristotelian metaphysics alike, since the "hypostasis" that exists in itself, here the Son, is patently *not* individuated by accidents or matter. We thereby introduce a new metaphysical principle of the subject. We seek, that is, a principle of the subject that makes this subject the most fundamental and *positive* metaphysical fact—namely a subject that is neither simply a more contracted instance of universal nature nor simply some spatio-temporal bundle of accidents. According to this bit of Christo-logic, *we require a positive principle that individuates and particularizes and that is utterly indifferent to—and so completes and actualizes—the universal (nature) and particular (characteristics) in and of every real being.* Said otherwise, we require this distinctive principle (or logic) of hypostasis if we wish to follow the Neo-Chalcedonians in their endeavor to render the individuating principle of Christ's flesh the same as that of every individual—that is, to make Christo-logic into cosmo-logic.[26]

1.1.2. Criticisms

Important scholars have lamented the conflation of hypostasis's two definitions. Charles Moeller, and Alois Grillmeier too, discerned here an illicit and "dangerous unification" of what had been kept judiciously discrete until the end of the fifth century: *theologia* (Trinity) and *oikonomia* (Incarnation).[27] Christological infelicities aside, Moeller praises Cyril and Severus of Antioch for at least grasping that concepts or terms in these separate domains must also retain separate definitions.[28] Chalcedon indeed forced reflection on the difference between nature and hypostasis in Christology proper, but the misstep many took, understandable at first blush, was to flee to Cappadocian Trinitarian terminology for uncritical succor.[29] Moeller means principally Nyssen's definition of hypostasis, "distinguishing characteristics," more than the second definition, "that which exists according to/in itself." Moeller maintains that only the second was necessary and that the first should have been "resolutely abandoned."[30]

Why? Recall Severus's dilemma: Was Christ's human nature universal or particular? This trap springs only if you define hypostasis as the "distinguishing characteristics" that constitute a concrete, particular instance of a nature or essence (it does not matter whether this "essence" is Aristotelian or Neoplatonic). If Christ's human nature is universal, then it lacks particularity and must simply comprise the whole lump of humanity; Christ would have assumed every human being. If his human nature is particular, then it bore a hypostasis after all that made it the concrete "this" that it was. Neo-Chalcedonians, Cyrillian at heart, had to reject this latter option as plain Nestorianism, while the first was sufficiently strange and therefore void. But now, warn Moeller and others, Neo-Chalcedonians were beguiled by a seductive resolution. They were led to say—and Leontius of Jerusalem here appears first and worst of the perpetrators[31]—that the human nature's individuating characteristics or hypostasis just *are* the very properties of the Word's eternal hypostasis.[32] The Word's very person makes his humanity both real and particular. Behold the "monophysite virus" injected into Neo-Chalcedonian Christology: now Christ's humanity cannot even be *conceived* apart from the distinguishing characteristics that make the Word who he is and how he is divine. For Moeller, apparently inspired by Thomas Aquinas, this whole line of thought collapses the individual integrity of Christ's humanity, since his human nature no longer remains a formal whole in itself considered separately from the Word's singularity:

> In other words, instead of strictly confining the role of the hypostatic union to the subsistence of the human nature conceived *as a whole*, Leontius [of Jerusalem] (perhaps unwittingly) verges very nearly upon a *mixture* of the human with the divine: those concrete, particularizing properties (Ἰδιώματα ἀφωρίστικα) which make Christ's human nature into a living reality imbued with a real psychological life rather than a mere optical illusion—these properties do not subsist *directly* in the Word's hypostasis. Rather they subsist in the concrete human *nature* of Christ. *It is the nature that subsists.* That the human nature lacks a human hypostasis does not mean the human nature is deprived of individuating characteristics. It means only that the human nature did not for an instant subsist separately or "by itself." The human nature subsists *ontologically* in the divine hypostasis. Thus those properties [i.e., the particularizing properties mentioned above] exist in the man, Christ, by *the intermediary* of the human nature's subsistence.[33]

It was the "awkward," unreflective use of the Cappadocian Trinitarian definition of hypostasis in Christology that inflicted monophysitism upon Neo-Chalcedonianism.[34] Abandon the first definition ("individuating properties") and retain the first ("subsistence" or "what exists in itself")—that is Moeller's antidote. But notice how his proposal already indulges the very language Neo-Chalcedonians meant to resist: if we conceive Christ's humanity apart from his person, then we see that the human nature is "a whole" *before it is Christ*. The Word's hypostasis, as mere "subsistence," toggles the existential switch that grants concrete being to an already conceived, distinct whole. Moreover, for Moeller it is the nature as a whole that initially subsists, as it were, in the Word, and only "then" do its particular properties (again already and separately conceived) subsist in the Word's own subsistence. Last comes the astounding claim that any Neo-Chalcedonian, Maximus above all, would have abhorred: the "subsistence" of Christ's whole humanity is "the intermediary" of its particular properties. The concrete person and the concrete humanity of Christ prove so distinct, at least formally or conceptually, that they must now relate through an intermediary—namely the phantom "subsistence" of the whole or abstract human nature as opposed to or different from the subsistence that the Word *is*. Here arises precisely the sort of surreptitious Nestorianism that Neo-Chalcedonians were wont to suspect and loathe.

Why palaver over an obscure scholarly trend? Because, obscure though it be, what is decided (or undecided) about these more conspicuous Neo-Chalcedonian trends fixes the parameters for what is possible or desirable to say about the fundamental relation between creation and Incarnation. A fault line already divides: conceptually and formally, the *fact* that Christ takes up even this human nature—his own, I mean—allegedly cannot in any way qualify or define or characterize its metaphysical content, namely what it is in power and how it will be in act. To put it bluntly, for Neo-Chalcedonianism's discontents *even the possibility (and certainly the actual creation) of Christ's individual human nature cannot be primordially linked to his very act of Incarnating into and as that human nature*. They have (perhaps unwittingly) decided that the event of Incarnation cannot unveil new and positive metaphysical content. That creation is not Incarnation here takes precedence over the potentiality and actuality of Christ's very flesh. Already the two tiers (nature and grace) of a certain Thomism,[35] or perhaps the weight of the "real distinction" between *esse* and *essentia* adopted in the high Middle Ages, emerges as the absolutely inviolable *Grundprinzip* of all creation, even of Christ's self-creation in Mary's womb.[36] But if we wish to grasp Maximus, at least, such a proscription will not suffice.

1.2. MAXIMUS'S FINE POINT: HYPOSTATIC IDENTITY

I discern in Maximus three features proper to hypostasis as it relates to nature. A hypostasis is *irreducible* to, *inseparable* from, and *indifferent* toward the nature it is.[37] This section lingers over the first and last features; the second feature returns in the next section on the concept of "the enhypostatic" (1.3). Together these help describe just what sort of identity obtains between different natures in a single hypostasis—in Christ, the identity of infinitely different natures, created and uncreated.

1.2.1. Irreducibility (or Positivity)

With all Neo-Chalcedonians Maximus insisted on the convertibility of terms in matters Trinitarian and Christological.[38] This univocity spans the two mysteries and reinforces the Chalcedonian distinction between οὐσία-φύσις and ὑπόστασις-πρόσωπον. The former pair predicates the common or universal, the latter the proper or particular. And that bit of tried traditional wisdom was of mainly Cappadocian deposit: "On the one hand, according to the Fathers the essence and the nature (for they say that these are the same thing) are common and universal, i.e. generic. On the other, the hypostasis and the person (for these too, they say, come to the same) are proper and particular."[39] That partition came hewn from solid dogmatic stone: were there no strict correlation of nature with commonality and hypostasis with property, the Christian doctrine of God as Trinity would implode. "My account," writes Maximus, "will dare to speak of the greatest: even with respect to the first, anarchic, efficient cause of all beings we do not contemplate the nature and the hypostasis as identical to one another."[40] God's very being proves and determines that these two logics of nature and hypostasis—and they are *logics*, they bear distinctive principles (*logoi*)[41]—are inseparable yet irreducible to one another.[42]

Thence follows a familiar deduction: if a person in the Trinity differs by hypostasis alone, and if a hypostasis is always what makes proper or individuates (or, as the first definition had it, "characterizes"), then the Son's hypostasis exists by an ineffable principle, an ineffable act of the Father.[43] The Son is *who* he is, is himself in all his personal distinctiveness, right there in the heart of the eternal Trinity. Few would deny this: vintage post-Constantinople (381) orthodoxy. But again, fewer still grasp the fairly massive implications this has for the concept of individuation in the Incarnation. The Son is already the singular hypostasis he is "prior" to his personal human existence in the historical Incarnation. His personal identity was certainly no product of some descending generic-to-specific "contraction,"[44] that is, an individual among other roots of Porphyry's tree. Still less could Aristotle's individuation by accidents apply, for the rather sane reason that God has no accidents at all.[45] The person of the Son, *that man* Jesus, the hypostasis he is, subsists by some other principle of individuation. If he is "not an individual" in Porphyry's sense, as Maximus reads Cyril to say,[46] this is exactly because "being individual" is for the Son an intra-Trinitarian act that bears its own unique principle (rather than the species-principle of genus plus differentiae or some variety of the bundle principle). But this is also the principle of Christ's human subsistence lest it be not the very Son in flesh. Thus in the Incarnation the divine principle of individuation extends to the created order itself: what alone is one in Christ, hypostasis, subsists in (and indeed grounds) his telluric life by a hitherto unthought individuating principle, a principle irreducible to the principle of either of his natures and yet, of course, inseparable from them as well.[47] In the Trinity and in Christ—that is, in God *ad intra* and *ad extra*—Maximus divines the surest warrant for distinguishing and describing the two logics of nature and hypostasis. In fact, he contends, failure to do so constitutes precisely the rotten root of otherwise opposed Christological heresies—no small matter.[48]

In Christological controversy everything comes down to the "mode of union."[49] Here you must discriminate the two logics. In their mutual inability to discriminate these logics Maximus perceives basic agreement between Nestorians and miaphysites of every sort. Whether two natures require two hypostases or one hypostasis/one nature, a tight correspondence between nature and hypostasis assumes that the mode (and so product) of the Incarnation must bend to "natural laws," to how any concrete synthesis supposedly occurs in nature.[50] Neither party sufficiently conceived hypostasis in its own positivity. Neither glimpsed that hypostasis bears a logic distinct from nature. Especially flagrant was the miaphysite concept of Christ's "composed nature," "the acropolis of Severus's reasonings."[51] For Severus Christ's one nature still retained something of a human "quality" and so is rightly considered "composed."[52]

Maximus tenders three arguments to the contrary.[53] First, the union of Christ's two natures becomes involuntary. It would have occurred, that is, with just as little intent involved as, say, the union of my body and soul: neither willed union with the other. Second, this union is simultaneous. Since neither "part" of Christ's one composed nature could really be what it is outside of that concrete whole (think again of human body and soul), either Christ's flesh must enjoy co-eternity with the Word or the very Word did not exist until birthed by the Virgin. Last and most significant, this union would complete or perfect both parts united. Christ would need both parts to achieve the whole he is by nature. His becoming would therefore be subject to a law or *logos* greater than either of his parts on its own, a *logos* corresponding to the perfected whole as such. Maximus defies all three necessary features of Severus's single "composed nature" and thereby denies that *Christ* names any kind of *natural* whole at all. And yet he remains the whole of these parts. In fact, Christ himself "is the limit, the principle [λόγος], and the law of every composed nature."[54]

A composed hypostasis, not a composed nature—this is Maximus's line.[55] Not without controversy.[56] Much of the worry, I think, comes from a failure to think through the two distinct logics of hypostasis and nature *and then* their peculiar relation (total indifference). The idea of a "composed hypostasis" is clear enough: it signifies that concrete whole apart from which its proper parts (or natures) could not subsist, and therefore a whole irreducible to and yet constituted by its parts.[57] Here we come upon a metaphysical axiom in Maximus. We already saw that it is an axiom grounded in the Trinity and now Christ: because both hypostasis and nature name positive features of all being—they name, that is, distinct logics or dimensions of being in their own right—they also act as the necessary and reciprocal condition for one another (this will become clearer in sec. 1.3). Christ the hypostatic "whole" is the sole and fundamentally positive oneness of divine and human natures. Their oneness, their identity, simply is their existential *fact* in Christ. But the hypostasis as such presents nothing natural, no formal or essential content of its own, which is precisely why it avoids all the absurdities of Severus's "composed nature."[58] Christ *qua* hypostasis contains absolutely no natural content that might in any sense stand in tension with (still less in contrast to) another nature: as nature's condition, hypostasis pretends no natural relation to nature at all, necessarily so. "Behold the paradox," says Maximus, "to contemplate a composed hypostasis without thereby predicating a composed nature of that hypostasis, as if of a species."[59]

1.2.2. Indifference

Hence Maximus's answer to Severus's dilemma. Are Christ's two natures universal or particular? For Maximus, both.[60] How? Recall hypostasis's two definitions or functions.[61] Hypostasis is the "this" that (1) grounds and (2) individuates what it is. The composed hypostasis of the Word, then, makes his natures simultaneously real and particular. In Christ divinity and humanity are single and factual—indeed, they are a single fact or event (not a nature, which apart from its fact/hypostasis is nothing at all). Again the singularity of a hypostasis bears its own positive principle, and yet this principle is decidedly not natural. The Son's hypostasis is therefore an existential fact that stands in no tension with nature. And for this very reason it can receive—and *be*—utterly incommensurable natures without diminishing them (hypostasis in itself possesses *nothing* natural to oppose any nature). The Word's reception of these natures is their very subsistence.[62] But it is indeed *his* reception; he, I mean, receives divine and human natures in his own distinctive way, his individual style, in the very concreteness of his own hypostasis—in his "this," if you will. Their personal identity in him just *is* their concrete particularity.[63]

So we meet once more that principal worry over Neo-Chalcedonian Christology, that the Son's own eternal property individuates his human flesh. But this point proves essential for Maximus. It discloses the Incarnation's very logic, its very possibility: "All this announces the true principle [*logos*] of the divine economy, of the Incarnation. For the properties by which his flesh differed, distinguishing him from us—by these his flesh possessed identity with the Word according to hypostasis. And the properties by which the Word differed from the Father and Spirit, distinct as Son—by these he preserved the monadic identity with the flesh according to hypostasis. No principle [*logos*] whatever divides him."[64] The point here, not entirely unique to Maximus,[65] is that the only thing the Son "has" that can be one with a nature infinitely different from his divinity is *himself*, his hypostasis; for his hypostasis certainly differs from the Father's and from divinity as such. This hypostasis is already "individualized" by his unique generation, already a distinct person in the Godhead. Therefore the Son who is very God becomes one with human nature only by instancing it in and as himself—by becoming the existential fact or event of both natures at once and as one. So while his divinity unites him to the Father and his humanity to us (by nature), he receives these two natural unities, Chalcedon's two "consubstantialities," only because of and in his hypostatic distinction from hypostases of both divine and human natures.[66] That hypostatic determination stands indifferent to nature is precisely what makes it wholly hospitable to nature.

A proper discrimination of the two logics, then, produces a clever circumvention of Severus's dilemma. Since it belongs to a hypostasis's principle to characterize and particularize and to a nature's principle to communize and universalize, an "individual nature" names a nature's universal power and actuality *in a personal mode*. A nature in that mode is no mere abstraction. That particular mode still bears the mode and quality proper to the nature as such.[67] In other words, nature in a personal mode remains a universal nature; it really actualizes and so displays properties common to all other individuals of the same kind (e.g., rationality in Paul is still the same essential rationality in me—however modally dimmer in me). And yet the very mode that concretizes these universal features is itself always individual, always of a certain person.[68] The positivity and total indifference of person to nature—its distinctive logic—make it possible for Christ to possess both a universal and a particular human nature.

Maximus helpfully clarifies all this when he confronts a monenergist proposal meant to mollify strict dyenergists like him. Since, they argue, an activity belongs properly to a person *qua* agent, and since Christ was undoubtedly one person, he possessed only one "hypostatic activity." Maximus thinks not. He responds to Theodore of Raithu's version:

> For [Theodore] obscured and in a certain sense destroyed the principle for these things [i.e., hypostasis and nature] by assigning to the person *qua* person the activity that characterizes the nature rather than [assigning to the person] the "how" and the "what sort of mode" of its [i.e., nature's] fulfillment [οὐχὶ τὸν πῶς καὶ ὁποῖον τῆς κατ' αὐτὴν ἐκβάσεως τρόπον]. In this way one recognizes the difference between those acting and those acted upon, possessing these with or against nature. For each of us acts principally as "what" we are rather than as "who"—that is, [we act] as man. And as someone, say Paul or Peter, he gives expression to the mode of the activity which he typifies through impartation, perhaps, or by progress in this way or that

according to his dispositive judgment. Hence, on the one hand, one recognizes difference among persons in the mode of conduct [ἐν μὲν τῷ τρόπῳ . . . κατὰ τὴν πρᾶξιν], and on the other, invariability in the *logos* of the natural activity. For one is not more or less endowed with activity or reason [ἐνεργὴς ἢ λογικός] but we all have the same *logos* and its natural activity.[69]

Positivity and indifference of person: positive, so it determines ("expresses" and "typifies") the peculiar mode of its nature; indifferent, so it perfectly preserves its nature's universal principle ("One is not more or less," "We all have the same *logos* and its natural activity").

The person of Christ is the principle of individuation.[70] Precisely because his hypostasis relates indifferently to nature it can welcome his human universality and particularity: hypostasis makes no natural determination that would qualify either pole of nature's modal determination, universal or particular, as if it were itself some principle of nature legislating one mode in place of the another. Christ grounds and determines his own humanity; he must therefore "precede" both its universal and particular dimensions. Now consider this: in Christ's case, at least (for now), Maximus sees no need for some other grounding and individuating principle— to take sides, as it were, on the great debate over immanent and transcendent universals.[71] Christo-logic relieves that sort of pressure. Indeed, it must.

At length we arrive at an anticipated claim: Maximus openly denies that any Porphyrian principle of individuation, Neoplatonic or Peripatetic, obtains in the Incarnation.[72] Curiously enough, he suspects Severus of just this.

And if he does not confess these [two natures] but really confesses the qualities alone, it is clear that, obliterating the natures, he teaches that Christ is an assemblage of qualities [ποιοτήτων ἄθροισμα τὸν Χριστὸν] just as we know the natures of material things to be: really established in a material substrate [ὑποκειμένῳ μέντοι τῆς ὕλης συνισταμένας] yet not contemplated in the sole and simple qualities, as indeed he depicts Christ. Which is why he calls him a composed nature—that, obviously, and does not conceive another fashioned and composed from simple qualities. For out of whatever things he says the difference is, of these plainly is the union too. For the difference is not of those things while the union is of others but [both] are of the very same things and not of others.[73]

A somewhat elliptical passage, but the basic claim is clear enough: it is wrong to conceive the "compositeness" of Christ in terms of nature or quality (itself of a concrete nature). Either fails to the degree that it virtually reduces Christ's "unity" to an assemblage of qualities around one material substrate. That is, Christ would be "one" and so "individuated" by matter such that we really only have one concrete nature ("which is why he calls him a composed nature") modified by the addition of accidents or qualities in the way a material substrate suffers alteration of its various qualities. Thus the subtle polemic in the closing lines: whatever differs—for Severus, merely qualities—is also what is united in Christ; and if the qualities alone differ, then the qualities alone can be united, and in the only conceivable way an "assemblage of qualities" is ever united, namely in a material substrate. But a material substrate (Maximus affirms in the next paragraph) is surely among the most divided unities. And this, Maximus argues, is the best sort of unity Severus can permit if he is to remain consistent.[74]

Successful or not, the argument nicely illustrates Maximus's rejection of the Porphyrian principle. A positive principle of hypostasis, Christ himself, and not some posterior assemblage of characteristics, grounds and individuates Christ's created nature.[75] He makes himself two.[76] In fact, to state the deeper insight, only such a principle of individuation proves Christ truly one.

1.2.3. Identity

In Christo-logic *hypostasis* names an individual positivity whose principle stands in a relation of utter indifference to the nature(s) it is. Its positivity and indifference are the exact properties that permit it to exist *as* the singular, concrete fact of two incommensurable natures—that is, to be their identity. Hypostasis is a *mode of union*, to reprise the Neo-Chalcedonian conviction.

Maximus (like Leontius) thinks this true even in the case of the human person.[77] The body-soul comparison, it is true, had by Maximus's time a somewhat fraught legacy. Apollinarius made much of it, as did Cyril. It was a miaphysite favorite.[78] Quite obvious why: a human person is a synthesis of two distinct natures, body and soul, and yet completes one nature, the human. So too in Christ. Divine and human natures, though two on their own, attain concrete identity as one composite nature. Maximus confronts the analogy's force in a way that seems counterintuitive. Rather than stress the inevitable dissimilarity to Christ's case, an exceptional one, Maximus extends the logic of Christ to the anthropological analogy itself. Even the body-soul unity in an individual human person does not yet constitute their true identity.[79] They remain—even in this or that person—essentially distinct in principle or by nature, a fact anyone "grasps clearly enough."[80] True, once they subsist and converge in a concrete person they enjoy relative commonality even on the level of nature: both are temporal, both are mutually affecting,[81] and both are of course natures.[82] Theirs is no absolute difference (as obtains among qualities, which are "mutually eliminating": triangular excludes circular, death negates life, and so on). Theirs is difference by "antinomy," a difference that "accepts separation" but only within a more fundamental community.[83]

Once body and soul unite in an individual, I said, *then* they achieve relative union in distinction. Only when real and really united, when they are brought into permanent "reciprocal relation" (τὴν εἰς τὸ πρός τι ἐξ ἀνάγκης ἀναφορὰν δέχεται) by the singular event of a person's historical birth (notice the anti-Origenism here)—only then do they receive each other in asymmetrical, essential union.[84] And so even in the case of a human person two natures find relation, actuality, and identity in hypostasis alone. More exactly: because their identity lies solely in the person, they retain their natural difference in principle.[85] Conceiving the human whole this way releases nature from having to achieve real identity between differing natures. Neither my soul nor my body nor some kind of natural mediation between them generates *me*—the concrete "I" who just *is* this body and this soul in this unity. Precisely here the comparison between anthropology and Christology truly obtains:[86] the singular identity of hypostasis, the only positivity that exists in itself (hypostasis's second definition), makes possible and actual the concrete union of my body and soul (first definition). And because of hypostasis's absolute indifference as the real identity of each, these natures, relieved of that burden (of achieving their own mutual identity), can preserve the universal principle that makes them what they are. The hypostasis itself is a mode of union granting absolute identity to essentially different realities. Only here and only in this way do they receive "identity with one another."[87]

And if this is so in the typical human case, *a fortiori* in Christ's. A human body and soul, once generated, still relate to one another naturally. They fit together *qua* nature(s). They form one human nature. But

Christ *qua* hypostasis—indeed, any hypostasis *qua* hypostasis—is no genus, no species, no nature at all. Actually for the same reason he is no mere individual either—if, that is, *individual* signifies the formal relations of the nature that a hypostasis instances.

> I hasten to add that Christ's composed person is not properly an individual [οὐδὲ ἄτομον κυρίως]. For [his composed person] possesses no relation to the division that goes from the most generic genus down through other subaltern genera all the way to the most specific species, finally proceeding into *him*, i.e. to that property defining [him]. Whence and for this reason, according to the most wise Cyril, the name "Christ" does not carry the power of definition since it is not a species [εἶδός] predicated of many differing in number. Nor obviously is it the essence of something. For he is not an individual referring back to a species or genus, nor is he circumscribed by these according to essence. Rather [he is] a composed hypostasis making identical to a supreme degree, in himself, the natural distinction of the extremes, even leading [these] into one by the union of [his] proper parts.[88]

Observe how the passage ends: with Christ's hypostasis as the identity "to a supreme degree" of "the extremes," of his two utterly incommensurable natures. That last part is absolutely crucial. Christ's case does not differ from that of the body-soul unity because in the latter the natures form parts of one hypostatic whole. Rather, it differs because Christ's parts are *absolutely* different from each other. Created and uncreated natures share nothing by nature.[89] Indeed, it is exactly because they attain identity only in Christ's person that they remain entirely different in nature.[90]

At last we meet the final and most urgent reason Christo-logic distinguishes the two logics of hypostasis and nature. Hypostatic logic, as the only licit logic of mediation between created and uncreated natures, therefore becomes the logic of salvation (cf. Eph. 2:16). Christ's person is the only place where divinity and humanity can be really, positively, invariably one: "It is therefore clear that, according to the one hypostasis that these [natures] achieve, the parts absolutely do not differ in any way."[91] He is not simply their "conjunction" or "composed nature" (Severus's natural fusion). He is their identity (ταυτότης). Nor is it muddled thinking to say so.[92] It would be muddled, indeed heretical, *not* to, as Cyril knew.[93] (After all, Nestorius was anything but unclear in his thinking. His fault lay not in clarity of thought but in failure to conform that thought to the matter itself, to the fact of Christ.) Anything less than concrete identity is less than true union, less than our salvation. He, as the determinate positivity that is also utterly indifferent (and so totally hospitable) to uncreated and created nature alike—he alone mediates between them as the impossible possibility of their real identity: "So in this way he is mediator, according to hypostasis, for those parts from which he is composed: *he comprises the interval of the extremes in himself*" (ἵνα ᾖ καθ' ὑπόστασιν μεσίτης τοῖς ἐξ ὧν συνετέθη μέρεσι· τὴν τῶν ἄκρων ἐν αὐτῷ συνάπτων διάστασιν).[94]

Christo-logic in Maximus comes to this: total symmetry of natures, total identity of person, and the total indifference of identity and symmetry that Christ is. Any other logic fails to describe the peculiarity of Christ. Demetrios Bathrellos, for instance, inspired by Georges Florovsky's idea of a Christological "asymmetry" between Christ's divine person and his two natures in union,[95] finds Maximus's talk of Christ's "composite hypostasis" slightly disturbing: this along with "the exceedingly symmetrical parallelism between Christ and man . . . seems to contradict the insistence that in Christ the hypostasis is divine."[96] If, Bathrellos worries, we stress the symmetry of natures *and then* identify Christ's very person with both natures ("composite" = natures, "hypostasis" = person), as Maximus often does, then we might stumble unawares into Nestorianism. Bathrellos strains to save the concept by distinguishing the dimensions of Christ's one hypostasis. The "material" aspect designates Christ in his two natures, and here it is proper to call his hypostasis "composite." But the "personal" aspect is the preexistent Logos himself, improperly called "composite."[97] Now, the thesis runs, Maximus distinguishes (in practice) these aspects of Christ's hypostasis, and so we need not suspect him of compromising the Son's true oneness when speaking of the Son's "compositeness" with regard to his two natures. His true oneness lies in "the personal" dimension of his, well, person.[98]

Something is amiss in all this. Bathrellos appears to make a distinction within the hypostasis itself. Viewed as "the end-product of the union of the two extremes," he assures, "'hypostasis' does *not* mean, strictly speaking, the 'person' (which is identical with the Logos), but *the one reality* in which the two natures are united."[99] What exactly is this "one reality" that differs from the very "person" of the Son—from the Son himself? It is as if the "material" hypostasis (*qua* two natures) is somehow in tension with the "personal" hypostasis, who is alone the true Word. Bathrellos concludes just so: "Maximus has rightly been very careful to keep these two aspects of the mystery of the hypostasis of Christ *in complementary tension.*"[100] How could these two aspects of Christ's one hypostasis stand in any relation at all, let alone any tension? Any relation (and certainly any tension) necessarily implies two some-things or someones related. To avoid one alleged Nestorianism must we risk another?

The governing assumption, I fear, is not altogether uncommon.[101] It is that Christ the Logos, because he "preexists" in his divinity, is somehow more divine than human—as if what "preexists" belongs to him more properly than what he becomes. Bathrellos finds support for this assumption in the following passage from Maximus:

> Thus even though we say "one and two" of the same, we do not say these in the same way of this "one and the same." In one way, accord-ing to the principle of nature, [we say] "two" of those things from which the union occurred. For we do not know God the Word as identical to His own flesh *by nature* [κατὰ τὴν φύσιν]. Yet in another way, according to the principle of hypostasis, we say "one." For we *have* known God the Word as identical to His own flesh *by hyposta-sis* [κατὰ τὴν ὑπόστασιν]. Therefore we do not mindlessly fuse the natures into one hypostasis by refusing to speak of Christ's natural difference, lest we introduce mutual alteration between the Word and the flesh. Nor again do we insanely divide [Christ] into two self-subsistences, assigning difference to the very principle of hypostasis, lest we refuse our own salvation.[102]

Bathrellos correctly notes that Maximus targets Apollinarian Christol-ogy here. While the Son is God "according to nature," he is man "ac-cording to hypostasis" rather than nature. But we should unlearn Bath-rellos's lesson—"There is a dissimilarity between Christ and man [i.e., the body-soul analogy] due to the fact that *the person in Christ is identi-cal only to the Logos*, who exists prior to his humanity"[103]—since, as we saw, Maximus perceives the force of the anthropological analogy to lie in just the opposite point: even a human hypostasis *qua* hypostasis is no more or less identical to either of its natures, body or soul. The hypostasis's indifference removes any need to distinguish its different "aspects." It suffers no tension with any nature, certainly not with its own natures, and even less with itself. More serious, "assigning difference to the very principle of hypostasis," as the last line here warns, seems to deny that Christ himself—that divine Son from eternity—is ever truly one with his humanity. Very God must be just as identical to his human nature as he is to his divine nature, "lest we refuse our own salvation."

The mode of union is not simply its product.[104] When Maximus denies that the Word is human "according to nature" and yet is so united to his divinity, he means to deny that identity with humanity occurs by a natural mode, not that the product itself is somehow less naturally human. The Word Incarnate is human by nature. Maximus very often calls Christ "double-natured"[105] and thinks his unqualified identity with both names the very content of salvation.[106] Here is the pith of the entire mystery of hypostatic identity, of the economy: "Christ is each according to nature."[107] In Christ the divine Son is no more divine than he is human, no more God than man, no more uncreated than created.

The tendency to think of Christ's "person" (or an "aspect" of it) as some prior or deeper reality than his human nature actually explains, I think, one of Maximus's signatures: to the Neo-Chalcedonian confession of Christ "out of two natures" (ἐκ δύο φύσεων) and "in two natures" (ἐν δύο φύσεσιν) he frequently appends the Antiochene phrase "*is* two natures" (αἱ φυσεῖς ἐστιν ὁ Χριστός).[108] By now we sense why. In Christologic you cannot have absolute identity apart from absolute difference. Divine and human natures stand in no essential relation to one another, no tension or asymmetry; they have nothing natural in common at all. Indeed, to effect their unqualified union they *must* not possess any natural commonality. Hypostasis designates a positivity that bears no natural relation to either nature (for it is itself no nature apart from its nature(s)!). And hypostasis is sufficiently indifferent so that it can become their concrete identity while exerting not a modicum of pressure on either nature in the process. Failure to speak of the Word's simultaneous, unqualified identity as and of both natures—(NB: He *is* both, but not as some third "thing."[109] The Incarnation is not a case of transitive identity: it is not "A = B, B = C, therefore A = C," but "A [hypostasis] = B/C [natures]" where the "/" itself only exists because there is nothing transferable in "A" as such to either "B" or "C" as such. So since he is both natures in *this* way, he is their "is" in a way transitivity simply cannot conceive)—this spells failure to speak most "properly" of the mystery of Incarnation.[110]

Natural and hypostatic logics enable each other. Nature never needs to answer for identity between different natures (especially absolutely different ones). Hypostasis never needs to answer for identity between concrete individuals (as with a crass "mixture"). Their ineffable discrimination within God himself—to come full circle—grounds the Son's ability, in his own hypostasis, to become the very ground of both concrete identity and essential difference between what he eternally is and what he becomes. So Christ is the ground, possibility, and actuality (in the historical Incarnation) of three identities at once: (1) natural identity with Father and Spirit (divinity); (2) natural identity with human persons (humanity); (3) hypostatic identity in himself (second definition of hypostasis).[111] Hypostatic logic, properly distinguished from natural logic, emerges as the condition of the possibility of natural difference to exist at all. In his economy the Son himself "made the union and distinction of the extremes" (οἷς τὴν πρὸς τὰ ἄκρα ἐποιεῖτο ἕνωσιν καὶ διάκρισιν). The Son proved to be more himself, more one, exactly to the extent that he preserved natural difference as their singular identity: "By preserving [the natures]" his hypostasis "preserved itself, and by conserving them it conserves itself. . . . If one ceases, the other is effaced in confusion."[112]

Balthasar called Maximus's Christ the (supposedly Hegelian) "identity of identity and nonidentity."[113] We can be more precise (and likely more Hegelian): Christ is the *hypostatic* identity of *natural* identity and *natural* difference. He himself, his very person, became an "is" otherwise unthinkable between created and uncreated nature. And yet his becoming that "is" is the ground and possibility of the most absolute and real natural difference. We might say that the Incarnation makes absolute natural difference thinkable for the first time in human thought. Hypostatic identity names the actuality or the fact of the very difference between God and man. If we were to grow hasty and expand Christo-logic to creation itself, we might even say this: the Son's hypostatic identity manifests, *is*, the very mode of *creatio ex nihilo*.

1.3. HYPOSTATIC IDENTITY GENERATES NATURAL DIFFERENCE

That bit of speculative haste invokes an exegetical dispute, albeit indirectly. The dispute concerns a concept, a single term, even, present before and in Maximus: τὸ ἐνυπόστατος. Behind the term lies a long and labyrinthine and mainly theological history.[114] It first emerges, it seems, "in

Christian circles in Origen's time or shortly before," chiefly in Trinitarian controversy to emphasize the concrete reality or distinct subsistence of the Son and the Spirit.[115] In the early development of Trinitarian thought, ἐνυπόστατος, ὑπόστασις, ἐνουσία, and οὐσία "were absolutely convertible":[116] they aimed to deny (against modalists) that the second and third divine persons *qua* distinct persons were "without hypostasis" (ἀνυπόστατος). At length the Word is described not merely as λόγος προφορικός ("an expressed word") or as λόγος ἐνδιάθετος ("an inner word") but as the ἐνυπόστατος Λόγος ("the really subsistent Word").[117]

Problems arise when pro-Chalcedonians, heirs to the Cappadocian-Chalcedonian legacy that distinguishes *ousia* and *hypostasis*, begin to employ the term ἐνυπόστατος to describe the metaphysical status of Christ's human nature. They did so to dissolve an already-familiar objection raised by both Severans and Nestorians: since there is "no nature without hypostasis [ἀνυπόστατος]," Chalcedon's "two natures" entail two hypostases.[118] From John Grammaticus on,[119] Neo-Chalcedonians countered that since Christ's humanity never had "subsistence" (τὸ ὑφεστηκέναι) or "distinct existence" (ἡ ὑπόστασις) apart from the Word, the Word's own hypostasis just *is* his humanity's. His humanity is indeed "not without hypostasis," but neither does it have its *own* (separate) hypostasis. It is ἐνυπόστατος because it subsists in the Word's hypostasis. But it is ἀνυπόστατος in itself.[120]

At this point *enhypostatos* means quite the contrary of what it meant in earlier Trinitarian theology. Then it signified a hypostasis, a distinct subsistence in its own right (Son and Spirit). Now it indicates a nature or essence that has no distinct subsistence in itself but rather in another (Christ's human nature in his person). Our exegetical dispute concerns this last claim. Friedrich Loofs argued in 1887 that Leontius of Byzantium distinguished a hypostasis from an enhypostatized essence in a novel way, specifically in Aristotelian terms:[121] as "second substance" is to "first substance," so stands the enhypostasized essence to its hypostasis.[122] This implies that Christ's human nature, as *enhypostatos* (second *ousia*), possessed a quasi-accidental ontological relation to Christ's person akin to an "essential quality."[123] It also implies that the activity of Christ's human nature, its existential integrity, was somehow "absorbed" (*aufnimmt*) into the divine nature, since its concrete actuality was dominated by the divine hypostasis as its sole primary substance.[124]

"One can hardly interpret Leontius worse than Loofs did"—thus thundered Grillmeier.[125] Inspired by Brian Daley,[126] and, as far as I can see, by a worry over a creeping monophysitism similar to what motivated earlier criticisms of Neo-Chalcedonianism, Grillmeier proposes that *enhypostatos* as applied to Christ's flesh means simply "real" or "subsistent." Leontius and others, they argue, do not with this word proffer an account of *how* Christ's human nature subsisted, just *that* it did so, and never apart from Christ himself. The etymology of the prefix *en-* indicates (solely?) the contrary of the *an-*prefix, an alpha-privative, so that, say, while accidents are *anhypostata*—not really subsistent in themselves—the flesh of Christ is *enhypostatos*—concrete, real, subsistent.[127]

I said this whole dispute concerns Maximus really but "indirectly," and for two reasons. First, more recent scholarship has shown, decisively to my mind, that Daley's etymological argument about what the prefix *en-* must always mean is certainly overstated.[128] The single and magisterial monograph on the subject by Benjamin Gleede proves that Leontius did instigate the critical change—a clear distinction between *enhypostatos* and *hypostasis*—that issued in what Gleede calls the "distinction tradition." This tradition self-consciously linked the in-subsistence of Christ's humanity—that it began to exist only *in* his hypostasis—with the concept (and term) of that nature's enhypostatic existence. And, second, Maximus stands firmly in and exemplifies precisely this tradition. In this tradition "a translation [of ἐνυπόστατος] as 'hypostatically realised,' 'enhypostatic' or 'enhypostasized' (as adopted especially by Maximus-scholars) would be preferable to the rather misleading 'hypostatical' or, even less precise, 'real.'"[129]

More significant, Gleede identifies two novelties in Maximus's own use of the term. The first has to do with its Trinitarian meaning. Maximus occasionally employs it in an earlier, more traditional sense: the Word is "really, personally distinct."[130] But he also uses it with the same sense it carries in Christology:

> For the Monad is truly a Monad: it is not the origin of the things that come after it, as if it had expanded after a state of contraction, like something naturally poured out and proliferating into a multitude, but is rather the *enhypostasized* being of the consubstantial Trinity [ἀλλ' ἐνυπόστατος ὀντότης ὁμοουσίου Τριάδος]. And the Trinity is

truly a Trinity, not the sum of a divisible number . . . but the *enessentialized* existence of the tri-hypostatic Monad [ἀλλ᾽ ἐνούσιος ὕπαρξις τριυποστάτου μονάδος]. The Trinity is truly a Monad, for such it is [ἐστίν]; and the Monad is truly a Trinity, for as such it subsists [ὑφέστηκεν], since there is one Godhead that is monadically and subsists trinitarianly [οὗσά τε μοναδικῶς καὶ ὑφισταμένη τριαδικῶς].[131]

Enhypostatos here refers to the divine, monadic, consubstantial essence. A crucial feature of the "distinction tradition," recall, was that the *enhypostatos* differs from hypostasis insofar as the former designates an οὐσία, what is common and universal *in* the hypostasis. So the two terms are "not convertible," as Maximus (following Leontius) said: hypostasis is all that nature is, not the reverse.[132] And the "tri-hypostatic Monad" has "existence" only as *enousios*, empowered and enacted as and through the consubstantial, divine essence.[133] That *enhypostatos* here responds to *enousios*—that the former refers to essence and the latter to hypostasis (three, of course)—just so Maximus manages to make Christological and Trinitarian terms more clearly univocal than they already were in Neo-Chalcedonian idiom.[134]

The second novelty effects a development of the in-subsistence theory itself. Maximus, Gleede observes, has a conspicuous penchant for λαμβάνειν ἐν when articulating the in-subsistence formula: Christ's flesh "takes" or "receives" subsistence or hypostasis in the very Word. And not only subsistence but τὸ εἶναι or τὴν φύσιν: in the Word's hypostasis humanity does not simply receive reality; it is actualized as the nature it is.[135] More precisely, Christ's human nature received concrete existence in the Word's own subsistence, yes, but also its very origin or the principle by which it is what it is. In Mary the Word becomes the seed of his own conception and gestation, the existence and natural formation of his own humanity.[136]

> Thus, "though He was beyond being, He came into being," fashioning within nature *a principle of generation* and a *different* mode of birth [γενέσεως ἀρχὴν καὶ γεννήσεως ἑτέραν [Wisd. 7:5] τῇ φύσει δημιουργήσας], for He was conceived having become the seed of His own flesh, and He was born having become the seal of the virginity of the one who bore Him, showing that with respect to her mutually

contradictory things truly exist together. For she herself is both virgin and mother, innovating nature by a coincidence of opposites,
since virginity and childbearing are opposites, and no one would
have imagined from nature their combination [ὧν ἐκ φύσεως οὐκ ἂν
τις ἐπινοηθήσεται σύμβασις].[137]

The mode of union is the mode of both of the Son's generations, and both
modes simply are him. Scarcely was there a starker reprisal of Chalcedonian symmetry. And yet this symmetry—of births, modes of existence,
natures—as before, proves possible and actual only by and because of
hypostatic identity. In other words, *because* these attain identity solely in
the singular hypostasis of the Word they can *therefore* retain all their own
natural properties undiminished. Nature, and indeed the very origin that
births it in both divine and human modes, never answers for its own subsistence or concrete being. Nature is only actualized in his hypostasis—
only ever *enhypostatos*. As divine nature subsists *in* God, so human nature subsists *in* Mary. Rather, because it is so in God, so it is in Mary.[138]

Now we can specify two elements of Maximian Christo-logic: in the
Incarnation hypostatic identity (1) enables and (2) generates absolute
natural difference. There in Christ we perceive not just the "conjunction"
or even "union" of natural extremes, but in fact "the generation of opposites" (τῇ τῶν ἐναντίων γενέσει).[139] Were these natures not hypostatically
identical, neither they nor their opposition would exist at all.[140]

1.4. PERICHORESIS IN CHRISTOLOGY:
A NEW MODE OF UNIFYING NATURES IN ACT

Those two elements of Christo-logic remain rather formal. They specify
that Christ is the generation and preservation of two incommensurable
natural principles, that is, of their absolute difference *in principle*.[141] But
natural principles are the principles of natural activities.[142] So Christ's
person possesses two natures, each with its own principle of activity.
When he acts, does he not unfold two activities? And if two activities, doesn't this imply that Christ is two *in actuality*? Just here Neo-
Chalcedonianism felt a certain pressure to stay true to its Cyrillian convictions. Karl-Heinz Uthemann has rightly argued that monenergism and

(soon after) monothelitism were understandable (though not inevitable) developments of Neo-Chalcedonianism itself.[143] Maximus championed another possibility. And yet his was no simple rejection of monenergism. Maximus's alternative, also a signature contribution to Christology proper, grew, I think, from a deep appreciation for what fundamentally motivated the insistence on "one activity." For the first time in Christian thought, Maximus made the peculiar logic of *perichoresis* the summit of Christo-logic.[144] This has not gone unnoticed.[145] What has, it seems, are the precise metaphysical implications of this innovation.

The monenergist intuition seems clear enough. We met it already in Theodore of Raithu: since Christ is one person, he is one agent, and a single agent enacts a single activity uniquely its own. Christ, though two in principle, must be one *in actu*. Here lay Pyrrhus's concern. After a lengthy dispute about Christ's wills, Pyrrhus, erstwhile patriarch of Constantinople, tenders a thesis about the logically prior question of Christ's two activities (since willing is a natural activity of rational beings): Christ possessed one "hypostatic activity."[146] One person performs one activity. Maximus rejects this view, not least because it would require three activities of the one Trinity (here again the Trinitarian-Christological univocity!).[147] He then offers an alternative proposal outfitted with a venerable analogy: *in actu*, Christ's activities unite in "their complete interpenetration into each other," like the burning cut and the cutting burn of a red-hot blade.[148] Pyrrhus immediately ripostes, "But the *agent*, is it not one?" Maximus concurs. A bit later Pyrrhus sharpens his criticism: "It does not necessarily follow that since he operates dually, he has two activities."[149] But even in union, Maximus follows, an activity must correspond to a nature, so that a single activity "dually" effected still implies a single (if composite) nature—an especially flagrant offense with respect to Christ's two natures, "since in general no mediator exists between the created and the uncreated."[150]

Pyrrhus pivots: "Do you not accept and agree with those who say that *the effect* of Christ's works *is one activity*?"[151] An evident motive: Pyrrhus wants to ensure that Christ's dual natures yet issue in one concrete reality, one actuality—in "the effect" (τὸ ἀποτέλεσμα).[152] Is Christ *really* one after all? Maximus notes a subtle distinction between "inner" and "outer" acts that appears to register the force of the underlying concern: "We are not discussing," he clarifies, "things external to Christ, but things within Christ himself, that is, the natural principle of Christ's essences, whether he was defective from the union or remained without defect."[153] The distinction chimes with Plotinus's doctrine of "double activity." An interior act perfects the very nature of the agent (or hypostasis), for example, the way thinking perfects intellectual nature. An exterior act is the separate effect issuing forth *from* that interior act, such as the way walking on a beach presses prints into the sand.[154] Maximus stresses the former: he wants to secure the perfect, undiminished actuality interior to each of Christ's natures. Their exterior effects are another matter.

Pyrrhus brandishes a second goad, one Maximus often felt—the weight of authority. Both Dionysius and Cyril appear to teach one activity in Christ: Dionysius speaks of "a certain new theandric activity" of Christ, Cyril of "the single, congenital [συγγενῆ] activity made manifest through both [natures]."[155] Now Maximus reprises his original proposal. What is "new," in Dionysius's terms, and what effects this unprecedented "congenital activity," in Cyril's, is precisely the new mode in which Christ's two natures relate *in actu*, the new way they are qualified in hypostatic union: "But if this newness [of Christ's 'theandric activity'] is a qualitative one [ποιότης], then it does not mean one energy. Instead it signifies both the new and the ineffable mode of the manifestation of Christ's natural activities—the ineffable manner of the *perichoresis* of Christ's natures into each other, and that manner of life that was proper to His humanity which, being foreign and paradoxical, is unknown to the nature of beings, and [signifies] the mode of exchange proper to the ineffable union."[156] Maximus plainly admits that the *perichoresis* of Christ's natures (in context, these natures *in act*) "is unknown to the nature of beings"—is, he indicates, something utterly unthinkable apart from "the ineffable union." What exactly is so new about this "mode of exchange"?

In *Opusculum* 5, a brief but suggestive text, Maximus registers and rejects three conciliatory proposals of the monenergists, three ways, that is, to confess Christ's activities as being in a certain sense "one and two":[157]: (1) divine activity overwhelms and dominates the human; (2) divine activity uses the human as "an instrument"; (3) there is one composite activity, the divine and human functioning as parts. The last first, and quickly. To this Maximus retorts that a "composed activity" carries the same absurdities as a "composed nature," since the former derives from the latter: it would be "simultaneous" and "involuntary," and it would itself be a *species* of activity that other individuals of that same composed nature would perform ("a plethora of Christs").[158] Of the second Maximus asks: This instrumental causality, is it natural or fabricated? If natural, then it would be "synchronous" (σύγχρονον), "like body and soul." That is, as with Severus's "composed nature," we would have to say that neither agent nor instrument exists as naturally distinct from the other.[159] If this causality is fabricated, Maximus sees only Nestorianism or Apollinarianism: if the two activities are not unified *naturally*, then the agent and instrument exist either in relative separation from each other as wholes (Nestorius) or else in a whole where the agent assumes the role of superior over the governed and inferior, so that while "this [instrument] is not always moved," it yet "appears to be taken up and moved by the hand of the actor" (Apollinarius).[160]

It is in his rejection of the first proposal, I think, that Maximus betrays his fundamental conviction about the unity of Christ's two activities. Even if the divine activity dominated the human in Christ, that divine activity would still itself suffer some degree of extrinsic qualification. The relation between the dominating and the dominated, Maximus observes, "has to do with things relative to another [τῶν Πρός τι]," and such things "always introduce, together, in themselves, things [by nature] mutually implicative [τὰ ἀντιδιαιρούμενα]."[161] This is an Aristotelian point. Aristotle launches his disquisition on the category of relation by noting that "all relatives are said having correlatives [ἀντιστρέφοντα]"[162] and, after discussing a number of examples, concludes that such correlatives naturally come into being "simultaneously."[163] The basic issue, unremitting here as ever, is that even natural dominance *in actu* still conceives a *natural* relation, as if the two activities were set in a certain tension, with the divine claiming a superior degree of being what both at some (specific or generic) level are.[164] Asymmetrical relation remains a natural relation; indeed, it *must* so remain if degrees of dominance be discerned at all. Once again Maximus knows no such asymmetry in Christ:

And then if you speak of one activity according to domination such that the human [activity] is denied because it is dominated, you introduce *diminution to both* [μείωσιν αὐταῖς εἰσάγετε]. For the one that dominates is always also itself among suffering things since it too is dominated by the dominated [καὶ αὐτὸ γὰρ κρατεῖται ὑπὸ τοῦ ἐπικρατουμένου]. Even if to a lesser degree, the [dominating] is yet certainly dominated, just as gold, for example, dominates the silver or the copper alloyed with it: here it is itself dominated even if to a lesser extent . . . since this has to do with *the degree to which it has been mixed* [ὅτι κατὰ τὴν ποσότητα τὴν προσμιγεῖσαν].[165]

What is new in Christ's actual existence then is this: two incommensurable natures (*logoi*), bearing their proper powers (*dynameis*) and activities (*energeiai*), which indeed express their proper *modes* of being (*tropoi*)—all of these are found in a singular and real identity (*hypostasis*) in such a manner (*perichoresis*) that they perdure utterly "without diminution," wholly untarnished and unqualified *in se* even as they wholly interpenetrate *in re*.

That last claim proves perhaps most astonishing against the backdrop of Neoplatonic metaphysics. Christo-logic must finally reject one standard account of "vertical causality" (which obviously funds the monenergist proposals here), in two ways: in Christ, unlike in Neoplatonic emanation, (1) higher and lower modes of activity interpenetrate each other *in both directions*, and yet (2) remain *perfectly whole* in their natural (interior) power, act, and mode.

Neoplatonism could never abide such perilous confusion.[166] Plotinus's doctrine of "double activity," a valiant attempt to combine Aristotelian and Platonic logics of act (horizontal and vertical, respectively), proscribes any symmetrical penetration of higher and lower levels of being.[167] Asymmetrical relation and mutual presence, certainly. The classic problem of participation just was the problem of how distinct existences might ultimately be one, and how that One reality, whatever and however it be, could be wholly present to the manifold of beings.[168] But as Proclus insists near the start of his *Elements of Theology*, although the One is wholly present to all as the very unity of the manifold, each instance of the manifold is itself "both one and not-one."[169] Higher beings or superior causes (and certainly the One) are "self-sufficient in essence and activity" and by that very self-sufficiency emanate inferior existences that depend on the higher for "completeness."[170] The essence or nature of every effect (pre)exists in its cause "in a primary mode" (πρώτως) and in this effect "in a secondary mode" (δευτέρως). Hence no effect—with its proper nature and activity—is ever simply identical to the cause, lest there be no discernible procession at all. But—and here lies the crucial matter—it is similarly impossible that there be "nothing in common or identical in both," lest the effect "not arise from [the cause's] existence."[171] What makes an effect an effect is that it possesses a nature and power identical to its cause but in a more determinate, lesser mode. It is "like" its cause.[172]

And so *modal asymmetry* characterizes the entire structure of vertical causality: the whole cause obtains in its effect in the effect's proper mode (procession) but is never the whole effect *qua* effect in the whole cause—since, of course, the whole effect is always in the whole cause "in a primary mode" (remaining) and, should it return to that whole cause, would simply *be* the cause itself, that is, assume its proper mode (reversion).[173] Hence Iamblichus, in reply to Porphyry's aversion to the idea that certain gods are assigned certain locales or elements, repurposes the asymmetrical structure of participation in order to defend theurgical uses of finite media (certain temples, certain words, certain materials). Just as sunlight "proceeds throughout the totality of existence" yet remains in its own prior mode, so too with the divine nature, which likewise stands in "no relation of symmetry" to its manifold participants.[174] Furthermore: "In respect of entities which are homogeneous in essence and potency, or indeed of the same species or genus, it is possible to conceive of some type of encompassing or direct control; but with regard to such beings as are completely and in all respects transcendent, how in this case can one properly conceive of any *reciprocal interchange, or total interpenetration*, or circumscription of individuals, or encompassing of localities, or anything of the sort?"[175]

But the Incarnation discloses just this: the divine Son's hypostatic identity with a nature infinitely different from his own divinity generates a lower (human) nature with its native powers, and when he acts through both his divine and human natures—precisely because *he* is the "is" of both in power and act—these otherwise incommensurable activities penetrate one another *symmetrically and wholly*.[176] In fact Dionysius as Maximus reads him precluded the possibility of understanding the Incarnation in terms of vertical causality and so cracked the door onto a deeper perception of that event: "'How,' you ask, 'is Jesus, who is beyond all things, ranked together with all men at the same level of essential being?' But here He is not called 'man' insofar as He is cause of men, but as being that which in the entirety of its essence is truly man."[177] Note the stress on *entirety* of essence (κατ' οὐσίαν ὅλην). Maximus does, and then takes the necessary step from whole essence to whole power and act: "The only valid proof that this 'essence' is present in its 'entirety' . . . is its natural constitutive power, which one would not be mistaken in calling a 'natural activity,' properly and primarily characteristic of the nature in question."[178]

How exactly does this surpass the logic of vertical causality? Because the Word's hypostasis bears divine nature, power, and activity from eternity; and because this very hypostasis is the "is" that generates his own human nature with its own power and activity; and because he is both at once—therefore he himself is the downward emanation, as it were, that causes or generates the inferior mode proper to his human nature *in actu*. His own higher power (divine) is present to his own lower power (human) in a way that requires no natural mediation whatever.[179] In Christ divinity and humanity both retain their own modes in the same, positive identity of his hypostasis. That hypostasis, precisely because it is both positive and yet not a *tertium quid* alongside the natures, relieves both natures of any contrast, any tension, any asymmetrical ratio, any pressure for one mode to give way to another in order for distinctive actualities to be. The vertical, asymmetrical relation of cause and effect implies "a shallow difference," not the absolute natural difference enabled by hypostatic identity.[180] The sole mediator of Christ's natures is Christ's own hypostasis, and since his mediating hypostasis *is* their mutual identity, they are immediately present to and in one another, entirely in each's entirety.[181] Again commenting Dionysius: "'And in a manner beyond man, he truly became man,' since he maintained the modes (which are above nature), along with the principles (which are according to nature), united and unimpaired. The conjunction of these was beyond what is possible, but he for whom nothing is impossible became their true union [ἀληθὴς γενόμενος ἕνωσις], and was the hypostasis in neither of them exclusively, in no way acting through one of the natures in separation from the other, but in all that he did he confirmed the presence of the one through the other, since he is truly both."[182]

1.5. INCARNATION: EVENT DISCLOSES LOGIC, LOGIC APPLIES SOLELY TO FACT

Daley characterizes Leontius of Byzantium's distinctive approach to Christology thus: the task is not to scrutinize divinity or humanity "in themselves," unmoored in abstraction, but rather "to look at the 'fact' of Christ, as faith perceives him—the fact of a single individual's being both God and a man—and to reflect on the 'mode of union.'"[183] So too for

Maximus.[184] When Paul Blowers appropriates Jean-Luc Marion's idea of "the saturated phenomenon" in order to describe "the saturating power of revelation," he means, I think, that the concrete *event* of Christ so overwhelms us with revelatory brilliance that only that event could have laid bare the mystery that, *in* its very revelation, proves still darker to our (abstract) gaze.[185]

Hence a final "feature" of Maximus's Christo-logic, one, though, that does not quite form a last link in the logical chain. It is more a feature of the whole logic. It is this: because we had first to apprehend the peculiarity of Christ's two activities to glimpse the peculiarity of the person behind them—and indeed to perceive the whole "mode of union" that was for us "new"[186]— the logic derived from this event must be as peculiar as the event itself. Maximus thinks that prior to the fact of the historical Incarnation very little could have been known about how God might realize the end of the universe, which is union with him. Only at the event of Christ's Transfiguration did Moses and Elijah (and so all who came before) first learn not just *what* and *how* union occurs but that this very *what* and *how* was, prior to the Christ facing them, itself shut up in impenetrable mystery:

> [Moses and Elijah learned] that the fulfillment of God's ineffable plan for the universe, contained within His divine dispensations [ἐπ' αὐτῇ θείων οἰκονομιῶν], was completely beyond the comprehension of beings. All that could be known was His great providence and judgment, through which the universe is led in an orderly manner to an end [τέλος] known in advance only to God. No one else knew what it would be, or how it would take place, or what form it would take, or when it would occur; the only ones who in truth knew simply that it *would* take place were the saints.[187]

How God's ineffable plan—the Incarnation (*Q. Thal.* 60)—was possible is disclosed only in its actuality. Thus the very incomprehensibility of God's union with the world was incomprehensible before Christ.

Christo-logic does not amount to a contemplative guess about the nature of things, their beginning and end. Its necessary source is the event of God's Incarnation. For instance, he was seen walking on water, speaking a cure, and, above all, dead and resurrected,[188] and only when we behold the peculiar mode of these whole and simultaneous and interpenetrating activities proper to incommensurable natures are we granted intellectual vision[189] into the logic of God's own identity with what he is infinitely not by nature. Maximus ceaselessly proclaims that revelation of Christ's person comes *through* his parts: "He revealed himself in the unicity of his person . . . by the personal identity of his own parts."[190] "What and who will He be known to be—He who is not subject to change—if this could not be confirmed by the works He performs naturally? And how will He be confirmed in His oneness—as out of and in and indeed as [the natures]—if He remained motionless and without activity?"[191] Hypostatic identity is an event. The identity of the Son's hypostasis with natures uncreated and created, that identity lived out in time and space, *in concreto*—precisely there first dawned the real identity and difference of created and uncreated natures. Should you want to penetrate the mystery of God's creation, you must do so by looking upon the mystery of God's Incarnation. That last implication, at any rate, will occupy us in the coming chapters.

The event is the singular "mode of the Lord's activities," his earthly existence. We perceive Christo-logic through this fact and in this order: activities reveal powers, powers reveal natures, natures reveal an ineffable and previously unthought identity between two realities that, on the level of nature, remain ever and absolutely different.[192] The concrete "mode of exchange" Christ effects within himself is the very mode he is from eternity, and so his historical acts ultimately disclose *him*, his very person.[193] And in apprehending his person we glimpse the entirety of the Godhead, all three persons, which is the "new proclamation of the truth" the Incarnation heralded in its very eventuation.[194] This new truth is precisely the truth of theology proper because the Incarnation, which achieves both God's identification with creation and creation's with God, is itself the "divine counsel" from all eternity. The Incarnation is the realization of that counsel, the infinite actualization of divine power, the absolute revelation of divine transcendence *as* God's power to be and thus deify what he is infinitely not by nature (true immanence). And this is so exactly because what God is by (abstract) nature does not at all exhaust the infinite positivity of who he is hypostatically.[195]

And so, to complete the revolution of Christo-logic, what appears finally dazzling about Christ is that he is and in this event becomes the only real and absolute identity of absolute (natural) difference. This is why even for Maximus the Greek the interpenetration of cross (death) and resurrection (life) reveals the deepest truth about the mystery of God's relation to the world. Precisely there, on the cross, you *must* say "suffering God" in the most intensely literal sense. Precisely there you *must* say "God suffered" and "died," for, as Cyril and Gregory of Nazianzus knew, just here the truth of the Word's identity with both natures strains nearly to the breaking point. There too, at length, we *must* learn to differentiate person from nature in their respective positivity, inseparability, and indifference. For the divine *nature* did not die, but *God* did: "Saint Gregory said these things so that we might not out of ignorance ascribe the properties of the person to nature [τὰ τῆς ὑποστάσεως κατηγοροῦντες . . . τῆς φύσεως] and, like the Arians, unwittingly worship a God who by nature is susceptible to suffering."[196] The basic discretion between hypostasis and nature demanded by Chalcedon was itself revealed only in the fact of Christ, above all in the event where death and life interpenetrated in the one God. From that discretion the entire logic followed.

· · ·

"The Incarnation to Maximus means precisely the hypostatic union of divine and human nature."[197] Assuredly. This chapter tried to specify further what this union means and entails. It did so by identifying three elements or moments in Maximus that together articulate his Christo-logic:

1. *Hypostatic identity* is the only real identity differing natures can attain.
2. *Generation* of created nature and its very difference from the uncreated comes in this hypostatic identity.
3. *Perichoresis* is the mode of relation between these incommensurable natures in act.

A fourth feature is that these three elements form a *logic* known only from an *event*. That event was the historical Incarnation of the second person of the Trinity, who, in and as himself, actualized all three in a single earthly existence. Hence:

*4. objective Christo-logic becomes subjectively grasped only through its singular actualization, above all in the Son's death and resurrection.

On Maximus's own terms, therefore, I think it misleading to describe an event as "an Incarnation" or to call some metaphysical doctrine "Christological" unless it actually bears the same logic as the very event that disclosed that peculiar logic. If, to take a clear example, Tollefsen (or Balthasar) is right that when Maximus describes the cosmos as God's universal Incarnation he merely indulges a bit of "metaphor,"[198] and if in fact this metaphor signifies exactly the vertical causality whose validity Maximus *rejects* in Christology proper, then Maximus's statements depicting creation as Incarnation would appear to be not only metaphorical but misleading.

They could be. It remains for me to argue the contrary. That requires investigating whether Maximus's Christo-logic accounts for his cosmology, his understanding of creation. So the following chapters correspond to specific elements of the Christo-logic: if Maximus inscribes creation with this logic, the "is" in "God *is* world" must signify (1) the Word's hypostatic (not natural) identity to created nature, which (2) generates the principles (*logoi*) and corresponding powers of all creatures—so chapter 2. Then these creatures would be destined for (3) a *perichoretic* union of their own creaturely modes and activities with that of God—so chapter 3. Then, finally, the entire logic of creation— protology and eschatology—must be (*4) just as peculiar an event as the historical Incarnation itself is, or even, perhaps, creation must be that very event—so chapter 4. Framed as a question: Does the peculiarity of Christo-logic disclosed in a particular event at history's middle really describe the peculiar onto-logic at history's beginning and end? Might it even characterize God's entire act of *creatio ex nihilo*?

CHAPTER TWO

The Beginning

Word Becomes World

"The Word of God, very God, wills that the mystery of his Incarnation be actualized always and in all things."[1] As I indicated from the outset, I aim in these remaining chapters to argue that this assertion means what it says. I try to trace how it shapes Maximus's distinctive view of God's creation of the world. I do so by reading Maximus's doctrine of the *logoi*—a doctrine Andrew Louth has called a "lonely meteorite" in the Christian tradition[2]—as the metaphysical inscription of the Christo-logic detailed last chapter. The *logoi* or metaphysical "principles" of all things define, generate, and sustain every conceivable difference and identity in creation, from the integral identity and proper difference of an individual subject (or hypostasis) to the arboreal network of generic and specific unities and differentiae (or natures).[3] Of each being and the whole cosmos, then, the *logoi* disclose the beginning and end of God's creative act. So we can approach the *logoi* from two distinct (though finally inseparable) vantages: protologically, they describe God's creation of the world from nothing; eschatologically, God's perfection of the world—its deification. This chapter treats the former, the next the latter.

I argue here that the first two elements of Christo-logic explain the rather peculiar protological role of the *logoi*, and I do so in three basic steps. First, I open with several passages where Maximus describes divine creation as Incarnation; the identification is not my own (sec. 2.1). Then I challenge the adequacy of (especially Platonic) "participation" to do justice to Maximus's view of creation. Maximus does speak of participation, no question. Nearly all modern commentators rest content to take it as a basically Neoplatonic way of describing the God-world relation.[4] But I identify and describe three qualifications of participation-talk that suggest a still more fundamental logic at work in his account of creation (secs. 2.2–4). Last, I collate the results of these qualifications into a protological overview of Maximus's logic of creation (sec. 2.5), and I conclude that this logic corresponds precisely to what I identified as Christo-logic.

2.1. UNQUALIFIED DESCRIPTIONS OF CREATION AS INCARNATION

That creation is Incarnation is a claim Maximus actually makes. We saw it at *Ambiguum* 7.22.[5] At first glance he does not appear to mean something different from what he means when he speaks of the historical Incarnation. They bear the same logic. An initial indicator that this is so: Maximus moves seamlessly between the Word's Incarnation in world and in Mary without the slightest proviso. It is an important point, especially because Maximus's commentators—from Eriugena to modern scholarship—routinely insert qualifications of their own, ones quite absent from Maximus's texts. Sometimes this takes the anodyne form of quotation marks around "Incarnation" when applied to the act (beginning and end) of creation.[6] Other times the qualifications are more explicit: Maximus's talk of creation as "incarnation" is clearly "metaphorical," obviously not intended to evoke the literal mode of the Word's personal presence in and as Jesus Christ.[7] This section treats five passages where Maximus more or less explicitly describes creation as Incarnation.

1. *Ambiguum* 33. In a passage as brief as it is celebrated, Maximus offers three explanations for Gregory of Nazianzus's remark "The Logos becomes thick" (Ὁ Λόγος παχύνεται).[8] It refers, first, to the Word's historical Incarnation, when he "deemed it worthy to 'become thick' through His

presence in the flesh [διὰ τῆς ἐνσάρκου αὐτοῦ παρουσίας]."[9] The Word
also "becomes thick" in human words, in language, and that is Maximus's
third instance.[10] The second occupies us here: "Or that, having ineffably
encrypted Himself in the *logoi* of beings for our sake, He is obliquely signified in a proportionate way through each of the things seen, as if through
letters—a most complete whole together in the wholes, and a whole according to each particular, whole and undiminished, the undifferentiated
in the differences and always self-same, the simple and uncomposed in the
composites, the one without origin in the things subject to origin, and the
unseen in things seen, and the untouchable in things grasped."[11] Consider
three features of this claim. The first is an obvious insistence on the integrity of wholes, both of the Word in the *logoi* and of the beings themselves.
A union or synthesis that leaves undiminished the nature and mode of the
things synthesized—this recalls the third element of the Christo-logic discussed last chapter (i.e., perichoresis of modes and acts in Christ),[12] and it
will become central in the next chapter on the deification of the world.[13]
Second, it is the Word "Himself," not, say, the divine essence as such or
God as the most indeterminate power of all things,[14] who is encrypted
in and as the *logoi* of created beings. It is his person or hypostasis; it is
him.[15] Hence a final feature: Maximus never qualifies the second and
third Incarnations—in world and in words—in a way that makes them
unlike the first, the historical Incarnation. Indeed, this *ambiguum* closes
with something like the fundamental axiom underwriting each Incarnation, what Maximus calls the "principle of condescension" (συγκαταβάσεως
λόγῳ):[16] "To the degree that, for His own sake, He contracted us in view
of union with Himself, to that same degree He Himself, for our sake, expanded His very self through the principle of condescension."[17] Creation's
most fundamental metaphysical principles, then, are instances of the
Word's own "expansion"—a theme I take up later (sec. 2.3).

2. *Quaestiones ad Thalassium* 60. This passage forms the centerpiece
of my final chapter, but I note it here because of how striking it is. Thalassius asks Maximus to interpret 1 Peter 1:20, which calls Christ "a pure and
spotless lamb, who was foreknown before the foundation of the world, yet
manifested at the end of time for our sake."[18] Who exactly, Thalassius
wonders, foreknew the Incarnation? The Trinity, that's who.[19] But what is
foreknown, exactly—that's more interesting. Maximus pairs this verse
with Colossians 1:26, where "the great Apostle" mentions "the mystery

hidden from before the ages." That mystery is for Maximus nothing else than "the mystery according to Christ" (τὸ κατὰ Χριστὸν μυστήριον).[20] Of course this mystery refers "clearly" to the historical Incarnation. Maximus recapitulates it with characteristic density: "This [mystery] is clearly the ineffable and inconceivable union of divinity and humanity according to hypostasis, which leads the humanity into identity with the divinity in every way through the principle of hypostasis, and effects one composed hypostasis from both [natures], without thus inducing the slightest diminution of their essential difference according to nature."[21]

The mystery signifies the Word's economy, which means precisely that God becomes in person and by nature what he is not by nature—and so preserves both natures entirely.[22] This union "into identity," he says, names the very union God foreknew and for which he created all things. Notice what Maximus is *not* saying here. He does not mean that creation merely sets the stage for the unrepeatable union between divinity and humanity that occurred in first-century Palestine, as if the fullest realization of the "mystery according to Christ" were restricted to a single climactic moment in creation's history (though there is indeed a certain primacy to that event).[23] Here and elsewhere Maximus clearly avers that the realization of the "ineffable union" effected in Christ is the *very same* destined for all humanity, for and in every person.[24] Thus the claim intensifies: "For because of Christ, or rather the mystery according to Christ, all the ages and everything in those same ages have received the beginning and the end of their existence in Christ."[25]

Every creature receives the very principle (ἀρχή) and end (τέλος) of *its own* existence in Christ. *Principle*, of course, in both philosophical and patristic literature, signifies a metaphysical origin, often the efficient, formal, and final causes (or all at once) of a thing.[26] Here Maximus locates that metaphysical principle, not just in a preexistent Logos, but, recalling one of Origen's more daring moves, in the Word *Incarnate*.[27] The very event of the historical Incarnation is in some sense the event that grounds (not just perfects) creation itself.[28]

3. *Capita theologiae et oeconomiae* 1.66–67. These two short "chapters" resolve a set of meditations that portray the soul's gradual deification in terms of Christ's Passion, burial, and Resurrection (1.59–67). Whatever interpretive risks I court by summoning texts of this genre, their intensely contemplative character makes them more, not less, interesting for my

purposes, since it is precisely the *mystery* "according to Christ" that is for Maximus the mystery of creation (as we just saw).[29] Maximus writes: "The mystery of the Word's Incarnation bears the power of all the enigmas and types according to scripture as well as the science of all created things sensible and intelligible. And whoever knows the mystery of the cross and tomb knows the *logoi* of those created beings just mentioned. And whoever is initiated into the ineffable power of the resurrection knows the principal purpose for which God gave hypostasis to all things."[30]

Notice that the principles of the Word's embodied existence—here the Triduum[31]—are precisely the principles of creation (as they were at *Amb.* 33). The Incarnation's "power" is actualized at the apex of mystical ascent, where, as Maximus teaches here and elsewhere, the rational soul's natural motions and activities come to rest in their proper limits.[32] At that point, he continues, "Only the Word exists, in Himself, just as He reappeared after He had been raised from the dead possessing all the things from Himself according to circumscription, since nothing at all possesses familiarity with Him by a natural relation. For the salvation of the saved occurs by grace, not by nature."[33] Two features. Creation's culmination—like its "origin" (ἀρχή) and principles (λόγοι)—evinces the logic of Christ. That means the identity between humanity and divinity that deification by grace achieves is, as with the Risen Lord, a hypostatic identity. This broader feature points up a second subtle but utterly crucial mark: creaturely perfection realizes *no natural relation* between God and creature. And yet there arises a concrete relation of identity.[34] The denial of any natural relation or "familiarity" (οἰκειότητα) between God and world (or One and Many) constitutes a distinctive element of both Christo-logic and Maximus's view of creation.[35]

4. *Ambiguum* 41. I address this *ambiguum* in detail next chapter, but, again, it is too weighty to neglect here. In this passage Maximus explicates his famous five divisions of being,[36] the first of which is the division of "the uncreated nature from the whole of created nature."[37] Early on Maximus makes the curious remark that unlike the other divisions (e.g., sensible/intelligible, heaven/earth), this first division between uncreated and created natures, though excluding "union in a single essence," knows no name among the seers who contemplate nature. In other words, "what it is that distinguishes creation from God" is not itself some sort of natural division, not a kind of natural *principle* or *logos* that clearly demarcates

the "created" category from the "uncreated."[38] The very act of creation—
God's act of producing a nature or essence altogether incommensurable
with his own—demands a mode otherwise inaccessible to natural contemplation or human philosophy.

God intended that the very divisions wrought in creation's beginning
be surpassed in its perfection, specifically in humanity. Adam was to
render even created and uncreated natures "one and the same"—a rather
provocative pronouncement.[39] For now, observe that Maximus then narrates how the Word's historical Incarnation actualized or "recapitulated"
(in biblical terms)[40] this final sublation of every division and that this
defines the very origin and purpose of creation: Christ initiated "the universal union of all things in Himself."[41] The exposition forms a chiasm:
Maximus introduces the five divisions from the highest (created/uncreated)
to the lowest (male/female), laments Adam's failure to unite them, and
then reviews how Christ overcame each in reverse order.[42] What proves
truly remarkable, though—particularly in light of the curious point at the
start about how the *logos* of the creative act has gone unnamed—is the
immediate conclusion Maximus draws from the historical Incarnation:
"And *He recapitulated in Himself*, in a manner appropriate to God, *all
things*, showing that the whole creation is one, just as if it were another
human being, completed by the mutual coming together of all its members, inclining toward itself in the wholeness of its existence, according
to one, unique, simple, undefined, and unchangeable idea: that it comes
from nothing. Accordingly, all creation admits of one and the same, absolutely undifferentiated *logos*: that its existence is preceded by nonexistence."[43] Incarnation discloses the principle of *creatio ex nihilo*. Maximus
extends Irenaeus and even Origen quite a bit further here. Like them he
maintains that we glimpse creation's purpose in Christ alone. Beyond
them he sees too that Christ affords the very principle and mode of creation from nothing—creation's *archê*, as he put it in *Quaestiones ad
Thalassium* 60.[44] No wonder, then, that when Maximus replays Dionysius's depiction of *creatio ex nihilo* as *creatio ex Deo*, he does so while
linking the divine ecstasy of creation to the Word's play in the historical
Incarnation.[45] Nor should it surprise that Maximus can quite comfortably
describe creation itself in eucharistic terms.[46]

5. *Ambiguum* 6. He also describes creation in Marian terms. Here
Maximus braves a remark at once profound and unsolicited. He aims
principally to explain that and how for Gregory of Nazianzus those who

are "dragged down" are different from those who are "bound," that these conditions indicate different levels of spiritual progress (of virtue and contemplation). The former designates those who may experience momentary lapses from contemplating God, a sort of infrequent backsliding. As for the latter, such people do not merely glance away from the vision of God occasionally but have desisted from even the ascetic labors necessary to secure virtue, an essential condition of contemplation.[47] So far, so monastically practical.

At one point, though, when Maximus commends the necessary transformation of the soul's "irrational powers" (anger and desire) into the power of love and joy, he appears spontaneously moved to offer a short meditation on the conditions of the soul's deification—that is, on the sensible world, how it can guide us through "reason" and "intellect" ultimately into this "joy." Joy, he recalls, was precisely John the Baptist's reaction when both he and Christ were still gestating in the womb. And in this world we gestate in the womb too:

> For many people this may be a jarring and unusual thing to say, though it is true nonetheless: both we ourselves and the Word of God, the Creator and Master of the universe, exist in a kind of womb, owing to the present condition of our life. In this sensible world, just as if He were enclosed in a womb, the Word of God appears only obscurely, and only to those who have the spirit of John the Baptist. Human beings, on the other hand, gazing through the womb of the material world, catch but a glimpse of the Word who is concealed within beings [τὸν ἐν τοῖς οὖσιν ἐγκρυπτόμενον . . . Λόγον]. . . . For when compared to the ineffable glory and splendor of the age to come, and to the kind of life that awaits us there, this present life differs in no way from a womb swathed in darkness, in which, for the sake of us who were infantile in mind, the perfect and super-perfect Word of God, who loves mankind, became an infant.[48]

Here again we meet the link between cosmic and historical Incarnation. In the former the Word "is concealed" or "encrypted in beings," quite as he was in the *logoi* of our first text (*Amb.* 33). Now, if the world's Marian figure were an isolated characterization, perhaps we might safely bypass it as a colorful way of making a simple point about God's immanence in creation. And yet, as we'll see later this chapter and in the next, the idea proves a common one and takes many forms: the very Logos of God dwells within us, whether through reason, "which lives like a child within us";[49] or through virtue, which is "the natural seed of the Good" in our nature;[50] or through grace, when "Christ Jesus becomes his own proper lamb" for those who are "able to contain and consume him"[51]—he who at creation's beginning "concealed the knowledge of Himself in each of the rational substances *as their first power*"[52] and who is therefore activated and indeed born in every deified soul at creation's end.[53]

· · ·

These texts show both that Maximus identifies divine creation as an act of divine Incarnation and that he never qualifies this in a way that would make the mode of the Word's presence in the world's womb somehow different from his presence in Mary's.[54] Yet this remains an argument from silence, though this silence gives pause. Indeed, it should give us pause. This silence murmurs if only because, as I tried to show in the last chapter, there *is* a distinctive—indeed qualitatively different—logic involved in Maximus's Christology contrasted with, say, your typical Neoplatonic vertical or emanative logic.[55] Hypostatic union differs from standard versions of Platonic participation. So the question becomes: Do the distinctive elements of Christo-logic appear in Maximus's theology of creation? If Maximus's unqualified declarations are more than metaphor, then Christo-logic determines the entire God-world relation. Talk of "participation" (understood Neoplatonically) would not be able to account for his unique protology or eschatology.

Scholars attentive to Maximus's participation language tend to assume its essential logic is something very like Neoplatonic participation, as I noted.[56] There is of course some merit to this. Dionysius weighs heavily on Maximus, as does 1 Peter 2:4 on the entire tradition of Christian Platonism. I do not wish to stave it off as if something insidious would thus be injected into otherwise pure Christian marrow.[57]

And yet it must be said that even in the philosophical milieu the logic of participation was never so monochrome. It could mean rather different things beneath different horizons of the God-world relation. Stoics, for instance, who outstripped even Aristotle in their rejection of a preexistent realm of Platonic ideas, still spoke of "participation" between particulars and the universal cosmic bond, the Logos.[58] Luminaries in the high Neo-platonic tradition such as Proclus know that vertical participation is not sufficient to account for the ontological character of at least the highest beings, the divine henads: they also are what they are because of their *horizontal* relation among themselves, a relation more like perichoresis than participation.[59]

It is even plausible that Plato penned his *Parmenides* to test the adequacy of his own solution to the One-Many dilemma—to expose, that is, the deceptive ease with which participation might skirt restive problems internal to any monistic account of the God-world relation.[60] It is rather striking that just after Plato has the young Socrates mock Zeno's confidence in the concept of participation to elucidate the One-Many relation—Who, after all, really denies that whatever is not the One must be in some sense many *and* one (i.e., participate the One's unity)?—he raises a single possibility that would stupefy him as a veritable marvel: "But," says Socrates, "if [Zeno] demonstrates that that which is One is *itself* many, and in turn that the many is One, then I will be astonished at that."[61] Plato himself knew that the idea of the One becoming one of the Many (and the reverse) would constitute something altogether beyond his account of participation.

So yes, Maximus employs the language of participation.[62] But can we assume he means what, say, Plotinus or Proclus means by it? I doubt it.[63] The next three sections (2.2–4) raise three qualifications to the God-world relation in Maximus. The latter two focus on protology, on features of Maximus's *logoi* doctrine that exceed standard accounts of participation. Together these qualify participation talk such that the logic at work corresponds to Christo-logic. They suggest, I mean, that Maximus circumscribes participation logic within a view of creation as Incarnation. Thus it is Christo-logic that ultimately determines the sense of whatever concepts he borrows to describe the God-world relation, including the very idea of participation.[64]

2.2. FIRST QUALIFICATION:
NO NATURAL MEDIATION BETWEEN GOD AND WORLD

One bracing feature of Maximus's Christo-logic is that there obtains absolutely no common quality between created and uncreated natures as such. The Word's hypostasis alone links and unifies them *in actu*.[65] It is thus significant that Maximus charges Greek philosophy and Origenism with precisely this error. Both fail to grasp that God and creation share nothing essential or natural whatever. Maximus does grasp it and indeed revels in it as the truth of *creatio ex nihilo*, and this portends a major modification of typical understandings of participation. First Maximus's accusation, then a word on how it qualifies participation.

Maximus critiques the way (he thinks) Greek philosophy conceives the God-world relation.[66] His charge goes something like this. Only God or "the divine essence" receives no contrary, yet creatures do and must.[67] Creatures receive both that and all they are. God is and is what he is from himself. And "to speak more truly," Maximus presses, God "transcends" the very things he "is," such as existence and goodness and wisdom. Or rather, he is what he is in a completely incomprehensible way, self-subsistently—which is at bottom a mere negation: God does not receive what God is.[68] Whereas what all creatures have, even existence itself, they have "by participation and by grace."[69] But the very fact that they *receive* being means that creaturely being stands in opposition to "not-being." I have being, but I did not always. Therefore in fact and in thought nonbeing negates my concrete being. It is not just my "existence" (ὕπαρξις, nearly like *esse*), notice, that courts a contrary and so fixes a great ontological distance between God and me. My very "essence" (οὐσία, *essentia*)[70] also admits of "privation." No such privation or contrary opposes "true essence," God's, while contrariety is "proper to being by participation."[71]

Hence Maximus's problem with the Greeks. They "maintain that the essence of all beings eternally coexists with God and that they have only their qualities from Him," since, in their view, "essence has no contrary" and "contrariety is found only in the qualities around the essence."[72] Maximus suspects Greek metaphysics of essential monism: "essence" is the very same in all things, only the qualities or modes change—more or less of this or that property or configuration of properties. And so the world's diversity and vertically variegated structure (the Many) are but the myriad qualitative determinations of a single truly real essence (the One). Maximus subtly concedes something to this view. He agrees that "true essence" admits no contrary. But he refuses to grant that this applies to *created* essence. Here *created* signifies precisely whatever is brought to essence and existence from nothing through the divine will and knowledge.

The lesson Maximus draws from *creatio ex nihilo* is not—as it is for much modern theology—that God might not have created anything at all. Maximus never says that; quite the reverse, actually, here and elsewhere.[73] He means rather to insist, as the word *coexists* (συνυπάρχειν) implies, that God's creative power can produce from itself an essence or nature utterly other than its own. Or to reprise earlier concepts, the God without contrary creates contrariety itself.[74] When God creates he does not simply modify himself, his essential being, and thereby produce something of himself in a new mode or determination. "He is Creator not of the qualities but of the qualified essences," as Maximus puts it.[75] God has no counterpart; nothing could complete or complement or even relate in any way to his very essence *qua* "the true essence."[76] This is why Maximus thinks the Greeks slight "the all-powerful Goodness" of God when they do not accept a creation at once from God and essentially nothing like him.[77] That he can do it—at this we stand "astounded."[78] That he unstintingly wills it—therein we behold "His infinite goodness."[79] How can this occur? Only hints here: when God created, he "sent forth His eternally pre-existent knowledge of beings." In fact, creation is precisely that knowledge receiving an essence, which, because received, admits a contrary (not-being) and, because a contrary, is not God's at all.[80] Creation from nonbeing comes by God's eternal will and knowledge. And these, Maximus later specifies, are the *logoi* of all things.

Maximus critiques Origenism similarly. Many commentators rightly see that Maximus corrects Origenist cosmology by reconfiguring its metaphysical triad.[81] Where the Origenist myth has rest (*stasis*), motion (*kinesis*), and only then becoming (*genesis*), Maximus reverses the sequence to initial *genesis*, historical *kinesis*, and final *stasis*. Origenism's was a tale about how rational beings originally enjoyed perfect unity (*henad*), suffered a tragic fall into corporeal multiplicity upon their failure to desire God alone, and, through the Word's economy, will regain their truest (if obscured) desire—oneness "in spirit" with the God who is spirit.[82] Maximus readily agrees that God is the highest and most natural object of desire for rational creatures. He makes this exact point a premise in some of his sharpest polemic against a preexistent henad.[83] And, frankly, at least compared to Origen himself, Maximus's insistence that whatever receives being cannot be on the same metaphysical plane as God registers a point of *agreement* between them.[84]

But Maximus divines a deeper issue than any of this. Beyond and beneath a faulty metaphysics of motion he sees the perennial problem of how exactly God can relate to what is both from him alone and yet not him.[85] So yes, Maximus agrees that God and world do not share the same metaphysical plane (in essence or in quality/mode). But then the question becomes: Is their relation in any sense a *natural* one? Maximus thinks Origenism falters here precisely to the extent that it does conceive the God-world relation as somehow a natural one. Notice the way he subtly characterizes Origenist protology when disputing an Origenist interpretation of Gregory's remark that we "are a portion of God that has flowed down from above."[86] Such would be a "facile interpretation," "which in fact is derived largely from the doctrines of the Greeks. According to the opinion of these people, there once existed a unity of rational beings, by virtue of which we were connatural with God [τήν τέ ποτε οὖσαν . . . τῶν λογικῶν ἑνάδα καθ' ἣν συμφεῖς ὄντες Θεῷ], in whom we had our remaining and abode. In addition to this they speak of a 'movement' that came about."[87] Origenists think we were (and are) "connatural" with God. This was Maximus's issue with "the Greeks" too.[88] Origenist protology, "after the manner of the Greeks, . . . mixed together the immiscible."[89] In other words, their protology tends to forge a natural or essential relation between, on one side, beings whose very nature (not simply their mode) necessitates a limited and self-contained process of actualization, and, on the other, God, whose nature not only is but transcends infinity itself.[90] For Maximus—and we will contemplate this in greater relief next chapter—there is absolutely no natural relation between created and uncreated natures *qua* natures.[91] A logic confined to essences or natures in themselves cannot conceive a natural God-world relation without thereby collapsing into essential monism or dualism, or perhaps retreating into an indefinite ignorance of any God-world relation whatever (recall *Amb.* 41.2).

Such passages might indicate Maximus's debt to the "closed world" view of creation articulated by his patristic forbearers in general and to fourth-century Nicene theology in particular.[92] For Maximus Greek metaphysics and Origenism alike seek to relax the radical difference between the natures of God and world.[93] "May divinity and humanity never become essentially identical, so that no created thing might be consubstantial and connatural with the divinity [ὁμοφυὲς καὶ ὁμοούσιον]! For we know that only an insane mind says these are consubstantial by nature."[94] And yet as we saw in the last chapter, proscribing any natural God-world property poses a major obstacle for any Neoplatonic version of participation. Proclus, for instance, regards it as plain nonsense to say there is "nothing in common or identical in both" participated and participant, cause and effect, because that would amount to denying any causal or dependent relation between them at all.[95] Indeed, it appears that the very heart of participation requires some sort of essential or natural commonality between the two, lest the entire notion of "likeness" among stratified levels derived from the One dissolve entirely (a notion, of course, dear to patristic doctrines of deification).[96] Put another way, Neoplatonic participation works precisely because higher and lower beings share a common essence (or essential property or essential power) and yet differ in mode. Participant and participated differ, that is, in *how* they possess and instantiate their common essence.[97] If, as Maximus contends, between created and uncreated natures no natural link of any sort abides, how could participation ever get under way at all?

At this point we might imagine Maximus to number among the staunchest advocates of *creatio ex nihilo* in Christian tradition.[98] There is certainly truth to the claim. It seems fairly typical to characterize patristic conceptions of creation like this: God posits an "outside" reality alongside himself, an "other" that, because it is ostensibly created by divine will rather than divine nature (unlike the Son's generation from Father), is wholly "dissimilar" to God's nature.[99] At least concerning the divine essence itself, Maximus may not even tolerate that much. After all, even a similar-dissimilar relation presumes common qualities. How then to bridge the "great chasm" Gregory of Nazianzus surveys, which "separates the whole of nature that has come into being . . . from that which is uncreated and at rest"?[100] When Maximus quotes this passage, he answers it with another from Dionysius: God, from the "overflow of His intense love for all things, *goes out of Himself* . . . to be in all according to an ecstatic and supraessential power which is yet inseparable from Himself."[101] That captures Maximus's underlying conviction as he wields his *logoi* doctrine against Origenist protology. "We consider" that "all things . . . come into being *from God*" (τῶν ἐκ Θεοῦ γενομένων . . . ἡ γένεσις).[102] So *creatio ex nihilo* entails an insuperable gap between the nature of God and that of the world, but, simultaneously, that the world's creation is God's becoming out of himself—*creatio ex Deo*. How both?

2.3. SECOND QUALIFICATION:
THE LOGOS BECOMES *LOGOI*, NOT IDEAS
(THE PARTICIPATED)

If Neoplatonic participation adequately explained the God-world relation, then you might expect the fundamental creative principles or *logoi* of all creatures to be the eternal ideas or forms participated by all things. Then the procession from One to Many would occur precisely *as* cascading iterations of more determinate or qualified essences, as, I mean, the egressive "limitation of act by power" that establishes every effect's hypostasis as a mixture of the One and not-One (i.e., as a determinate configuration of variously participated higher principles).[103] Maximus's *logoi* do generate the species and forms of created hypostases as well as the very individuality of each hypostasis. They make all things "related to" God, though not by a natural relation.[104] But the *logoi* are not forms or ideas. Nor does Maximus ever identify them as such.[105]

He could easily have done so. John of Scythopolis (*sedit* 536–ca. 548) was the first commentator of the Dionysian corpus.[106] Maximus would later add his own scholia to John's, which led to a long history of conflating the two under Maximus's name.[107] John did identify Dionysius's *logoi* and "paradigms" with the preexistent "forms" and "ideas" in the mind (or Logos) of God.[108] For John a Dionysian *logos* is "an idea, that is, a paradigm," "an eternal production of the eternal God which is complete in itself."[109] This definition points up the precarious station that divine ideas occupy. As eternally complete productions (ποίησιν αὐτοτελῆ ἀίδιον) they are not the divine essence, yet as eternal with and internal to God they are not quite creatures either. They are "thoughts of God," and though not worshipped as very God,[110] they are nothing other than him. They constitute the stuff of God *qua* "pure mind":

> Since God is also the creator of beings, he will think them in that which does not yet exist. But he is the archetype of this universe. And these things he thinks not by receiving types from another, but by himself being the paradigm of beings. Thus, he is neither in a place, nor are things in him, as if in a place. But he has them, in so far as he has himself and is one with them—since all things, on the one hand, exist together and exist in the indivisible in him; and since, on

the other hand, they are distinguished indivisibly in the indivisible. Accordingly, his thoughts are beings, and these beings are forms.[111]

These forms or ideas are like the "incorporeal matter of the things which participate in those ideas."[112] So for John the *logoi* are the preexistent ideas that result from God's simple act of thinking himself, the forms participated variously by creatures.[113]

Not for Maximus. "Who," after contemplating the latent unity under-girding the "infinite natural differences" in creation, would "fail to know the one Logos as many *logoi*, indivisibly distinguished amid the differences of created things," and conversely would fail to know that "the many *logoi* are one Logos, seeing that all things are related to Him without being confused with Him"?[114] The one Logos "is manifested and multiplied [πληθυνόμενον]" in and as the *logoi* of all beings.[115] They preexist "in" and "with Him,"[116] ineffably precontained in Him from eternity.[117] Through the "creative and sustaining procession [πρόοδον] of the One to individual beings," "the One is many." And through "the revertive, in-ductive, and providential return of the many to the One," "the many are the One."[118] The Logos is the *logoi* and the *logoi* the Logos.

Plotinus said the same.[119] The Intellect, the second of the three primary hypostases,[120] "is like one great complete *logos* embracing them all," embracing, that is, the *logoi* of the highest intelligible realities down to the *logoi* of particular "living beings" (i.e., particular souls). And these *logoi* are "what the Intellect wills and is [ὅ θέλει νοῦς καὶ ἔστι]." Intellect is therefore "one and many."[121] One and many, because intellectual power is the power to receive the form of the object known and so become identical to that object in actuality.[122] So when Intellect contemplates the *logoi* of all things—themselves the productive principles issuing from Intellect's restive labors to image the imageless One[123]—it becomes identical to them. Intellect's very nature comprises the perfect union of "otherness" (ἑτερότης) and "sameness" (ταυτότης), which forms the ground of all creaturely "difference" (διάφορα).[124] Plotinus's Intellect is the *logos* that generates difference by self-identifying with many *logoi*. Quite like Maximus, it appears.[125]

Recall, though, that for Plotinus the divine Intellect is not the One. There can be no difference in the One, since to be different is to be other than one. The One somehow possesses all created beings beforehand, yet

"in such a way as not to be distinct [μὴ διακεκριμένα]: they are distinguished on the second level, in the *logos* [ἐν τῷ δευτέρῳ διεκέκριτο τῷ
λόγῳ]."[126] Creatures gain their definitional difference by *not* being the One,
that is, in the Intellect's *logoi*. Ever since Clement and Origen firmly
planted the *logoi* of creatures in the Second Person of the Trinity, the Word
and Wisdom,[127] Christians were obliged to waver here. After Proclus's proliferation of causal intermediaries (the henads),[128] Dionysius again pressed
the Christian intuition: "The whole good processions and the Names of
God, celebrated by us, are of one God."[129] If the Christian Creator is *sole*
cause of the Many, he becomes, in the creative act, One and Many.

Maximus identifies God the Logos (not the Father, not the Spirit)
with the creaturely *logoi*, so this must mean that the Word is somehow
both one and many in such a way that it transcends the logic of Neoplatonic procession (which is the logic of participation from above, as it
were).[130] He speaks of the Word's "procession" (πρόοδον) into all beings,
true.[131] But we should not take this to imply what it must if this were Neoplatonic procession, namely, either (1) that this procession somehow diminished the Word (making the Logos essentially subordinate to the One)
so that the "identity" of Logos and *logoi* would obtain only "by derivation,"[132] or (2) that the very Word would not be really identical to creaturely *logoi* after all (as Plotinus's One is not essentially Intellect-*logos*).[133]
No, this procession of One Word to manifold world proves at once vertical and horizontal. It designates the Word's vertical descent who yet remains the same hypostasis.[134] It indicates a horizontal multiplication and
yet no inner perfection of any hypostasis.[135]

Actually, if we seek philosophical precedent for that type of causal
procession we should look not to Neoplatonism but to Stoicism. Consider
one ancient summary: "The Stoics made god out to be intelligent, a design-
ing fire which methodically proceeds towards the creation of the world,
and encompasses all the seminal principles [τοὺς σπερματικοὺς λόγους]
according to which everything comes about according to fate, and a breath
pervading the whole world, which takes on different names owing to the
alterations of the matter through which it passes."[136] And not only does the
Stoic Logos-god contain all "seminal principles within," but, as "the seminal *logos* of the cosmos,"[137] this Logos "brings forth [the world] from himself"[138] and simultaneously "comes to be in its parts."[139] The Stoic Logos
does not proceed into the *logoi* of all things through declension.[140] In every

logos dwells the same Logos, whose very identity constitutes both the universal identity and the particular difference of all beings.[141]

Now compare all this to an ostensibly odd feature of Maximian protology. There is another metaphysical "movement" besides procession and return in Maximus: "expansion" and "contraction."[142] Maximus knows a "principle and mode of expansion and contraction," the "simple essence" that pervades and binds all genera, species, and individuals into a single world.[143] Again we meet similar ideas in Stoic physics.[144] The Word "expands His very self" into and as the creative *logoi*.[145] And so the Word's "procession" (*Amb.* 7) and "expansion" (*Amb.* 33) ultimately name the same creative movement. They name the way God brings the world into being from nothing, from himself.[146]

Two crucial metaphysical features emerge from this comparison. Both features differentiate Maximus and the Stoics from Neoplatonic participation/procession. First, each retains the order or sequence of Neoplatonic procession *without* a gradual, vertical chain of self-subsistent intermediaries. The one Word "preexists" the manifold cosmos.[147] And yet unless the very Word becomes the undiminished, immanent, and personal presence in and as the principles of everything, we have no cosmos at all. Second, this more "horizontal" creative procession does *not* preclude some version of a vertical, cosmic hierarchy. The point is rather that this hierarchy emerges *from within* the sole world that subsists—the cosmos. In neither Stoicism nor Maximus do we encounter a "world of ideas" akin to Platonic forms.[148] Rather, both envision only the eternal Word and the temporal world, which together form a single subsistent cosmos because the Word is both at once.[149] The Word constructs the very world of ideas from within this world. Stoicism can "combine pantheism and cosmic hierarchy"[150] precisely because when their Word processes he remains the Word he is, and, being himself in and as the world, he gives "form and figure to every particular thing [εἰδοποιεῖν ἕκαστα καὶ σχηματίζειν]."[151] Maximus employs these exact terms: "What are these *logoi* that were first embedded within the subsistence of beings, according to which each being is and has its nature, and from which each was formed [εἰδοπεποίηται], shaped [ἐσχημάτισται], and structured, and endowed with power, the ability to act, and to be acted upon . . . ?"[152] The *logoi* are not separately subsistent, participated forms. They are the personal Logos crafting all things within himself, within them.[153]

So then, the second qualification to participation logic comes from the side of the participated. The *logoi*, which are the Word's self-willed procession as the "infinite identity" of all things[154]—of their most generic kind to their most individual difference, and of the manifold relations among all universals and particulars—are not participated forms. They do not subsist in themselves or in some separate realm. They subsist in only two realities: eternally, in and *as* the very hypostasis of the Word; and simultaneously, in and *as* the very principles that cause and sustain the entire world. Both realities are the one Word. The *logoi* refer to the fact that the Logos becomes and is the "is" of both uncreated and created natures.[155]

2.4. THIRD QUALIFICATION:
THE *LOGOI* OF CREATED HYPOSTASES
(THE PARTICIPANTS)

Now consider participation from the opposite vantage, from the side of the created individuals or hypostases—the participants. Here we meet a qualification from below, as it were. You might state it like this: one reason that participation, an activity, cannot account for the whole creative act (and so the whole God-world relation) is that it cannot explain the creation of the positivity of participants as such. A picture captivates us: "The creation of the world . . . is to bring God's eternal knowledge of beings into a temporal dimension. Beings have their design in the *logoi*, and creation is precisely this, that entities are called into the temporal sphere . . . of participation in God's activity in accordance with these designs."[156] But if participation names the "sphere" into which God's creative act moves the beings he has always had in mind, how could the dynamics of that very sphere explain a movement *into* that sphere? How do you get a participant "before" participation? Or how is there participation "before" participants? The movement into participating God must itself precede and (and so exceed) participation lest we coil ourselves into a circular argument. The circle would run thus: creation is the transitive movement from nonbeing into participating God (Tollefsen's "sphere"); but that very movement is itself a participation in God; therefore creation is participation in participation—a vacuous notion.[157]

Matters worsen if you believe with Maximus that individual participants *qua* hypostases bear their own distinctive, whole, existential positivity. We saw how that idea results inexorably from the basic distinction between nature and hypostasis in Maximus's Christo-logic.[158] But it exacerbates the problem of participation "from below" in that it means that a hypostasis, which bears absolutely no formal content as such, still bears *some* sort of positivity requiring a causal act that *intends that very individual*. Now, for Maximus a hypostasis *simpliciter* is an effect in its own right, with its own integrity, rather than merely the fleeting residue of ever more contracted and higher subsistent forms or ideas. All this becomes clearer if we return to Maximus's *logoi* doctrine, this time from the standpoint of the participants these *logoi* ground and effect.

A thing's *logos* comprises and establishes the whole ontological continuum of its nature, its determinate and innate power and activity.[159] There is a *logos* of each participated nature (one of angels, one of human beings, and so on) and a *logos* of each individual's way of participating its nature(s), and these together constitute an individual creature's proper *logos*.[160] A *logos* indeed for every branch of Porphyry's tree: the *logos* of a genus allows it to exist "as a whole indivisibly and really in the whole of those things subordinate to it," while the *logos* of a particular is contained by the *logoi* of "what is universal and generic."[161] The preexistent *logos* of an individual creature necessarily includes its formal content, what sort of thing it is, up to the most generic level. Its "*logos* of being" makes it the sort of thing that is.[162]

More often Maximus invokes the *logoi* to secure the integrity of creaturely difference. This certainly includes the differences among natural genera and species, and even the categorical distinctions embedding a creature in space and time—all of which contribute to the unique identity of that creature, something close to Porphyry's "bundle of properties."[163] Close, but not quite. Maximus knows a deeper individuality, the difference of the differing thing itself. For "if we wish to have a complete knowledge of things," he says, "it is not enough to enumerate the multitude of characteristics," that is, "whatever is around the subject." Rather, it is "absolutely necessary that we also indicate what is the subject of these characteristics, which is the foundation, as it were, upon which they stand."[164] No creature simply "coincides in its essence with what is and is called the assemblage of characteristics that are recognized and predicated of it." The inmost identity of the individual creature "is something different from these characteristics," something "which holds them all together, but is in no way held together by them" and so "is not derived from" or "identical with them."[165] The *logoi* together carve out the individual difference of the differing thing—quite Platonic. But Maximus also attributes a *logos* to the difference of the individual as such, what he calls the "*logos* of hypostasis." Whereas a thing's "nature" "comprehends the common *logos* of being," its "hypostasis" "comprehends also the *logos* of being for that very individual."[166] A creature's uncreated *logos* grounds its identity as *that* individual—none of which should surprise us given Maximus's Christo-logic.

We can appreciate Maximus's originality here if we contrast his *logoi* to Plotinus's particular forms, especially since the two are often compared.[167] Richard Sorabji rightly observes that Plotinus's concept of particular or individual forms "can provide no help with the differentiation of *persons*, since the individuals in question are *souls*."[168] A particular soul is a fixed nature, more precisely a preexistent form, which contains as *logoi* the potential for "all the individuals it animates in succession." These *logoi* permit reincarnation. The same soul can now be Socrates and later Pythagoras.[169] I concede that Plotinus does not conceive the relation between an individual and its form in *simply* formal terms, "as portraits of Socrates are to their original."[170] The *logoi* of a soul (indeed, the *logoi* of the whole world soul) shuffle down, as it were, into the material realm, and by their "unequal predominance" together with matter constitute an individual. The mother transmits now these *logoi*, now those, the father these, now those; certain *logoi* predominate during this particular time period, others at another, still others at this place, others elsewhere—and so ever on through myriad individual combinations *ad infinitum*.[171] A circuitous route to be sure, but where individuals are generated by *logoi* "the difference must [still] be linked with the form."[172] An individual preexists only as a potency of its particular form. To the extent it is an individual it is not its form. And so, as Proclus later perceives, Intellect does not know the individual "before" the individual comes to be. Intellectual activity, after all, finds perfection in formal content—in an idea or concept or the like. But the individual as such has no form. Whatever Intellect knows in the individual is itself not individual. Intellect's ignorance of individuals is no defect, then. There is simply nothing there to know.[173]

Maximus agrees that an individual *qua* hypostasis is unknowable. A hypostasis certainly *possesses* form, bears a particular nature, but is not itself form. No form means no intelligible content. Again, a "nature" has to do with "a *logos* of form," and while a hypostasis as such lacks formal content it still has a *logos* of some kind.[174] Of what kind? Of *no* kind! A "*logos* of hypostasis" necessarily indicates no formal principle at all. This goes for every creaturely hypostasis. Since "every divine energy indicates through itself the whole God, indivisibly present in each individual thing, according to the *logos* through which that thing exists in its own way [ἐν ἑκάστῳ καθ' ὅνπερ τινὰ λόγον ἐστὶν ἰδικῶς]," then no mind can fathom "precisely how God is whole in all things commonly, and in each being in an irreducibly singular way [ἐν ἑκάστῳ τῶν ὄντῶν ἰδιαζόντως]." Intellects "are incapable of understanding even the lowermost creature in terms of the *logos* of its being and existence."[175] In each thing's *logos* God is, as scripture attests, truly "all things in all" (1 Cor. 12:6, 15:20; Eph. 1:23)—from the most universal participation (Being itself) to what is most particular (the participant or hypostasis).[176] Where some saw only intelligible dearth Maximus glimpsed the fundamental mystery that every single creature is: the *logos* of what is necessarily unintelligible *qua* abstraction and thus unknowable by adequation—the hypostasis, the concrete participant[177]—this God foreknows "as only he knows how."[178] There, where "the intellect finds nothing to grasp," where formal procession can account for nothing of what is truly subsistent—I mean the individual or person—precisely there we encounter perhaps the most palpable preeminence of "divine power."[179]

All this explains why Maximus never says creatures participate their *logoi*. A creature's *logos* is the principle "by which" it participates divine perfections (Being, Goodness, Immortality, etc.). It is *how* a creature participates at all, not *what* it participates.[180] An individual's *logos* of hypostasis not only facilitates participation, but, as we saw, establishes the participant herself. Maximus can even say that we "receive participation."[181] My *logos* is the eternal principle that determines what I participate and the very I who participates.[182] It is God the Logos predetermining and preestablishing the *power* to be *me*—my nature and my person united in their ineffable and fundamental and singular "is."[183]

2.5. THE WORD PROCEEDS: ONE ACT IN TWO MODES

Participation in Maximus has now received three vital qualifications. (1) The world's essence enjoys no abstract natural mediation with or relation to divine essence; (2) the *logoi* that establish the world's essence are the Word himself and not participated forms or ideas that subsist on their own; (3) participants *qua* hypostases cannot come to be, cannot receive their concrete positivity, through participation (understood Neoplatonically as the formal, successively determinate limitation of higher acts by lower powers). What then is the divine act of creation? And what could "participation" signify in this radically qualified schema? In reply I limn a brief but instructive portrait of what sort of ontology emerges from the protology just considered.

Consider two characteristics of this portrait. First, divine creation is a single and inevitable act. Second, this one act generates two infinitely different natural modes (and so their very difference).

1. *One inevitable act.* Maximus conceives the act of creation in both aorist and present tense. Wisdom 9:1 says God "created" or "made" all things, yet in John 5:17 Jesus says: "My father continues to work even now, and I too am at work."[184] Maximus thinks this indicates two moments of a single creative act. God "completed" or "fulfilled" the foundational *logoi* of creatures "all at once" (ἅπαξ).[185] And these *logoi*, we saw, constitute the *power* of every creature to be who and what and at all.[186] But the actualization of these powers, the arboreal "extension of the ages," implies that God continues to create at every moment.[187] The *logoi* of identity and difference, the very lineaments of created being, show themselves "one in power" though they "assume a different and multi-modal activity."[188] Creation is a work of the entire Trinity, to be sure, but a work carefully distributed: the Father "approves" (εὐδοκῶν), the Son "actualizes it from himself" (αὐτουργῶν), the Holy Spirit "completes" (συμπληροῦντος) the roles of both.[189] And I must note *en passant* that Maximus uses exactly the same schema to describe the act of the historical Incarnation.[190]

I mentioned above that Maximus thinks creation inevitable. He could never agree with Florovsky, for example, that "the world could have not existed."[191] Here Maximus's doctrine appears diametrically opposed to Florovsky's, since the latter confuses creation's inevitability with its self-sufficiency and then accuses such a view of "introducing the world into the intra-Trinitarian life of the Godhead as a co-determinant principle."[192] Maximus instead thinks that a supposed *indeterminacy* on God's part toward the world would itself introduce another principle into God, a shadow side, as it were, of God's unmoored and aleatoric will. Strange to say, but Maximus even considers this among the most flagrant results of a certain Origenism and Manichaeanism.[193] It is the Origenist myth, Maximus notes, that imagines God having to "react" to the downward inclination of primordial souls and thereby to create something he never intended to create: a proliferation of bodies. Not only would this mean attributing to sin (as an essential condition) the beauty of the corporeal cosmos. It would imply the sudden emergence of *logoi* or "wills" in God that he did not intend from eternity, from the unqualified goodness of his nature. Maximus doesn't even consider this line. To him one thing remains surest of all: "The purpose of God, who created all things, must be changeless concerning them."[194] Ultimately the Word's Incarnation defines for us God's unwavering and irrevocable disposition toward creation. The Incarnation reveals that God is "truly Creator by nature."[195] Thus Maximus joins those venerable voices of patristic tradition who affirm creation's "sublime necessity,"[196] rarely defended in contemporary theology with the exception of another great Russian theologian, Florovsky's master, Sergius Bulgakov.[197]

2. *Two infinitely different natural modes.* In *Capita theologiae et oeconomiae* 1.48–50 we come upon a schema of participation that seems obviously Neoplatonic at first glance. Any determinate thing (τι) is qualified by (at least) the predicate "to be," and any such thing is a "work of God."[198] Works of God fall into two categories: those that "began" and those that "did not begin" or, more precisely, works generated "temporally" (χρονικῶς) and those "eternally" (ἀϊδίως). Temporally effected works designate "all participating beings [τὰ ὄντα μετέχοντα], such as the different essences of beings."[199] Works produced eternally are "participated realities" (τα ὄντα μεθεκτά) that participants participate "by grace."[200] The latter category of divine works comprises participated realities such as "all life, immortality, simplicity, immutability, infinity," and even "being itself."[201] And the God who works "incomprehensibly eludes infinitely all beings, participating and participated."[202]

Three levels, then: God the unparticipated,[203] his eternal works (participated), and his temporal works (the participants). A rather neat and apparently straightforward (if simplified) appropriation of Neoplatonic participation, Proclus's in particular.[204] But some oddities yet lurk. Maximus calls both types of divine works "beings" (τὰ ὄντα). Fine enough for participants generated in time, but what to say about "beings" eternally wrought? Perhaps this recalls Proclus's henads, causal mediators who share a single essence yet emanate different participants. Jonathan Greig has given the lie to this ostensible parallel, since, of course, Proclus's henads are whole and "self-subsistent" hypostases.[205] God's eternal works, though they have being, are nowhere called hypostases. And this would violate Maximus's first qualification denying any natural mediation between created and uncreated essences.[206]

Tollefsen argues that the "being" of God's eternal works puts Maximus in opposition to the Dionysian priority of Good over Being: "For Maximus, then, Goodness embraces the other activities and is itself embraced by Being."[207] Thus Tollefsen conceives the "being" of participated works as itself an instance of participation. I noted before some metaphysical problems with this line of thought, but here an exegetical point suffices: the participated works of God *include* "being itself."[208] Being itself *is*. The "is" of being itself therefore cannot be by participation. For what "being" would participated-being-itself participate? All that subsists above, we saw, is "true being" never participated—that is, the divine essence.[209] So what constitutes the "being" of God's eternal works?[210] Or since the participated works are also the one God,[211] we might reformulate the problem from the other metaphysical perspective: How can the imparticipible God become participible in his eternal works?

A hint: Maximus says here that the participated (eternal) works have "by grace been implanted in originated beings [temporal works/participants], as if a kind of implanted potentiality, loudly proclaiming that God is in all beings."[212] Again we sense Neoplatonic reverberations. Proclus too teaches that separately participated realities are "present to the participant through an inseparable potency which it [i.e., the participated] implants."[213] This power subsists in the participant alone, and yet, as the transference point of participation between higher act and the lower internal act, it is the "medium" of the two terms.[214] Again the comparison misleads. Not only are Maximus's "participated realities" *not* themselves hypostases, but the "power" within participants must furnish them the power to be more than *what* they are; it must also grant the power to be *who* they are, that is, to be hypostases. And hypostases exceed form in Maximus, we just saw (sec. 2.4). But Proclus's implanted "power"—here is the critical point—rehearses the very mechanism that is both essential to Neoplatonic participation and proscribed by Maximian *logoi*. Proclus's "power" emanates solely as a qualified and more determinate instance of the higher and "more perfect actuality" of its cause.[215] In other words, this "power" is the cause's natural activity in a lesser mode. A Maximian *logos*

emanates, not by a process of formal modification or participation—
indeed, we saw that it *establishes* that very process—but rather in a still
more fundamental, more mysterious way.

All these oddities and divergences make good sense if we make
proto-logic Christo-logic. This very text (*CT* 1.49) intimates the way: it
begins with the God who infinitely transcends both participated and participating works and then resolves in the assertion both that this "power"
implanted within each participant is God's participated work *and that it
heralds God himself in all beings*. We have here the divine *procession*
into all beings. This "power" names the term of that procession. God's
eternal works dwell within me as my very power to be all I am, and they
do so because God himself dwells within.[216] Maximus specifies the peculiar character of this procession in *Ambiguum* 7:

> When, however, we exclude the highest form of negative theology
> concerning the Logos—according to which the Logos is neither
> called, nor considered, nor is, in His entirety, anything that can be
> attributed to anything else, since He is beyond all being [ὡς ὑπερού-
> σιος], and is not participated in by any being whatsoever [οὐδὲ ὑπό
> τινος οὐδαμῶς καθ' ὁτιοῦν μετέχεται] . . . the one Logos is many
> logoi and the many are One [πολλοὶ λόγοι ὁ εἷς Λόγος ἐστὶ καὶ εἷς οἱ
> πολλοί]. According to the creative and sustaining procession of the
> One to individual beings, which is befitting of divine goodness, the
> One is many [τὴν ἀγαθοπρεπῆ εἰς τὰ ὄντα τοῦ ἑνὸς ποιητικήν τε καὶ
> συνεκτικὴν πρόοδον πολλοὶ ὁ εἷς]. According to the revertive, in-
> ductive, and providential return of the many to the One [τὴν εἰς τὸν
> ἕνα τῶν πολλῶν ἐπιστρεπτικήν τε καὶ χειραγωγικὴν ἀναφοράν τε
> καὶ πρόνοιαν] . . . insofar as the One gathers everything together, the
> many are One.[217]

The *logoi* are and issue from the Logos himself becoming the causal
principles of the world. They institute both participant and participated
(for he is both). Which is to say they effect a single activity in two infinitely different natural modes. And though these modes disclose one
divine act constituting "a single world," they themselves remain infinitely
different by nature.[218] Creation, then, is a non-natural (or supranatural)
procession of the Word that generates an essence utterly different from the
divine essence. And yet these same *logoi* bear within and make accessible

to creatures "the infinite divine activities of God,"[219] which, as *Capita theologiae et oeconomiae* 1.49 just mentioned, are implanted within us. Herein lies the marvel: somehow the *logoi* introduce the eternal works of divine essence (participated) into created essence (participants), though the latter enjoys no *natural* mediation with that same divine essence. Somehow the *logoi*, I mean, make the imparticipable God participable in a way that exceeds any natural process abstractly conceived.

Wasn't that exactly the logic of Incarnation? The second person of the Trinity, the Word, condescended to make himself identical to human nature, and that act was the very creation of that human nature (sec. 1.2). And yet, because created, his human nature bore nothing natural in common with his divinity, only the positive identity of his own hypostasis (sec. 1.3). Hypostatic identity generated natural difference and the consequent difference of natural powers and modes. These powers, recall, when reduced to concrete actuality in the doings of Christ's historical life, proved that the proper modes of infinitely different natures can interpenetrate one another, whole in whole, in perichoretic union (sec. 1.4). His existence revealed that "divine and human activity coincided in a single identity."[220] The "mode of exchange" between Christ's two natures was not natural for the simple reason that it was his person alone that united them.[221] And so, though Maximus might indulge in participation language even in a Christological context,[222] his fundamental logic comes ever to this: hypostatic identity generates infinite natural difference, and the modes of each nature, when perfected, interpenetrate one another symmetrically rather than, say, merely "by derivation."[223]

I therefore contend that the "being" attributed to the eternal mode of God's creative activity is the "tri-hypostatic existence" of the divine essence (itself imparticipable).[224] That explains why eternal works are at once "beings" and not self-subsistent (*anhypostatos*), namely because they are hypostasized in the Word.[225] It also explains how those works can retain their proper mode even while "implanted" in the participant's created nature, which still possesses its own infinitely different mode. These modes, that is, are brought into a single subsistence with one another without the slightest modal diminishment—without altering their *logoi*. And those sorts of conditions and characteristics make sense only if they bear the very logic that obtained between created and uncreated natures in Christ himself.

No wonder Maximus dares to describe the *logoi* of created beings as "the body of Christ."[226] When he meditates on John 1:14, "the Word became flesh," and then considers other scriptures that speak of Christ's blood and bones, he begins as always at the historical Incarnation and then goes cosmic: "The super-essential Word and Creator of all beings, wishing to come into [created] essence, bore the natural *logoi* of every sensible and intelligible being along with the inconceivable intellections of his own divinity." Because of this Incarnation, writes Maximus, we must contemplate the *logoi* of sensible creatures "as flesh to eat," and the *logoi* of intelligible creatures "as blood to drink," and the unbroken bones "the *logoi* concerning his divinity."[227] Once more the *logoi* of creation—*creatio ex nihilo*—just are the logic of Christ. The Word's act of self-identification with created essence generates it at all, grounds the participants, and makes God's own activity participable (since it is not by essence). After a reflection at length on what it means to consume Christ, Maximus draws all these threads together:

> But who would be able to enumerate all the aspects of God our Savior, which exist for our sake, and according to which *He has made Himself edible and participable to all* in proportion to the measure of each [καθ' ἃς ἐδώδιμον ἑαυτὸν καὶ μεταληπτὸν ἀναλόγως ἑκάστῳ πεποίηκεν]? . . . Proper and profitable communion in these is attained by those who assimilate each member in light of the spiritual meaning signified by each. In this manner, according to that holy and great teacher, the Lamb of God "is eaten, and given up to spiritual digestion," assimilating to Himself, through the Spirit, *those who partake of Him* [μεταποιῶν πρὸς ἑαυτὸν τῷ Πνεύματι τοὺς μεταλαμβάνοντας], for He guides and transposes each one to the place in the body that corresponds to the member that was spiritually eaten by him, so that in a way befitting His love of mankind *the Word becomes the essence in concrete wholes, the very Word who alone is above nature and reason* [ὥστε φιλανθρώπως τὸν ἐν τοῖς ὅλοις Λόγον τοῖς πράγμασιν οὐσίαν γίνεσθαι τὸν μόνον ὑπὲρ φύσιν καὶ λόγον].[228]

• • •

I maintained in this chapter that Maximus's *logoi* doctrine, protologically considered, differs in crucial respects from Neoplatonic participation and that these anomalies indicate the way God's creative act corresponds to the first two elements of Christo-logic. The anomalies are three:

1. *Creatio ex nihilo* means uncreated and created natures share absolutely no natural principle, quality, power, or mode, and so their relation cannot be described as a *natural* procession from higher, less determinate to lower, more determinate modes of the same essence.

2. And yet there is a procession from One to Many. But it is specifically the Logos who makes himself hypostatically identical to the *logoi* of the created world and so generates it. Thus the activity of the essentially imparticipable God becomes participable through the only possible medium: the person of the Word.

3. The Word's procession penetrates deeper than formal principles (the *logoi* of natures) to establish the nonformal identity of creaturely hypostases as such (the *logoi* of hypostases). It grounds, that is, the very participants who participate the eternal works the Word bears in himself, *in them*.

(1) and (2) match the first two elements of Christo-logic in reverse order. Christo-logic's first element dictates that the only concrete identity must be hypostatic (not natural)—this occurs at anomaly (2). The second element dictates that this hypostatic identity is the fundamental cause and condition of essential difference, as with the enhypostatization of Christ's humanity—this explains anomaly (1).

The latter observation is no mere surmise. Maximus says it aloud. If Maximus faults Greek philosophy and Origenism for failing to conceive a God-world relation that is not some sort of *natural* relation (which would demand a procession according to the logic of natures or essences), he himself does not fail to conceive a real relation in its place—a relation of hypostatic identity.

> The aim is that "what God is to the soul, the soul might become to the body," and that the Creator of all might be proven to be One, and through humanity might come to reside in all things in a manner appropriate to each, so that the many, though separated from each other in nature, might be drawn together around the one nature of man [τὰ πολλὰ ἀλλήλων κατὰ τὴν φύσιν διεστηκότα περὶ τὴν μίαν τοῦ ἀνθρώπου φύσιν ἀλλήλοις συννεύοντα]. When this happens, *God will be all things in everything* [1 Cor. 15:28], encompassing all things and hypostasizing them in Himself [πάντα περιλαβὼν

καὶ ἐνυποστήσας ἑαυτῷ], for beings will no longer possess indepen-dent motion or lack any portion of God's presence [καὶ τῆς ἄμοιρον παρουσίας]. . . . We are, and are called, *Gods*, *children of God*, the *body*, and *members of God* [Eph. 1:23, 5:30], and, it follows, "por-tions of God," and other such things, in the progressive ascent [ἀναφορᾷ] of the divine plan to its final end.[229]

As I said at the outset of this chapter, to verify that Christo-logic is truly creation's logic in Maximus we need to approach his *logoi* doctrine from both the beginning (protology) and the end (eschatology). Do all the elements of Christo-logic play out to the very end of the God-world rela-tion, to the fullness of the creative act? We have contemplated hypostatic identity and infinite natural difference in protology, at the beginning. If, though, Christo-logic should determine the final form of the God-world relation, then it must evince what we saw was the culmination of that logic: perichoresis of natural modes and activities (already intimated by anomaly [3]). It does, as it happens, and the next chapter's task is to show how.

CHAPTER THREE

The End

World Becomes Trinity

Excepting his contribution to the monothelite controversy, Maximus is perhaps best known for his doctrine of deification. It "represents the true climax of the patristic tradition."[1] So it makes sense that several scholars have studied this theme in great detail, crafting, as it were, veritable compendia of Maximus's thinking on the subject.[2] I make no such attempt here. I seek rather whether and how Maximian deification means what it must if it is to be the perfection of creation *as Incarnation.*[3] The previous chapter argued that Maximus's *logoi* doctrine presents a protology that bears the first two elements of Christo-logic: the *logoi* name (1) the Word's hypostatic condescension in becoming identical to the creative principles of created nature, a self-identification that (2) generates that very nature. Now to see if the third element—perichoresis of natural modes and activities—characterizes Maximus's eschatology.

Before that I briefly review Christo-logic's three elements and their interrelations. The Word's hypostasis names the only concrete, positive, and real identity of infinitely different natures (created and uncreated), an identity that is itself the condition for the possibility of infinite natural difference as such. Next, Christo-logic requires a third element tailored to meet the monenergist challenge. Suppose we grant one hypostasis and two natural principles (or *logoi*) with their respective powers. What then happens as these two natural powers reduce to the activity of a single personal existence? How do they remain distinct in natural power and mode and activity and yet describe a single reality or actuality? Maximus replied with one of his own Christological signatures—the perichoresis of Christ's activities. True to its proximate Trinitarian provenance, peri-choresis here has two necessary features. It indicates an interpenetration of otherwise infinitely different natural modes and activities, such that (i) the whole integrity of each remains undiminished and (ii) the whole of each utterly pervades the whole of the other so that there is no sense in which the consequent reality is *positively and separately* two. Perichore-sis of activities completes Christo-logic as its third and final element (3), its peculiar mode of actuality.[4] And this final element assumes the prior two elements as necessary conditions because the second person of the Trinity, the Word, is himself the "is" of both natures and their attendant modes, powers, and acts—only thus do his two natural activities con-cretely exist. And since the selfsame hypostasis just is their concrete ex-istence—so that their sole existential mediator is the Word himself—those activities cannot but finally exist as essentially distinct yet really one, that is, in the mode of "whole in whole" in actuality.[5]

So this chapter must establish that Christo-logic's third element also describes the completion of God's act of creating the world. Does the perichoresis of infinitely natural modes and activities characterize the world's deification? Do the *logoi*, the principles of creation, prescribe an eschatological existence in a perichoretic mode of actuality?

Discerning this third element may in fact prove the most convincing bit of evidence that Maximus conceives creation as Incarnation—more persuasive, even, than the presence of the first two elements presented in the last chapter. After all, Neoplatonism in general and Dionysius in par-ticular say things that sound very much like Maximus's protological de-scriptions of the Logos-*logoi* relation.[6] An example from Dionysius: God's mode of "being" is properly "super-essential." But since that same God donates being "to beings and produces whole essences," then "That 'Being-One' is said to be multiplied in the production [or derivation] of all beings from Itself, remaining no less Itself and One in this multiplication, being unified [with all beings] according to this procession and utterly plentiful even in division—[all this] due to Its separation from all beings in Its super-essential mode, even in Its unitary production of all whole things [or of the universe] and in the unstinted effusion of Its undiminished communications."[7] As this passage illustrates ("separated from all things in Its super-essential mode"), Dionysius indulges in talk of "self-multiplication" while preserving a more Neoplatonic modal dualism, if you will. God creates all things from himself and so in some sense distributes himself in creation. But as far as I can see, this never disposes Dionysius to claim that God's "superessential" mode of being and a creaturely mode of being are simultaneously present to one another as "whole in whole."[8]

On the contrary, when Dionysius turns to the matter at hand—to our deification and filiation as "sons of God"—he hastens to add that "there is not an exact likeness between effects and causes." Two reasons: "On the one hand, the effects possess *potential* images of the causes," and on the other, "The causes in themselves remain separate and established above the effects *according to the principle of their own origin*."[9] Principle or *logos*, itself granted by origin or beginning, determines the inviolable modal boundaries of a being's activity. Those bearing superior principles, and certainly the divine principle itself, remain ever in their own mode and interior activity even as they are present to their derived effects according to the latter's own modality. Hence a great Dionysian axiom: "For though the Trinity is present to all things, not all things are present to the Trinity."[10]

I said Dionysius never affirms the simultaneous and whole presence of created and uncreated modalities to one another. Not entirely true. He acknowledges one exception that proves the rule: the Incarnation. Note again the context. This concession comes as he is rehearsing what I called modal dualism or vertical asymmetry, which is of course integral to the dynamics of Neoplatonic emanation or participation.[11] He reprises a standard trope in the long Platonic tradition. The causal "archetype" remains one and the same even as it is "imprinted" on its many participants, like a signet ring's seal pressed upon waxes of varying consistencies. The trope denies that participants differ from their archetype because of the archetype itself. That difference is instead a modal one: it is due to what is proper to derived essences, and, of course, to the extent that these participants actualize their own receptivity to the archetype. So while the seal "gives all of its very self to each," it is "the participants' own difference that makes those imprinted dissimilar to the one, whole, and selfsame archetype."[12] "But there is a difference," Dionysius continues, "between the divine activity that acts towards us in a manner befitting the Good, and the fact that the super-essential Word wholly and truly became essentialized for us, and enacted and suffered many eminent, exceptional things from his divine activity in a human manner."[13] As Maximus interprets Dionysius to teach elsewhere, because the Word became wholly man in a way unlike the way cause "becomes" effect by procession, Christ's divine activity *wholly* manifests itself in his human activity.[14] The difference is that Dionysius appears to think this an isolated instance; Maximus does not.

On my reading, Maximus agrees with Dionysius both that the Incarnation introduces something new and that this innovation cannot consist in a sameness or confusion at the level of essence or the "*logos* of origin," as Dionysius phrased it. Rather, the newness disclosed in the Incarnation issues in a perichoresis of modal activities grounded in hypostatic identity (as distinct from natural identity). Therefore Maximus's view of the God-world relation does not simply negate Dionysius's (or Neoplatonism's) but exceeds it according to Christo-logic. If at the world's end the Word "embraces and hypostasizes all things in himself,"[15] and if enhypostatization makes possible a new mode of concrete relation and mediation among differing natures—between infinitely differing natures, even—then Maximus can conceive cosmo-logic as Christo-logic without repudiating Dionysius's core convictions concerning *natural* metaphysical relations. Hypostatic identity and perichoresis of modes open upon a new horizon, as it were, for Christian metaphysics, and thus a new possibility for contemplating the logic of creation as the logic of Christ.

And so this chapter completes the task of tracing the three elements of Christo-logic in Maximus's cosmo-logic. It demonstrates that and how the third element proves fundamental to creation's perfection, its end. Two lines of evidence prove this. The first is textual. Maximus explicitly evokes perichoresis and its distinctive features to characterize creaturely deification—and was indeed the very first to do so.[16] There emerges also significant conceptual evidence. There are several aporiae or extreme tendencies in Maximian deification that we can explain and even expect if we read them by Christological canons. Three in particular:

1. Maximian deification aims for the very hypostatic *identity* between created and uncreated natures that Christ's historical Incarnation accomplished.
2. Human deification, or becoming "God by grace," as Maximus often phrases it, is both utterly non-natural and yet *innate* or "implanted" within human nature from creation.
3. Deification of individual humans is simultaneously incorporation into Christ's one Body, and this is really what it means to speak of our "analogous" relation to Christ (and his to us)—not that we are similar to him within ever greater dissimilarity but that we are him in our own personal ways.

Christo-logic as a whole, with perichoresis as its culmination, explains all these apparently "hyperbolic"[17] components of Maximian deification and indeed renders them plain sensible.

I begin with the first two aporiae, namely that the ground and goal of deification are hypostatic identity (sec. 3.1) and that this involves a process simultaneously innate and supranatural (sec. 3.2). I then linger over passages where Maximus evokes perichoresis as the logic of actual or experienced deification (sec. 3.3). At length I return to the third aporia, that the perichoretic logic of deification becomes for Maximus the logic of Christ's own Body, at once individual and cosmic, such that perfected creation's "analogous" relation to its creator actually presupposes its hypostatic identity with him (sec. 3.4).

3.1. HUMAN VOCATION: HYPOSTATIC IDENTITY OF CREATED AND UNCREATED NATURES

Maximus never thinks of the world's end apart from the historical Incarnation of the Son.[18] That event, and that event alone, has definitively disclosed the "plan" or "purpose" or "scope" or "end" of God's creative activity.[19] And since that event discloses the end of all creatures, it follows that the end of the world is hypostatic identity between God and the world.

In *Quaestiones ad Thalassium* 60 Maximus identifies the "mystery hidden from the ages" that "has now been manifested" (1 Pet. 1:20) with the "pure and spotless lamb, Christ," who "was foreknown before the foundation of the world" (Col. 1:26). "Christ" here comprises at once the historical (particular) and cosmic (universal) achievement of a single mystery, "the mystery according to Christ." This mystery is for Maximus "the ineffable and incomprehensible union according to hypostasis of divinity and humanity" that brings created and uncreated natures "into perfect identity."[20] In this very identity—the one wrought in history from conception in Mary's womb to cross to Resurrection to Ascension— every being (not just the man Jesus) "receives its beginning and end."[21] I quote at length Maximus's insistence on this point, since its full import often goes underappreciated:

> This is the great and hidden mystery. This is the blessed end for which all things were brought into existence. This is the divine purpose conceived before the beginning of beings, and in defining it we would say that this mystery is the preconceived goal for the sake of which everything exists, but which itself exists for the sake of nothing, and it was with a view to this end that God created the essences of beings. This is, properly speaking, the limit of providence and of the things preconceived, according to which occurs the recapitulation into God of the things made by God. This is the mystery that circumscribes all the ages, and which reveals the grand plan of God, a super-infinite plan infinitely pre-existing the ages an infinite number of times. The essential Word of God became a messenger of this plan when He became man, and, if I may rightly say so, revealed Himself as the innermost depth of the Father's goodness while also displaying in Himself the very goal for which creatures manifestly received the beginning of their existence.[22]

That "very goal" toward which all things were made reemerges in a passage glossed in the previous chapter, which serves here as overture for this entire chapter. In *Ambiguum* 41 Maximus recounts his five natural divisions of being only to say that it has always been humanity's (Adam's) vocation to unite these in itself, even the first and highest division between created and uncreated natures. Indeed, man, "like a most efficient workshop sustaining all things," has "by nature the full potential to draw all the extremes into unity" because of "his characteristic attribute of being related to the divided extremes through his own parts."[23] The human being intrinsically relates to and therefore can unify all five divisions.

Consider the second. Even if malformed or not yet properly actualized, a human being is already body and soul (and hence is related to the second division between sensible and intelligible)—already, that is, potentially greater than either as their unity.[24] So too was Adam already somehow related to both created *and* uncreated natures, the first division. I return below to what it could possibly mean that Adam "naturally" bore such a relation to divinity (sec. 3.2). But we spy a hint in the next line: "Through this potential, consistent with the purpose behind the origination of divided beings, man was called to achieve within himself *the mode* of their completion, and so bring to light the great mystery of the divine plan."[25] Actualization of the divine mystery occurs in the metaphysical field of *modes*, not in (natural) principle.

From this context sounds the overture:

> And finally, in addition to all this, had man united created nature with the uncreated through love (oh, the wonder of God's love for mankind!), he would have shown them to be *one and the same* by the state of grace, the whole man pervading the whole God, and becoming everything that God is, without, however, identity in essence, and receiving the whole God instead of himself, and obtaining as a kind of prize for his ascent to God the absolutely unique God, who is the goal of the motion of things that are moved, and the firm and unmoved stability of things that are carried along to Him, and the limit (itself limitless and infinite) of every definition, order, and law, whether of mind, intellect, or nature.[26]

This passage sounds four significant themes. First, deified Adam would have achieved an *identity* between created and uncreated natures, would have proved them "one and the same" (ἓν καὶ ταὐτὸν). And yet this would be no "identity in essence" (χωρὶς τῆς κατ᾽ οὐσίαν ταὐτότητος)— a qualification Maximus systematically makes,[27] and one we should expect from Christo-logic.[28] Indeed, how could there ever occur natural identity with divinity as such, which is, as the end of this passage again affirms, properly above "nature"?[29] Second, and despite the insistence on non-natural identity, the potential for attaining such identity is in some sense *innate* to the human person (here Adam). Context made this plain.[30] Third, the identity of deification refers to a "state" or "condition" brought about *by grace* (κατὰ τὴν ἕξιν τῆς χάριτος). Finally, this non-natural but concrete identity whose potential reverberates within human nature like an innate calling or commission realized by grace alone—this identity, I note, reduces *in actu* in the form of a *perichoresis* of natural activities, divine and human (ὅλος ὅλῳ περιχωρήσας ὁλικῶς τῷ Θεῷ, καὶ γενόμενος πᾶν εἴ τί πέρ ἐστιν ὁ Θεός).

Those four themes recapitulate the entire logic of Maximian deification: we become identical to God in all but essence; we possess the innate power to do so; we realize this power through and in grace alone; and we concretely manifest it in and as the complete interpenetration of created and uncreated qualities, powers, modes, and activities.

The contours of Maximian deification originate from and retrace those of the Word's deified humanity. Granted, Christ's flesh did not undergo the process of deification in the way ours does and will.[31] But that concerns the question of deification's *how*, not *that* or *what*, a question of process rather than product. Certainly the humanity the Word assumed was deified from its conception while ours must become deified.[32] Yet even here the two ways of deifying created flesh share a crucial feature: neither is natural. I suspend this point until the next section. The main matter for now is that Maximus thinks the historical Incarnation, the ground and goal of creation, notates the themes of creaturely deification. Maximian deification signifies a non-natural "identity" between created and uncreated natures.

No surprise, then, that Maximus everywhere keys this identity to Christ, the Incarnate Word and Son of God. His identity, the one wrought in the historical Incarnation, is ours too in deification.[33] To become God we must become Christ—for no other mediator exists between God and man, creator and creation.[34] Here we meet some of Maximus's most provocative expressions, many of which say not just that we become "identical" to God in some nondescript sense but that we become Christ himself.

Actually this identity claim is surprising. It is, I mean, if you draw back a little and consider the rather hostile atmosphere surrounding such a doctrine—particularly its possible prominence and fate in the Origenist tradition.[35] Whether Origen and Evagrius themselves propagated or prepared the grounds for the later "isochrist" crop of sixth-century Origenism,[36] the latter proved particularly toxic to anti-Origenists of the period. We know little more than what the calque suggests: some (not all)[37] sixth-century Origenists held that our eschatological destiny was to become "equal to Christ," united to God as much as he.[38]

In 552, the year before the Fifth Ecumenical Council (Constantinople II) convened, Theodore, bishop of Scythopolis, addressed a *Libel* against Origenist errors to the Emperor Justinian and the four Eastern Patriarchs. It promulgates twelve anathemas, nine of which simply restate Justinian's own from his 543 edict. Three appear original to Theodore. These reflect the dawning sense among anti-Origenists that Origenism's enduring appeal (and so its fundamental challenge) lay not simply in its speculative protology or eschatology but in its compelling Christology—especially of the isochrist variety.[39] One of the three added anathemas reads: "If anyone should say, think, or teach that we will become equal to Christ our Savior and God who was born of the holy and ever-virgin Theotokos; and that God the Word must be united to us as he was to the animate flesh that he assumed from Mary according to essence and hypostasis—let him be anathema."[40] Nearly a year later Justinian's own letter to the council reprises and expands this charge. He urges the swift condemnation of those who teach that all men, dissolute and deified alike, "will enjoy the same union with God that Christ too enjoys, just as in their preexistence, with the result that there will be no difference at all between Christ and the remaining rational beings, neither in substance nor in knowledge nor in power nor in operation."[41] Two of the anti-Origenist canons associated with Constantinople II surface the same concern. Anathema be anyone who says all rational beings "will be united to God the Word in just the same way as the mind they call Christ" (can. 12), or anyone who "says that there will not be a single difference at all between Christ and other rational beings," neither in "substance," "knowledge," "power," nor "operation" (can. 13)!—much as Justinian had it.[42]

These are powerful witnesses to the growing worry over the isochrist eschatology of certain Origenists. They appear anxious over Christ's uniqueness or primacy among rational creatures, which tends to evaporate into sheer oneness at the edges of creation, at the beginning and end of all things.[43] This anxiety will linger in later Maronite (Syrian monothelite) polemics against Maximus.[44] Note here just two relevant features common to Justinian and the canons.

First, the fundamental concern is one familiar to Neo-Chalcedonian orthodoxy—the *mode* of union. The way the Word is united to Christ in isochrist thought seems to assume some essential relation or mode, since the Christology targeted portrays Christ as a mind separate from the Word, who then becomes that mind only to absorb it in the end (can. 12:

"The kingdom of Christ will have an end"). Obviously Maximus sides with the canons here: no essential or natural identity, ever. Second, although Theodore of Scythopolis specified a mode of union either "according to essence *or hypostasis*," the latter precision is missing in Justinian and the canons. Essence, knowledge, power, and activity are said to differ between Christ and the saints—but nothing references hypostasis. Maximus, I show below (sec. 3.3), actually agrees that deification does not imply our absorption into the Word's hypostasis; we are not obliterated for the sake of hypostatic identity. Yet it is notable that this precision has disappeared in the official condemnations; it means the logic of hypostasis is not clearly in view here.[45]

Now consider the following passages from Maximus. In *Ambiguum* 21, Maximus strives to resolve what appears to be an evident historical error or rare slip-up in one of Gregory of Nazianzus's orations. Gregory refers to "John, the forerunner of the Word"—naturally John the Baptist (Matt. 3:1–3; John 1:23)—but then attributes to him a line from John the Evangelist (John 21:25).[46] Rather than concede misattribution, Maximus reads Gregory's remark to invite the hearer into Gregory's own spiritual interpretation of scripture's literal expression.[47] Gregory means what he says, namely that John the Evangelist, "by means of his Gospel, is forerunner of a greater and more mystical Word."[48] Thence ensues an elaborate meditation on how scripture, especially the four Gospels (and especially John's), correspond to and coalesce with the four elements that constitute the physical cosmos, and how all these together reveal the Word within them.[49] The last third of this *ambiguum* turns to the "inner cosmos," as it were, the soul seeking union with God. Maximus notes that the Word who inhabits things external to us also dwells silently within our own souls. There he longs to cooperate, as grace, with our labors in virtue, labors by which our soul—in a stunning expression—grants "hypostasis" to the virtues themselves.[50]

After another meditation on our deification from this interior vantage—particularly that love is the greatest unifying power we have[51]—Maximus culminates his lengthy lucubration with a traditional trope: our deification glides along a trajectory of increasing intensity from the primordial "image of God" to ever-greater "likeness" to him.[52] True, Maximus can comfortably and occasionally wield this trope in its traditional sense.[53] But not here. Inspired by Hebrews 10:1, he sets it on a more lateral or historical trajectory that moves from shadow to image to truth—all of the one Word, of course. Maximus assigns the Word's "shadow" to the Old Testament (represented by John the Baptist), his "image" to the New Testament (represented by John the Evangelist), and his "truth" to our future union with him in deification. "The Gospel," writes Maximus, "possesses the image of true things" to come,

> And it is through this image that those who choose the pure and un-defiled life of the Gospel, through their strict exercise of the com-mandments, take possession of the likeness of the good things of the age to come, and are made ready by the Word through the hope that they will be spiritually vivified *by their reception of the archetype* of these true things, and so become living images of Christ, or rather *become identical to Him through grace (rather than being a mere simulacrum)*, or even, perhaps, *become the Lord Himself*, if such an idea is not too onerous for some to bear.[54]

By now we see pretty clearly why this might be "too onerous for some to bear."[55] It rings isochrist. Surely it is significant that Maximus himself anticipates an unsettling effect—as in fact he does on several occasions around this theme.[56] But it is not simply that Maximus here trespasses into Origenist precincts. The logic and even the wording of this passage might seem curiously transgressive to those expecting a more Platonic or Dionysian description of deification. Two insights illu-minate the point: the archetype's *downward motion* and the image's *iden-tity that supersedes likeness*.

(1) At least in this passage the archetype, the Word, does not merely hover in a purely ideal modality only to be approximated by its permuta-tions, confined as they are to spatio-temporal vicissitudes. Union with the archetype is simultaneously the archetype's own advent in the imitator. The downward condescension of archetype to image derives, as Élie Ayroulet has recently shown, from a distinctly Aristotelian rather than Platonic conception of the archetype-image relation. Aristotle thinks a work of art—a poem or play, say—achieves its completion solely in its reproduction or imitation in the onlooker, so that the archetype-image relation enjoys a kind of "existential simultaneity": the archetype pos-sesses the power of this act *in itself*, to be sure, but attains actuality only

in the imitator.[57] Clearly Maximus does not mean that the Word's divine essence as such is realized only in the image or imitator. Yet there is more to God than the divine essence as such. And this "more"—the person of the Word (or any and all of the Three)—is what allows and even requires, if not an essential, still *a real* sense in which the divine archetype must condescend to complete the "truth that is to come," the deification and perfection of all creation. In fact Maximus seems to detect exactly this concern and immediately adds: "For even though He Himself is always the same, and is beyond all change or alteration, becoming neither greater nor lesser, He nonetheless *becomes all things to everyone* [1 Cor. 9:22, 12:6, 15:28; Eph. 1:23] out of His exceeding goodness: lowly for the lowly, lofty for the lofty, and, for those who are deified through His grace, He is God by nature, and Deity beyond all knowledge as God beyond God."[58] Incarnation demands that God, by essence immutable and remaining in himself, can yet really, in person, identify himself with lowly creatures in such a way that he who cannot be essentially completed by any finite creature is in fact realized in those very creatures.[59] Christo-logic demands even that God show himself all the more transcendent by nature precisely to the extent that he becomes truly identical to created nature in person.[60] The two distinct yet inseparable logics of nature and hypostasis prove once more to open new possibilities, here for our deification. We do not receive merely the activities or qualities of the transcendent archetype in our own natural or finite mode; we receive the very archetype.[61]

(2) The archetype condescends into the imitator to make the two "the same" (ταὐτὸν)—a claim already familiar from *Ambiguum* 41. Amazing here is how Maximus qualifies and presses into this identity: we do not, by grace, remain "a mere simulacrum" but "become the Lord Himself." Becoming Christ achieves an identity that surpasses that of a "simulacrum," an ἀφομοίωμα. A significant word, that, and intentionally to exceed it more significant still. Not only does this outstrip Proclus's henads, described in just those terms.[62] It appears to aim beyond Dionysius's own definition of deification: "Theosis is the likeness [ἀφομοίωσίς] to and union with God, as far as possible."[63]

Since Dionysius's definition comes from a liturgical and sacramental context, it is fitting that our next set of passages treat the identity with Christ that occurs through the sacraments, especially baptism and the Eucharist. In *Ambiguum* 42 Maximus confronts the following difficulty.

Gregory of Nazianzus identifies three human births—"from bodies, from baptism, and from the resurrection"—but later adds a fourth, more mysterious one: "the original and *vital inbreathing* [Gen. 2:7; Wisd. 15:11]."[64] Why? What follows is an elaborate theory of humanity's original becoming (*genesis*) as distinct in mode from its postlapsarian becoming (*gennesis*), both of which Christ assumes in his act of becoming man. An interesting and relevant disquisition, to be sure, but what concerns us here is the question Maximus raises late in this *ambiguum*. He notices and asks why Gregory links baptism to the Incarnation.[65] He answers by invoking the image-likeness trope. But again this quickly drifts toward a more extreme sense:

> Those who interpret the divine sayings mystically . . . say that man in the beginning was created *according to the image of God* [Gen. 1:27], surely so that he might be born of the Spirit in the exercise of his own free choice, and to acquire in addition the *likeness* by the keeping of the divine commandment, so that the same man, being by nature a creation of God, might also be Son of God and God through the Spirit according to grace [ἵνα ᾖ ὁ αὐτὸς ἄνθρωπος πλάσμα μὲν τοῦ Θεοῦ κατὰ φύσιν, Υἱὸς δὲ Θεοῦ καὶ Θεὸς διὰ Πνεύματος κατὰ χάριν].[66]

How can Maximus move seamlessly from likeness to identity? Consider two aspects of Maximus's reasoning here, both of Irenaean vintage. First there is the more subjective concern to respect human freedom even when we have to do with realizing humanity's natural vocation. Nearly everywhere that Maximus treats baptism he stresses its voluntary character—as if birth by baptism surpasses bodily birth to the extent that the former is freely elected, the latter not.[67] This recalls Irenaeus's response to the question why God did not make us gods from the very beginning: "So that no one might think him invidious or less than most excellent," God "graciously granted a great good to human beings, and made them like himself, [that is,] possessing their own power."[68] For Irenaeus a creature unfree is a creature unlike God. For Maximus baptismal birth makes us God's adopted children; it is how we freely answer our vocation and indeed ultimately how we cooperate in our own primordial generation.

There is also the more objective theory, Irenaeus's recapitulation idea (cf. Eph. 1:10), which stipulates that Christ heals and saves (preserves) all things by remaking and re-sourcing them in himself.[69] But notice what this becomes when combined with the Neo-Chalcedonian precisions about hypostatic identity detailed earlier (sec. 1.2). Where are all these things "summed up" and stitched together if not in the *person* of Christ? So when Maximus says, as he does soon after this text, that "He who is God by essence and the Son of God by nature was baptized for our sake, voluntarily subjecting Himself to the spiritual birth of adoption," he intimates, I think, that all human adoption by the Spirit (through baptism) subsists directly in the one who recapitulated it in himself—in the composed hypostasis of Christ.[70] Christ becomes and is, in very principle (*logos*), the identity of human regeneration—the universal principle active in every individual's adoption by grace:

> On account of my condemnation, the Lord first submitted Himself to Incarnation and bodily birth, after which came the birth of baptism received in the Spirit, to which He consented for the sake of my salvation and restoration by grace or, to put it more precisely, *my reformation* [ἀναπλάσεως]. In this way God joined together *in me* the principle of my being and the principle of my well-being, and He closed the division and distance between them that I had opened up, and through them He wisely drew me to the principle of eternal being, according to which man is no longer subject to carrying or being carried along.[71]

For Maximus the power implanted or nascent in baptism must be nursed to fullness by a person's own deeds.[72] And no deed proves more effective than receiving the Eucharist. On the two occasions in his *Mystagogy* where Maximus remarks on the "holy communion" of the synaxis—curtly and cryptically[73]—he makes bold to speak of "identity" with God through Christ. After the "Our Father," which sustains our adoption as God's offspring, we hymn the "One Is Holy," an ancient chant about Jesus Christ,[74] which makes us "like him by participation in an indivisible identity according to each one's power."[75] Later Maximus warns his readers against laxity in attending the divine liturgy exactly because, there and then, the Holy Spirit's grace is present "in a special way," a grace that "transforms [μεταποιοῦσαν] and changes [μετασκευάζουσαν] each person who is found there and in fact remolds [μεταπλάττουσαν] him in proportion to what is more divine in him and leads him to what is revealed through the mysteries which are celebrated"—even if the participant himself "does not feel this" because he is but an infant in Christ, unable to perceive what really takes place.[76] What takes place is this: "By holy communion of the spotless and life-giving mysteries we receive both fellowship with him by participation through likeness, and identity, by which man is deemed worthy to become God out of man."[77] More precisely, we become identical to God because identical to Christ: "Then we shall pass from the grace which is in faith to the grace of vision, when our God and Savior Jesus Christ will indeed transform us into himself [μεταποιοῦντος ἡμᾶς πρὸς ἑαυτὸν δηλαδὴ τοῦ Θεοῦ καὶ Σωτῆρος ἡμῶν Ἰησοῦ Χριστοῦ] by taking away from us the marks of corruption and will bestow on us the archetypical mysteries which have been represented for us through sensible symbols here below."[78]

Maximus's mention of the "Our Father" (*Myst.* 13) recalls his formal commentary on that prayer. Here again we find identity claims. Maximus's principal premise is that the Lord's Prayer teaches us to pray for the "good things that are themselves actualized from the Word incarnate."[79] The "good things" are seven, of which the second and third pertain here.[80] The Incarnation grants humanity "equality in honor with the angels" (third) and "adoption in grace" (second).[81] Adoption and participation in divine life surpass even angelic equality to the extent that they make us equal to God. This occurs because in the historical Incarnation the Word "makes Himself edible—as He Himself knows how," and thus "mixes with a divine quality those who eat for their deification, since He both is and is clearly called Bread of Life and of power."[82]

Here we have the very logic of participation operative in Maximus's protology (sec. 2.5): (1) the Word condescends to identify his person with created nature, which generates that nature; (2) the Word's generative self-identification with created nature opens for the latter a "new," non-natural mediation or relation by which to participate the "good things" or "eternal works" of the divine nature; (3) so participation through this supranatural mediator—the hypostasis of the Word—enables otherwise inconceivable modes of perfection and real relation between God and world: a single perichoretic or a "whole in whole" modality of two infinitely different modes and acts. So here:

(1) [Christ] sets in movement in us an insatiable desire for himself who is the Bread of Life, wisdom, knowledge, and justice. When we fulfill the Father's will he renders us similar to the angels in their adoration, as we imitate them by reflecting the heavenly blessedness in the conduct of our life. (2) From there he leads us finally in the supreme ascent in divine realities to the Father of lights wherein he makes us sharers in the divine nature by participation in the Spirit according to grace, (3) through which we receive the title of God's children and *become, ourselves [still] wholes, clothed with the whole and very author of this same grace, without limiting or defiling him who is Son of God by nature*, from whom, by whom, and in whom we have and shall have being, movement, and life [cf. Acts 17:28].[83]

So exactly does the logic of deification conform to the logic of Christ that Maximus can even apply a classic passage on Christ's kenosis (Phil. 2:6) to the deification of our soul and thence make some incredible claims:

[The soul] becomes a radiant abode of the Holy Spirit and receives, if one can say it, the full power of knowing the divine nature insofar as this is possible. By this power there is discarded the origin of what is inferior, to be replaced by that of what is superior, while the soul, *equal to God* [ἴσα θεῷ—Phil. 2:6] keeps inviolable in itself by the grace of its calling the hypostasis of the gifts that have been given. By this power [or: "according to this hypostasis"], Christ is always born mysteriously and willingly, becoming incarnate through those who are saved. He causes the soul which begets him to be a virgin-mother who, to speak briefly, does not bear the marks of na-ture subject to corruption and generation in the relationship of male and female.[84]

We could adduce several other passages that make identity claims like those canvassed here.[85] Instead I terminate this catalog to consider how Maximus could safely venture such statements, particularly given the deep concern around Origenist isochristism. Notice first that Maxi-mus had before him other authorities whose writings brandished similar convictions, authorities not obviously of the Origenist stock. Take the simple but vigorous Christ-devotion of the Macarian homilies—an influence Maximus definitely imbibed.[86] There you read that "the heavenly Image, Jesus Christ, now mystically illumines the soul" of the saint from within;[87] that "perfect Christians" who by grace receive the "heavenly anointing" that makes of them "sons and lords and gods" must be "bound and held captive, crucified and consecrated" with Christ;[88] that we are like "burning lamps" lighted from a single flame, "the Son of God," so that when anointed with the same oil and enkindled with the same fire as Christ himself "we should become Christs—of the very same essence and of one body, as it were";[89] that even as one Body we need not think our bodies melt away at the resurrection, since "all are being transformed into a divine nature, becoming christs and gods and children of God" (εἰς θεϊκὴν γὰρ φύσιν ἅπαντες μεταβάλλονται, χρηστοὶ, καὶ θεοὶ, καὶ τέκνα Θεοῦ γενόμενοι);[90] and that God dispatched the scriptures as letters beckoning human beings to "receive the celestial gift out of the hypostasis of God's divinity," which is "immortal life" or simply "Christ."[91]

Maximus exemplifies the vitality of this tradition. So too was he shaped by his affinity for the (especially Evagrian) Origenist legacy, both directly and as it animated the Cappadocians.[92] And yet I think Maximus's courage regarding identity between Christ and the saints is not entirely explicable as a mere epiphenomenon of various traditional compounds. He had dogmatic reason for such fortitude. In other words, Maximus's developments of and supplemental burnishes to Neo-Chalcedonian Christology—especially Christo-logic's discrimination between hypostatic and essential logics along with the new modal possibilities that this distinction entails—allowed him to retain a "structural isomorphism" to isochrist Origenism even as he infused it with the dogmatic content of Neo-Chalcedonianism.[93]

And this constitutes, I suggest, the great significance of Maximus's celebrated *tantum-quantum* (or τοσοῦτον-ὅσον) principle.[94] This principle prescribes that to the *same* degree that God became man in the historical Incarnation we become God in deification. Here we move beyond (not against) the Irenaean-Athanasian axiom that God became human so that humans might become gods.[95] That axiom posits an intimate causal link between Incarnation and deification. But the *tantum-quantum* principle, which Maximus inherits but forges into a veritable *Grundprinzip*,[96] commends something like a formal and even "mutually proportional" relation between them.[97]

Consider two features of this fundamental principle. First, it is not an abstract axiom. Axiomatic, certainly, but it could not be *less* abstract, really, since one of its terms is precisely the historical Incarnation of the Word. Even when Maximus emphasizes the cooperative work of the soul in the process of its deification, the referent and measure is the actual Christ-event:

> He gives adoption by giving through the Spirit a supernatural birth from on high in grace, of which divine birth the guardian and preserver—along with God—is the free will of those who are thus born. By a sincere disposition it cherishes the grace bestowed and by a careful observation of the commandments it adorns the beauty given by grace. And by emptying itself of the passions *it takes on divinity to the same degree that the Word of God willed to empty himself in the incarnation ["economically"] of his own unmixed glory in being reckoned and truly becoming human.*[98]

Little doubt that the final line refers to the historical person of Christ.[99] That matters because, as Maximus reminds us just before another *tantum-quantum* passage, the only way the Word becomes man at all is in his own hypostasis.[100] Hypostatic identity remains ever the sine qua non of the *communicatio idiomatum* in Christo-logic. There is no exchange without the factual identity sustaining and indeed generating that very created nature whose qualities the Word assumes. Nor does there exist by any other means that supreme degree of communication wrought and displayed in the Word's kenosis unto death. If our reception of the fullness of God proves somehow lesser in degree than God's assumption of the fullness of man in the Word's historical, hypostatic identity with human nature (particular and universal), then we must admit that this principle, as systematically expressed, lapses into sheer nonsense.[101]

The second feature: since we become truly and wholly God to the same degree that the Son became truly and wholly human,[102] and since we remain ourselves whole while becoming the whole God (sec. 3.3), then the Word still incarnates, still *gains bodily existence*, in the ongoing mutual assimilation between God and man—what Maximus calls the "ages" of deification.[103] Thus emerges a profound characteristic of Maximian deification, namely the symmetry and even mutual conditioning or fulfillment between God's becoming creature and the creature's becoming God. "From the mystical vantage of man's personal perfection," Larchet writes, "[deification and Incarnation] even become reciprocally dependent and mutually condition each other. For not only does man become God in respect of the hominization of God, but indeed God, by a supreme manifestation of his love, becomes human in respect of the deification of man insofar as he incarnates himself mystically in every deified person."[104] That this reciprocal fulfillment occurs "mystically" makes it no less concrete or extreme. Rather more so, since, of course, the historical Incarnation itself is the greatest among and source of all mysteries.[105] The *tantum-quantum* principle therefore posits the profoundest possible identity between Incarnation and deification—that both achieve the complete perichoresis of created and uncreated natures possible only in the Word's person. He himself becomes the continuity of extremes so that realities infinitely different by nature can *now*, in a totally supranatural manner, become each other's terms, as if they inhabited the same metaphysical mode of existence. The deified "as wholes," says Maximus,

> were deemed worthy to be wholly intermingled through the Spirit with the whole of God, and thus were *clothed* (so far as humanly possible) in the whole *image of the heavenly man* [1 Cor. 15:49], and to the extent [τοσοῦτο] that they drew to themselves the manifestation of God, to that very same degree, if it be permitted thus, they were drawn to God and united to Him [εἰ θέμις τοῦτο εἰπεῖν, ὅσον ἑλχθέντες αὐτοὶ τῷ Θεῷ συνετέθησαν]. For they say that God and man are paradigms of each other, so that as much as man, enabled by love, has divinized himself for God, to that same extent God is humanized for man by His love for mankind; and as much as man has manifested through the virtues God who is invisible by nature, to that same extent man is rapt by God in mind to the unknowable.[106]

• • •

I sought to establish two basic points in this section. First, Maximus understands deification to achieve an identity between God and the world, however fraught that idea's legacy by his day. And second, this identity is nothing else than that wrought in the historical Incarnation,

namely hypostatic identity. Yet everywhere and always Maximus qualifies deific identity as a product of grace, as we heard in the overture (*Amb.*
41). Maximus's own iteration of Dionysius's definition of deification runs:
"The work of theological mystagogy is to establish one *by grace* in a state
of being like God and equal to God"—where "grace" and "equal," note
well, are Maximus's elaborations.[107]

But doesn't the former vitiate the latter? If "by the state of grace"
I become "one and same" as God and "everything that God is, without,
however, identity in essence,"[108] then can I really say my eschatological
identity with God is *identity* in any meaningful sense? Doesn't "God by
grace" instead of "God by nature" finally just mean never quite God? What
does grace mean to Maximus? This immediately evokes another aporia.
Its resolution, I propose, resolves these larger objections too.

3.2. GOD BY GRACE:
AN INNATE AND SUPRANATURAL PROCESS

The aporia of deifying grace comes to this: grace is a power primordially
present *in* human nature, yet it activates a completely supranatural process and state. I study both in reverse order and then propose a resolution
according to Christo-logic.

1. *Grace is not a natural power.* I hope to have said enough in the
previous two chapters to make this point evident and expected: if creation's logic is Christ's, then there is never a question of essential or natural identity (or even relation) between God and world. Hypostatic logic
completely relieves nature of that burden. We heard Maximus offer some
rather unequivocal remarks along those lines in protology. There at the
beginning of the God-world relation Maximus openly denied any natural
relation—however mollified through modal declension—between God's
eternal, participated "works" and their historical participants. Here at
creation's end, where "actual identity" occurs, no less, no natural mediation exists between nature and grace.[109]

At times Maximus expresses this infinite difference with nearly
formulaic pairs correlated to discrete spheres.[110] Or he can distinguish
the "three laws"—the natural, the written, and the gracious.[111] Still another schema springs from his *logoi* doctrine, where the common *logos*

of all rational beings makes them exist according to three modes: "being, well-being, and eternal-being."[112] Each successive mode assumes those prior, such that the prior modes bear in potency what the next mode actualizes—sort of. A complication arises between the second and third modes, nature (which for rational creatures includes a volitional faculty) and grace:

> And the first [mode] contains potential, the second activity, and the third, rest from activity. This means that the principle of being, which by nature possesses only the potential for actualization, cannot in any way possess this potential in its fullness without the faculty of free choice. That of well-being, on the other hand, possesses the actualization of natural potential only by inclination of the will, for it does not possess this potential in its totality separately from nature. That of eternal-being, finally, which wholly contains those that precede it (that is, the potential of the one, and the activity of the other), *absolutely does not exist as a natural potential within beings, nor does it at all follow by necessity from the willing of free choice*. (For how is it possible for things, which by nature have a beginning and which by their motion have an end, *to possess as an innate part of themselves* that which exists eternally and which has neither beginning nor end?)[113]

Rational being, a created essence, possesses a power actualized through will; when that power is discharged, it is. So the first and second modes relate more or less as potency to act. They imply each other in principle. Not so with the third mode, eternal well-being or grace. If rational nature's concrete end were an automatic outcome of its own power—even of the volitional power proper to it—then that end would come by nature and not by grace. The end of creation proves just as supranatural as its beginning. Creation's edges, as it were, cannot by definition be *natural*. Otherwise they would not be given or created in any meaningful sense. And if not natural, then their brute facticity evidently does not concretize through any natural relation to the source of that truth, God. The *logos* of divine infinity, as Maximus says near the end of this passage, could never be "an innate part" of a rational creature's *logoi*.[114]

So severe is Maximus about grace's *supra*-natural character that some of his statements might make even the most stolid two-tiered Thomist blush. A creature's ecstasy and "experience" (πεῖρα) in deification, both significant motifs in Maximus,[115] stem precisely from the conviction that our union with God happens by no natural medium at all, and certainly not through any *potentia obedientialis*. Observe how Maximus glosses Gregory of Nazianzus's mention of "the things [Paul] experienced" when rapt to the third heaven (2 Cor. 12:2):

> A name is indicative of grace when man, who has been obedient to God in all things, is named "God" in the Scriptures, as in the phrase, *I said, you are Gods* [Ps. 81(82):6], for it is not by nature or condition [οὔτε κατὰ φύσιν οὔτε κατὰ σχέσιν] that he has become and is called "God," but he has become God and is so named by placement and grace. For the grace of divinization is completely unconditioned, because it finds no faculty or capacity of any sort within nature that could receive it, for if it did, it would no longer be grace but the manifestation of a natural activity latent within the potentiality of nature. And thus, again, what takes place would no longer be marvelous if divinization occurred simply in accordance with the receptive capacity [εἰ κατὰ δεκτικὴν δύναμιν φύσεως ἡ θέωσις ἦν]. Indeed, it would rightly be a work of nature, not a gift of God, and a person so divinized would be God by nature and would have to be called so in the proper sense. For natural potential in each and every being is nothing other than the unalterable movement of nature toward complete actuality. How, then, divinization could make the divinized person go out of himself [ἐξίστησιν ἑαυτοῦ], I fail to see, if it was something that lay within the bounds of his nature.[116]

Becoming God by grace names a process activated neither by nature nor by "condition" or "relation" (σχέσις). Not by nature, since then we are "God by nature." And not by relation—say, as the simultaneous relation between my body and soul (both essentially different) makes them naturally fit for each other.[117] But for the process and deed of deification there is no natural fit at all.[118]

Nor is there a natural fit for the "experience" of deification. Maximus knows two kinds of knowledge, "relative knowledge" (τὴν . . . σχετικήν) and experiential or participative knowledge. Relative knowledge "is based on reasoning and concepts" (ὡς ἐν λόγῳ μόνῳ κειμένην καὶ νοήμασιν), similar to what many today would call theoretical knowledge.[119] This grace neither is nor provides. Rather, "There is knowledge that is true and properly so called, which is gained only by actual experience [τὴν . . . ἀληθινὴν ἐν μόνῃ τῇ πείρᾳ κατ' ἐνέργειαν]—without reason and concepts—and provides, by grace through participation, a whole perception of the One who is known [ὅλην τοῦ γνωσθέντος κατὰ χάριν μεθέξει παρεχομένην τὴν αἴσθησιν]."[120]

The mystery of this passivity, this "suffering of divine things,"[121] lies in the fact that what is suffered is without abstract or discursive relation to our nature. It occurs without any part of our essence anticipating it whatever—not body or soul or intellect. *And yet it occurs.* It is a concrete experience, a fact, an event, a most palpable happening wherein the entirely impossible transpires: "According to a simple union, without relation and beyond all thought, on the basis of a certain unutterable and indefinable *logos*, which is known only to the One who grants this ineffable grace to the worthy, that is, it is known only to God and to those who in the future will come to experience it."[122] Experience is immediate. Nothing intervenes as arbiter or hybrid or unifying third term of a triad—at least nothing related by or within the essential order.

Rather, God himself is the medium. Therefore and once more, right here at creation's far edge, its end, the operative logic exceeds that of Neoplatonic participation or the limitation of act by power. Three characteristics of deific passivity make the point. First, the deifying act is suffered by the saint, not performed by her. And yet, second, that is precisely why her deification is infinite: it happens to and in her according to no natural principle of her own that would legislate limits or delimit its activity by any determinate proportion.[123] "And we will become the very thing that is not in any way the outcome of our natural capacity."[124] The concrete *that* and *there* of deification—the state *that* the deified person *is*—is itself as restricted by the natural (finite) mode of that person as divine infinity, which is to say, not at all. Just here a certain Thomist reading proves inadequate: "For no created thing is by its nature what effects deification, since it cannot grasp God. For this is the property of divine grace alone, that is, to grant the gift of deification proportionately [*analogos*] to created beings, brightly illumining nature by a light that transcends nature, making nature [to be] beyond its own proper limits through the excess of divine glory."[125] Deification is not a supernatural mode *of* a creature's natural activity. It is not a created activity or mode at all. In deification a person's natural mode and act receive a relation to God's totally unlike that of mode to act, however stratospheric the new heights reached by the latter's proportions.[126] *Super*-natural for Maximus does not mean "some degree higher than what is natural." It means *not* natural at all, a mode and state operative above nature of whatever level—a process and result for which nature could never answer. Deification is a process that occurs according to another logic altogether, Christ's.[127]

After all, Maximus also says the Word's historical Incarnation happened "in a supernatural mode."[128] And surely that mode was not a matter of qualifying the degree (in this case to a lesser one) of any nature's mode or activity. That supranatural mode was *him*, his very hypostasis.[129] So far is "the whole Christ" from being a state negotiated by any natural or modal settlement between created and uncreated natures that the fact of Christ demonstrates how the person of the Word "truly transcends all humanity *and divinity*."[130] The logic of nature simply cannot comprehend the fact of Christ.

Christo-logic abides no modal hybrid, even when (and indeed because) infinite natural modes and acts become one actuality. Nature need never mediate between a higher and lower version of itself. This is not because Maximus simply failed to develop the categories necessary to elucidate grace's presence in and perfection of nature. Rather, the logic of Christ does not and cannot permit any mediator but the Word.[131] Supranatural modality just is that of divine economy—of Incarnation.[132] When you behold Christ rightly, you do not perceive created (human) nature outfitted by grace with a superadded mode that imbues this nature with the power to attain otherwise unnatural (divine) proportions. What you behold is far more magnificent because what he displays is far more symmetrical and identical: whole humanity and whole divinity, each wholly possessed of its natural powers perfected in and manifested through whole activities, so completely indifferent to one another that they completely interpenetrate *exactly as they naturally are*—and all this solely because they are he and he is they.[133] The only supranatural mode is Christ's person.

Hence a final characteristic of deific passivity: the permanence of created nature (and mode and activity) in immediate union. The hypostasis, the Word, mediates non-naturally between infinitely different natures and therefore establishes a naturally *im*mediate identity between them. Hypostatic identity is the only way a finite nature can be identical to the infinite without being obliterated by it. Christo-logic is the logic of deific "ecstasy" and "experience": when the saint suffers immediate union with God, the very medium through which such an identity occurs is simultaneously the medium that preserves the saint's own created nature.[134] So the natural activity of the saint's nature is "not suppressed," Maximus assures, though it indeed ceases or stabilizes in its limit.[135] We do not receive the divine activity of grace through our nature at all. The "sole, super-essential power capable of deifying" does come to be [true] "of those deified."[136] Just here we glimpse grace's miraculous work. Grace makes divinity's entire and proper activity—including the mode of that activity[137]—the saints' very own even as it leaves nature's proper mode and activity entirely intact. Grace is not nature, first and last.[138]

2. *Grace is an innate power.* And yet somehow this non-natural, deifying power (and activity) is "inscribed into human nature as a vocation."[139] If two-tiered Thomists could blush a bit over Maximus's rigid partition between nature and grace, now even the *nouveaux théologiens* might incline to temper his claim about grace's universal presence in nature. Again contemplating Melchizedek:

> And you must not think that no one else can have a share in this grace simply because Scripture speaks of it solely with respect to the great Melchizedek, for in all human beings God has placed the same power that leads naturally to salvation [Πᾶσι γὰρ ἴσως ὁ Θεὸς τὴν πρὸς σωτηρίαν φυσικῶς ἐνέθηκε δύναμιν], so that anyone who wishes is able to lay claim to divine grace, and is not prevented, if he so desires, from becoming a Melchizedek, an Abraham, or a Moses, and from simply transferring all the saints to himself, not by exchanging names or places, but by imitating their manner and way of life.[140]

Grace names a power equally "implanted" in all. It is innate, present from the beginning *in potentia*. Given Maximus's near-obsessive discrimination between nature and grace above, how can he make of grace a germ so successfully inseminated into nature that its accessibility proves as universal as human nature itself? In no uncertain terms: Maximus is saying that the power of grace—which configures the rational soul through virtue to the point that "the Holy Spirit of God naturally becomes its intimate companion, and fashions it into a divine image, according to the likeness of the Spirit's own beauty" so that the soul "lacks nothing of the attributes that belong by nature to the Divinity"[141]— lay dormant in nature itself, always and everywhere.

Grace and its effects therefore do not come to us from without. At first blush this might not seem so. Take baptismal grace. Maximus assigns it a particular moment. Baptism is "when each person received the grace of adoption."[142] 1 John 3:9 claims that the one born of God sins no more because "God's seed remains in him" (ὅτι σπέρμα αὐτοῦ ἐν αὐτῷ μένει). Maximus argues that this "seed" takes root at baptism and blooms thereafter through the believer's voluntary praxis in cooperation with the Spirit.[143] It would appear, then, that the Spirit does not arrive until the time of baptism.

Not so. Elsewhere Maximus tries to reconcile one scriptural passage that says the Spirit is present to all things (Wisd. 12:1) and another that the Spirit absconds from the impure (Wisd. 1:4). Here Maximus portrays an unbroken and gradual presence of grace within nature. He narrates three stages. If we work backward the thread becomes very clear. (3) For those who "through faith have inherited the divine and truly divinizing name of Christ," the Spirit is present "as one creating the adoption given by grace through faith."[144] The Spirit is "productive of wisdom" (σοφίας ποιητικὸν), working through the pure to cultivate virtue.[145] (2) For those under the Law, the Spirit convicts hearts and foretells the coming salve for their soul's ongoing wounds, the Christ.[146] (1) But for everyone and all, the Spirit who providentially permeates "all things with His power"

> stirs into motion the natural inner principle of each [ὅτι θεὸς καὶ θεοῦ πνεῦμα κατὰ δύναμιν προνοητικῶς διὰ πάντων χωροῦν καὶ τὸν ἐν ἑκάστῳ κατὰ φύσιν λόγον ἀνακινοῦν] through which He leads a man of sense to consciousness of whatever he has done contrary to the law of nature, a man who at the same time also keeps his free choice pliant to the reception of right thoughts arising from nature. And thus we find even some of the most barbarous and uncivilized men exhibiting nobility of conduct and rejecting the savage laws that had prevailed among them from time immemorial.[147]

"Consequently," he goes on, "the Spirit is in all things in a simple way," awakening and succoring powers already universally implanted in every creature.[148] Grace's immanence to and actualization within all creation appears rather like the Word's own birth: by Mary's delighted consent the Spirit elicits a totally supranatural power *from within* the Virgin herself in order to conceive and gestate the Lord—but more of that presently.

The principal point for now is that grace's deifying potential already indwells everything from creation's dawn. Two more themes everywhere linked to grace further substantiate this account—faith and virtue.

Consider faith first. Faith for Maximus is always a power.[149] Its end or final deed is "the salvation of souls."[150] It is the root of all union with God—the first contact and caress, as it were.[151] Through faith the Spirit births virtue, actualizes in the soul every divine property—indeed, "hypostasizes" an immediate unity with God—for faith "is the hypostasis of things hoped for," as Hebrews 11:1 says.[152] This is why the knowledge (of God) that faith affords outstrips intellection and dialectic:[153] its power is the subjective condition for that unmediated experiential knowledge we considered before, rather like knowing a person, face-to-face recognition. And this power is "an innate good" (ἐνδιάθετον ἀγαθὸν), the invisible kingdom of God within (cf. Luke 17:21) that takes form through virtue and practice of Christ's commandments. Therefore "Faith is not outside us" but already given within the intellect, awaiting actualization: "If, then, the kingdom of God is actualized faith, and if the kingdom of God brings about an unmediated union of God and those in His kingdom, faith is clearly demonstrated to be a relational power, or a relationship that effectively realizes in a manner beyond nature the unmediated, perfect union of the faithful with the God in whom they have faith."[154] Faith names the supreme subjective power objectively given to all by grace alone,[155] which (always with love's succor)[156] opens an *immediate* relation to divine power in a way that once again circumvents Neoplatonic limitation of act by power. God gifts faith directly and *as* God himself, in the very act of creation. Faith is ours to vitalize, ours to thicken by deed.

So too with virtue, a primary way faith takes flesh. Although "virtue itself" (as opposed to its instances) numbers among those "works of God" eternally subsisting in him by nature and which we participate by grace,[157] Maximus states they are "natural things" (φυσικαί) for us too. When he says this to Pyrrhus, the latter wonders why virtue isn't equally manifest among all humans and why we must undertake ascetic struggle to acquire it at all. "Asceticism," Maximus retorts, "and the toils that go with it, were devised simply in order to ward off deception, which established itself through sensory perception. It is not [as if] the virtues have been newly introduced from outside, for they inhere in us from creation. . . . Therefore, when deception is completely expelled, the soul immediately exhibits the splendor of its natural virtue."[158] In another place Maximus even calls knowledge and virtue "powers of the rational soul" (δυνάμεις ὄντας ψυχῆς λογικῆς). But he does so, significantly, only as these arise from the *logoi* planted in nature, the principles according to which knowledge and virtue "exist and subsist."[159]

It is a significant point because the link to the *logoi* both exacerbates and begins to resolve the restive aporia we have been studying. That aporia presents grace as simultaneously a supranatural and an innate power in created nature. Virtue, for instance, a work of grace, is both "against" (or "over") nature and "an innate movement of nature."[160] The *logoi* intensify the apparent contradiction because they are *divine*—indeed, bear divinity itself within them[161]—and yet are, as grace was said to be, "implanted" or "placed in" nature in the very act of its creation from nothing.[162] Thus Maximus glosses the unbroken "bones" of the Word: "And after the manner of bones, which are constitutive of blood and flesh, the *logoi* of His divinity, which transcend all intellection, exist within beings and create—in a manner beyond our cognition—the essences of those beings, and preserve them in existence, and are constitutive for all knowledge and all virtue."[163]

Creation's *logoi* are the way uncreated grace exists as a supranatural power in nature. They establish faith's first and immediate contact with divine knowledge. They are and possess the power that makes God's eternal works—by essence imparticipable—participable by his finite works.[164] They institute the mode of deific union.[165] And the general "*logos* of nature" constitutes the open threshold between a rational creature's finite nature and the infinite works of God; if she would but join her will in love to that *logos*, she would have the Logos himself.[166] In a word, nature's *logos* functions as mediator because it is "a law both natural and divine" (ὃς καὶ νόμος ἐστὶ φυσικός τε καὶ θεῖος).[167] And that, I suggest, reveals the logic that explains and even necessitates the anomaly grace is.

3. *Grace is the Logos, as logoi, bearing and immediately presenting divinity from within nature.* Christo-logic explains why divine grace is a power and activity utterly without natural relation to our own essential

power and activity, and yet lies latent everywhere as nature's profoundest depths—the cause of its power and promise of its perfection. The
anomaly of grace describes the actualization of the Word within created
nature, the very Word who has already made himself hypostatically
identical to created nature's proper power and thereby generated it at all.
The Logos is the *logoi*.

In the *logoi* the Logos offers his own person as the immediate link
between uncreated and created power. Hence grace's source and logic
are the historical Incarnation: "But the Lord set forth the manifest might
of His transcendent power, having hypostasized an unchanging birth
in the nature of the contrary realities by which He Himself experienced. For by giving our nature impassibility through His Passion, relief
through His sufferings, and eternal life through His death, He restored
our nature, renewing its habitual dispositions by means of what was negated in His own flesh, and through His own Incarnation granting it that
grace which transcends nature, by which I mean divinization."[168] Grace
inhabits nature as the personal Word. The condition or *hexis* of the deified soul is in fact Christ's personal stamp, his stability, his character,
himself.[169] He "hypostasizes" what he experiences. Therefore what he
experiences—the entire existential range of human nature ("the contrary realities," pleasure and pain)—simultaneously comes to be possible at all and possible to be perfected, by no natural mediation, in identity with the divine activity.

Here again Maximian virtue proves an illuminating case. Its character makes no sense unless the Word condescends to become the immediate and real identity of virtue in two infinitely different natural modes.[170]
Recall that Maximus summons human growth in virtue as another way
to grasp his *logoi* doctrine. Just before the famous passage (*Amb.* 7.22) he
repeats what we saw in the *Dispute with Pyrrhus*, that virtue is natural
because entirely present in all human beings—never "more or less" universally there in power.[171] Here he specifies why. We do well to read it at
some length:

> The essence in every virtue is the one Logos of God—and this can
> hardly be doubted since the essence of all the virtues is our Lord,
> Jesus Christ, as it is written: *who was made for us by God wisdom,*
> *righteousness, holiness, and redemption* [1 Cor. 1:30]. . . . Which is to

say that anyone who through fixed habit participates in virtue, un-questionably participates in God, who is the substance of the vir-tues. For such a person freely and unfeignedly chooses to cultivate the natural seed of the Good, and has shown the end to be the same as the beginning, and the beginning to be the same as the end, or rather that the beginning and the end are one and the same [μᾶλλον δὲ ταὐτὸν ἀρχὴν οὖσαν καὶ τέλος]. . . . For it is from the beginning that he re-ceived being and participation in what is naturally good [εἰληφὼς πρὸς τῷ εἶναι καὶ τὸ κατὰ μέθεξιν φύσει ἀγαθόν]. . . . Having com-pleted his course, such a person becomes God, receiving from God to be God, for to the beautiful nature inherent in the fact that he is *God's image*, he freely chooses to add the *likeness* to God by means of the virtues, in a natural movement of ascent through which he grows in conformity to his own beginning.[172]

Track the logic closely. I recount it in reverse order of its appearance in this passage, which is the typical order of its phenomenological appear-ance in human life. Virtue inheres in human nature such that the ascetic ascent from image to likeness reveals virtue's hidden and hitherto buried beauty.[173] To cultivate that virtue—to reduce it to concrete deed by free choice—is to participate God himself. Existential, historical, *horizontal* acts of virtue somehow perform what is normally regarded as the more ontological, metaphysical, and *vertical* act of reverting to one's begin-ning (*arche*), which is also one's end (*telos*). Thus Origen favored a meta-physical axiom, "The beginning is like the end."[174] Maximus reprises and intensifies it here to stress the singular identity of beginning and end, the very identity ubiquitously latent within nature as the power of virtue, of deification.[175]

This identity is Jesus Christ. How so? Maximus reads the Apostle literally and metaphysically: "By God he was made for us wisdom" means for Maximus that the Word "was made" universal wisdom and virtue—indeed, all the participated works of God—in just the way he "was made" at all, that is, by Incarnation,[176] by making his hypostasis the "is" of what he is not by nature in order to make that nature both be and be his in a single creative act. Clearly Maximus operates according to Christo-logic here. In the preceding paragraph he explicitly distinguishes the Word's divine essence from his hypostasis precisely to claim that the

Logos—this hypostasis considered apart from divinity—is identical to the *logoi*.[177] Divine essence as such could never become anything, let alone created. But Jesus Christ can and did—here "the essence of all the virtues" (οὐσία γὰρ πάντων τῶν ἀρετῶν). A truly remarkable claim, particularly when you realize what Maximus is *not* saying. He does not mean that Christ "as Word," say, is the self-subsistent exemplar participated piecemeal by lesser participants. He might have easily taken this route. In this very passage (in the first ellipsis) he evokes the classical distinction between "Wisdom itself" (αὐτοσοφία) and specific instances of wisdom, "a wise man" (σοφὸς ἄνθρωπος), and initially identifies Christ with the former.[178] But then "Wisdom itself" appears entirely inherent within the participant, still, mind you, the very wisdom and virtue essentially identified with Christ's person. Wisdom's vertical, downward movement into its participants is Christ's own, which yields a feature totally foreign to standard philosophical models of participation: when the soul consumes the "lower members" of Christ's body, through virtue "it completely forms within it the *whole Word* who became flesh."[179]

We saw in the previous chapter that God is participable only because the Word deigns to bring down his proper (divine) activity with his own person (since divinity is no abstract thing), joining that activity to the nature he becomes according to hypostasis. Now here, as the lower, finite nature's own power reduces to act—a human soul's, say—it "mixes" with the divine activity fully present within itself.[180] The deified soul participates an interior activity whose power is not its own by nature and yet is entirely present because it belongs by nature to the Word within that soul, the Word who has given himself to be the concrete identity of two infinitely different natures—to be their *logoi* while also remaining himself in nature and person. And so when that soul actualizes its power in its proper (human) mode, the Word assumes *that* particular mode of created nature as well. In that sense the Word *gains* a modal instance or iteration he did not actually possess before (or rather besides) that person, since every instance bears a character and modality as individual as the person who "typifies" it.[181] You "lavishly show forth in yourself," writes Maximus to Thomas, "by means of the marvelous mixture of opposites—God incarnated in the virtues."[182]

Consider another individual, Melchizedek. Maximus does intently, we noticed, and in doing so resplendently illustrates grace's Christo-logic.

Maximus makes his start from scripture itself, which asserts that Melchizedek was "without father or mother or genealogy, having neither beginning of days nor end of life" (Ἀπάτωρ καὶ ἀμήτωρ καὶ ἀγενεαλόγητος, μήτε ἀρχὴν ἡμερῶν, μήτε τέλος ζωῆς ἔχων).[183] Maximus thinks this indicates Melchizedek's deified state. God made him "worthy to transcend time and nature and to become like the Son of God," that is, "He became by grace what the very Giver of grace is by essence."[184] What Melchizedek, a human person, was by nature certainly included things like having a temporal beginning and end, wielding dialectic to ascertain the truth of creatures, and so on. But what he becomes by grace comprises nothing less than the entire set of divine properties, undiminished. Grace, specifically "divine and uncreated grace" (τὴν χάριν τὴν θείαν καὶ ἄκτιστον), makes Melchizedek's own what he is not by nature. And it manifestly must be *uncreated* grace: if grace were created it would no longer be divine—at least not modally divine. But Maximus reads scripture and the Word's economy alike to aim at nothing less. Therefore only that grace which exists "eternally and is beyond all nature and time" renders Melchizedek "begotten" of God.[185]

Like Father like son:

> And so transcendentally, secretly, silently, and, to put it briefly, in a manner beyond knowledge, following the total negation of all beings from thought, he entered into God Himself, and was wholly transformed [ὅλος ὅλῳ ποιωθείς τε καὶ μεταποιηθείς], receiving all the qualities of God, which we may take as the meaning of *being likened to the Son of God* [ἀφωμοιωμένος δὲ τῷ Υἱῷ τοῦ Θεοῦ] *he remains a priest forever* [Heb. 7:3]. For every saint who has made exemplary progress in beauty is thereby said to be a type of God the giver. Consistent with this principle, the great Melchizedek, having been imbued with divine virtue, was deemed worthy to become an image of Christ God and His unutterable mysteries, for in Him all the saints converge as to an archetype, to the very cause of the manifestation of the Beautiful that is realized in each of them, and this is especially true of this saint, since he bears within himself more prefigurations of Christ than all the rest.[186]

Observe first that Maximus here defines "likeness" (again from ἀφομοίωμα) as "receiving all the qualities of God." We already attended to Maximus's rather strong sense of deific likeness (sec. 3.1). There and here you almost get the sense that deific "likeness" signifies something closer to the way the Word is "image of God" (Col. 1:15) or "the exact character of the Father's hypostasis" (Heb. 1:3)—which is to say, not by (essential) modal qualification.[187] In fact, just such an extreme sense emerges in a passage immediately prior to the one at hand: "The divine Melchizedek unfolded his intellect to the divine, beginningless, and immortal rays of God the Father, and was begotten out of God through the Word in the Spirit by grace, so that he now bears within himself, unblemished and fully realized, the likeness of God the begetter, for every birth creates identity between the begetter and the begotten [ἐπεὶ καὶ πᾶσα γέννησις ταὐτὸν τῷ γεννῶντι πέφυκεν ἀποτελεῖν τὸ γεννώμενον]."[188] Maximus reveals here what "by grace" means: to be born *from* God, *in* the Spirit, and *through* the Word, to such a degree that an "identity" obtains between the person become God and God. Grace forges an identity with God through the Word.

That this identity comes through the Word explains a second unique feature of grace's logic. We watched it at work in the *tantum-quantum* principle. Deification names a simultaneous, double movement of our ascent into God and God's into us—indeed, our ascent *is* God's into us and the reverse. The passage above (*Amb.* 10.45) describes our ascent: all the saints converge on Christ "as to an archetype." Even here we can discern the downward movement: Melchizedek "bears *within himself*"—so that his "self" still endures and houses the manifold "prefigurations" of Christ. A few paragraphs later we find that the *descent* was all along the mutual condition for ascent:

> Whoever casts aside this present life and its desires for the sake of the better life will acquire the *living, and active*, and absolutely unique *Word of God*, who through virtue and knowledge *penetrates to the division between soul and spirit*, so that absolutely no part of his existence will remain without a share in His presence, and thus he becomes without beginning or end, no longer bearing within himself the movement of life subject to time, which has a beginning and an end, and which is agitated by many passions, but possesses only the divine and eternal life of the Word dwelling within him, which is in no way bounded by death.[189]

At length we see how Melchizedek won the heights he did—even becoming "without beginning" (ἄναρχος), a predicate Maximus usually reserves exclusively for the divine essence itself.[190] Our ascent cannot occur except as an ascent *into the divinity already innately present in us*. The Word initially dwells in us that we might in him. There exists no divinity, no "divine and eternal life," that is not precisely "of the Word dwelling within" (τοῦ ἐνοικήσαντος Λόγου).[191]

Now too we can glimpse the distinctively Maximian sense of a theme dear to Origenism, the birth of the Word in the deified soul.[192] It bears the unmistakable marks of Christo-logic. Observe its first two elements (hypostatic identity generates infinite natural difference): the Logos condescends to identify his person to created nature; he becomes the *logoi* of all and each. That includes the *logos* of every human being. This generates the human being, nature and person. Indeed, it is the "hypostasis of [divine] gifts,"[193] the person of the Word, that establishes the (natural) potency of that person's being, well-being, and eternal well-being— which is to say the entire existential continuum of that person: beginning, middle, end.[194] The Word's person remains divine by nature even as it becomes this human being's natural power and principle. So now the Word bears two principles within that person (the divine and *this* human's) along with their respective natural modes and activities. Manifestly the indwelling Word's divine nature is always and infinitely actualized; it awaits no further reduction to act. But the Word's human nature remains in potency in each human being—rather, *is* that person's whole potency.[195] And since the Word is as much *that* human nature as he is divine, that human nature's actualization (its gradual, freely elected perfection through a person's proper and integral activity) is his as well.

And so I think we can take Maximus's statements literally: "Christ is always born mysteriously and willingly, becoming incarnate in those who are saved."[196] This is our adoption, how we become God's children. As it was in the historical Incarnation, the Holy Spirit, who dwells perichoretically (wholly) in the Son, is "the one creating" (δημιουργικὸν) the Son's birth in and as us.[197] So exactly does our deification hew to Christo-logic that the birth of Christ in our soul even evinces the basic causal reciprocity that obtained between Christ and his Mother:

> The mother of the Word is the true and unsullied faith. Just as the Word, who, as God, is by nature the creator of His mother who gave birth to Him according to the flesh, and made her His mother out of

love for mankind, and accepted to be born from her as man, so too the Word first creates faith within us, and then becomes the son of that faith, from which He is embodied through the practice of the virtues. And it is through faith that we accomplish all things, receiving from the Word the graces necessary for salvation. For without faith, through which the Word is God by nature and a son by grace, we have no boldness of speech to address our petitions to Him.[198]

The very Word becomes "a son by grace" in *our* adoption. Scarcely could his identity with us appear more starkly—his identity with our individual finite essences, powers, modes, and activities. He really does "become flesh" in our virtue (not merely in some abstract realm where Virtue lives).[199] On one occasion Maximus praises his addressee for "always conceiving and bearing the pious *logos* of your understanding, which is like a womb made capable by grace of manifesting the supra-natural Word." The Word manifests because the Word *increases*. "By your generous dispositions, which were born from your heart," Maximus continues, "you nourish the Word in accordance with right praxis and contemplation—as if from breasts—and you nurse along the Word to growth in the abundance of pious conceptions and modes [of life] so that, paradoxical as it sounds, his own growth becomes the deification of the very mind that nourishes him."[200]

Just as the Virgin's own free power to bear and to birth the Word was itself a power given by the Word, so too is grace's. When the Mother consented, the Word became his own seed in her in an utterly supranatural way.[201] When I consent to the Word's invitation, coursing as it does through creation's very veins as the *logoi*[202]—mine too!—then the Word realizes himself in me, assumes my own nature and mode in its every general and particular dimension. This then reveals a most stunning culmination of grace's Christo-logic:

> Jesus my God and Savior, *who is completed through me who am saved*, brings me back to himself who is always filled to overflowing with plenitude and who can never be exhausted. He restores me in a marvelous way to myself, or rather to God from whom I received being and toward whom I am directed, long desirous of attaining well-being. Whoever can understand this by having had the

experience of these things will completely come to know in clearly having recognized his own dignity already through experience, how there is rendered to the image what is made to the image, how the archetype is honored, what is the power of the mystery of our salvation, for whom it was that Christ died, and finally *how we can remain in him and he in us,* just as he said (John 15:4).[203]

· · ·

That final line opens upon the logic of the actual, deified state—perichoresis. I return to that shortly. But I want to terminate this discussion of the aporia of grace as the indelible index of its Christo-logic by lingering a bit over one of Maximus's favorite formulations of our deification. He often says we become God "by position" (θέσει).[204] The expression κατὰ θέσιν can refer to adoption, the legal rather than biological mode of gaining a child.[205] That idea is certainly present in Maximus, but, as Larchet observes, θέσει probably does not take that as its principal sense, not least because Maximus often employs another (biblical and technical) term for "adoption."[206] Both of course indicate a process outside of nature, something non- or supranatural: θέσει opposes φύσει.[207]

But θέσει expresses more than the process's character. When a fact or state results from a process that occurs "by position," it tells you something remarkable about that very state too. What comes to be "by position" is a state or fact *just like* the fact that comes to be by nature. Becoming God by position, as it were, makes us just as much God as God is by nature (i.e., *tantum-quantum* principle). "By grace," which also means "by position," does not make us less God just because the process is utterly supranatural. Hence Maximus can gloss the Christological claim of Colossians 2:9 with this remarkable claim: "In Christ, on the one hand, who is God and Word of the Father, the whole fullness of divinity dwells by essence in a bodily manner. But in us the fullness of divinity dwells *by grace* at the moment we gather within ourselves every virtue and wisdom—such that, to the extent possible for a human being, nothing in any way lacks in the true imitation with respect to the archetype. For it is not unfitting that, *by the principle of position,* the fullness of divinity dwells in us too, a fullness consisting in various spiritual contemplations."[208] The *logos* of "position" describes the way grace makes the whole divinity inhabit us as it inhabits Christ. The process is not natural. But the outcome exists *in fact* just as if it were.

I think that another, more distant horizon might illumine Maximus's affinity for θέσει: ancient Greek prosody (right pronunciation).[209] There we encounter a fairly direct replication of Maximus's use. More evidently than in any other of its contexts, "by position" in prosody immediately opposes "by nature." The Alexandrian grammarian Dionysius Thrax (d. 90 BC), whose *Ars grammatica* marked the first systematic grammar treatise and would become "a text-book in the schools of the Roman Empire,"[210] allots two categories of instances where one must pronounce long syllables. "A long syllable may come about in eight ways," Dionysius writes, "three by nature and five by position" (Μακρὰ συλλαβὴ γίνεται κατὰ τρόπους ὀκτώ, φύσει μὲν τρεῖς, θέσει δὲ πέντε).[211] You pronounce a long syllable "by nature" when, for instance, the syllable contains a long vowel or diphthong (these are already long by nature), and "by position" when, say, the syllable ends in two consonants or is followed by a double consonant (as with ἔξω—"ξ" is a result of the palatal stop "χ" before "σ"). In fact pronouncing "by position" seems not to yield any exact or universal rule precisely because its art is not natural (and so is not abstractly proscribed). Or to put it another way, a general rule in prosody condenses by convention, not by the very essence of the syllables themselves. Syllables come arranged, and pronunciation introduces yet another level of ordering. Prosody deals with the direct deed wrought and performed by the speaker in concert with generations of other speakers. From prosody, Dionysius thus teaches, we learn "the art of the reader."[212]

I claim no direct textual dependence here. Yet the picture conjured proves compelling enough to take seriously. Maximus does sometimes say θέσει in an apparently prosodic register. Those who consume the Eucharist "can be *and be called gods by position* through grace" (δύνασθαι εἶναί τε καὶ καλεῖσθαι θέσει κατὰ τὴν χάριν θεούς).[213] The deified receive the "name" of God,[214] and the mysteries to be revealed in that final state which transcends every written and spoken word will then sound forth as "a masterly articulated speech" (ὡς πρὸς τρανὸν λόγον).[215] Deification by grace and "by position," then, delightfully expresses that supranatural process according to which the very Word who dwells within and assumes form in all creatures makes those very creatures *in fact* what they could never be "by nature"—divine.

That we become identical to and equal with God through Christ and in the Spirit—this describes a literal, actual state of the creature's *being* God, though, unlike God, that creature certainly had to *become* God.[216] This supranatural process transpires solely by the art of the reader: the Word is the reader, and what he reads is himself in and as us, in and as the *logoi*.[217] In them he enunciates himself as us by convention, as it were, free of every natural necessity. Yet what and who is spoken is no less him. We are short by nature, and likely less. But in the *logoi*, creation's "scripts,"[218] the Word masterfully speaks us long and thereby displays the sublime art he is. We become the Word when we willingly give ourselves to be pronounced by, in, and as him. "Blessed therefore is the one who through wisdom has actively made God man in himself, who has brought to fullness the inception of this mystery, and who passively experiences becoming God by grace, for this experience will never come to an end."[219]

3.3. PERICHORESIS, THE LOGIC OF DEIFIED CREATION

Passive experience, remember, characterizes the existential state of Maximian deification. Maximus's meditation on Melchizedek begins: "This, I think, is what that wondrous and great man, Melchizedek . . . knew and learned through experience [γνοὺς καὶ παθὼν]."[220] What did he experience? The preceding paragraph strains to say: "Having been wholly united with the whole Word, within the limits of what their own inherent natural potency allows . . . [the deified Old Testament saints, such as Melchizedek] were imbued with His own qualities, like the clearest of *mirrors* [Wisd. 7:26], they are now visible only as reflections of the undiminished form of God the Word, who gazes out from within them, for they possess the fullness of His divine characteristics, yet none of the original attributes that naturally define human beings have been lost, for all things have simply yielded to what is better, like air—which in itself is not luminous—completely mixed with light."[221]

The term *perichoresis* is absent here, though not its logic. In chapter 1 (sec. 1.4) and in the introduction to this chapter (sec. 3.1) I noted two characteristics of perichoresis. First, it describes a union of two distinct wholes that retain their integral identities even as they exist as one and the same reality. This feature betrays perichoresis's remote provenance in the "mixture" of Stoic physics.[222] I leave "wholes" ambiguous, since of course what the two "wholes" are depends on context. In the Trinity the wholes are persons.[223] In Christ they refer to his natures, or more exactly to his natural activities.[224] Second, these wholes interpenetrate every part of each other to the point that a modal and actual symmetry or reciprocity emerges.

That last characteristic definitely distinguishes perichoretic logic from, say, Neoplatonic emanative or participative logic. For the latter, I remarked already, the Plotinian doctrine of double activity necessitates a *modal asymmetry* in order to explain why anything proceeds at all and yet remains essentially related to its superior, subsistent cause.[225] If therefore Christo-logic culminates precisely in an actuality or existential reality whose logic is perichoretic, and if that logic is creation's too, and if deification is creation's perfection—it follows that deification's logic must also terminate perichoretically.

It does, incontrovertibly. Unlike anyone before him,[226] Maximus makes perichoresis the intractable and characteristic logic of the deified creature's concrete condition.[227] He summons the technical term to describe that state, in both its verbal and nominal forms.[228] A creature's deification occurs "through the grace of the Spirit" and manifests "God alone acting within it"—not, Maximus carefully clarifies, in such a way that the creature's natural power and activity vanish. Rather, God "in a manner befitting His goodness wholly interpenetrates all who are worthy" (ὡς ὅλον ὅλοις τοῖς ἀξίοις ἀγαθοπρεπῶς περιχωρήσαντος).[229] "Unconfused union," sometimes thrown about abstractly in the literature,[230] retains its exact Christological meaning even in our deification. It designates actual perichoresis grounded in hypostatic identity: "In assuming both of these for our sake, God renewed our nature, or to put it more accurately, He made our nature new, returning it to its primordial beauty of incorruptibility through His holy flesh, taken from us, and animated by a rational soul, and on which He lavishly bestowed the gift of deification, from which it is absolutely impossible to fall, being united to God made flesh, like the soul united to the body, wholly interpenetrating it in an unconfused union [δι' ὅλου περιχωρήσασαν ἀσυγχύτως κατὰ τὴν ἕνωσιν]."[231]

Perichoresis's two signature traits crop up again and again. Whether the technical term appears, the idea that the deified state involves the "whole" God in the "whole" creature and the reverse—"whole in whole, wholly"—suffuses Maximus's oeuvre.[232] But it is the modal symmetry, the second trait, that really reveals perichoretic logic at work. This symmetry shows us that the deified state consists in two simultaneous, vertical movements (both realized horizontally)—God's descent and our ascent. Both transgress Neoplatonic participation. They make it so that the very mode (and act) of divinity descends into the finite mode (and act) of the creature just as much as the latter ascends into divinity's; that both modes exist as one reality; and that in this single reality both modes perdure entirely undiminished—neither's natural power limits the other's act in and through it.[233]

Consider God's descent. God does not come to be in a deified person in the way a Platonic cause dwells in its effect. Indeed, what would it mean to say such a cause "comes to be" in anything, since such a "coming to be" just *is* the effect—the procession "out of" the cause that differentiates effect from cause in the first place?[234] If there is any sense in speaking of the cause's "coming to be" in its effect, this would amount to either pure metaphor or pure Aristotelian efficient causality (i.e., potency terminates its act in the passive recipient). The second cannot by itself explain God's creative act because God's proper mode and activity naturally precede all effects (divinity's *natural* activity is not completed in created effects, not even in their perfection).[235] The first is possible. But it would obviously violate Christo-logic. That "God became man"—a finite effect—is no mere metaphor. And yet Maximus claims God "comes to be" in the deified.

Take, for instance, the way he adjudicates two apparently contradictory scriptures. The apostle John says "God is light" (1 John 1:5). But two verses later he exhorts, "If we walk in the light, *as He is in the light*" (1 John 1:7). What does it mean to say God both *is* and *is in* light? Maximus replies:

God, who is truly light according to His essence, is in those who "walk in Him" through the virtues, so that they too truly become light. Just as all the saints, who on account of their love for God become light by participation in that which is light by essence, so too that which is light by essence, on account of its love for man, becomes light in those who are light by participation. If, therefore, because of virtue and knowledge we are in God as in light, God Himself, as light, is in us who are light. For God who is light by nature comes to be in that which is light by imitation, just as the archetype [comes to be] in the image.[236]

Two critical points here. First, Maximus does wield the "by essence" versus "by participation" distinction. Ostensibly we have to do with vertical, Platonic (or exemplarist) causality. But then, second, the archetype does a most un-Platonic thing: it *descends* or "comes to be" or even "becomes" (γίνεται) participated light (i.e., light in a qualified or finite mode). There is no hint that this is metaphor. Quite the opposite, really, and for two reasons. For one thing, the context of the second scripture ("as He is in the light") clearly refers to Jesus Christ.[237] And then Maximus assigns a clear motive to Light's descent, namely "on account of its love for mankind" (διὰ φιλανθρωπίαν)—a motive everywhere linked to the Word's historical Incarnation.[238] The logic of descent here is not simply Platonic. Nor is it simply the Aristotelian logic of the archetype's realization in the imitator—what we saw at *Ambiguum* 21.15. Rather, it is both at once. It is Christo-logic. It is the *tantum-quantum* principle. It is a claim that in the deified person God descends and "becomes" the very participated mode (and activity) of that person, all while retaining the divine mode unmuted and unqualified and unmediated.

Maximus underscores that last claim fairly often. I mean the claim that when God descends he continues to bear and to be in the complete modality proper to the divine essence. Rational creatures are never truly free (or rational) "until the law of nature is completely swallowed up by the law of the Spirit, just as the death of the wretched flesh will be swallowed up by life everlasting, that is, not before *the entire image* of the unoriginate kingdom is clearly revealed, mimetically manifesting in itself *the entire form* of the archetype."[239] Christ's "form" comes to be in every deified person. And to emphasize the fact that it is *not* limited to finite nature's mode, Maximus calls it "unvarying."[240]

Now consider our ascent. In Maximian deification we behold "the whole man pervading the whole God" (ὅλος ὅλῳ περιχωρήσας ὁλικῶς τῷ Θεῷ).[241] Again, in a celebrated passage on deification—a running catena of its deifications, as it were—Maximus makes the splendid remark that the "true revelation of the object of one's faith is the ineffable *perichoresis* with that object according to the proportion of one's faith."[242] Remarkable here is that he indexes the degree of God's self-revelation (descent) directly to the degree that we—as individual persons—penetrate God (ascent).[243] God dwells wholly in the deified person *because* the deified person dwells wholly in God, and the reverse.[244] Chalcedon's symmetry recurs in the deified state as the latter's very logic.

And this is indeed Chalcedon's symmetry. It describes a modal and actual symmetry grounded in and revealed by Christo-logic. Modal perichoresis never floats free of hypostatic identity. Only the Word's hypostasis can be and so establish the nonessential identity of realities infinitely different by essence. Hypostasis names a non-natural, existential positivity that—precisely because it is *not* natural in itself—is in no way limited to natural relations or modes in order to bring creatures to be at all and to be one with him. Hypostatic identity relieves nature from having to achieve such identity. It therefore circumvents standard philosophical negotiations between created and uncreated natures, finite and infinite modalities, that is, how these can or must be identical to and distinct from each other. Witness again Maximus's precisions about actual and modal perichoresis in Christ:

> "And in a manner beyond man, He does the things of man," according to a supreme union involving no change, showing that *the human energy is conjoined with the divine power* [συμφυεῖσαν δεικνὺς τῇ θεϊκῇ δυνάμει τὴν ἀνθρωπίνην], since the human nature, united without confusion to the divine nature, is *completely interpenetrated by it* [ἡ φύσις ἀσυγχύτως ἑνωθεῖσα τῇ φύσει δ' ὅλου περικεχώρηκε], with absolutely no part of it remaining separate from the divinity to which it was united, having been assumed according to hypostasis. For "in a manner beyond" us, the "Word beyond being truly assumed our being," and joined together the transcendent negation with the affirmation of our nature and its natural properties, and so became man, *having united His transcendent mode of existence with the principle of His human nature* [τὸν ὑπὲρ φύσιν τοῦ πῶς εἶναι τρόπον ἔχων συνημμένον τῷ τοῦ εἶναι λόγῳ τῆς φύσεως], so that the ongoing existence of that nature might be confirmed by the newness of modes of existence, not suffering any change at the level of its inner principle, and thereby make known His power that is beyond infinity, recognized in the generation of opposites.[245]

The three italicized parts illustrate the exact Christo-logic of perichoresis: *because* of their hypostatic identity,[246] which puts divine and human principles and powers into immediate union (so circumventing limitation of act by power), the modes and activities of both natures can entirely interpenetrate each other. They are unrestricted by the supposed finality of any essential restriction. Christ's modal and actual perichoresis discloses a new existential possibility, what Maximus just before this passage simply calls "the unified mode of the Lord's activities."[247]

Notice too how Maximus introduces here a deeper Trinitarian ground of Christological perichoresis: since Christ's person is the second person of the Trinity, and since he truly identifies himself with the created mode of his human flesh, we rightly say that the Word "united His transcendent mode of existence" to the very "principle of his human nature." That "mode of existence" is of course the "tri-hypostatic mode" of the divine essence itself, namely the *personal* perichoresis of Father and Son and Spirit.[248] Because Christ reveals himself through the unbroken perichoretic mode of his human and divine modes and acts (he walks divinely on water and heals humanly with the spoken word), and because such perichoresis derives solely from Christ's hypostatic identity as the "is" of both natures, and because hypostatic identity can be distinguished from essential identity only if hypostasis and essence bear different logics even in God, and because these logics differ in God only as inseparable and *essentially* one in a single mode of existence that *is* three persons— therefore, Maximus concludes, only the economy, the Incarnation, could have taught true theology, God's "mode of existence" (τὴν πῶς ὕπαρξιν), the Trinity.[249]

·   ·   ·

All this raises a major objection to my thesis, though. If hypostatic identity grounds modal perichoresis in our deified state too, doesn't our deification imply our personal obliteration? In Christ there is but *one* hypostasis that is the identity of the two natures. But in me, say, if the same hypostatically grounded perichoresis of modes should occur, either "I" (my hypostasis) simply becomes "him" (Christ's hypostasis), or he comes actually to reside *in* me. Not the former, at least not if we wish to avoid the Origenist problem of eschatological absorption.[250] And not the latter if we wish to maintain Neo-Chalcedonian Christo-logic—for then there would be *two* hypostases in my deific state. In that case wouldn't Maximian deification prove Nestorian?

Before replying I note two historical points in order to intensify the objection. The first is that several had flagged and rejected the idea of personal perichoresis between created and uncreated hypostases, which a certain Origenism did seem to enjoin in a way that entailed the destruction of the former as such.[251] Some of Maximus's traditional authorities repudiated it. Diadochus of Photice, for example, wrote that even though baptism forges a strong personal link between soul and Spirit, the baptized soul cannot contain "two persons" (*prosopa*) in view of its "simple form."[252] And the Macarian homilies worry at the status of individuals after the general resurrection: "All things will become light. All are immersed in light and fire and are indeed changed, but are not, as certain people say, dissolved and transformed into fire so that nothing of their nature remains. For Peter is Peter, and Paul, Paul, and Philip is Philip. Each person in his proper nature and hypostasis remains, yet filled by the Spirit."[253] Maximus actually agrees with the motive behind these cautions. He does not envision the annihilation of created hypostases any more than they.[254]

And yet the second point is that Maximus does think perichoresis of persons characterizes the deific state. Our opening text spoke of "the undiminished form of God the Word, who gazes out from within" the saints, and it did so, as with the Macarian homily, in the context of describing an eschatological oneness wherein all things mix with the divine light.[255] Or in a passage that drifts in quite a different direction from Diadochus's above, Maximus lauds Dionysius and Gregory of Nazianzus, whose excessive wisdom shows that they "set aside a life conformed to nature" and "occupied themselves with the essence of the soul and so took hold of the living, unique Christ, who—to say what is even greater—became the soul of their souls." Thus identified with Christ, they penned words that "were authored, not by them, but by Christ, who by grace has exchanged places with them."[256]

In a text flanked on both sides by deific perichoresis, Maximus adduces "conjecturally" the character of that state. It eludes all conception and description, of course. It is a state that surpasses our original "participation in goodness" and relies directly on the Son's historical Incarnation to come about. There, at the decisive moment of his earthly sojourn and recapitulation of human nature, the Son "typifies our own [voluntary subjection] in himself" (αὐτὸς ἐν ἑαυτῷ τυπῶν τὸ ἡμέτερον) as he cries, "Yet not as I will, but as you will" (Matt. 26:39). The Son's subjection to the Father hypostasizes the full potential of our own subjection to God. Thus we can become by grace (as we saw with its aporetic process) what the Son is by nature, but only because he first became by nature what we are. Now our nature, unimpeachably united to and "characterized" by his personal mode of existence[257]—personal perichoresis with Father and Spirit—possesses the conditions that allow us to receive the Trinity's existential mode (by grace, no doubt). Which is why Maximus immediately equates the Son's self-offering with the apostle Paul's own, citing Galatians 2:20: "It is no longer I who live, but Christ who lives in me."[258]

These texts suggest that Maximus took the same sort of risk by affirming personal perichoresis in deification as he did with isochrist identity statements. And if any doubt yet lingers, one passage in particular settles the matter. It portrays nearly the contrary to what the Macarian homily just did.

In *Ambiguum* 47 Maximus interprets Gregory's figurative reading of the Passover, especially this line: "We need not be surprised that, first and foremost, a lamb is required in each and every house [κατ' οἶκον ἕκαστον]."[259] This short *ambiguum* is itself an excellent performance of perichoretic logic, wherein our ascent through Christ—through our incremental ascent to his body, then to his mind, finally into his divinity—appears seamlessly and simultaneously as Christ's descent into us—like an immolated "lamb" for each to ingest and so become. Maximus resolves his meditation like this:

> Thus it happens that *each* of us *in his own rank* [1 Cor. 15:23] . . . sacrifices the Divine Lamb, partakes of its fleshes, and takes his fill of Jesus. For to each person Christ Jesus becomes his own proper lamb, to the extent that each is able to contain and consume Him. He becomes something proper to Paul, the great preacher of the truth, and again, something distinctively proper to Peter, the leader of the apostles, and something distinctively proper for each of the saints, according to the measure of each one's faith, and the grace granted to him by the Spirit, to one in this way, and to another in that, so that Christ is found to be wholly present throughout the whole of each, *becoming all things to everyone* [1 Cor. 9:22].[260]

Behold Maximus's astounding claim: when the whole God, in and as Christ, becomes "the whole of each," this whole includes the very person of the deified. His language is strong and exact. Christ Jesus "becomes the *proper* lamb *of each*," so that he becomes, literally rendered, "a proper *of Paul*" (ἴδιος Παύλου) and what is "distinctively proper *of Peter*" (ἰδιοτρόπως ἴδιος τοῦ . . . Πέτρου) and precisely "in the proper mode *of each*" (ἰδιοτρόπως ἑκάστου). It is not merely that Christ accommodates himself to the personal proclivities or abilities of each—though deification includes that too. He becomes the very "proper(ty)" that distinguishes Paul's person from Peter's, and each from all.[261] Christ becomes their very hypostatic difference, the very property that makes each the person he or she is.

Maximus's pregnant statements here anticipate my response to the objection about obliterating created hypostases. It runs roughly thus. Maximus takes a hard line on Platonic Ideas: he doesn't have them.[262] He does have eternal "divine works" that are participated, but, as we saw in the last chapter, these are not self-subsisting and are participated only within the peculiar conditions of Christo-logic. Moreover, Maximus holds the fairly idiosyncratic but somewhat predictable view (given his position on Platonic Ideas) that universals are created and consist and indeed "subsist" *in* the total set of their particulars.[263] For Maximus there is no such thing as a generic or universal created nature existing somewhere other than in the created hypostases that bear and exemplify it.[264] The only world that exists is the world made in and through and as the determinate panoply of its actual denizens.

This view of universals carries massive soteriological implications. Christ, as Larchet rightly argues, assumed *universal* human nature just as much as a particular one; assuming one is assuming the other, really.[265] He therefore assumed (and continues to assume) *all* human particulars, every human person, since universal humanity does not exist separately from the sum of human individuals. So Maximus reads Gregory's remark that Christ "bears the whole of me in Himself" to mean "He bears the totality of human nature" (τὴν ἀνθρωπείαν φύσιν ὁλόκληρον).[266] Indeed, Christ "as man is the *first fruits* of our nature in relation to God the Father, and a kind of *yeast that leavens* the whole *mass of humanity* [Rom. 11:16, Maximus adds τοῦ ὅλου]," so that his own personal death and resurrection becomes the universal power of humanity's—every human being's—resurrection. Those perfected in Christ are *"natural outgrowths of His resurrection."*[267]

How does this meet the objection? Because universal created nature subsists only in and as particular created hypostases, Christ cannot identify himself with created nature without also identifying himself with every individual creature. Maximus's *logoi* doctrine already taught us as much. In everything there is a *"logos* of the common [essence or nature]" and a *"logos* of hypostasis."[268] Both condition each other. The *logos* of a created hypostasis constitutes a particularly arresting display of divine power because it is a fundamental and immanent causal principle that no process of declension by formal or modal qualification can illumine. I am the person I am, but "I" names a *non*-natural mode (hypostasis bears no natural content) that yet instances or "typifies" nature in an utterly unrepeatable and inexplicable manner.[269] My person's "ability" to typify or affect at all discloses the existential positivity of hypostasis as such. A hypostasis, like a black hole, signifies that inconceivable reality whose gravity is yet sensed in the way it pushes and pulls nature, as it were. Personal style marks every instance of universal nature. And yet you cannot speak of that style without predicating either natural qualities (intelligent, loving, hospitable, beautiful, well-formed, etc.) or accidental properties. You can only speak a proper name: "It is very *Paul* to say or do this or that." That distinction, that property, that irrepressible yet inexpressible positivity that a person is—it is precisely this reality that, since it too comes from God, *has a principle* or *logos* as such. And it is this that God in Christ also *becomes*. The Logos is the *logoi*—all of them.[270]

If the Logos, Christ, has identified himself with even the principle of a created hypostasis as such—and so generated it—then he has become the very power of that person to become who and how (not just what) she is. As she actualizes her personal potency (always through and with her natural potency, of course), which exists in her personal *logos* and which the Logos became, the Logos assimilates her body—her entire life—as his own: "taking a body in a variety of ways, as only he knows, in each of the saved."[271] Personal perichoresis is the eventual mode of existence prepared in the very act of the Logos becoming the *logoi*. It is Incarnation, for the Word assumes universal created nature. And it must climax in a state of personal perichoresis, for created nature subsists only in created hypostases. When the Word became a creature, then, he planted the very mode of his personal existence into the principles of all creation—the potential for every creature's personal interpenetration of and by the Three. For the whole Father and the whole Spirit are in the whole Son who is Christ, and in Christ alone the *logoi* live.[272]

3.4. CHRIST'S BODY AND ANALOGY

Maximus regards this entire schema of creation as Incarnation as basically just good Pauline theology. No reason to rush to Plato or the Stoics for the idea that the world is God's body.[273] Colossians 3:11, for example, plainly states that "Christ is all things and in all things."[274] The Logos is the *logoi*, first and last.

Maximus punctuates his *logoi* treatise (*Amb.* 7) with scriptural citations, especially from Paul about the Body of Christ. After a lengthy explication and defense of the *logoi* as the proper way to read Gregory's remark that we are "portions of God," Maximus repairs to crucial New Testament texts to make some rather amazing claims of his own. Witness how Maximus embosses these texts around his bold eschatological portrait of all things *hypostasized* in Christ. I quoted it near the end of last chapter, but we must read it again:

> The aim is that "what God is to the soul, the soul might become to the body," and that the Creator of all might be proven to be One, and through humanity might come to reside in all things in a manner appropriate to each, so that the many, though separated from each other in nature, might be drawn together around the one nature of man. When this happens, *God will be all things in everything* [1 Cor. 15:28], encompassing all things and hypostasizing them in Himself, for beings will no longer possess independent motion or lack any portion of God's presence, and it is with respect to this presence that we are, and are called, *Gods* [John 10:35], *children of God* [John 1:12], the *body*, and *members of God* [Eph. 1:23, 5:30], and, it follows, "portions of God," and other such things, in the progressive ascent of the divine plan to its final end.[275]

Creation's contours appear ever more like a continuous human nature or Body, the personalized bond of all things sundry by nature, whose unifying power is that of a divine person who assimilates and "makes all things his own" such that none of what he assumes—even other human bodies—suffers violation in principle when transposed into perichoretic mode.[276] The world is born like a Seed generating the very womb in which it gestates. It is born again and again as the particular seed of this or that creature, and, because it retains all it has hypostasized, gains in each actualized creature a new member of its Body.[277]

At the apex of his reflection on the *logoi* Maximus invokes scripture once more: "The basic argument [proves to] be more persuasive when supported by the inspired words of Scripture, in particular those of the holy blessed apostle Paul."[278] He then quotes Pauline texts extensively, Ephesians especially. These he selects to link the world's *logoi* to Christ's ecclesial Body and his "recapitulation" of every creature into that Body. A sampling: "*And He has put all things under His feet and has made Him the head over all things for the Church, which is His body, the fullness of Him who fills all things in every way* [ends Eph. 1:17–23]."[279] And: "*Rather, speaking the truth in love, we are to grow up in every way into Him who is the head, into Christ, from whom the whole body, joined and knit together by every joint with which it is supplied, when each part is working properly, makes bodily growth and upbuilds itself in love* [from Eph. 4:11–16]."[280] From such passages Maximus adduces exactly how we become "one and the same" (ἓν καὶ ταὐτὸν) with God—the very goal of creation announced in our overture (*Amb.* 41.5):

[These words show] that we are the *members* and the *body of Christ*, and that we constitute *the fullness of Christ God* [Eph. 1:23], who *fills all things in every way* according to the plan *hidden in God the Father before the ages* [Eph. 3:9], with the result that [or "the *skopos* being"] we are being *recapitulated into Him* [Eph. 1:10] through His Son and our Lord and God Jesus Christ. For *the mystery hidden from the ages* [Col. 1:26] and from all generations has now been revealed through the true and perfect Incarnation of God the Son, who united our nature to Himself according to hypostasis, without division and without confusion. In and through His holy flesh—which He took from us, and which is endowed with intellect and reason—He has conjoined us to Himself, as a kind of *first fruits*, making us worthy to be one and the same with Him, according to His humanity, since we were *predestined* before the ages [Eph. 1:11–12] to be in Him as the members of His body. Just as the soul unifies the body, He joined us to Himself and knit us together in the Spirit, and He leads us *to the stature of the spiritual maturity according to His* [i.e., Christ's] *own fullness* [Eph. 4:13].[281]

We are "one and the same" with God "according to his humanity" (κατὰ τὴν αὐτοῦ ἀνθρωπότητα). For Maximus, Paul himself teaches that our deification is God's Incarnation. In the previous chapter we saw that the Word's protological condescension in identifying his person with the world's *logoi* is itself the condition for the possibility of any participation in his divine activity. He brings down in person what is imparticipable in essence. But since hypostatic *identity* alone establishes creation's power to participate God, it must *also* and simultaneously reveal a necessary condition in the reverse direction, as it were: God grants "hypostasis" to creation by identifying himself with it in the Word's hypostasis.[282] God creates by assuming a Body. Therefore the Body he assumes is creation— its process (*logoi*) and perfection (modal perichoresis). And since he identifies himself in person with what he creates by nature, and since what is created begins necessarily in motion (*Amb.* 7.3–14), then creation's existential movement into ever more perfect actuality is the Word's too. That the world is literally Christ's Body is the deepest ground for Maximus's bold and consistent insistence on the God-world reciprocity.[283] "For inasmuch as He came to be below for our sakes . . . it follows that we too, thanks to Him, will come to be in the world above, and become gods according to Him through the mystery of grace, undergoing no change whatsoever in our nature. . . . The world above will again be filled, with the *members of the body* being gathered together *with their head* . . . filling *the body of Him who fills all in all*, which fills and is filled from all things."[284]

Christ's Body grows or is knitted together or gains modal iterations precisely through and as every member of the cosmos. His own person constitutes the base of every creature as its individual and generic *logoi*, yet he never relinquishes the *individual* body he assumed from Mary and is. Here we approach admittedly bizarre and nearly incomprehensible claims. That is as it should be, of course, and it is why Maximus pressed the point that the deified state can finally be known only by experience. The same might have been said about the world's middle, about the very idea that God became man. And yet by faith we must say something about it, even if with a strained voice speaking fragile words and concepts. Bear that in mind here at the world's end. Its logic is just as enduringly mysterious and necessarily sayable as Christ's at the middle (for they are the same). "The body of Christ is either the soul, or its powers, or sensations, or the body of each human being, or the members of the body, or the commandments, or the virtues, or the *logoi* of created beings, or, to put it simply and more truthfully, each and all of these things, both individually and collectively, are the body of Christ [ἰδίᾳ τε καὶ κοινῇ, ταῦτα πάντα καὶ τούτων ἕκαστόν ἐστι τὸ σῶμα τοῦ Χριστοῦ]."[285] Everything is his Body. Even "the body of each human being" forms part of Christ's Body. "Every man," Maximus resumes just after this passage, "who possesses an addition of faith and knowledge, and who is augmented by the modes of virtue . . . is a spiritual Joseph [of Arimathea], able to receive the body of Christ and bury it properly, placing it in the niche that faith has hewn in his heart, *by grace making his own body as the body of Christ* [τὸ τε σῶμα τὸ ἑαυτοῦ ὡς Χριστοῦ σῶμα διὰ τὴν χάριν]." So grows "the mystical body of Christ."[286]

Christ's actual recapitulation of the entire world into and as his Body reveals "that the whole creation is one, just as if it were another human being, completed by the mutual coming together of all its members."[287] Maximus frequently evokes the whole human person to depict the world's deification.[288] He seems fond of saying God will become to us as the soul is to the body, for instance.[289] Given Maximus's Christological account of the human person—where body and soul are at once essentially different and yet never concretely whole outside of the unifying positivity of a hypostasis—we must take sufficient account of two significant features of Christ's Body.

For starters, hypostatic identity grounds and conditions whatever else we might say about elements within Christ's Body. A person's parts, even her essential parts (body and soul), do not exist at all or together as an ontic whole except *as* her.[290] Maximus distinguishes the "principle of becoming" from the "principle of essence" (Οὐχ ὁ αὐτὸς γὰρ γενέσεως καὶ οὐσίας λόγος) to make just this point.[291] The latter has to do with a thing's natural "what" (τί) and "how" (πῶς), the former with its existential "when" (πότε) and "where" (ποῦ) and, most significantly, "its reciprocal relation" (πρὸς τί ἐστιν).[292] In other words the *logoi* of various essences only generate their respective realities through *particular* individuals—the individual human being, say, who bears an entire complex of spatio-temporal-personal

relations by birth. The consequent and concrete "coexistence" and "reciprocal relation" of a hypostasis's natural parts is the *logos* that generates
"the completion of a single human being."[293] In Christ's Body, then, to the
degree it is potentially the entire cosmos, we should contemplate the various relations among his members (i.e., every creature) as predicated upon
his single hypostasis. He is the very *logos* that unifies all things and
grounds the reciprocal relation or basic symmetry or sympathy among all
Christ's parts, even his created and uncreated natures.[294]

Second, all Christ's parts will finally assume his own personal perichoretic mode of actual existence even while remaining distinct in their
own *logoi*. Here Maximus sounds most Stoic. In *Ambiguum* 17, for instance, he marvels at length at how the *logoi* can even "constitute a single
world" at all. This consideration moves him forthwith to wonder at our
own bodies, at "this complexion of opposites blended together in a synthesis,"[295] which "brings things separated by nature into an amicable community, subduing, by virtue of the mean, the severities of the extremes, leading each to inhere within the other without the loss of integrity [καὶ χωρεῖν
δι' ἀλλήλων ἀλυμάντως], but rather preserving the elements of the synthesis, which is the *perichoresis* of one extreme in the other by virtue of the
blending [τὴν τῶν ἄκρων κατὰ τὴν κρᾶσιν εἰς ἄλληλα περιχώρησιν]."[296]
Stoics evidently thought that a certain process of "mixture" (κρᾶσις) could
allow two or more bodies to occupy the same physical space without
obliterating any parts' "own essence" or "proper hypostasis" or "qualities."[297] Maximus too, it seems, but only because something else—namely
a hypostasis—relieves nature from having to achieve the kind of "whole"
that would permit such *perichoresis* among the parts. And in Christ's
Body, which is one with itself and with all other entities exactly because
his hypostasis is the identity of his parts, those parts preserve their whole
integrity *and* interpenetrate one another. Indeed, as they become both
more themselves and more he who sustains them by subsisting as them,
they *must* so pervade each other as they are "gathered together with their
Head" and "become one flesh" (Col. 1:18; Eph. 5:30–31).[298]

•   •   •

These two traits of Christ's Body explain how "analogy" in the deified
state retains its distinctly Pauline sense. In conformity with that state's

Christo-logic, which is also the body-logic of Christ, analogy does not preclude hypostatic identity. Rather, the former presumes the latter. True, Maximus very often qualifies the process of deification by saying it occurs "analogously" or "in proportion" to the person deified. Many have read this to imply something like what "by grace" allegedly implied—that our deification makes us still a bit *less* God than Christ is in his own humanity.[299]

Philip Gabriel Renczes and Ayroulet, for instance, propose two ways that the deified person's union with God is analogous to Christ's union with humanity.[300] There is "the essential divergence" between Christ and ourselves and then "the differences among human beings with respect to their personal mode of collaborating in the realization of their deification."[301] I return to the second shortly, which seems right to me. But the first falters. It falters in that it deduces from an absolute *ontological* difference between created and uncreated essences the impossibility of their concrete and *real* identity.[302] In this way it rehearses the error of Christological asymmetry familiar from chapter 1, but from the opposite vantage. If before Christ was conceived as somehow more divine than human, now we are conceived as more human than divine.

This would of course make nonsense of Maximus's claim that the identity achieved in the deified state is the very same achieved in the historical Incarnation—a conviction crystallized and intensified in the *tantum-quantum* principle (sec. 3.1). It elides too the distinction between process and product or state, so that the necessity of our *becoming* God is misread as our perpetual failure to *be* him (sec. 3.2). And, last, this version of "analogical difference" also assumes that modal perichoresis amounts to the kind of reciprocity that might obtain, say, between two magnetic poles, one smaller (humans) and one much bigger (God). Yet as I have stressed time and again, modal perichoresis finds its ground solely in hypostatic identity and thus culminates in complete, actual symmetry (sec. 3.3).[303] Christo-logic belies any asymmetrical relation between created and uncreated natures for the simple reason that they share no natural (abstract) relation at all. And yet, by and as God's grace, the Word becomes the hypostatic identity and essential symmetry in a single concrete reality—his Body.

We fare better with the second sense of "analogous" deification. Each person, each created hypostasis, does in fact differ from Christ and from each other person in principle—not essentially (as regards Christ's humanity) but according to each's individual *logos* of hypostasis. Significantly, nearly every time Maximus speaks of "analogy" or "proportion" in deification it is "in proportion" to *each individual* deified.[304] And yet an individual *logos*, we know, is the Logos as well. Each person is a member of the Word's Body. Analogy, the "logic of proportion," therefore emerges as a body-logic.[305] That was just how Paul used it,[306] and others too.[307]

Hence predicating "analogy" in deification, as in any body, actually demands both hypostatic identity (for no body subsists as a real whole except as a hypostasis) and a perichoretic symmetry among any and all its parts. That includes its "extremes," created and uncreated natures. And so I recognize two senses of eschatological analogy in Maximus.

First, it means that I am and manifest the Word of God in my own personal way. This holds generally for every creature, actually.[308] "Each person," writes Maximus, "according to his own power, and according to the grace of the Spirit that is granted to him with respect of his worthiness—has Christ in him, and in proportion to him, leading him through increasing mortifications to ever more sublime ascents."[309] Just "as the soul reveals itself as active in the parts of the body according to the capacity underlying each part," so too do I manifest the Word's divine activity and person in me in a manner "in proportion" to my power, my desire, my love, my passion.[310]

That last text points up a second sense of analogy. Again, I can manifest the Word who has become all that I am in principle (all my *logoi*) only because he has made every creature himself, his Body. Analogy in this context becomes a two-way channel, a true symmetry. In fact, the Word *becomes analogous to me*.[311] Since he can become in person what he is infinitely not by (divine) nature, the Word makes himself the hypostatic, concrete identity of every creature precisely *as* that creature (its natural and hypostatic modes—its entire finitude). So it is with a human hypostasis and its body: I am as much my finger as I am my hair, as I am my heart, as I am my eyes.[312] My toe only *is* to the degree it *is me*. If then we are members of Christ's Body, it follows that he is *us* in just that way—hypostatically.

Only thus, I submit, do Maximus's extreme articulations of the God-world *symmetry* make any sense. God and man "are paradigms of each other"—we read that before.[313] We also read in Maximus that the Incarnate Word, because he is truly and really man, taught us in deed and even in word that a human person can become God's own model: "And for God he makes himself an example of virtue, if one can say this, and invites the inimitable to come imitate him by saying [καὶ τῷ θεῷ καθίστησιν ἑαυτὸν ἀρετῆς ἐξεμπλάριον, εἰ τοῦτο θέμις εἰπεῖν, πρὸς μίμησιν ἑαυτοῦ τὸν ἀμίμητον ἐλθεῖν ἐγκελευόμενος, λέγων], 'Forgive us our trespasses as we forgive those who trespass against us.' He summons God to be to him as he is to his neighbors."[314] The Word identifies himself with us and thus generates us. But his primal self-identification with all creation and its every creature does not dissipate after a while. Rather, it extends into every mode and actuality—even, stunningly, into the very heart of finitude, *our suffering.*

> For the Word has shown that the one who is in need of having good done to him is God; for, he says to us, as long as you did it for one of these least ones, you did it for me—and God himself says this!— then, he will much more show that the one who can do good and who does it is truly God by grace and participation because he has taken on in happy imitation the energy and characteristic of his own doing good. *And if the poor man is God, it is because of God's condescension in becoming poor for us and in taking into himself the sufferings of each one sympathetically* and "until the end of time," *always suffering mystically through goodness in proportion to each one's suffering.* All the more reason, then, will that one be God who by loving human beings in imitation of God heals by himself in a God-fitting way the sufferings of those who suffer and who shows that he has in his disposition, in due proportion, the same power of sustaining Providence that God has.[315]

Analogy in Christ's Body means inconceivable symmetry. The Word becomes analogous to me—even *suffering* and *mortal* me! It was exactly his own brutal death on the cross that fully revealed God's ineffable modality as a trinity of hypostases in and as one divine essence (Christologic's two logics). We saw that in chapter 1.[316] Discerning and following through the distinction between those logics has at length led us to this mystery, which comes to the same: "In accordance, then, with one of the aforementioned contemplations, whereby we are 'crucified with Christ' [τῷ Χριστῷ συσταυρούμεθα], let us endeavor, for as long as we are in this world, to propitiate the Word who is crucified together with us [τὸν συσταυρούμενον ἡμῖν ἱλεώσασθαι Λόγον]."[317] A notion dear to Paul, of course (Gal. 2:20; Col. 1:24).

. . .

This chapter has gone to considerable lengths to show that and how Maximian deification demonstrates the Christo-logic of creation. The Word of God has made his own person the identity of God and the world. That names the primordial principle and goal of creation (sec. 3.1). That identity grounds and reduces to modal perichoresis between God and every creature, a total symmetry that makes what is proper to God "improperly proper" to creation and the reverse (sec. 3.3).[318] We thus become identical to God not just in principle but in our eschatological, existential, concrete state. And so while we *become* God by an utterly supranatural process—"by grace"—we along with the world prove no less God in eschatological fact (sec. 3.2). For we are his Body (sec. 3.4).

Just as the Lord's particular body welcomed the "whole Father" and "the whole Spirit" into itself, which the Son had "actualized in himself"[319] (κατ᾽ αὐτουργίαν)—so too will the whole world, his mystical Body, become and manifest the Trinity.

> One and the same *logos* will be seen in all things. . . . In this way, the grace that deifies all things will manifestly appear to have been realized—the grace of which God the Word, becoming man, says: "My father is still working, just as I am working" [John 5:17]. That is, the Father bestows His good pleasure on the work, the Son actualizes it in himself, and the Holy Spirit essentially completes in all things the good will of the former and the work of the latter, so that the one God in Trinity might be "through all things and in all things" [Eph. 4:6], being wholly contemplated in proportion to each of those made worthy by grace, and wholly complete through the whole of them, in the same way that, in each and every member of the body, the soul exists naturally and without diminution.[320]

There in the Son's one Body not only will the Trinity be present to all things, as Dionysius said. All things will be, by grace, the Trinity.

CHAPTER FOUR

The Whole

Creation as Christ

The logic of creation is the logic of Incarnation. The Logos, Jesus Christ, is the truth of both. As Eriugena perceived with great clarity, only this Maximian insight accounts for the riddle of the world's being. That riddle runs thus. If creation proceeds from God alone—lest the "nothing" whence creation comes prove a "something" alongside God—creation is simultaneously identical to and different from God. Here one tends to invoke "participation" to name and perhaps explain this paradox. But the problem is that the dynamics of participation simply assume the very positivity that creation from nothing means to valorize permanently—the positivity of the *participants*, of the created subject(s) as such. The mystery of creation *ex nihilo* is that a world proceeds from God as what differs infinitely from God, and yet what proceeds bears such absolute ontological stability that, even in its final return to God, this world will not cease to differ essentially and infinitely from the same God whither it has returned.

Hence Eriugena perceives that creation's mystery requires that the predicates proper to created nature—genus, species, spatiotemporal location, accidents, being caused at all—must themselves inhere in a subject just as absolute as God. Why? Because only a subject that is at once God and the world, uncreated and created, could render the world's subject permanent and yet dependent upon God *alone* as its beginning and end. If, I mean, the created world bore an underlying subject that was itself positively not God, then the world, precisely as essentially and positively different from God, would owe its positive distinction to some cause other than God. The mystery of creation is precisely the mystery of the *communicatio idiomatum*—the mystery of Christ.[1]

All this, though, remains admittedly abstract. So long as it lives in abstraction, the idea of creation as Incarnation faces two distinct but related problems. The first problem has to do with the primacy of Christ, or, more exactly, with the meaning of Christ as an event in history. Does my reading of Maximus thus far reduce Christ to a particular instance of some more universal logic of creation? The second problem is still more serious: If creation is Incarnation from its beginning, why the Fall? The first asks after Christ in history; the second after Adam, specifically Adam's (humanity's) historical failure from the very outset. I offer here a brief word on each issue and thereby introduce this chapter's critical themes.

First, one might justifiably think that the argument up to this point basically amounts to tracing Maximus's meticulous analysis and extraction of the historical Incarnation's logic and then expanding it into something like a new generic principle of all creation, an abstract logic of the God-world relation. This sort of abstraction would betray the very Christo-logic I have articulated. Recall that Christo-logic's fourth element, which is not a discrete element but instead a characteristic of the whole, was exactly that the event in and by which this logic emerges is peculiar and unique. This event is the enhypostatic *act* of the Word of God in history (sec. 1.5). Like any event, the historical Incarnation is also the disclosure of the person who acts and is acted upon. Every event contains and is contained by a person whose whole truth resists reduction to either an abstract genus or an abstract instance of some generic principle. The Christ-event is a happening every bit as resistant to abstraction as the logic it discloses is. Maximus denies, remember, that "Christ" names either an essence *or* an individual.[2] Christ is neither simply a general, metaphysical rule (essence/nature) nor a mere individual that appears only as an exception to that rule—an instance of something more common whose individuality emerges merely as what is particular or not-common. Christ's person, which alone constitutes the concrete identity of his two (abstract) natures, is no simple negation of a genus *qua* genus; his person reveals and is a nonformal positivity. In fact, the positivity he himself is establishes the very condition for the (existential) possibility of any further abstraction about him whatever.

Worrying at Christ's primacy or exceptionality, then, does not really raise a vital objection to creation's Christo-logic. It remains a worry about the relation between universal principle and particular instance, neither of which touches the principle of hypostasis, namely the very principle of Incarnation.[3] This worry is itself an abstract one; it presumes to know a priori the way Christ's primacy must behave. It presumes that primacy must oppose all else as an exception.[4] But that is merely the obverse of the abstract stipulation that what is primary must be universal. And yet as the principle, unity, and end of the universal-particular dialectic itself— which remains a dialectical movement *within* abstractions about nature (that is, "humanity in general" and "a particular human" alike treat human nature as the main content)—the person of Christ proves exceptional precisely because he is neither simply universal nor simply particular, nor even their inner dialectic. In Christ particulars and universals and their mutual dependency are *created*.[5]

Second, there is the related but more acute problem if we consider my thesis in view of the concrete world: If creation is Incarnation, why the Fall of creation? How could Adam descend so swiftly and entirely into "the misery of this present life"?[6] The chaos of this world cries out that whatever "the world" is, it is not obviously the Word's Incarnation "always and in all things" (*Amb.* 7.22). The absurdity intensifies when Maximus claims, as he does on three separate occasions, that creation fell "at the very instant it came into being."[7] Jesus Christ lived a sinless human life, from conception to ascension. Maximus famously deprives Christ of a gnomic will. And yet creation itself, which I have argued is integral to the whole mystery of Christ, failed instantaneously? Doesn't the particular, concrete, undeniable history of actual human beings refute this whole way of construing things?

This chapter assays an exegetical and constructive response to these two fundamental problems. We will discover once more that Maximus's thought never departs from the basic conviction that the truth of creation— its "extremes," its beginning and end—has been fully revealed in the person of Jesus Christ. A good deal of his retort to the two problems as presented will consist in questioning our most basic and cherished assumptions about creation itself—the very assumptions animating the objections.[8] What, after all, makes a "beginning"? What is the truth of "history"? Is a true "event" simply what appears to us, either firsthand or as a historical happening? Does God create all that appears? Is God's single act of creating the world really still an intelligible act so long as the world that appears is not yet the world God wills, the world as the fullness of Christ's Body?

I begin with Maximus's view of Adam and the Fall. I devote special attention to the way sin illicitly "creates" a "world" and a "history" that are not truly God's creation. This analysis uncovers that for Maximus Adam (or the concrete human being in history) has received two fundamentally opposed beginnings. We have the fantastical but self-actualized "human," on the one hand, and the true human being, Jesus Christ, on the other. So what we uncritically assume to be creation's concrete "history" turns out to be, from the vantage of Christ as creation's true origin and end, not yet truly creation or history at all (sec. 4.1).

Thence we circle back from Adam to the historical Incarnation. Maximus reconfigures the Origenists' most paradigmatic metaphysical pairing, providence and judgment, around the Christological themes of the Word's embodiment and Passion. Analyzing this unprecedented reconfiguration concretizes a suggestive theme we already encountered on the abstract level of Christo-logic: the fundamental God-world reciprocity or symmetry. Here that reciprocity emerges as the very dynamic of God's creative act (sec. 4.2).

These peculiar themes invite us to rethink what we naturally presume are obvious and absolute features of the God-world relation. That Christ is, in his very person, the identity that generates difference and symmetry reveals that the truth of creation unfurls existentially in a series of reciprocities or interpenetrations. Universal and particular, eternity and time, even theology and economy—these unfold according to the reciprocal logic of the God-world relation. This logic reveals that our true beginning and end need not and indeed should not appear in a manner subject to time. That the historical Incarnation eventuates in the middle of this world's seemingly senseless flux of phenomena should not therefore disqualify it from being identified as God's singular and true act of creation. Rather, we should come to expect precisely this sort of peculiarity (sec. 4.3).

4.1. ADAM'S TWO BEGINNINGS

Humanity as it has actually appeared in history derives from two beginnings. We can schematize them abstractly and even mythically, as Maximus seems ready to do.[9] Adam's true primordial origin is to be born "by
the Spirit." His false, self-deluded origin is to be born "from the flesh"—
from, that is, a comprehensively enthralling yet irrational motion toward
bare phenomena, an acquisitive act of desire occasioned by his own ignorance of God, creation, and his own self. The Fall signifies the ubiquitous
and false deification of the phenomenal world, a disposition and act that
fabricate the world itself as something other than God's true world.

If we survey the contours of concrete history, we behold a world
dominated by diastemic disjunction, fragmentation, illusion, and ironclad
conformity to the abrupt limits of sheer finitude. Our world's serial beginning, at least the little we can make out, appears to Maximus as if the Fall
was simply coextensive with the very moment of creation. We do not even
really perceive in this fallen world our historical or metaphysical origin.[10]
This portrait of things, as many have noticed, is an extremely dismal one.
"For Maximus," writes Balthasar, "the bronze doors of the divine home
are slammed remorselessly shut at the very start of our existence."[11]

My first task, then, is to trace how Maximus's thought stoops to such
a nadir. Doing so demonstrates that the failure of the postlapsarian world
to be, as yet, the Word's Incarnation always and in all things—to become
the whole Body of Christ—does not disprove the thesis that creation is
Incarnation. Quite the contrary: that we can "create" a counterfeit world
by incarnating, in ourselves, our own impassioned delusions proves possible only because creation's very logic is already that of the Word's *actual* Incarnation in and as all things. A small seed of truth lies buried in
even our idolatrous worship and illicit creation of the phenomenal world,
whose tyrant is, of course, the devil himself (John 14:30).

This section commences with the two-origin schema (birth by Spirit
vs. birth by body). I then concentrate more fully on the creation-Fall simultaneity, followed by an analysis of the pseudo-incarnational structure of sin
and the false world that sin hypostasizes. At length I terminate with a development on true and false history. My hope is that this confessedly idiosyncratic presentation of Maximus's startling insights into the fallen world
might unsettle our assumption that whatever appears to us personally or

historically is necessarily God's creation. If creation does not seem to us the sublime Incarnation of the Word "always and in all things," perhaps that means not that creation is something other than Incarnation but rather that "creation" as it appears is not yet truly creation, not yet God's finished work, not yet the world.

4.1.1. Birth by Spirit

On several occasions Maximus voices the peculiar claim, reprised from Gregory of Nyssa,[12] that human beings were originally meant to propagate not by the familiar mode of sexual copulation but instead "according to Christ in the Spirit" (τῶν κατὰ Χριστὸν ἐν πνεύματι γεννωμένων).[13] I do not here launch an exhaustive disquisition on all the pertinent and often-vexed issues related to this idea.[14] Instead I treat four features more pertinent to our purposes. These features intimate the degree to which Maximus's reconceiving of "creation" as occurring through the historical Incarnation challenges our own assumptions about what exactly the act of creation is.

So the four salient features of birth by Spirit: it designates (1) a necessary condition of the deification process, (2) which is itself the process of creation, (3) which double process requires complete freedom at every stage, even the "first" one, (4) all of which depends entirely on the conviction that the historical Incarnation is Adam's true creation, his true origin and end.

Consider a passage near the end of *Ambiguum* 42, a text I treat at some length in the next section (4.2). Here Maximus countenances the first three features.

> Those who interpret the divine sayings mystically . . . say that man in the beginning was created *according to the image of God* [Gen. 1:27], surely so that he might be born of the Spirit in the exercise of his own free choice, and to acquire in addition the *likeness* by the keeping of the divine commandment, so that the same man, being by nature a creation of God, might also be Son of God and God through the Spirit according to grace [ἵνα ᾖ ὁ αὐτὸς ἄνθρωπος πλάσμα μὲν τοῦ Θεοῦ κατὰ φύσιν, Υἱὸς δὲ Θεοῦ καὶ Θεὸς διὰ Πνεύματος κατὰ χάριν]. For there was no other way for man, being created, to become Son of God

and God by the grace of deification, without first being born of the Spirit, in the exercise of his own free choice, owing to the indomitable power of self-determination which naturally dwells within him.[15]

First note that "being born of the Spirit" is the sine qua non of deification. One must "first" be born of the Spirit to commence the deification process. Birth by Spirit grants one the power to become God, a power that, as I discussed in some detail (sec. 3.2), lies utterly beyond (and yet universally present within) humanity's natural capacities. And it is evident, second, that the process from spiritual birth to achieving the full stature of divine filiation is itself the process of creation. Maximus's proximate concern here is, after all, to explicate what it means that humanity was "created according to the image of God" (Gen. 1:27). In other words, he contemplates the proper conditions for the realization of that primordial vocation which constitutes Adam "in his beginnings" (κατ' ἀρχὰς). Finally and most prominently, the entire process unfolds only by the free consent (κατὰ προαίρεσιν) of the one thus created and deified—by, I mean, the determinative volitional actualization of one's "indomitable power of self-motion" (διὰ τὴν . . . αὐτοκίνητον καὶ ἀδέσποτον δύναμιν). One must assent to being sired by Spirit.

These three features recur with some regularity across Maximus's writings and are worth tarrying over for a moment (we return to the fourth feature later). That third feature, birth in and by freedom, proves especially critical. One might take Gregory's and Maximus's aversion to propagation by bodies as a regrettable sign that they suffered the undue influence of this or that Platonism, or of their general monkish prudishness.[16] And I do not dispute the suspicion entirely. But I also suspect a more subtle Christological intuition at work.

Maximus everywhere insists upon the voluntary and rational character of birth by Spirit. This is evident both positively in what Maximus says of spiritual generation and negatively in the way he contrasts this mode with our current servile, irrational, and necessity-driven mode of generation. Consider the positive first. As I mentioned briefly last chapter, Maximus divides the "grace of adoption" into two aspects or modes or stages. They relate as potency to act. The initial stage, itself composed of faith and baptism, renders spiritual birth "entirely present in potential" (δυνάμει). And the second, freely elected obedience embodied through ascetic practice and concrete acts of love, renders generative grace "entirely present in actuality" (κατ' ἐνέργειαν).[17]

It is not difficult to see that and how the movement from the first to the second stage requires free will. Virtue and knowledge are rational activities. In cooperation with them grace transforms "voluntarily the entire free choice of the one being born so that it conforms to the God who gives birth."[18] This prepares the way for Maximus's response to Thalassius's question of why we can still sin after baptism even though John says that someone born of God through baptism and Spirit no longer sins, for "God's seed is in him" (1 John 3:9; John 3:5–6). The potency or seed sown in one's being through water and Spirit must be actualized by one's own consent, one's own spirit. "For the Spirit," writes Maximus, "does not give birth to a disposition of the will without the consent of that will, but to the extent that the will is willing, He transforms and deifies it."[19] Hence postbaptism vice occurs because we still lack "the unequivocal desire to surrender our whole selves, in the disposition of our will, to the Spirit."[20] Maximus elsewhere declares that "free will" (προαίρεσις) "along with God" is the "guardian and preserver" of our divine birth.[21]

Negatively, the voluntary character of birth by Spirit contrasts sharply with the mindless multiplication of bodily generation. Adam rejected "this deifying and divine and nonmaterial birth" and preferred the immediate pleasure of sensible things to spiritual delights "that were not yet fully evident to him." He was thus "condemned to a material, mortal, and corporeal birth, outside the power of his free choice [ἀπροαίρετον]." The Fall happened when he willingly exchanged "his free, impassible, voluntary [αὐθαιρέτου] and chaste birth for an impassioned, servile, coercive birth *after the likeness* of the irrational and *mindless beasts* of the earth [cf. Ps. 48 (49):13]."[22]

Two paradoxical but significant implications emerge here. First, Maximus conceives these two births as absolute antitheses in that they vie against one another as humankind's primordial beginning. He follows the passages just cited, for instance, with the Christological point that in the historical Incarnation—particularly in view of his conception, bodily birth, baptism, fulfilment of the commandments, death—the Son "voluntarily subjected himself to the spiritual birth of adoption, *so that bodily birth might be abolished*."[23] He then claims that this is also why Gregory of Nazianzus linked Incarnation with Christ's baptism:

[The Word] accepted the birth of baptism unto spiritual adoption . . .
so that baptism might be considered as the abolition and release from
bodily birth. For the very thing which Adam freely rejected (I mean
the birth by the Spirit leading to deification), and for which he was
condemned to bodily birth amid corruption, is exactly what the Word
assumed willingly, out of his goodness and love for humanity, and,
by becoming man in accordance with our fallen state, willingly subjected himself to our condemnation (though he alone is free and sinless), and consenting to a bodily birth, in which lay the power of our
condemnation, he mystically restored birth in the Spirit.[24]

The Word freely consented to be born of the Spirit. This free act established, in the very flesh born of the body, the inherent power of all Adam's
progeny likewise to be born in the Spirit.[25] "Because of Christ," Maximus
elsewhere remarks, "those who in the Spirit are willingly reborn of Christ
'with the bath of regeneration' [Tim. 3:5] are able by grace to put off their
former becoming from Adam based on pleasure."[26] The abolition is absolute. There can be only one *primordial* beginning for Adam: the deifying
grace that the historical Incarnation sows into all humanity, a grace "rendered effective by the voluntary keeping of the commandments," makes
these persons "possess their becoming solely in the Spirit" (μόνην τὴν ἐν
πνεύματι γένεσιν ἔχοντες).[27]

So one paradox of birth by Spirit is that, even though it seems to
occur at a temporal moment quite distinct from one's phenomenological
beginning in time (i.e., bodily birth),[28] it is for Maximus our primordial,
true, and absolute becoming—the way God *actually* creates us. That my
temporal start appears as a wholly discrete phenomenon from my spiritual generation is in some sense a *result* of my own sin, of my own deluded attempts to make myself into what I irrationally imagine "me" to
be. And so when I freely desire and love Christ in the act of receiving
adoption in the Spirit (at baptism) I undergo not simply restoration but, "to
put it more precisely, my re-creation [ἀναπλάσεως]." "In this way God
joined together in me the principle of my being and the principle of my
well-being, and he closed the division and distance between them *that I
had opened up*, and through them he wisely drew me to the principle of
eternal well-being, according to which human beings are no longer subject
to carrying or being carried along, since the sequence of visible realities in

motion will reach its end in the great and general resurrection, through which human beings *will be born into immortality* in an existence not subject to alteration."[29] Below we will consider how sin severs one's phenomenological beginning from one's true beginning in Christ, who unites all beginnings in himself (even our own fantastical one). For now the essential point is that Maximus regards birth by Spirit as our true creation, our actual beginning. This the Word wrought in his historical Incarnation. Becoming human, he thus "created for our nature another beginning of becoming through the Holy Spirit."[30]

Another paradox of birth by Spirit is that it would appear to demand a logical impossibility: that in order truly to *be*—to be created in Christ by the Spirit—I must first freely desire this creation, this "to be." But how could I desire anything if I am not yet truly created? Still more vexing (and with strange Kantian resonance), how could I, by failing to desire my true creation in the Spirit, thereby *cause* the stunted condition by which I appeared at all, namely my birth from another body?[31] We should not rush too quickly to resolve the apparent contradiction here. In fact it is worth wondering why Maximus invites the contradiction at all.

We have seen repeatedly that for Maximus the distinctive characteristic of spiritual birth is freedom, principally "free choice" (προαίρεσις).[32] Analyzing this mode of rational freedom reveals that there is more to Maximus's preference of spiritual over bodily birth than visceral and puritanical disdain for sexual procreation. In a later *Opusculum* Maximus had occasion to clarify various aspects or modalities of rational freedom. There he identifies the "natural appetitive faculty" (θέλησις), the "imaginative intention" toward some general end (βούλησις), the act of deliberative judgment or "counsel" with respect to a general end (βούλευσις/ βουλή), the particular "free choice" that determines the course of action with respect to the desired end, the consequent disposition or inclination toward the desired end (γνώμη), and so forth.[33]

Crucial for our purposes is that free choice comprises a "mixture of several ingredients," specifically a combination of "desire and counsel and judgment."[34] Free choice is, Blowers glosses, "the ultimate intersection of reason with underlying desire, committing the soul to a course of action."[35] Maximus portrays the volitional process passing through increasingly determinate stages, a movement from general (or "simple") desire to a particular end achieved by concrete means. The ends and means are freely chosen through rational deliberation. But the stages do not merely succeed one another; at each point a new modality comes to characterize what preceded it. Free choice is neither abstract desire nor counsel nor judgment but rather their decisive configuration by a person's interior (i.e., self-determined) act of intending a determinate end along with the best way to gain it. Choice names the very "combination" of indeterminate and essential powers into a concrete intending, rather like the way "the 'human' is a synthesis of soul and body" in a concrete human being.[36] That is, the very act of intentionally directing the more general modalities in a determinate fashion becomes its own product: the transitive "choosing" becomes—indeed *is*—the objective "choice."[37]

Thus free choice presupposes and produces determinate objects of rational desire, objects that grow ever more determinate in the very act of freely intending. This emerges clearly in perhaps Maximus's subtlest portrayal of the process surrounding free choice:

> For they say that general intention [βούλησιν] is not simply a nature-level [activity][38] but is always of determinate quality; that is, it is a natural appetite [θέλησιν] for a certain object. If one intends, one seeks; and if one seeks, one investigates; and if one investigates, one deliberates [βουλεύεται]; and if one deliberates, one judges [κρίνει]; and if one judges, one freely chooses [προαιρεῖται]; and if one freely chooses, one moves to act [ὁρμᾷ]; and if one moves to act, one enacts one's desire [κέχρηται]; and if one enacts one's desire, one brings the desiring motion to rest. For no one enacts desire without first moving to act; and no one moves to act without first freely choosing; and no one freely chooses without first judging; and no one judges without first deliberating; and no one deliberates without first investigating; and no one investigates without first seeking; and no one seeks without first intending; and no one intends without first reasoning; and no one reasons without first desiring [ὀρεγόμενος]; and no one desires rationally without first being rational by nature. Therefore the human being, by nature a rational animal, is a being who desires and reasons and intends and seeks and investigates and chooses and takes action and enacts a desire.[39]

Free choice is the interior termination of a person's rational act of intending. It is, in other words, the perfection of an entire series of moments, the intentional closure of an appetitive motion solicited by a definite object of rational desire (i.e., an object that is perceptible and attractive to a person precisely through his or her own natural appetite as that appetite is directed and stirred by reason itself). Free choice functions like the immediate mediator of an exterior act that, successfully executed, finally sates the rational desire that prompted the whole process to begin with.[40] Actualizing freedom is always a motion from the depths of one's own being to a determinate end known and loved as one's own fulfillment. So absolutely is this the case when that end is God himself, the ultimate object of rational desire, that our free choice for God realizes our very creation—to be born by the Spirit in the Son.[41]

And so I propose that for Maximus the deepest regret about our postlapsarian mode of birth is not simply that it renders us more beastly. The problem is that this bestial condition subjects us to irrational and unintentional and thus unfree movements, and is for that reason a departure from our true creation as concrete spirits in Christ. In this world, which appears a seemingly ceaseless and chaotic parataxis of the generation and destruction of discrete phenomena, my own creation also *appears* to be mindless and unintended, a tiny and ephemeral eddy in the immense flow of finitude.[42] The embarrassment of bodily propagation lies not in bodies themselves; Christ was born of the Virgin's body, after all.[43] Nor is there inherent shame in pleasure as such, as if the sexual act is sinful because it is delightful.[44] Nor does it fall afoul of God's intention for creation that persons come from other persons (again the paradigm is Christ's birth from Mary and perhaps, I would add, the Son and Spirit's derivation from the Father).[45]

Rather, the truly lamentable character of sexual generation—what distinguishes it from spiritual birth—is that it neither expresses nor perfects the human spirit at all. It is not free; there is no reasoning or intending or deliberating or judging or free choice about it. Contemplated as yet another phenomenon in the interminable chain of phenomena, I do not appear to will my own creation, nor do my progenitors will *me* (even if they will a child generally), nor do I choose to possess God as my own ultimate end and thus receive him as such.[46] The paradox of birth by Spirit, then, turns out to be the very paradox of created freedom: my inability freely to become that and who I am is somehow already a consequence of my ignorant misuse of freedom. If God intends to create not just an abstract order of things that unfolds by impersonal necessity,[47] but *spirit*—not, say, just "humanity" but concrete human persons—then creation should occur as a free act of both God and Adam. Hence Adam wields, even if with near-inevitable folly, an almost primordial creative power. This is why Adam's primordial transgression does not merely disorder creation. Rather, it "introduced another beginning of becoming [ἄλλην ἀρχὴν γενέσεως]."[48] Adam's sin corrupts God's creation by illicitly "creating" or sourcing a false world radically hostile to God, a world into which we are born and because of which our very mode of becoming becomes damaged.[49]

Birth by Spirit, paradoxical as it seems, is for Maximus the necessary issue of that fourth feature listed above, namely that the historical Incarnation reveals and is Adam's true, primordial creation. "When the Thearchic Word clothed Himself in human nature without undergoing any change," writes Maximus, "and became perfect man like us in every way but without sin, He possessed the first Adam, manifesting him in both the mode of His becoming and the mode of His birth."[50] Christ "manifests" (φαινόμενον) Adam; he makes Adam into a real historical *phenomenon* at long last. This ought not to surprise. After all, we heard Maximus declare that "all the ages and the beings existing within those ages received their beginning and end in Christ."[51]

It is precisely due to his unwavering conviction that the Christ-event is Adam's true creation that Maximus identifies spiritual birth with Adam's true creation. The pattern is clear: whatever characterized the Word's becoming in history is what characterizes our primordial becoming, since the Word's becoming *is* ours. Not that this characterizes our appearance in this phenomenal world. The two beginnings remain absolute antitheses. No possible compromise can be brokered between them, since they oppose one another as what God does and does not create—surely an absolute distinction. Christ entered existence by a seedless conception and was born of Mary in such a way that she suffered no bodily toil. In fact, "and this is really a wondrous event and report," Christ came forth from Mary "without the seals of His mother's body being opened," and his birth even "bound the bonds of His mother's virginity more tightly."[52]

Here, then, we encounter the creation of a human being that is at once the result of that person's own free choice (since the Word *willingly* condescends to becoming human);[53] is the result of his mother's deliberate choice (since she heard and accepted whom she was to conceive);[54] is therefore the cooperative work of two spirits in the creation of concrete spirit (hence the whole process is realized by the Holy Spirit);[55] and yet does not efface but transfigures the body's proper role in human propagation. Only here did the human body, Mary's virginal body, "give flesh without seed." And that presents us a modal miracle every bit as constitutive of the mystery of Incarnation as the Word's self-identification with created nature.[56] In his historical Incarnation "Divine Reason" thus "abolishes" these "laws of nature," these "laws of irrationality" that were "added externally" to our nature because of sin—for instance, bodily birth, sexual propagation, corruption, and really any impersonal or necessary law by which creation appears to proceed without intent[57]—and he also "renews" the "laws of the first and truly divine creation."[58]

Birth by Spirit is nothing other than birth "according to Christ in the Spirit,"[59] or—which comes to the same (sec. 3.3)—living in a way that allows Christ's own births (both of which find their term in his hypostasis) to take place in you. Christ now appears as the ground of the second paradox, which was that I must choose to become truly created and yet somehow already be in order to so choose. Christ, who has and *is* both created and uncreated natures, is in himself the generation or becoming of opposites, the very possibility that I can be and yet need to become. There is no reason that Christ, who is the new and true Adam "bearing within Himself the first Adam,"[60] could not also bear and perfect me in eternity even as I must freely cooperate to become through time the "me" that Christ, with my cooperation, always already is.

So too is Christ the ground of the first paradox—that human beings as they currently exist possess two "beginnings," each vying for primordial priority. That seems especially odd. Maximus entertains the oddity exactly because he never relinquishes the conviction that the true world, divine creation, is accomplished only through and as Jesus Christ, the Incarnate Word.

God, then, truly became man and gave our nature another beginning of a second becoming [δέδωκεν ἄλλην ἀρχὴν τῇ φύσει δευτέρας γενέσεως], which through pain ends in the pleasure of the life to come. For our forefather Adam, having transgressed the divine commandment, introduced into our nature another beginning of

becoming—in opposition to the first [beginning/becoming]—
constituted by pleasure, yielding to pain, and ending in death [Ὡς
γὰρ Ἀδὰμ ὁ προπάτωρ, τὴν θείαν ἐντολὴν παραβάς, ἄλλην ἀρχὴν
γενέσεως, ἐξ ἡδονῆς μὲν συνισταμένην, εἰς δὲ τὸν διὰ πόνου
θάνατον τελευτῶσαν, τῇ φύσει παρὰ τὴν πρώτην παρεισήγαγε].[61]

Note that the beginning that Adam's sin introduces stands "in opposition to the first" beginning given only in the historical Incarnation. In the
latter event, putatively a phenomenon posterior to Adam, the Word "creates within our nature a beginning of becoming and a different mode of
birth"—that of the Spirit.[62]

Thus both paradoxes of spiritual birth are somehow grounded in the
historical Incarnation. This insight throws a little light on the emerging
gestalt we have seen throughout this study: the beginning (Adam) and the
end (birth by Spirit/deification) are but moments of the singular act even-
tuated in the middle (Christ). Christ is the whole. Before limning the
shades of those relations a bit more, though, I spend the remainder of this
subsection contemplating just how radically Maximus conceives Adam's
Fall, that fantastical and fatal "beginning."

4.1.2. The Fall at the Moment of Becoming

On three separate occasions Maximus asserts that Adam, despite his
natural desire for God, fell "at the very moment of his coming into being"
(ἅμα τῷ εἶναι), so that his true beginning became utterly dark to his own
gaze.[63] Those passages, along with Maximus's almost stratospheric manner of interpreting Genesis's opening chapters, led Balthasar to conclude
that the paradisiacal state was for Maximus "pure imagery," a "myth" in
the sense of "a prehistorical or metahistorical reality."[64] Most scholars
have since demurred.[65] Larchet, to take the most ardent dissenter, even
insists "that we must understand ἅμα not as simultaneity but as a brief
lapse of time,"[66] and this despite the fact that ἅμα never means this generally, certainly not in Maximus.[67] Larchet wants to resist the idea that Maximus, "in the manner of the Origenists or of certain Gnostics," treats bodily
becoming or perhaps becoming itself as a lapse—the idea that evil, in
other words, might be native to creation itself. That would implicate
God's goodness, of course. It would also diminish the personal character

of Adam's transgression by reducing it to "an ontological 'fault.'"[68] Indeed, our earlier discussion of προαίρεσις shows sufficiently that this cannot be the way Maximus conceives the Fall.

Yet I think Balthasar was nearer the mark, for three reasons (beyond the meaning of ἅμα). The first is a negative point addressed to Larchet's chief worry. It seems odd to deny the Fall's simultaneity with the generation of this phenomenal world[69] on the grounds that this would vitiate Adam's personal choice in the matter, only then to affirm that the "ancestral sin" consequent upon Adam's transgression creates conditions that virtually necessitate the sin of all Adam's progeny. For Maximus the primordial disobedience meant that "henceforth sin originates in the passible part of our nature, associated with birth, as if by a kind of law, under which no one is sinless [καθ' ὃν οὐδείς ἐστιν ἀναμάρτητος], for all are subject by nature to the law of birth," itself a "consequence of sin."[70] Not that Maximus imagines Adam's *guilt* extends to his descendants; they too choose vice.[71] But their desperate circumstance is hardly Adam's own. He had it "in his power of self-determination" to become one with God "without obstacle";[72] yet for his offspring "there was no hope of freedom, since human nature was bound in the disposition of its will by an indissoluble bond of evil."[73] Larchet's momentarily actualized, pristine, individual Adam whose personal fault alone summons evil and its subsequent tyrannical march merely pushes the problem one step back, at least from the vantage of personal sin. Every person posterior to Adam's disobedience finds her own choice all but determined by the concrete conditions within which alone she chooses anything. Doesn't this approximate Larchet's "ontological fault," if not for Adam the individual then for essentially everyone else?

A second and more constructive reason: it does seem that Maximus instinctively handles the paradisiacal narrative as "myth" in Balthasar's sense. The prelapsarian story is a useful device for contemplating not humanity's historical beginning but its true end, which is its true beginning.[74] Hence it is not necessarily a point in favor of a historical, individual Adam to note that evil makes its appearance only through Adam's personal freedom. After all, "Adam" might just as well symbolize that evil enters the world through everyone's personal freedom. In one of his most extensive meditations on the Fall—an interpretation of Jonah's tale—Maximus glosses that "Jonah, then, signifies Adam, that is, the common nature of human beings [Σημαίνει γοῦν τὸν Ἀδὰμ ὁ προφήτης, ἤγουν τὴν κοινὴν φύσιν τῶν ἀνθρώπων], and in himself he mystically figures our nature, which slipped away from the good things of God."[75] If Adam is human nature, then Adam, as demanded by Maximus's Christological metaphysics of any nature or essence or universal, subsists only in the entire set of all human hypostases.[76] So construed, the Fall names not principally an ancient event, nor simply an event simultaneous with becoming as such, but an event that occurs at all moments of becoming in this world—in the generation, conduct, corruption, and death of every person. Thus "The nature of human beings perpetually flees Joppa, like Adam from paradise."[77] Far from diminishing the personal character of sin, Maximus now imbues it with primordial significance. "I was subject to two curses," he writes, "one was the fruit of my own free will, that is, sin. . . . The other was death, to which nature was justly condemned on account of my free will, pushing nature by necessity, and apart from its own wishes, to that place where the movement of my own free choice had sown it by the inclination of my free will."[78] Again, somehow my freedom (here its misuse) both causes and is caused by the Fall: *I* pushed "nature by necessity" into its sullen servitude to death and corruption.[79]

The third reason proves at once less conspicuous and more decisive. Had Maximus taken the prelapsarian narrative to prescribe a literal sense for at least the historical or phenomenal order of things, it seems fair to assume he would have understood Adam's "becoming" (γένεσις) to precede his "birth" (γέννησις) in actual fact.[80] The "vital inbreathing" that constitutes Adam (Gen. 2:7) obviously precedes Adam's Fall and consequent adornment with the "garments of dead skin" (Gen. 3:21). After all, Maximus understands the latter event to signify God's act of "mixing" the soul with the body after such a fashion that both consequently display the "capacity to suffer" and "undergo corruption" and the like.[81] In that case Adam *qua* historical individual would have come into concrete being apart from bodily birth and a male's seed, just as Christ did.[82] But no: elsewhere Maximus openly declares that "Christ *alone* has been made by God without seed according to the flesh" (Οὗτος γάρ ἐστιν ὁ πεποιημένος ἄνευ σπορᾶς ὑπὸ θεοῦ μόνος τὸ κατὰ σάρκα).[83] This is no small point. It is, we saw, the very condition of Christ's becoming our true beginning and end, our true creation, our birth in the absolute freedom of the Spirit.

Actually there remains another reason to doubt that "Adam" designates a literal, historical progenitor who enjoyed some fleeting but pristine state of union with God. And this reason uncovers a far more radical relation between the Fall and creation. Primordial sin is motion, a movement of human reason and volition away from the very end that would make humanity truly rational and free.[84] Sin's consequence, at the same time its cause, is a "motion that easily inclines to rush into every passion," man's insane pining after "the relative deformity of the material nature surrounding him." "It was thus that man plucked the fruit."[85] Hence one of Maximus's most concise formulas of "evil" or "vice" (τὸ κακὸν): "Evil is the irrational movement of natural powers toward something other than their proper goal, based on an erroneous judgment."[86]

I return below to the significance of error or ignorance. Here I wish to consider the implications of Maximus's broader understanding of creaturely motion for the Fall.[87] In the opening sections of the seventh *Ambiguum* Maximus crafts an entire polemic designed to refute the Origenist thesis of a primordial "henad of rational beings . . . connatural with God," which (inexplicably) fell into a "motion" away from God, away from unity, and into the diverse and variegated bodies God graciously generated as "this corporeal world."[88] Maximus marshals about four distinct arguments to prove that this "windily iterated 'unity' does not exist."[89] In other words, Maximus contends that there has never yet existed a complete rational being or unity of rational beings that, as actually perfected, enjoys perfect rest.

His first argument maintains that any being created *ex nihilo* (which he also depicts as *ex Deo*)[90] possesses its true beginning and end in God alone, who is for that reason the ultimate object of its rational desire. Therefore "Nothing that moves has yet come to rest, because its capacity for appetitive movement has not yet come to repose in what it ultimately desires," and, of course, "Nothing but the appearance of the ultimate object of desire can bring to rest that which is carried along by the power of its own nature."[91] Note two immediate implications here: every real creature must begin in motion (there is no *real* neutral state),[92] and if a creature—say, a human being—appears in motion, then it has never in fact known perfection (there has never *really* been a perfect state). And the perfect state wherein our rational activities—our desiring, our knowing, our loving—attain their limit in the limitless God,[93] once realized, is irrevocable. That segues to Maximus's second argument against an erstwhile state of perfection: if we spurned it once, we will "find no reason to cease from doing so for all eternity"—a truly damnable and hopeless prospect.[94]

In the third and fourth arguments Maximus shows that, besides inducing despair, the postulate that there once existed a perfect state demeans God himself. For starters, even the bare possibility that we might experience the perfection of our faculties in God and yet move away from him belies God's own beauty, indeed that God is beauty itself, since "whatever is not good and desirable in and of itself" and "does not attract all motion to itself, strictly speaking cannot be the Beautiful."[95] But suppose we could know God, reject him, and regain him after experiencing the sufferings and evils of life apart from him—what then? "Those who espouse such a theory would be indebted to evil"! That is Maximus's final blow. If rational beings ever existed in a concrete state of perfection, lapsed, and strive now to return with more resolve than before, then this would mean that "evil is of necessity the origin of the Beautiful." Evil, that is, would have served as the bitter but necessary contrast by which God's beauty became more beautiful to us than it ever was on its own. Thus evil would have given "birth to the most precious of all possessions, I mean love," which is the most effective power uniting and holding us to God.[96]

All this, I suggest, carries great significance for those rare passages where Maximus does portray prelapsarian Adam in what approximates a perfect state. This is especially so for *Ambiguum* 45, a classic text on paradisiacal Adam. There Maximus explicates Gregory of Nazianzus's description of Adam as "naked in his simplicity and in a life devoid of artifice, and without any kind of covering or barrier. For such was fitting for the primal man [τὸν ἀπ᾽ ἀρχῆς]."[97] Maximus confects several contemplations of this remark, each meant to describe Adam "before the transgression."[98] Adam's bodily constitution, for instance, did not suffer the "flux and reflux" autochthonous to matter as we know it, since "surely man was not without a share in immortality by grace."[99] He was utterly free of distraction by anything save God, so that, "for his perfection" (πρὸς τελείωσιν), he possessed "the unconditioned motion of the whole power of his love for what was above him."[100] And, "being impassible by grace" (Ἀπαθὴς γὰρ χάριτι ὢν), he "was not by pleasure moved to accept the deception of passions in his imagination." He was "free of the necessity, imposed by circumstances, to make use of arts and skills." And in his great wisdom "His knowledge placed him beyond the contemplation of nature." In general "The first man possessed no barrier between himself and God, which might have veiled his knowledge, or hindered his kinship with God, which was to have been realized as a freely chosen movement to Him in love."[101]

Here Maximus says things of Adam that (in *Amb.* 7) he denies ever to have occurred in fact. Take, for example, the claim that the "primal man" was "not without a share in immortality by grace." But that immortality—bodily immortality—cannot actually occur until human beings reach the state Maximus just argued could have never yet been. The grace of immortality comes only when God will "be present in the body (in a manner that He knows), so that the soul will receive immutability and the body immortality." "In this way," he continues, "man as a whole is deified, being actualized as God by the grace of the God who became man."[102] It's rather difficult to see how Adam could have partaken of the same immortality that cannot be actualized until the resurrection and deification of human nature—an immortality that, once realized, cannot be forfeited.

Or consider the claim that Adam was "impassible by grace." Again Maximus's anti-Origenist polemic terminates in the antithesis: "Nothing that has come into being is impassible, for this belongs only to what is unique, infinite, and uncircumscribed."[103] As creatures we do not naturally possess our own sufficiency, our own satisfaction, our state of infinite fulfillment. This is why actual deification alone makes us impassible. When the rational soul at length suffers ecstasy for God alone so that God alone slakes its every desire, it then lives "in no way subject to the movement of the passions, for there is nothing that it desires, neither can it be moved by desire toward something else." And "Therefore no created being which is in motion has yet come to rest."[104] That rest is "impassibility" and "immobility," and these are but "the fruit" of a motion that has actually terminated in God.[105]

And what to make of the claim that "the first man possessed no barrier between himself and God" so that nothing "veiled his knowledge"? We will very soon see that, to the contrary, ignorance and error constitute necessary conditions of primordial sin. But again and beyond that, Maximus's refutation of an Origenist paradise led inexorably to the conclusion that if there really is "no barrier" that prevents knowledge of

God—not even, as it seems here, a fallacious judgment—then Adam should have freely and necessarily attained perfection rather than fall the very instant he came into being. God is our beginning and end; the former because he is the source of the very faculties by which we move toward him, the latter because he is the infinite horizon of the particular ways we are moved and perfected. A rational being moves toward and is moved by God rationally, which is to say that knowing God unveiled means experiencing him as the infinite end of both desire and reason. Therefore if a rational being

> knows [God], it surely loves that which it knows; and if it loves, it certainly suffers an ecstasy toward it as an object of love. If it suffers this ecstasy, it obviously urges itself onward, and if it urges itself onward, it surely intensifies and greatly accelerates its motion. And if its motion is intensified in this way, it will not cease until it is wholly present in the whole beloved, and wholly encompassed by it, willingly receiving the whole saving circumscription by its own choice, so that it might be wholly qualified by the whole circumscriber, and, being wholly circumscribed, will no longer be able to wish to be known from its own qualities, but rather from those of the circumscriber.[106]

Nor will it suffice to observe that this entire process unfolds *freely*, as if everything said of Adam in *Ambiguum* 45 was available to him in potency and could have passed into actuality had he chosen it. We just saw that, on Maximus's terms, without a veil Adam would have necessarily chosen God, since God is the ultimate end of rational (and thus *free*) desire. More profoundly, we find ourselves before the same paradox we met in birth by Spirit. Suppose the grace of impassibility was available to individual, historical Adam only in potency. That is no different from saying that impassibility did not yet exist in actuality; and if not in actuality, how in history? History or time, to the degree it measures motion, must appear from the start with creatures in motion. There is no *actual* state of Adam's pure potency. No motion, no existence (and this in no small part because there is no realm of self-subsistent Forms or Ideas).[107] As it was with spiritual birth, so it is here: Adam must first be in order to move, and yet if he is not already moving he is not yet in being.

All these considerations demonstrate, I think, that Maximus reads the opening chapters of Genesis in the way Balthasar proposed (à la Alexandrian tradition). And so Maximus seems to have two principal motives in contemplating Adam and his Fall. On the one hand, the Adam story represents our true beginning and end—Gregory's "primal man" or, more literally, humanity "from its beginning" (ἀπ' ἀρχῆς).[108] Adam possesses only one primordial generation and true creation: to be born of the Spirit according to Christ the Image of God.[109] On the other hand, Maximus perceives in this same narrative our false beginning and end, our universal and personal Fall. Now the story reflects our collective Fall refracted in a darkened mirror and reveals it as the generation of a false world, a false incarnation always in all things—about which I say more below.

The paradoxes dwelling at the heart of the Adam story render it apt for contemplation of the paradox of this phenomenal world. This world's Fall, it bears repeating, appears to Maximus to have occurred "simultaneously" with its beginning. There lurks in this extreme notion an extraordinarily profound dilemma operative in Maximus's understanding of creation.

The dilemma runs thus. Maximus's opposition to any primordially realized state of perfection moves him very close to Irenaeus's view that original imperfection is an ontological (and logical) feature of creation as such. For Irenaeus too it follows "from the very fact that" creatures naturally *receive* their beginning and end outside themselves, namely in God, "that they are not uncreated."[110] And since Irenaeus likewise sees in Jesus Christ the "perfect human" who is also perfect God—so that humanity's end is to become uncreated[111]—he regards Adam's initial imperfection as a blameless and infantile state, yet imperfect nonetheless.[112] Being created necessarily means making one's start in a condition of relative ignorance, in need of becoming "accustomed" to one's own divine destiny "throughout a long course of ages."[113] Or to reprise Maximus: being created necessarily means being in motion toward (or against) the state of divine rest. This renders humanity from its natural and serial beginning vulnerable to error, misuse of desire, and the wiles of diabolical powers.[114] "The first man," writes Maximus, "being deficient in the actual movement of his natural powers toward their goal, fell sick with ignorance of his own Cause, and, following the counsel of the serpent, thought that God was the very thing of which the divine commandment had forbidden him to partake."[115] So, then, humanity naturally begins in actual but deficient motion and must therefore traverse the precarious course of becoming accustomed to God (its true beginning and end).

But the dilemma's other horn is that, in fact (not by essential necessity), infantile human beings appear incapable of rightly traversing that course until they are already accustomed to God, already deified. Here Maximus's diagnosis of the primordial transgression proves at once very subtle and profoundly somber. To grasp this I turn to what amounts to Maximus's minitreatise on evil and the Fall in the introduction to *Quaestiones ad Thalassium*.

There Maximus proffers two "definitions" of evil (τό κακόν). The first is a version of the classic privation theory. "Evil neither was," he begins, "nor is, nor ever will be an existing entity having its own proper nature, for the simple reason that it has absolutely no essence, nature, hypostasis, power, or activity of any kind whatsoever." Evil in no sense belongs to the fundamental whole of any being. Nor does it naturally inhere in any attendant properties, a point Maximus stresses by depriving evil of all Aristotelian categories (quality, quantity, relation, place, time, position, activity, passivity, state—he adds "motion"). In short, "Evil is nothing other than a deficiency of the activity of innate natural powers with respect to their proper goal."[116]

This first attempt at formulating evil does little to indicate how evil appears. It says what evil is not. So Maximus gives another definition, one we read above: "Evil is the irrational movement of natural powers toward something other than their proper goal, based on an erroneous judgment." Ignorance now emerges not just as a necessary concomitant of created nature but as the fundamental occasion for a primordial error of judgment. The error is about God, "the Cause of beings, which all things naturally desire." The devil, feigning kindness while burning with envy, devised "a ruse to persuade man to move his desire to something in creation instead of its Cause" and thereby "created ignorance of the Cause."[117]

We gain some ground. Evil in itself is nothing at all (first definition) yet appears and wreaks havoc through the deception and misjudgment of rational beings (second definition).[118] But note the nature of the error. Adam misjudges God, yes, but that mistake simultaneously constitutes a grave mistake about created nature as such. Exactly because "the first man" was "deficient in the actual movement of his natural powers toward their goal," he knew neither God *nor* God's creation in truth: he "thought that God was the very thing of which the divine commandment had forbidden him to partake," namely merely finite pleasure.[119] Adam mistakes sheer phenomena for his ultimate object of desire, a misapprehension at once dependent upon and generative of ignorance of his ultimate object of desire, God, the true beginning and end. "Becoming thus a transgressor and having not known God [τὸν θεὸν ἀγνοήσας], he completely mixed the whole of his intellective power with the whole of sensation, and drew into himself the composite, destructive, passion-forming knowledge of sensible things."[120]

From this primordial and devastatingly fatal double error springs an indomitable dialectic, a harrowingly endless cycle of ignorance and self-deception and desire and pleasure and pain. It pays to read Maximus's own description at some length:

> Thus the more man was preoccupied with knowledge of visible things solely according to the senses, the more he bound himself to the ignorance of God ['Όσον οὖν κατὰ μόνην τὴν αἴσθησιν τῆς τῶν ὁρωμένων ἐπεμελεῖτο γνώσεως ὁ ἄνθρωπος, τοσοῦτον ἐπέσφιγγεν ἑαυτῷ τοῦ θεοῦ τὴν ἄγνοιαν]; and the more he tightened the bond of this ignorance, the more he attached himself to the experience of the sensual enjoyment of material objects of knowledge in which he was indulging; and the more he took his fill of this enjoyment, the more he inflamed the passionate desire of self-love that comes from it [τοσοῦτον τῆς ἐκ ταύτης γεννωμένης φιλαυτίας ἐξῆπτε τὸν ἔρωτα]; and the more deliberately he pursued the passionate desire of self-love, the more he contrived multiple ways to sustain his pleasure, which is the offspring and goal of self-love. And because it is the nature of every evil to be destroyed together with the activities that brought it into being, he discovered by experience that every pleasure is inevitably succeeded by pain, and subsequently directed his whole effort toward pleasure, while doing all he could to avoid pain, fighting for the former with all his might and contending against the latter with all his zeal. He did this believing in something that was impossible, namely, that by such a strategy he could separate the one from the other, possessing self-love solely in conjunction with pleasure, without in any way experiencing pain.[121]

A series of dialectical manacles forms a great chain shackling this world to its present bondage. Ignorance of God links together with ignorance of visible creation ("*solely* according to the senses"), since attempting to know creation apart from its true beginning and end leads inevitably to knowing something other than creation. Ignorance of creation intensifies ignorance of God. Knowing neither God nor creation, Adam cannot know himself; he, in his deluded self-love, fancies himself fulfilled by bare sense pleasure.[122] Such pleasure always disappoints. Pain follows hard upon pleasure because no finite phenomenon can sate infinite desire. Thus the whole of this miserable existence, which vacillates pitilessly between pleasure and pain, relies first and last upon ignorance of God, creation, and the self. Yet Adam strives still more defiantly by "believing in something that was impossible," namely that he has the power to make creation satisfy him in a way only God can. His striving makes him prodigious in inventing all manner of vice.[123] Vice makes him increasingly ignorant of pretty much everything. And so ever on. Even the self that Adam loves is a mirage.[124]

"Evil," Maximus concludes, "is ignorance of the benevolent Cause of beings," an ignorance that "blinds the human intellect and opens wide the doors of sensation." Adam knew not God, so he knew not this phenomenal world. He knew not this world, including the truth of his own body, and so "became a lover of his own self, always eating from the Tree of Disobedience, which tree [made him] possess the knowledge of good and evil thoroughly mixed into one, in the act and experience of sensation."[125] And that, to Maximus, is what the Tree of the Knowledge of Good and Evil represents: it is either "the visible creation" (τὴν φαινομένην κτίσιν), which naturally yields pleasure and pain, or something subtler still, namely visible creation contemplated through its immanent "spiritual *logoi*" (the Good) in lieu of experiencing it in a purely "corporeal manner" (the Evil).[126]

Maximus makes the following remark about this Tree: "It was perhaps for this reason that God temporarily forbade man to partake of it, rightly delaying for a while his participation in it." That is, God knew that human beings could not safely experience visible creation in ignorance of God, since this would produce the very dialectic of delusion just traced. Rather, "Having already become God through deification, man might have been able without fear of harm to examine with God the creations of

God, and to acquire knowledge of them, not as man but as God, having by grace the very same wise and informed knowledge of beings that God has, on account of the deifying transformation of his intellect and sensation."[127] At length we perceive the whole intractable dilemma. On one side, being simultaneously created and destined to become uncreated necessitates an initial (and in itself blameless) state of imperfection, including actual ignorance of God (incomplete rational motion). On the other, considering the concrete judgments of created rational beings when they confront visible creation in ignorance of God, it appears virtually inevitable that these persons should lapse into the dialectical prison of misapprehending God, the world, and themselves. We must become accustomed to God, but we must also become accustomed to creation and to ourselves, and we cannot really do one without having done the other. Is it any wonder that Adam fell at the moment he first appeared?

Are we to conclude that Maximus thinks evil necessary to creation? Clearly not, as his stringent opposition to a perfect primordial henad of rational beings demonstrated. There is nothing about nature as such, whether created or uncreated or the infinite difference between them, that forces creation to assume the form of the Fall. But then contemplating nature as such is scarcely ever Maximus's chief concern. Nature as such does not and could not exist (even in God).[128] Just here we must recall, I think, the fundamental role of personal free choice (προαίρεσις) in our true creation, in spiritual birth. Adam represents the *universal* fact that every *person* causes the Fall, and that therefore every person, empowered by Christ's personal human freedom, must freely undo that Fall.[129] After all, God's intention and will and desire (his *logoi*) in creating at all is not principally to make a created order, an impersonal hierarchy of variously arranged essences. His goal is to create concrete, free, unique, ultimately deified persons. There is a *logos* of every person, and every person's *logos* is also Christ the Logos. Creation's perfection, its true beginning and end, is nothing less than the personal perichoresis of God and creation—beholding God "face to face."[130]

God wants to create spirits by birthing them through the Word and in the Spirit. He seeks to generate persons from his Persons. And that demands we move beyond generalized dilemmas when we speak of God's creative act. The dilemma indulges an abstraction of what is actually the case. It is true so far as it goes, but only because the actual persons that make up humanity have made it true. And yet *those* are the very persons God wills to create; there is no other set of persons whom he begrudges the gift of being.[131] We fashion a false world of the true one and thus prevent the arrival of the true world. The deep significance of Adam's Fall being also the beginning of this phenomenal world is that what appears as our beginning is nothing of the sort. God is not constrained to become our true beginning in the way that we have made (and that he allows) our false beginning. In fact, when God makes himself our true beginning in Jesus Christ, he simultaneously enables and overcomes our false beginning. Before plumbing that quite unexpected insight, though, I wish to say a bit more about the radical sense in which we ignorantly "incarnate" our false beginnings, our false worlds.

4.1.3. Sin Hypostasized

Adam misjudges the phenomenal world out of ignorance of God. Ignorance in itself is no more blameworthy than our natural passivity toward the true beginning and end. Passion itself lies at the heart of creation.[132] But actual rational beings "always" eat of that Tree whose fruit is "mixed knowledge" of this visible world.[133] All of us, in the irrepressibly singular course unfolded in our personal decisions, are "perpetually fleeing" paradise, always making Adam fall.[134] In our naïveté we encounter phenomena and imagine them to be what they are not—sufficient in themselves. We believe the "impossible," that we can deify creation without the deity becoming created, that we can engineer sheer phenomena to yield infinite satisfaction without transcending its natural limits. An absurdity, that; the mad rush for sense pleasure and the visceral evasion of all pain spins a holographic web whose gossamer threads are so many insane fantasies, above all the judgment that phenomena themselves can remain as they are (finite) and yet become our absolute beginning and end (infinite).

As rational beings, we never experience phenomena in a purely sensible way. We try, but that too spells delusion. To imagine phenomena as mere phenomena is to *image* the world. It involves crafting an intellectual judgment and picture of the way things are.[135] Thus "the movement of the intellect gives a form to the passions, and fashions beautiful images that give pleasure to the senses." For "no passion," notes Maximus, "would ever arise without the intellect's conceptual capacity to fashion such forms."[136] The mind "invents" interpretive schemas for the phenomena it experiences, without which it would not perceive anything at all.[137] Hence the absurdity of our "impassioned disposition"[138] toward brute phenomena: the very judgment that sense phenomena and their attendant pleasures should consume our "whole being," its every activity, indulges an intellectual interpretation of the world that ignores the intellect itself (and thus the world's truth).[139]

When Adam generates in his own intellect false images of what phenomena are and can offer, he is "moved . . . by the irrational fantasies of passions, being deceived by his love of pleasure."[140] Adam desires and suffers passion for *nothing* in the guise of self-generated fantasies about himself, the world, and God, and so moves (or rather, is moved) to *realize* this fictitious picture of things.[141] He strives to embody his own world, a world of sheer phenomena laid out on a tray from which he might sample and so satisfy his self-love. Adam's Fall is the struggle to call forth this world. It is the fight to incarnate false forms, to make error true. "In the beginning, sin enticed Adam and persuaded him to transgress the divine commandment, and through transgression sin hypostasized pleasure [τὴν ἡδονὴν ὑποστήσασα], and through pleasure sin affixed itself to the very foundations of our nature, condemning the whole of our nature to death, and through man it was pushing the nature of all created beings away from existence."[142]

The Fall appears coeval with this world's generation because, in an absurd yet real sense, *it is this world's generation*. Adam introduced "another beginning of becoming,"[143] recall, which means that creation as it seems to us is not yet creation. We drive "the nature of all created things away from existence," away from true creation.[144] The Fall does not merely *happen* at the moment of creation; it is itself the falling away from creation. The Fall is false incarnation, anticreation.[145] It is the monstrous eventuation of what is no real event. We, each and all, endeavor to incarnate in ourselves—in our concrete existence, in our hypostases—what is in itself pure illusion. Evil possesses no essence or hypostasis or power or activity, certainly. But the "dishonorable passions," which constitute the mixed fruit of our erroneous judgment about this world, acquire in us "a dependent, parasitical subsistence" (παρυπόστασις). Those evils "were not generated from God" (τῶν ἐκ θεοῦ μὴ γεγονότων);

they come from us, for we give our very selves—our *hypostases*—in order illicitly to grant life and concrete existence to what is in itself nothing but our own madness.[146]

Adam errs in ignorance of God, the world, and himself. The portrait of the world for whose existence he lends his very person imagines pure finitude as the ultimate object of rational desire. He eats of the Tree, and "by partaking of this fruit he set in motion the whole cycle of bodily nourishment, thereby exchanging life for death, having created a living death in himself for the whole temporal duration of the present age [ζῶντα τὸν θάνατον ἑαυτῷ κατὰ πάντα τὸν χρόνον τοῦ παρόντος καιροῦ δημιουργήσας]."[147] This present age exists as both condition and effect of Adam's transgression, that is, of the actual sins committed by every human being.[148] Sin's structural motion is incarnation: we "hypostasize" our imagined delusions. Demonic powers are actualized *in* us, as Maximus also teaches.[149]

And so we become counterfeit creators of a world of bare phenomena, of absolute limit, of false beginnings (merely corporeal birth) and ends (death, "the corruption of becoming").[150] For Maximus as for Origen and Gregory of Nyssa,[151] nature's hideous "mutation" (μεταποίησις) in the direction of merely finite phenomena—whence come passion, corruption, death—was not something God created in Adam; "It was rather man who made it [ἐποίησε] and knew it, creating [δημιουργήσας] the freely chosen sin through his disobedience."[152] It is Adam—all of us—who through the soul seduces the soul into the body's bondage, its isolated delights. My soul turns from life "according to nature" and "becomes the *demiurge* of evil, which has no substantive existence."[153]

4.1.4. History as Bad Infinity

Senseless "incarnation" generates a senseless world. A world without apparent meaning is a world conceived solely according to its natural limits, since of course the "meaning" or "sense" of anything necessarily transcends the phenomena whose sense it provides.[154] Adam's error makes him "dependent on things that by nature can never be stable." So he suffers the natural fate of mere phenomena: "subject to change together with those things that break up and scatter the disposition of his soul" (ἐξηρτημένος τῶν φύσει στῆναι μὴ δυναμένων). He is "ceaselessly tossed about like a ship on a sea of perpetual flux and change, while he himself fails to perceive his own destruction, for the simple reason that his soul is completely blind to the truth."[155]

A subterranean reciprocity underlies the relation between this "world," this "region of death and corruption," and Adam's transgression, which is really "our interior attachment to the world based on pleasure."[156] Finitude as such, the world of sheer phenomenal limitation and pointless parataxis, is not, I repeat, inherently evil. That was clear in Maximus's refutation of a primordial state of perfection. But the world becomes the Fall "on account of sin."[157] Again, we see it is our personal freedom that renders the created world a fallen world. More precisely, it is our free, impassioned *attachment* to pure phenomena, our deluded judgment that sheer limitation might yield limitless bliss—it is, I mean, our frenzied strife to make this contradiction *actual* that prevents the world's true creation and generates in its place a world of our own making, a world of brute boundary.

And so the world we experience is "subject to time and flow."[158] It is "a definitively bounded state" (τὴν πεπερασμένην στάσιν). All the world's denizens naturally commence in this state of circumscription, but, as we have seen (sec. 3.3) and will once more (sec. 4.3), the true termination of God's creative act is nothing less than modal, actual, existential unboundedness for all creatures. "If, then, the world is a place that is definitively bounded, and a state that is circumscribed, and if time is circumscribed motion, it follows that the movement of things living within it is subject to change."[159] Beginning in motion (potency to act) and therefore in time is perfectly natural and innocent. But it proves just as true that cleaving to anything less than infinity falls short of true creation.

When, however, nature in actuality and thought will pass beyond place and time [Ὁπηνίκα δὲ τὸν τόπον διελθοῦσα καὶ τὸν χρόνον κατ' ἐνέργειάν τε καὶ ἔννοιαν ἡ φύσις] (in other words, beyond the necessary conditions without which it could not exist, that is, the limits of stasis and motion), then, without any intermediary, nature will be conjoined to providence, finding providence to be a principle that is naturally simple and stable, without any kind of circumscription, and thus absolutely without motion. This is why, as long as nature exists in this world being subject to chronological duration, its motion will always be changeable, on account of the world's definitively bounded state and the alternating character of the movement of time. When, however, it comes to be in God, having arrived at Him who by nature is a Monad, it will acquire an ever-moving stasis and a stable movement identical with itself.[160]

God's mode of being—call it the good infinity—is the very origin and term of created being itself. Anything less is bad infinity. We meet the phenomenal world in a state of natural limitation and then mistake this limitation for its truth. We seize finitude, we know it "solely according to the senses," and lapse inevitably into despair. Despair arises from the very perception that occasions our Fall; that is, from the correct perception that mere finitude signifies *nothing at all*. In this too Maximus follows Origen and Gregory of Nyssa, for whom there is but one true creation: "In the case of the first creation," says Gregory, "the final state appeared simultaneously with the beginning, and the race took the starting point of its existence in its perfection."[161] So certain is Gregory that "creation" names only this singular beginning and end that he can remark elsewhere (commenting Eccl. 1:9–11): "There exists nothing outside its original state. For *there is nothing new*, he says, *under the sun*, as if he were saying, 'Unless something exists in its original state, it does not exist at all, but is only thought to exist.'"[162] He even dares to say that this world, to the degree it departs from its true beginning and end, will dissipate into the nothing it is:

When our nature inclined to evil we became forgetful of the good; when we are set free again for the good, evil in turn will be veiled in oblivion. For I think this is the meaning of the text, *There is no memory for the first, and indeed for those who come last there will be no memory of them*. It is as if he were saying that the memory of events which followed our blessed state at the beginning, through which humanity has come to be among evils, will be obliterated by what again supervenes at the End. For *there will be no memory of them with those who have come to be at the last*. That means, the final restoration will make the memory of evil things utterly vanish in our nature, in Jesus Christ our Lord, to whom be the glory for ever and ever.[163]

Maximus invokes these very verses when glossing Gregory of Na-zianzus's remark that "the sublime Word plays in all kinds of forms, judg-ing His world as He wishes."[164] This prompts Maximus to contemplate this world, which he calls the "mean terms" between the "extremes" (i.e., the true beginning and end), as a sort of bad infinity. The "game of God," writes Maximus, is "perhaps the conspicuous position of the mean terms, which maintains an equal distance from the extremes on account of its fluid and mutable state of rest." Really this pseudo-world is "a state of rest that is forever flowing and being carried away, a flowing that is unmoved"—a mirage of fixity that, scrutinized with more care, proves only a sea of endless and aimless phenomena.[165] For such a world "the only thing it has that can be called permanent and stable is its impermanence and instability."[166] Of course, God makes providential use of this flux and by it rears his wayward children.[167] But the means are not the extremes, and only the extremes are "the *hypostasis* of coming realities that are not visible [τῶν μὴ φαινομένων] but will without fail come to be around man." The extremes alone "have properly and truly been created and have come into being in accordance with the ineffable and primal purpose and *logos* of divine goodness" (which refers, mind you, to Jesus Christ).[168]

> In the same way, when the wise Ecclesiastes, with the great and clear eye of his soul, looked beyond the coming into being of visible and transitory things [τῶν ὁρωμένων τε καὶ ῥεόντων ὑπερκύψας τὴν γένεσιν], and beheld, as it were, the vision of what had been truly created and brought into being [τῶν ἀληθῶς πεποιημένων καὶ γεγενημένων], he said, *What is this that has been brought into being? It is the same as that which will come into being.* . . . He clearly had in mind the first things and the last things, inasmuch as they are the same things and truly exist [τῶν αὐτῶν ὄντων καὶ ἀληθῶς ὄντων], but of the things in the middle, which pass away, he makes no men-tion here whatsoever.[169]

He later concludes, just as Gregory of Nyssa had, with the obliteration of what was all along only a positive nothingness: "When the arrangement of present, visible things is compared to the truth of what in fact are di-vine and archetypical realities, it will not even be reckoned to exist in the eyes of those who have been made worthy to behold. . . . In the same way, when a child's plaything is compared to anything true and real, it is not reckoned as having actual existence."[170]

The great paradox of this world is that it is not yet the world. I do not mean Maximus was an absolute dualist, of course. Adam's campaign to establish himself and his ignorant fantasies as the world's true, primordial beginning is, in the end, entirely vain. That is good news. It means that there yet lay in the very depths of our deception the deepest truth of all things, the *logoi* who are the Logos. But because the Word who gestates within us can be born only through our own freedom, our spiritual birth, and since we instead fall headlong into bodily birth and corruption and have, in a word, become mad with mere finitude and bad infinity—we have become the creators of this phenomenal world. It is not true creation. Creation eagerly awaits and groans for the children of God to be born and thereby to liberate being from nonbeing.

All this elucidates Maximus's frequent portrayals of our deification—and indeed the world's—as liberation from *nature*'s bondage. The Fall is "slavery to nature and time," to pure *limit*.[171] "Deification," writes Maximus, "is the compass and limit of all times and ages, and of everything that exists within them." And that "limit" is in fact "the unity unbroken by interval [ἀδιάστατος ἑνότης] . . . of the true and proper beginning with the true and proper end." And that in turn describes the "surpassing exodus of those who by nature are essentially measured by a beginning and an end."[172]

Some scholars rush to mitigate Maximus's more extreme statements about nature's necessary sublation.[173] Maximus, they note, very often grants a positive sense to nature. They do concede that he sometimes asserts that the ascetic struggle or our embodiment of virtue runs "against nature" (παρὰ φύσιν).[174] But more often he commends virtue as the life "according to nature" (κατὰ φύσιν).[175] True enough. To my mind, however, the positive sense of nature in no way vitiates its negative potential to beguile Adam, for the very reason that it is relatively good and desirable.

Maximus is eminently clear about all this in a letter addressed to his faithful pupil Thalassius the hegumen. "They say there are three things," begins Maximus, "that move human beings; or rather, human beings are freely moved through their judgment and inclination by three things: God, nature, and the world."[176] He then says that when one of these draws us, we drift from the other two, and that whichever moves us "makes us,

by position, into the very thing it is by nature."[177] Now, human beings remain what they naturally are even if they chase the "extremes" (world or
God). Nature as such occupies the "middle" and marks the "boundary"
(μεθόριος) of the other two.[178] Striving after the world renders us "car-
nal," after nature "psychical," after God "spiritual" (σαρκικὸς, ψυχικὸς,
πνευματικὸς). The worldly person seeks pure evil (i.e., sense pleasure
"against nature") while the spiritual person pursues only good. But the
psychical person—"natural man," Maximus calls him—occupies the putatively prudent middle ground: he wants neither to become God nor to
wallow in the world. Natural man just wants to minimize physical corruption (avoid pain) and enjoy physical well-being (seek pleasure).[179]

"If, therefore, you long to be moved by the Spirit of God," Maximus
advises, "drive away from yourself the world and nature. Or better: sever
yourself from both."[180] Maximus does not simply detest nature. Nor does
he merely repeat the true but elementary point that the misuse of nature
can divert you from God. Rather, the very fact of the Incarnation—its
supranatural identity of phenomena and infinity *within* the phenomenal
world itself—reveals the extent to which the natural limits of finite beings
quickly become the occasion of our Fall. "Beholding Jesus, the author of
our salvation," we know that "the purpose of the Giver of the commandments is to liberate humanity from the world and nature."[181] Presuming
that bad infinity is the truth of creation betrays our refusal of its true beginning and end, Jesus Christ. Only "ignorant people, in an iniquitous
manner," try to subject even the God-world identity that Christ actualized
to "natural boundaries."[182] But no: nature as such is a false figment. For
Adam, for us, there exists only one world, one true creation: the hypostatic identity of God and creation.

> And, just as in the beginning He brought it into being out of nothing, so
> too now His aim is to rescue and restore it from its fallen condition,
> preventing it from falling again by means of immutability, and to real-
> ize for nature the entire design of God the Father, deifying nature by
> the power of His Incarnation. For Scripture says that the "hands" of the
> spiritual "Zerubbabel have established this house," the "house" being
> the human being; and that "his hands shall bring it to perfection,"
> which refers to the initial formation and the perfect re-formation,
> which takes place within Him according to the ineffable union.[183]

4.2. CHRIST AS PROVIDENCE AND JUDGMENT

Adam makes of himself a false beginning by reducing creation to pure nature. As he strives to embody what he fancies in his soul, he fabricates a counterfeit world entirely bounded by abrupt limitation—from (merely) corporeal birth to tragic death. History, or what appears to us when we scan the phenomenal world, menaces us as a senseless and therefore bad infinity. This, I think, begins to resolve a potential objection to my interpretation of Maximus's view of creation as Incarnation. Far from discerning in this world some sublime, cosmic, and deifying Incarnation of the Word always and in all things, we typically meet ephemera, flux, deceit, self-love, greed, corruption, death—in a word, "slavery to time and nature." Maximus concedes and raises the stakes: the Fall occurred at the very moment this world appeared. One is tempted to say that, for Maximus, we are thrown into existence, caught up in apparently aimless motion—downward motion—from our very origins.

But even this aleatoric life (and with it our infantile yet real freedom) is made possible only by the historical Incarnation. That, at least, is what my thesis implies. Said differently, if creation and Incarnation name a single act, then the historical Incarnation must be the actualization of the world's universal potency. Jesus Christ, from conception to ascension, makes himself the actual potential of every principle (*logos*), every creature, every motion, every act, every passion, every time, every place, every relation, every reality. If, as we just read Maximus saying, the "the perfect re-formation" comes to be "within Him, according to the ineffable union," if "the whole mystery of Christ" is precisely that "all the ages and the beings existing within those ages received their beginning and end in Christ,"[184] and if indeed our very potential to resist the Word's Incarnation and thereby illicitly hypostasize a counterfeit creation—if, I mean, even this slavish passion to sheer finitude—is itself made possible by God's veritable act of creation in and as Christ, then we should expect to find Maximus making explicit this *concrete reciprocity* or *simultaneity* at every level of his contemplation of the historical Incarnation.

We do. This reciprocity emerges most evidently in the way Maximus reconfigures the Origenists' architectonic pair, "providence" (πρόνοια) and "judgment" (κρίσις). Though formalizing these nowhere near as much as Evagrius does, Origen does couple the two ideas when presenting his more notorious speculations about the beginning, middle, and end of all creatures. "And since," he writes, "this fall or lapse, by which each one departs from his original state has in itself the greatest diversity, according to the impulse of the intellect or intention, one falls slightly, another more seriously, to the lower things: in this is the just judgment of the providence of God [*in hoc iam iustum iudicium dei providentiae est*], that it should happen to everyone according to the diversity of his conduct, in proportion to the merit of his declension and revolt."[185] I do not here wish to wade into the troubled waters surrounding Origen's precise view of creation, the so-called preexistence of incorporeal beings, or the relation of either of these to human beginnings.[186] I note simply that in this passage divine judgment and providence describe God's comprehensive response to the errant motion of rational beings away from their "original state." Providence and judgment are at once protological, eschatological, and ontological terms. They also implicate each other: God's distribution of beings, which appears simultaneously as the result of and response to primordial sin, unfurls within the greater providential aim of realizing his eternal will that all creation be one with itself and God.

Balthasar already observed that it was Didymus the Blind who made this pair shorthand for God's whole activity toward and in creation, and that with Evagrius it becomes a veritable *Grundprinzip*.[187] Evagrius joins Didymus in this counsel to the "knowers": "Exercise yourself continuously in the *logoi* of providence and judgment." Evagrius defines them: "And you will discover the *logoi* of judgment in the diversity of bodies and worlds [τῇ διαφορᾷ τῶν σωμάτων καὶ τῶν κόσμων], and those of providence in the means by which we return from vice and ignorance to virtue or knowledge."[188] Judgment and providence name two of five contemplations the knower must exercise (the others are Trinity, incorporeal beings, and corporeal beings).[189] As for Origen and Didymus, for Evagrius they indicate the whole divine activity in creation and for that reason function as metaphysical and soteriological principles. Judgment is "the creation of an age which distributes to each of the reasoning beings a body corresponding to its state."[190] Providence, which circumscribes judgment as the more comprehensive aspect of God's activity,[191] executes two purposes: it "preserves the substance" of all creatures and—a note we just heard—it "urges on rational creatures from evil and ignorance to virtue and knowledge."[192]

Evagrian judgment and providence represent not simply what God does in response to the free motion of rational beings. They are the immanent principles (*logoi*) that work "within" creatures, responding to and empowering every movement unto the greater purpose of complete union in the Trinity.[193] Evagrius follows Origen in linking the manifold distribution of beings—especially their variegated bodies (i.e., their space-time coordinates)[194]—with the work of judgment, which distribution serves too as God's providential means. Providence "accompanies the freedom of the will."[195] Judgment is order; it establishes one's station along with the myriad relations among all stations. Providence attends to the singular path each person treads in concert with every other path underway. Archangels, "heavenly powers," spiritual masters, and even the celestial luminaries all constitute and contribute to the realization of God's providence in creation.[196] Above all it is Christ who, through the *logoi* of providence, creates and "leads the rational nature through various aeons toward union in the holy Unity."[197]

Now we face the issue of how exactly the Origenists' providence and judgment construe the very act of creation. Perhaps the most intuitive (and so most common) way to interpret the schema here is to treat it as a metanarrative proceeding from beginning to middle to end. Granted, there could be many "beginnings" and "ends" in the middle. Maybe there was an initial state of perfection from which rational beings freely defected, which prompted God's discriminatory judgment (i.e., the distribution of beings in a hierarchical array of essences and bodies), which is itself a judgment made in view of God's providential aim of drawing all beings back into union with himself. And maybe this takes a while: God creates an age populated by a vast multitude of variously arranged beings, then that age terminates in a provisional judgment that prepares the next age's initial order, then providence guides that age (in cooperation with free will) to its relative end, then another judgment—and so ever on. "Thus, every judgment comes between the movement of free will and God's providence."[198]

Of course, the other way is Gregory of Nyssa's. His account too can be read as a sort of metanarrative. Only with him the sequence of scenes does not exactly reflect the truth of creation. Gregory famously proposes the so-called double creation theory. When we interpret Genesis 1:26–27, he cautions, we must make the crucial distinction between "the human being" made "in accordance with the image of God" and the "male and female" that God permitted from this world's beginning. "For we find," says Gregory, "that what is made *in accordance with the image* is one thing, and what is now manifest in wretchedness is another."[199] He adds immediately that this distinction derives not simply from the text's repetition (though that is its sign) but—to take the most notorious example—from Paul's remark (Gal. 3:28) that in Christ there exists no longer male and female. Christ is "the Prototype" of true humanity; therefore true humanity does not divide into gender.[200]

Humanity's true creation comes about perfectly and instantaneously in its "first formation." Gregory characterizes this primal creation as the realization of humanity *qua* "universal," which, with respect to creation, designates the actualized universal potency determinative of every particular human being that will come to be at its appropriate moment.[201] But first creation is not strictly coeval with the phenomenal world's beginning. Specifically, humanity's initial appearance in concrete history did not manifest true humanity. Consider again the gender distinction: God, "since he foresaw by his visionary faculty the human would not keep a straight course towards the good" but indeed "would fall away . . . from the angelic life," implanted "in humanity, instead of the angelic nobleness of nature, the animal and irrational mode of succession from one another."[202] And so God, by "the activity of his foreknowledge," implants *from the serial start* the very occasion of concrete human sin—our "animal-like," irrational nature—even as that preemptive implantation is itself a response to (and thus an effect of) fallen humanity.[203]

In later writings Gregory uses the analogy of a seed to sketch the same picture. Primordial creation, true creation, was generated entirely and perfectly in an initial state of actual potential, rather like the "seminal power" (σπερματικὴ δύναμις) present latently in a seed that will unfold stepwise unto concrete perfection.[204] The true world is "thrown down" (καταβολή). It is, as Köckert remarks, "generation in the primary sense of the word."[205] Its "successive formation" (κατασκευή), its arboreal ramification through space-time, proves necessary only because of primordial evil (again as both cause and effect). "For when it was first created," Gregory elsewhere declares, "since evil did not yet exist, there was nothing to prevent the race's perfection from going hand in hand with its birth, but in the process of restoration, lapses of time necessarily attend those who are tracing their way toward the original good."[206]

And yet Gregory also asserts that the same humankind characterized by diastemic conditions from this world's beginning "took the starting point of its existence in its perfection."[207] Once more Gregory presents our phenomenological origins as simultaneously (not serially) God's act of creation and salvation, of initiative and response, or, to put it terms he himself never uses but that chime rather well here—of judgment and providence.[208] There lingers a sense in which judgment is secondary, as it was in Evagrius. It is a kind of reaction engineered into the primal act of creation. God's creative act actualizes the very power to overcome the primordial failure that itself foils that same creative act from attaining perfection from its first concrete instant. Thus the story's logic, its truth, appears rather more complicated than the ordering of its scenes. It is not as facile as perfection, deviant motion, order by judgment, progress by providence, judgment again, providence again, and at length ultimate restoration. It is rather judgment-providence from this world's first dawn, a dawn constituted by both God's primordial creative intent and its provisional (but real) resistance by rational creatures.[209]

Gregory's ingenious insight into the dual or reciprocal character of the creative act remains, however, slightly abstract. We hear only that such reciprocity resulted from the "the activity" of divine foreknowledge and will.[210] Scarcely do we glimpse the positive relation or the form of the unity presupposed in the reciprocity itself—the determinate link, I mean, between Adam's two beginnings (first/final creation and this provisional world of phenomena).

Brilliantly, Maximus integrates both Evagrian and Gregorian approaches. Doing so, he brandishes them in a stunningly idiosyncratic manner. To be sure, Maximus can give providence and judgment the same sort of general or philosophical acceptation that the terms carry in many late antique schemas.[211] And he betrays Evagrius's unmistakable influence, even to the point of counseling the same five contemplations for ascent.[212] Thus Maximus too can define providence as "the revertive, inductive, and providential return of the many to the One."[213] The *logoi* of judgment and providence are immanent in all things, ever at work sustaining the ordered differentiation and the existential unification of every creature with respect to all others, in the one Word. He even intensifies the providence-judgment schema as God's comprehensive activity in creation. "Now by providence," he says, "I do not mean 'convertive' providence," a crude reactive influence upon wayward creatures in an effort to return "whatever has gone astray to its proper course." And "by judgment I do not mean retributive action," the reactive chastisement of sinners. Providence and judgment secure in principle (*logoi*) the total unity and inviolable distinction of creatures, respectively. "Thus I am not saying that there are two kinds of providence and judgment, for they are one in power, but insofar as they relate to us, they assume a different and many-moded activity."[214]

Old Testament saints, and really any conscientious intellect, perceive these immanent principles in the flittering interplay of universals and particulars. They recognize in universals the inherent impulse in all things toward providential unity, in particulars the restive stability of decisive difference, and then the dialectical simultaneity of both universals and particulars in their mutual dependence and destruction.[215] This mesmerizing display, we just heard, indicates obliquely the "one power" of God's providence and judgment, a power whose peculiar effect is to accomplish total unity and irreducible difference in a single act.[216]

So far, so Evagrian. But we also find in Maximus Gregory's marked divergences from the metanarrative approach. Of course, Maximus too opposes a primordial state of realized perfection from which rational beings sank. And the phenomenal world begins proleptically devised in response to the Fall. One of the rare occasions when Maximus names Gregory, in fact, is to commend the latter's teaching that the irrational passions—sense pleasure, grief, desire, fear—"were introduced on account of the fall from perfection, emerging in the more irrational part of human nature [διὰ τὴν τῆς τελειότητος ἔκπτωσιν ἐπεισήχθη ταῦτα]," so that through such passions, "at the very moment of transgression, the distinct and definite likeness to irrational animals appeared in man instead of the divine and blessed image" (εὐθὺς ἅμα τῇ παραβάσει διαφανὴς καὶ ἐπίδηλος ἐν τῷ ἀνθρώπῳ γέγονεν ἡ τῶν ἀλόγων ζῴων ὁμοίωσις).[217] Adam's false beginning appears designed by divine foreknowledge in order to initiate his long pedagogical return to the true beginning and end. Matter itself meets us as a bad infinity, yet its very vanity can serve to reform us.[218] Death wields the sternest instruction. Its "law" absolutizes the dialectic of pleasure and pain. Certain death portends the unforgiving finitude of merely paratactic pleasure—surely a valuable lesson.[219]

Thus Maximus codifies in Evagrian terms many instincts common to Evagrius and Gregory even as Gregory's "reciprocal causality" prevails when it comes to our phenomenological origins. But this creative confection is not yet the most distinctive feature of Maximus's providence and judgment. In one passage Maximus glosses the presence of Moses and Elijah at the Transfiguration with these words:

> [There they learned] that the fulfillment of God's ineffable plan for the universe, contained within His divine dispensations [ἐπ' αὐτῇ θείων οἰκονομιῶν], was completely beyond the comprehension of beings. All that could be known was His great providence and judgment, through which the universe is led in an orderly manner to an end [τέλος] known in advance only to God. No one else knew what it would be, or how it would take place, or what form it would take, or when it would occur; the only ones who in truth knew simply that it *would* take place were the saints.[220]

Natural contemplation of the principles of providence and judgment intimates their true realization. It does not disclose that realization apart from the event itself. Saints of the Old Covenant attained only the abstraction *that* the mystery would occur. But what form would it take? What would it be? When? Only the event could reveal the *way* God's creative act truly eventuates—how it is, we might say, that God manifests himself as our true beginning and end right in the midst of our false beginnings and ends.

Maximus identifies God's providence and judgment with the historical Incarnation. We might have sensed this in the famous *Question* 60. There we read that the "great and hidden mystery," the "blessed end for which all things were brought into existence," the "divine purpose conceived before the beginning of the ages," the "preconceived goal for the sake of which everything exists, but which itself exists on account of nothing"—likely an Evagrius-mediated definition of "end"[221]—is the God-world hypostatic identity wrought in Jesus Christ, which is "the limit of providence and of the things preconceived, according to which occurs the recapitulation into God of all the things made by God" (τὸ τῆς προνοίας καὶ τῶν προνοουμένων πέρας, καθ' ὃ εἰς τὸν θεὸν ἡ τῶν ὑπ' αὐτοῦ πεποιημένων ἐστὶν ἀνακεφαλαίωσις).[222] But he makes it utterly manifest in the following passage, a contemplation of the two "olives trees" in Zechariah's vision (Zech. 4:2– 3), which I must quote at considerable length:

In the midst of these—I mean in the midst of the holy Catholic Church, or in the soul of each of holy person—as if upon a golden lampstand spreading the light of the truth to all, stands the Word who, as God, contains the universe, revealing and binding together the true and most general *logoi* of beings—providence and judgment. It was according to these *logoi* that the mystery of our salvation, foreordained before all the ages and completed in these last times, was realized. Thus we behold providence, as if it were an olive tree standing to the right of the light, in the ineffable manner of the Word's hypostatic union with flesh rationally endowed with a soul, and we see this by faith alone. And to the left, in a manner beyond words, we recognize judgment in the mystery of the Incarnate God's life-making sufferings, which He underwent for our sake. Inasmuch as He is good, the former [i.e., providence] came about principally according to His will, for by nature He is Savior of all. Inasmuch as He loves mankind, He consequently endured the latter [i.e., judgment] consensually and with forbearance, for by nature He is clearly Redeemer of all. For God did not become man principally so that He might suffer, but so that He might preserve mankind through sufferings—in subjection to the very sufferings that resulted from the transgression of the divine command and to which man, being impassible in his true origins, yet made himself subject.[223]

Earlier we heard Maximus concede that one might well discern, philosophically, that divine providence and judgment exercise an immanent activity from "one power." Here he specifies that the actualization of that one power is Jesus Christ—an insight perceptible "by faith alone." More, Maximus assigns providence and judgment to particular aspects or dimensions of the historical Incarnation. Providence is the union itself, the God-man; judgment is the Passion, the suffering God. And Maximus could scarcely be clearer about the fundamental reciprocity characteristic of the whole mystery. The union reveals divine goodness and "will" (θέλησις), God's absolute desire, while the Passion evinces Christ's concrete love for human beings in his "consensual" (καθ᾽ ἑκούσιον) or voluntary response to a determinate phenomenon—our transgression, the actual sins of all persons. Attend carefully to the reciprocity, the symmetry: God's pre-eternal foreknowledge comprises the *logos* not only of providence (his primary, unitive intention in creating) but also of judgment (his differentiated, singular response to personal sin).

"This mystery was predetermined before the ages [πρὸ τῶν αἰώνων προορισθείσης τῶν σῳζομένων θεώσεως]," Maximus continues, "and absolutely no principle of beings can approach it by nature." The judgment rendered in Christ's Passion and cross "brings about the utter destruction of all the properties and movements contrary to nature that were introduced through the primal disobedience."[224] In his providence God wills absolutely to become essentially human. But in his judgment God's will is only ever determinative of and determined by actual, individual, concrete human beings. In his divine counsel God knows Adam's true *and* false beginnings because—and this is truly critical—God knows and wills *Adam*. Which is to say, God wills and thus creates not an abstract arrangement of essences or mere instances of nature but actual, individual, free persons, the very persons who in themselves freely hypostasize something other than themselves. God wants to become and so create human beings (and the reverse). But human beings do not want to become God and so be truly created. Incarnation makes God human and actualizes the principles of every being in which he wishes to accomplish this mystery. But human persons make God a *suffering* God-man. The Passion at once establishes and responds to actual persons, since, of course, God's judgment sustains the singularity and distinctiveness of all persons—even in and through the depths of their deluded self-destruction.

In this way providence, the infinite power of the God-world identity in and as Christ, really is "primary." Incarnation names the ultimately invincible realization of the pre-eternal divine will; it is what is "seen" or "conceived" "before," what faces God in his own act of creating and indeed in his own act of being God. In Christ we therefore discern the deepest reciprocity: he concretizes, in himself, the essential paradox of human freedom, the possibility of both our primordial error and our eventual embrace of God, our "initial" and "perfect" formation. "But the Lord set forth the manifest might of His transcendent power, having hypostasized an unchanging becoming in the nature of the contrary realities by which He Himself experienced. For by giving our nature impassibility through His Passion, relief through His sufferings, and eternal life through His death, He restored our nature, renewing its habitual dispositions by means of what was negated in His own flesh, and through His own Incarnation granting it that grace which transcends nature, by which I mean deification."[225] The "contrary realities by which" the Incarnate Word "experienced" are, context reveals, the same pleasure-pain dialectic of which our primordial transgression is cause and consequence. Note Maximus's precision here. In the historical Incarnation the Word "hypostasized"—gave his subsistence and person to—the very conditions which *all of our personal sins* cause and within which they occur. Bodily birth (our false beginning) and death (our false end)—in a word, the bad infinity we ignorantly desire and deify—only become *real* possibilities because the Word himself *experiences* them. In his Passion he makes himself, freely and out of profligate love for every person, the actual possibility of every person's rejection of him. The Passion is the metaphysical principle of divine judgment. Not only is it the generation of the infinite difference between created and uncreated natures (a crucial element of Christo-logic), but here, in the darkest depths of divine kenosis,[226] the suffering God-man also generates the potential for all the differences we "create," illicitly and stupidly, through our personal sin, our primordial Fall.

By thus "becoming sin for us" (2 Cor. 5:21) the Word immediately (for he is the sole mediator) realizes his divine and providential mode and activity within the very principle of judgment. The *logos* of providence— the Word's hypostatic union (and thus generation) of all things, in principle and in fact—remains ever primary to and directive of the *logos* of judgment. What he "hypostasized," we just read, was precisely "an unchanging becoming" (γένεσις) into the origins of a "nature" in the throes of pleasure and pain.[227] That nature is Adam's, which is to say, all of ours collectively. Natures (or universals or essences) subsist only in and as hypostases. Were it therefore confined solely to *our* hypostases, perfected human nature would never truly come to be. But since Christ actualizes in himself both a particular instance of humanity *and* its universal potency,[228] he has thus endowed even the possibility of our sin—more exactly, our freedom *qua* spirits—with the indestructible principle of providence. By "his own power he freed—as if through the 'first fruits' of his own holy flesh (which he took from us)—the whole human nature from the wicked power that had been mixed into its condition of possibility."[229] Even if individual persons are moved by pure nature or the "world" and not God, the principle of human passibility retains the immanent power of Christ's Passion, which is the power of Resurrection. To whatever de-

gree it is disfigured by Adam's "characteristic marks,"[230] you will encounter not a single instance of human nature that is not, at least in concrete principle, personalized in principle by Jesus Christ. After all, it was
precisely Adam's corrupted flesh that the Word became and to which he
united his divinity. "He is Pentecost," Maximus writes in another place,
"inasmuch as He is the beginning, the end, and the principle of beings, in
whom all things subsist by nature."[231]

And so the Word's historical Incarnation makes it universally and
immanently possible for any human being in any age to be born of the
Spirit. Christ "is 'ruddy in appearance,' suffering death 'with the beauty
of His eyes' [1 Kings 16:12]," Maximus comments, "with the glory of the
loftier principles of providence and judgment, for the 'eyes' of the Word
are judgment and providence, through which, even in His suffering for
us, He conducts His universal oversight."[232] The Word hypostasized the
very "possibility" or the conditions of Adam's transgression by suffering
the bad infinity of sheer phenomena—death itself. That action is simultaneously a reaction, a passion. But also, since Christ *is* Adam's true beginning and end, which is nothing less than the modal and actual perichoresis that Christ's identity realizes (*Q. Thal.* 60.3; *Amb.* 41.5), Christ
becomes the immediate mediator, in the very principle of human passivity (which itself subsists nowhere except in the principle of every individual person), of our providential end in deification and spiritual birth—our
true, personal, sole creation.

This explains how Christ's historical Passion is simultaneously the
judgment and providence of every concrete person ("Adam"). We saw in
the last chapter that creation's Christo-logic opens upon an ultimate reciprocity and perichoresis, not only of "modes" abstractly considered, but
indeed of persons with the Word (and thus the Three). We saw too that
one consequence of this perichoresis was that, as members of Christ's
Body, Christ "takes into himself the sufferings of each one" and, "until
the end of time, always suffers mystically through goodness in proportion to each one's suffering."[233] Now we see that the historical Incarnation
(providence) and the Incarnate God's concrete sufferings (judgment) actualize the universal principles immanent within and already responsive
to every particular being. We see, in other words, that Christ's personal
sufferings hypostasize and for that very reason *potentially overcome* the
personal sins of all. Our recognition of this fundamental reciprocity and

the various ways we respond to it together name the very process of judgment and providence.

It is a process of coming to see that my own sin causes the Passion of Christ, the same suffering that, because it is *his* personal experience, enables and annihilates my sin in principle. The judgment of the Passion thus restores my freedom and invites me to choose to be created, to be born of the Spirit rather than from my own primordial delusion. I must come to recognize the depths of God's love in the fundamental God-world reciprocity generated in the Word's historical experience.[234] That reciprocity creates the freedom to undo my own misuse of freedom exactly because the Word's identification with the false world is simultaneously his identification with the true one. He made himself the hypostatic identity of bad and good infinities. That is, he received, in his Passion, the entire burden of the errant motions of every individual rational being, and by making them *his own*—he who is essentially God—endowed the very false "principles" our sin falsely incarnate, namely the "law of death," with the deeper principle of providence, the complete deification of even *this* universe and of the "me" I make in vain. His true Incarnation, always and in all things, destroys all false incarnations from true beginning to true end—for he is both.

Judgment, then, converts the grief generated by our inability to absolutize merely finite pleasure into the grief generated by our ability to see that the Word suffers personally in our personal grief. Such purgative grief grows in proportion to our love for the Christ who suffers, since, of course, the more we love someone the greater our pain at his or her suffering. And greater still if we cause that suffering, if that suffering is *ours*.[235] Anyone "who has been overtaken by the deception of material things," writes Maximus, "receives the Word of God as something smiting his conscience like a worm [cf. Jonah], devouring his attachment to pleasure like the root of the gourd plant." "But with the perfect rising of the illumination of the teachings of the Spirit, the Word of God withers the activity of sin; and through the memory of eternal punishments [τῇ μνήμῃ τῶν αἰωνίων κολάσεων], like a wind of burning heat, it smites—as if it were a head—the origin of the evil passions in the provocations of the senses. And this happens so that we might come to learn the principles of providence and judgment, which give priority to eternal things over what is transitory, the privation of which typically causes the human race to grieve."[236] Our conscience burns; we grow sickened by mere finitude. We burn because pure nature cannot truly satisfy, yes, but also because our lust for it crucifies God. Recognizing this, our love increases, disabuses us of deception, stirs our desire for nothing less than true infinity. But again we behold infinity suffering in mere finitude. We intensify in disgust for the latter and in love for the former—and so on through the long pedagogy that characterizes this "world."[237] And we see too that God preserves every person even through that person's self-destruction, and that every other person (indeed every creature) is created in Christ for actual infinity.

All this indicates something of what it means to "come to learn the principles of judgment and providence." It means learning that "He did not hesitate to make our condemnation His own condemnation, and to make us Gods by grace to the same degree that He undertook in His economy of salvation to become man by nature."[238] And so, as Maximus says of divine judgment in commenting Jonah's "Nineveh"—which signifies fallen humanity, each soul, and this current world—"God in truth both destroys and saves the same city."[239]

4.3. TIME AND THE INCARNATION

One might object that creation cannot be Incarnation for the simple reason that creation is presupposed by the historical Incarnation. The Word "becomes flesh" (John 1.14), and, since he takes our flesh, his becoming seems to presume us. The world is already there. Into this world the Word is born. Whatever happens to it or within, even deification, presumes it.

We already noted one problem with this line of reasoning, at least as it relates to Maximus's view of things. What has appeared is not necessarily God's creation. Adam's false beginning, which he both causes and is caused by, raises the paradoxical possibility that the mere fact that something is a phenomenon might not prove it is truly created. Insofar as it *is* a true work of God, it finds itself always already in motion on the long course of providence and judgment, which will involve the destruction of what it falsely incarnates and the perfection of the Word's true Incarnation in it (these are really the same process).

Another problem with the objection can be framed negatively. The Word's "becoming" flesh is an event that cannot be subject to the logic of events *qua* phenomena. His historical becoming is a "movement"[240] from his essential pre-eternity into time, not a transition from one temporal state to another. The Word "becomes" amid the very flux of becoming; therefore his becoming becomes in a mode necessarily different from our assumptions about what it means to become. His "before" is not some prior time period but his divinity. His "after" is not a subsequent state but his humanity. He is the "is" of both—that is his becoming. Thus "the union of nature with the Word according to the design of providence" is "a union in which there is no imprint of time or becoming."[241] The Son, precisely in his historical kenosis, "possesses the circumscriptive limit of all ages."[242] Such kenosis could not therefore be an event whose logic simply obeys the logic of events. In fact subjecting the true eventuation of the Incarnation to the dictates of the temporal flow within which it appears verges perilously close to repeating the primordial sin: it is to judge the whole mystery of Christ as if it conformed to mere finitude.

Nor would we evade this temptation by conceiving eternity strictly negatively, say, as not-time. For the question arises whether the referent of "not-time," the ostensible "before" creation, *is*. If not-time does exist, even if not in a chronological or finitely-measured mode, then one wonders whether this atemporal mode isn't just a surreptitious conception of "before-" or "above-" time every bit as finite as our apprehension of time itself. If, after all, "beginning, middle, and end are identifying marks of things divided by time,"[243] and if what exists in an atemporal mode necessarily *presupposes* time itself as its negation, then I cannot see how we are any better off conceiving the Word "before" time than we supposedly were in presupposing creation to Incarnation. Only, on my reading of Maximus, we can embrace the mutual presupposition of creation to Incarnation and Incarnation to creation exactly because it reveals the very identity that generates opposites—the Word who, since he *is* both, makes both interpenetrate in and as his personal modes and acts. Christo-logic entails just that (secs. 1.4 and 3.3).

Were we to conceive the matter exclusively through the logic of essence or nature, we would concede that there are but two ways to exist: as God or as not-God. The corollary for created nature is that it exists immediately in time, in motion, and anything that exists otherwise is just God. It is well known, for instance, that Maximus (like John Philoponus) denied the eternity of this world.[244] And in this sense—that is, according to the logic of essence—God is the beginning, middle, and end of nothing at all. "God is neither an essence, meant as unqualified or qualified essence, and therefore not a beginning [ἀρχή]; nor a potentiality, meant as unqualified or qualified potentiality, and therefore not a middle [μεσότης]; nor an actuality, meant as unqualified or qualified actuality, and therefore not the end [τέλος] of the essentializing motion that is conceived prior in terms of potentiality."[245] All beginnings familiar to us, chronological or essential, presuppose an essence, a "what." A qualified essence—human, angelic, equine, et cetera—comes pre-equipped with or predetermined by a specific set of formal principles or faculties by which it acts according to what it is. Since this essence is *given*, it functions as an essential beginning. But God receives no essence from something prior (again, chronologically or essentially) and so never begins in that sense at all. Maximus further denies that God is essence "unqualifiedly" (ἁπλῶς). God names not even an indeterminate "what." Hence it follows that God possesses no essential potency (beginning), so no essential motion (middle), and so no essential state of having fulfilled an essential motion (end). He causes these in created beings; but, understood solely as essence, he is none of these.

Considered essentially, not just time but eternity too possesses a beginning. "For time [ὁ χρόνος], which is measured motion, is circumscribed by number, whereas eternity [ὁ αἰών], possessing the category of 'when' as conceptualized together with its existence, undergoes distension, since it receives an *arche* of being." And "if time and eternity are not without first principle [οὐκ ἄναρχα], all the more the things contained within them."[246] Time is an epiphenomenon of finite motion.[247] Its appearance corresponds, then, with the sheer fact of phenomena. Eternity or the age, like other intelligible realities,[248] seems to us transcendent of time because it lacks the parataxic character of temporal phenomena. But eternity too "suffers distension" (πάσχει διάστασιν) as soon as we conceive it as existing at all for concrete beings in such a way that it could not really subsist apart from those beings who began to be. The age thus appears determined (and limited) by at least one Aristotelian category: "when" (πότε).[249]

It belongs to the *essence* of created being, we saw earlier, to begin in motion. Here we see that to begin at all necessarily implies a "when" and a "where," which for Maximus constitute "necessary conditions" (τῶν οὐκ

ἄνευ) of created nature.[250] Subject, beginning, motion, where, when—all
of these name mutually entailing "relations."[251] They are "naturally simultaneous" (συνεπινοεῖσθαι πέφυκεν), dialectically determined, always
predicated *toward* another determinate conception (πρός τι).[252] You cannot coherently conceive someone in motion without immediately presupposing a "where" from which that someone moves (again, chronologically or ontologically), nor a "where" without a "when" (even if your
conception is a static one, say, that of McTaggart's famous description of
the B-series, you presuppose a when-where coordinate always in *relation*
to other such coordinates).[253] Being created thus immediately implicates
an entire network of necessary relations, among them phenomenological
ones (such as time) and logical ones (such as eternity).

Beginning amid necessary conditions is in itself innocent. But for
Maximus the historical Incarnation has disclosed that creation's true beginning and end—which is to say, *true creation*, God's finished act—is a
reality "beyond place and time."[254] God's Sabbath rest signifies this:
"Whatever things exist in time are being fashioned in accordance with
time and, having been perfected, they are brought to a standstill, thereby
having ceased from growth according to nature."[255] Time and eternity are
essentially created. But the latter—the "age to come"—is in fact the perfection of the former. And the age names the deified state that bears the
character of a total and actual and modal perichoresis between God and
the world. "For [the age] has Jesus [= Joshua], who is the successor of all
time and every age," so that, as with Moses and the Promised Land, "the
Law" marches thither even as Moses [= time and nature] remains behind.
"For when its motion is stilled, time is the age, and the age is time as carried along and measured by motion." Concisely put, "The age is time de-
prived of motion, whereas time is the age measured by motion."[256]

Against a certain Origenist tendency to perceive in the final God-
world union the necessary annihilation of ages, plurality, distinction,
bodies, number, and so forth, Maximus's "age" preserves all difference
and identity.[257] This much was clearly implied in his account of divine
judgment and providence. And as with those concepts, he can maintain
this ultimate paradox precisely because he believes that the age itself,
true creation, occurs in the historical Incarnation.[258]

Consider the way Maximus answers Thalassius's question about
how Paul could speak of "the coming ages" (Eph. 2:7) and yet claim that

"the ends of the ages have come upon us" (1 Cor. 10:11).[259] Maximus begins by repeating that the divine counsel "before all the ages" determined that humanity would receive "a true union according to [the Word's] hypostasis" and that we must thus distinguish two types of ages: "Some would be for the activity of His becoming man, and others for the activity of making man God."[260] The end of the ages is actualized in the historical Incarnation "through the events themselves" (δι' αὐτῶν τῶν πραγμάτων λαβούσης τὴν ἔκβασιν). These ages designate "not simply 'ages' as we ordinarily understand them, but clearly those which, *intended for the actualization of the mystery of embodiment*, have reached their proper limit according to the purpose of God."[261] This is almost exactly Maximus's terminology in *Ambigua* 7.22: "The Word of God, very God, wills that the mystery of his embodiment be actualized always and in all things."[262]

At length a vision emerges. The very "events" of Jesus's historical life are what actualize the universal principles (*logoi*)—above all of providence and judgment—of every true age, and indeed of every creature that, since it must begin in motion, dwells within and is a vital constituent of that age. Every creature's motion, sinful or not, generates time. False motion renders existence more crudely finite, slavishly borne along with the flux of phenomena. True motion—the motion of virtue, knowledge, love of God in Christ—brings creaturely motion nearer its term, its Sabbath cessation, and hence takes leave of the provisional necessities of spatiotemporal existence.[263] And so the perfection of creaturely *logoi* is the age. But those *logoi* carry potentialities that are themselves actualized for the first time in one hypostasis, Jesus of Nazareth. Outside of his historical existence—or rather the union that existence *is*—no creaturely principle *actually is*. Conversely, the actualization of all the principles he himself hypostasizes—through the correction of his Passion and the attainment of his providential union (which bears, recall, "no imprint of time or becoming")—is also the universal actualization of the mystery of his Incarnation. Thus Maximus does not name only "God" as our true beginning, middle, and end.[264] But also, "Since our Lord Jesus Christ is the beginning, middle, and end of all the ages past, present, and future, one could say that through the power of faith, 'the end of the ages'—I mean that end which will be actualized by grace according to its proper form in the deification of the worthy—'has already come upon us.' "[265]

• • •

Beyond the logical issue raised by the idea that creation is Incarnation, namely the worry that it reduces Christ to a universal principle of particular instances, I admitted that the far more difficult objection asks how creation could be the Word's Incarnation given the devastated condition of this world. I offered two basic responses.

The first challenges our assumption that all phenomena we encounter in this world necessarily qualify as God's creation. Maximus's radical portrayal of Adam's beginnings, both the spiritual birth we have yet to achieve and the fantastical becoming we strive vainly to incarnate within ourselves, should caution us against the easy assumption that what we experience must be a true creature. And conversely, of course, it should also lead us to consider that the entirety of God's creative act—even of this age and all its creatures—is, from our deluded and faithless perspective, still to occur. If this phenomenal world is not yet truly creation, then creation is an act whose perfection is yet to be (sec. 4.1).

Another challenge to our assumptions came in the profound reciprocity Maximus perceived in creation as the Word's historical Incarnation. Here the God-world symmetry becomes utterly concrete and irrepressibly personal. Because God's aim is to create free and rational persons (spirits), and because these particular persons freely prefer fantasy to the Word, then God's reaction to human sin already determines the very form of God's creative action. Maximus borrows the Evagrian dialectic of divine judgment (which determines all space-time difference) and divine providence (which determines the course of unitive restoration) even as he adopts and concentrates Gregory of Nyssa's doctrine of "reciprocal causality" in the generation of *this* fallen world. For Maximus Christ hypostasizes the universal principle of providence in his identity as the God-man and the principle of judgment in his Passion. Since he never ceases to be the former even through the latter, he endows all human passivity—down to the false motions of every last person— with the power of his invincible divinity, the power of Resurrection and thereby liberation from all time and nature. Christ hypostasizes the very possibility to reject him and therein creates the *logoi* of all concrete rational beings. He suffers in all persons in order to meet all persons in their deluded self-destruction, which is paradoxically the very guarantee that their personal distinction will forever persist in him—that they shall be saved (sec. 4.2).

All this challenges the very idea that Incarnation must presuppose rather than be creation. The truth is both. Of course Incarnation presupposes creation, since it is an identity that generates the very difference between created and uncreated natures. And of course creation presupposes Incarnation because a God-world hypostatic identity is what Christ revealed to be the pre-eternal counsel of the Godhead. The modal and actual perichoresis that characterizes deified existence constitutes "the age" toward which all motion (and so time) must move and in which it must repose. There every age—all necessary relations and persons and desires and beauty and individuality and oneness—is perfected (sec. 4.3). To demand that God's creative act adhere to the strictures of mere finitude, of time, of seriality, of phenomena, is to perform the primordial error anew. In Maximus's grand vision, creation is a finished work of God only when it no longer exists merely *as* created nature. The truth of creation, the only true creation, is therefore nothing less than the mutual and total interpenetration of God and the world.

Conclusion

The Whole Mystery of Christ

RECAPITULATION

I have tried to justify and to perform a literal interpretation of Maximus's declaration that "the Word of God, very God, wills that the mystery of his Incarnation be actualized always and in all things" (*Amb.* 7.22). I admit that the justification lies mostly in the success of the performance. There is some prima facie warrant for this performance in the very fact that Maximus himself never qualifies this statement (or the many others documented and discussed throughout) in the way nearly all his later commentators do. Not once does Maximus say, for instance, that the mystery of the Word's Incarnation into all the world differs from the mystery wrought in Jesus Christ.[1] Maximus never says the Word is somehow more or differently immanent or present to Christ than he is in the *logoi* of every creature—even though many had and would after.[2] As far as my exegetical argument goes, that is a negative point in my favor.

But I also pursued two positive and more substantive points. On the one hand, I tried to show that Maximus views the logic of creation as the logic of Christ. On the other, I explained how this identification accounts for and even necessitates many of the putatively hyperbolic or extreme or anomalous aspects of Maximus's thought (especially on deification and the Fall). In the first instance, I can state my argument in three contentions. For Maximus, (1) God's Incarnation in the middle of history reveals a logic that differs from all other conceptions of vertical causality, particularly Neoplatonism's; call this "Christo-logic" (chapter 1). (2) The peculiarities of Christo-logic appear in and adequately explain creation's peculiarities: its beginning *ex nihilo* (chapter 2) and end in deification (chapter 3), as well as the current counterfeit, phenomenal world, which nevertheless contains the *logoi* of God's one true creation already begun and destined for consummation in the whole mystery of Christ (chapter 4). (3) Since therefore Christo-logic constitutes the literal meaning of "Incarnation," and since that same logic is creation's—then "Creation is Incarnation" states the literal truth of Maximus's vision.

As I made this somewhat rigidly linear case, I had numerous occasions to garner credibility for my interpretation by indicating how it clarifies many basic anomalies in Maximus's theology. If God, in and as the Word, can make himself hypostatically identical to that from which he infinitely differs by nature; and if that basic element of Christo-logic applies to the entire God-world relation—then this resolves the apparent contradiction between the assertion that while uncreated and created natures bear absolutely no common property, created nature proceeds from uncreated nature alone (secs. 2.2–5). This is precisely the lesson Eriugena learned from Maximus. Again, if Maximus really conceives creation as Incarnation, then his famous *tantum-quantum* principle—which claims that in deification we become God to the *same* extent that God became human—is not only audacious but literally true (sec. 3.1). Or take his doctrine of grace. For Maximus grace is at once a power whose act has no relation to our nature and a power that is innate to created nature. But if that power is the very Word in creatures, the Word who makes himself identical to creatures even as he still bears his divine properties—and so becomes the supranatural and sole medium between us and divinity—then the apparently nonsensical aporia dissolves (sec. 3.2).

Or again, consider a particularly odd feature of Maximus's thought, namely that this phenomenal world lapsed "at the very moment it came to be." If creation is the whole mystery of Christ, the perfect realization of the Word's Incarnation always and in all things, then Maximus's nearly unprecedented view of the Fall does not at all render evil coextensive with creation. The world that began in free fall is not yet the actual world (sec. 4.1). Nor are the phenomenological strictures of temporality the final truth of phenomena (sec. 4.3). That truth, that one creative act of the Trinity that makes a world from nothing, is Jesus Christ. Creation from nothing is nothing else but the communication of idioms between God and the world. Creation is the fundamental coincidence of the most extreme natural opposites. Yet God, who wills not merely some abstract natural order but every face, every atom, every particle, every true and good and beautiful moment and thing and event—that God, Maximus teaches, has abased himself to such a degree that he receives even the false opposites we illicitly incarnate in and as this world of devastation. He thereby overcomes our false world in the very act whereby he creates the true world. In the historical Incarnation the Son becomes the principles of both judgment and providence, of failure and perfection, of suffering and salvation. So utterly ineffable is his love for us that he does not even create the world apart from us. And he is patient with us as we gestate in the womb of this world, which is also the womb of his Mother, as we learn obedience through suffering—for he did too. But only because we needed it (sec. 4.2).

THE WHOLE MYSTERY OF CHRIST

Suppose the vision thus depicted really was Maximus's. There is no denying its speculative élan. Were one to discover this vision relayed in the books of other kinds of thinkers—those of the speculative idealists, say—the Christian theologian might be tempted to detect clear divergences from what he or she regards as the rightful parameters of traditional or conciliar Christian thought. Indeed, I have heard more than a few times the understandable and predictable objection: But does this not do away with the absolutely fundamental distinction between the Creator and the creature? Do you not risk confusing categories here? How can the uncreated and infinite be in any way *identical* to the created and finite? At which point I am tempted in turn to quote Hegel, that specter whose speculative vision I met only after being warned that this reading of Maximus sounded a bit like him.

We must long since have finished with such categories. The usual practice, however, is to base oneself on them in order to oppose the concept, the idea, rational cognition. These categories are employed entirely uncritically, in a wholly artless fashion, just as if Kant's *Critique of Pure Reason* were nonexistent, a book that put them to the test and arrived in its own way at the result that they can serve only for the cognition of phenomena and not of the truth. In religion, however, one is not dealing with phenomena but with the absolute content. How totally improper, indeed tasteless, it is that categories of this kind are adduced against philosophy, as if one could say something novel to philosophy or to any educated person in this way, as if anyone who has not totally neglected his education would not know that the finite is not the infinite, that subject is different from object, immediacy different from mediation. Yet this sort of cleverness is brought forward triumphantly and without a blush, as if here one has made a discovery.[3]

There is of course no need to make Maximus into a mere proto-Hegel. But Hegel's point here remains relevant for the natural objections to Maximus's vision as I have understood and presented it. It will not do simply to repeat what Maximus never disputes—that, for instance, since the uncreated is not the created, God could never enjoy essential identity with the world he makes from nothing. Maximus even intensifies their natural contrast by denying any commonality between them whatsoever (secs. 1.3, 2.2). But Maximus knows that every attempt to conceive the God-world relation according to the abstract logic of nature or essence will necessarily (if unreflectively) introduce their dialectical, mutual determination, so that really both categories remain finite even as one of them is "infinite" (secs. 1.4, 2.3). Thus Maximus knows what Hegel claims few do: "That these forms [e.g., finite vs. infinite, subject vs. object, and so forth] are different everyone knows; but that these determinations are still at the same time inseparable is another matter."[4] You cannot meaningfully predicate infinity of God without simultaneously referring to infinity's negation, the finite. The abstract meaning of infinity is itself negatively determined by the concept of finitude. Abstract infinity remains a finite predicate, since it positively depends for its sense on its *not being* whatever we mean by "finite." While these categories are indeed different, they are also inseparable. Their very difference unites them.

We naturally resort to these dialectical pairs because it is more intuitive to grasp at a fragment than to aim for the whole. Grasping at a fragment is in itself harmless. Problems arise, at least from the perspective of Maximian Christo-logic, when we wish to absolutize the part as if it were the whole. This is no less true when we try to do so negatively. If, I mean, we were to propose an abstract but absolute axiom that proscribed all claims of a God-world identity even before we investigated just what sort of identity was meant, this would be just as much an instance of absolutizing a part as anything else (here "finitude" as *opposed* to "infinity," or "created" as *opposed* to "uncreated"). One point Hegel's remark reveals about Maximus, I submit, is that the boldness of Maximus's speculative vision and asseverations might be the greatest index of his profound spiritual humility before the whole mystery of Christ.

Maximus lets the Logos's self-disclosure in the historical Incarnation instruct us as to what is finally logical, possible, and actual. It is true that this perfection of logic, as it were, does not occur merely on the level of what is abstractly logical, possible, and actual. But Maximus's Christo-logic does insist that what is abstractly impossible is not actually impossible. Nor is it impossible for speculative logic, perfected by the Incarnate Logos as faith, to see this mystery for itself. "Christ" does not name a genus. Neither does "Christ" name an "individual."[5] That is a crucial point. Maximus denies genus and individual of Christ because both presume Christ can be adequately conceived according to the logic of substance or nature (which, admittedly, happens to predetermine the very form of basic predication: "X is Y," where Y names some qualification of the subject *qua* instance). If you say Christ is a genus, then you make the sheer fact of Christ an abstract principle or form. If you say Christ is an individual, where "individual" denotes a mere instance of some formal principle, then you do the same, oddly enough, but from the bottom up. In that case, the fact of Christ reduces to a mere instance of some repeatable, higher principle.

Perhaps this is why many prefer to make Christ an exception to the logic of creation rather than its rule.[6] That, they think, is the best way to protect his primacy. Only as an exception is Christ exceptional. But as I indicated before, that very judgment presumes some canon of exceptionality, doesn't it? It appears to know the conditions that must obtain for Christ to be the exception he is. It presumes, for instance, that what is exceptional bears a contrary relation to what is repeatable, as a particular is particular precisely to the extent it is not universal. Thus it seems even to presume some kind of antagonism between particularity and universality, the unrepeatable and the repeatable, the primary and the rest. When Maximus denies that Christ expresses either genus or individual, he means precisely to deny that *any* formal judgment adequately accounts for the whole mystery of Christ. Christ is no form or nature or essence, neither mere principle nor mere instance. He is at least these: he obviously bears a form (two or three, depending on how you count) and is a particular instance (in first-century Palestine).

But his "is" entails more. It entails his "who," his hypostasis, his person, *him*. Christ is neither mere individual nor mere genus because the genus-individual relation is purely formal, and Christ is more than either of his forms or natures. If then we assert that the mystery of Christ *must be* unrepeatable in order to be exceptional, "exceptional" here still means particular. Particularity predicates a formal relation and is therefore not the final or even the main criterion of Christ's exceptionality. Rather, Christ is exceptional precisely because he can *be* both universal and particular in his own person (sec. 1.2). No surprise there. If his "composed hypostasis" is the identity "to a supreme degree" of the greatest imaginable "extremes"—of created and uncreated natures—it is not so remarkable that Christ is also the very identity of all merely created particularity and universality.[7] He therefore does not need to be unrepeatable to be exceptional. His exceptionality lies in the fact that the very mystery he *is*, is repeatable in a nonformal way in and as all creation.

If the principle of *creatio ex nihilo* is manifest and actualized in the very event of the historical Incarnation, then Christ would prove so primary that the truth of his mystery would occur both particularly and universally. In fact, he would be the fundamental and concrete identity of every formal principle and every possible instance. A more exceptional reality is rather difficult to conceive.

For Maximus Christ determines the very limits of theological predication. The Word of God is both unmade and made. Being made and being unmade are essential predicates. That is, "created" and "uncreated" qualify natures.[8] They are predicated of hypostases only to the extent that hypostases are really identical to the natures of which "created" and "uncreated" are predicated. And so the Word, the second person of the Trinity, "*made* himself man."[9] He is himself both subject and object, agent and recipient. If one wished to "clarify" this statement by adding, say, a *secundum humanitatem*, that would be correct so far as it went. But it would not be the whole truth of Christ. The whole Christ is the hypostasis who is both created and uncreated natures in a manner that no essential predicate can capture; Christ's hypostasis is the concrete identity of both natures. If he is the "is" of both natures, then whatever logic forbids one nature's abstract predicate from being properly predicated of the other nature cannot really and finally forbid this of Christ. It can indeed properly forbid it. But that proves of little consequence, since Christ names a fact that exceeds what seems to us naturally proper anyhow.

Maximus's Christo-logic—and arguably Chalcedon's—actually requires what we might call "properly improper predication." In John 20:17, for example, Christ speaks of "your God and my God, your Father and my Father." Maximus knows that "when I contemplate the difference of the natures, and mentally conceptualize their distinction [τὴν αὐτῶν κατ' ἐπίνοιαν ποιοῦμαι διάκρισιν]," Christ says these things improperly according to nature.[10] For "the Father is neither the God of the Word nor the Father of the flesh." And yet the "whole" hypostasis of the Word is both God and flesh. The fact of Christ demands a "reversal" or "inversion" "'with respect to what may be properly said' [κυρίως] and what may 'not properly be said' [οὐ κυρίως]."[11] Abstract natures admit of what is generally "proper" to predicate in a given case. But for Maximus the "unconfused reality" (τὴν ἀσύγχυτον ὕπαρξιν) of the created and uncreated natures—which the whole Christ is—makes it proper to predicate improperly:[12] to say of one and the same reality that it is both mortal and immortal, passible and impassible, created and uncreated. In principle the first predicate cannot be predicated of what the second is predicated of. But Christ's truth is no mere principle—not even the principle of his Godhead (abstractly conceived). It is not muddled thinking, then, to say that in Christ "God created himself" any more than it is to say "God died." Really, if all we said was that "God created himself *according to his human nature*," and said nothing much more, we would fall rather swiftly into muddled thinking of another sort. There is no such *thing*, after all, as an "according to human nature." There is only the one God-human Jesus Christ. In all this Maximus reveals himself a champion of Cyril's old worry that many, captivated by dialectical abstraction, "speak with undue precision" (especially of Christ's sufferings), "as if they separate [his humanity] from the Word and set it apart by itself."[13]

Now apply this Christo-logical predication to the entire God-world relation. The only way we fall into either idolatrous pantheism or world-denying theopanism in affirming the literal truth of "God is the world" is if we assume a priori that creation is not Incarnation. That assumption could arise from an obsession with the way divinity as such overwhelms us as being ever greater than any similarity we might note between uncreated and created nature.[14] For if creation is Incarnation—if creation's logic is the whole Christ—then what is naturally improper to predicate of the world determines the world's whole truth no more than the fact that corpses do not rise from the dead determines the truth of Christ's resurrected flesh—which is to say not at all. Overly quick and unreflective labels like "pantheist" or "theopanist" are just so many ways to assert that creation could never be Incarnation. But assertion is not demonstration.

One often hears that a major achievement of Nicene orthodoxy was that it articulated and fixed the unbridgeable ontological gap between the created and the uncreated. Yet too many have concluded, from the great labor Nicene theologians undertook first to make an absolute distinction between created and uncreated natures and then to push the Son on the latter side of the divide, that Christianity's profoundest genius was to recognize this absolute natural difference between God and the world.[15] This story misses the fairly evident reverse implication of fixing the Son on the side of the uncreated: that same Son, very God, is *also a creature*. No truly Chalcedonian Christo-logic can fail to notice that the more you make Christ's two natures differ, the more you must simultaneously admit the utterly new way God was identical to "being created." Making the Son very God also makes very God a creature. Total symmetry in natural principle, utter identity in concrete fact, modal and actual perichoresis in final condition—anything less is, by the canons of Christo-logic detailed in this study, one-sided to the point of distorting the truth of the matter.

On this telling, Christianity's genius is rather that it conceives the most absolute natural difference between God and the world only *through* their ineffable and hypostatic identity, such that neither created nor uncreated nature need forfeit anything of its own modal or essential integrity in the final union of all things, when "God is all in all" (1 Cor. 15:28). And that, perhaps, is what Maximus finally teaches us: that God, precisely in order to "save" or "preserve" even the most apparently incidental attribute of every last created being, must really *be* all things.

Major Christological developments always appear initially unbeliev-able, always a scandal.[16] Nothing less than the kenosis of God the Son, who in his ecstatic, indeed erotic love for creation became what he loved, could have disclosed the truth of the God-world relation. There yawns after all a "great chasm" that "separates the whole of nature that has come into being and is in a state of flux from that which is uncreated and at rest," as Gregory of Nazianzus put it.[17] But then, to come full circle to that insight Eriugena gleaned from Maximus and Dionysius, this same yawn-ing chasm not only is overcome but is made possible at all precisely be-cause God in infinite ecstasy "goes out of Himself in His providence for all beings, and is, as it were, spellbound by goodness, love, and longing, and is led down from His position above all and beyond all, to be in all."[18] Maximus adds the crucial insight: God's providence is Jesus Christ (sec. 4.2). Not only does God identify himself with and so generate the world; he offers himself even to the false world we have fabricated for ourselves.

> For the Word has shown that the one who is in need of having good done to him is God; for, he says to us, as long as you did it for one of these least ones, you did it for me—and God himself says this!— then, he will much more show that the one who can do good and who does it is truly God by grace and participation because he has taken on in happy imitation the energy and characteristic of his own doing good. And if the poor man is God, it is because of God's con-descension in becoming poor for us and in taking into himself the sufferings of each one sympathetically and "until the end of time," always suffering mystically through goodness in proportion to each one's suffering.[19]

God suffers in and with and as us because his personhood is infinite, and so he can, and his will is infinite love, so he wants to. Hence Maxi-mus can again match Hegel: the whole mystery of Christ has obliterated the finality of all our abstractions, positive and negative, and thereby re-vealed that the logic of creation culminates in a truth beyond all dialecti-cal truth. When at length the Word who is and is in all creation van-quishes all suffering, sin, ignorance, and natural limit—then at last the universe will be recapitulated in him, truly "enhypostasized in him."[20] Then at last will the world be created.

This is because everything that is now reckoned by us to be truth is in fact a type, and the *shadow* and *image* of the greater Word. For the Word, who created all things, and who is in all things according to the relation of present to future [Ὁ ἐν ὅλοις κατὰ τὸ παρὸν πρὸς τὸ μέλλον καὶ τῶν ὅλων ποιητικὸς Λόγος], is comprehended as both in type and in truth, in which He is present both in being and manifestation, and yet He is and is manifested in absolutely nothing, for inasmuch as He transcends the present and the future, He transcends both type and truth, for He contains nothing that might be considered contrary to Him. But truth has a contrary: falsehood. Therefore the Word in whom the universe is gathered transcends the truth, and also, insofar as He is man and God, He truly transcends all humanity and divinity [Ὑπὲρ ἀλήθειαν ἄρα ὁ πρὸς ὃν τὰ πάντα συνάγεται Λόγος, καὶ αὖθις, ὡς ἄνθρωπος καὶ Θεὸς ὑπάρχων, καὶ ὑπὲρ πᾶσαν ὢν ἀληθῶς ἀνθρωπότητά τε καὶ θεότητα].[21]

ANALYTIC APPENDIX
OF KEY CONCEPTS

Near the start of Maximus's *Dispute with Pyrrhus*, engaging the once-patriarch of Constantinople and monenergist-monothelite proponent, Maximus inveighs against conceptual obscurity in Christology. His recommendation is fairly intuitive: define your terms. "To state something and not first to distinguish the different meanings of what is being said invites confusion, and ensures that what is under investigation remains obscure, which is foreign to a man of learning."[1] Maximus counseled his own habit. A number of his *epistola* and *opuscula* are mere lists of definitions: "Various definitions" (*Opusc.* 14/*Add.* 21), "Definitions of Distinction" (*Opusc.* 17), "Definitions of Union" (*Opusc.* 18), "Definitions of the Will" (*Opusc.* 26b/*Add.* 24), "Definitions of Activity" (*Opusc.* 27/*Add.* 25), "On Quality, Property, and Difference, to Theodore, Priest in Mazara" (*Opusc.* 21), and so forth. Often too Maximus inserts analytic definitions of crucial concepts in the course of extended dogmatic and polemical argumentation.[2] So important were precise definitions for grasping Maximus's thought that either he himself or some astute reader attached logical compendia to his corpus, short chapters on the ὅροι of Aristotelian categories and Porphyry's *quinque voces*—sometimes even outfitted with diagrams mapping the subtle relations among them.[3]

And so I furnish here a restricted list of significant terms, ones that my argument takes up again and again. The list derives mainly from Maximus's own *Opusculum* 14, though I supplement it with a few other significant terms. It serves two purposes. First, it is a reference guide the reader may find useful at various points throughout the argument.

Chapters 1 and 2 especially rely on Maximus's technical use of these terms, and so it seems helpful to be able to repair back to this list when things get dicey. Second, this list constitutes something like a general (not exhaustive) optics of Maximian metaphysics. Here one spies the fundamental principles isolated and related in the form of an esquisse. This courts the liability, true, of extracting the principles from their native soil where they flourish organically (in Christology proper, for instance). Yet doing so, I hope, also trains the reader's eye to detect these principles when she comes upon them in their natural habitat—in the thick, often vexing density of Christological and Trinitarian metaphysics. Bones and animate flesh together make a living being. Here lie the bones.

Essence (οὐσία) or **nature** (φύσις)

"The same thing."[4] Always in Maximus correlated to the "common" (κοινόν) and "universal" (καθόλου).[5] These disclose "what" something is rather than simply "that" or "how" or "who" it is. A specific "nature" or species is a genus (τὸ γενικόν) with differentiae (e.g., human or angelic), and this specification has its own principle (*logos*) that makes it what it is and no other.[6] In this Aristotelian and Porphyrian sense, an "essence" or "nature" is also a "form" (εἶδος).[7] Though these are always *in themselves* "universal" or "common" or a "form"—which therefore must be known in several individuals[8]—Maximus does know "proper" or "individual" or even "particular" natures.[9] But a nature is not particularized or individualized *in itself.* It must be so determined by another, positive, metaphysical principle—that of hypostasis.

Hypostasis (ὑπόστασις) or **person** (πρόσωπον)

"The same thing."[10] Always in Maximus correlated to the "particular" (μερικόν) and "proper"—or better, the "idiomatic" (ἴδιον)[11]—though not simply *reducible* to particularity or an individual assemblage of properties.[12] These disclose first "that," then "how," and most fundamentally (for rational beings) "who" one is.[13] A hypostasis is therefore the concrete existent, the existential *fact* of this or that singular being; it bears no formal or essential content as such.[14] Unlike nature, hypostasis "exists in itself."[15] In the singularity of hypostasis both particularity and concrete existence are a single fact. But the *fact* of a singular is not yet its *principle* (cf. "Logoi" below). Hypostasis is not the principle of individuation but the thing individuated. A hypostasis stands "before" or "under,"[16] as it were, any sign of its distinctive existence; indeed, it just *is* this or that distinctive existence. Maximus presses this point with special vigor in Christology, where predicating number of Christ (e.g., "two natures," "one person") reveals nothing about the thing numbered except that there is something there to be numbered. The referent already *is* by some prior principle—however and whatever it is—before it is recognized: especially so for a singular existent that is first there, then numbered.[17] In sum, hypostasis as such bears at least five distinctive features:

1. It is always associated with the *particular*, proper, and idiomatic (as opposed to the common, universal, and generic).
2. It presents no formal, essential, or natural content; its content is *not predicable*.[18]
3. It is nevertheless a *positive* ontological and existential reality; it *determines* "to be" (τὸ εἶναι) and "nature/essence" as their irreducible, most singular determination.[19] This determination itself betrays two properties:

    3.1. Hypostasis *unifies* realities that differ essentially. In this sense it is considered the concrete "whole," a determinate unity of essentially distinct realities.[20]
    3.2. Hypostasis *distinguishes* an individual from every other. Thus arises a typical definition of hypostasis, "an essence with idioms."[21] So it is too that the "hypostatic principle" (not strictly the hypostasis itself) is the deepest ground of absolute "difference."[22]

4. It is the basic existential *fact* yet not itself the principle of singular (or specific) facts. It *possesses* an eternal principle that makes it such.[23]
5. It never exists separate from an essence or nature, so that although it does not itself possess predicable or formal content (2), it is *not actual* except through and "in" some nature (see "en-natured" below); for nature bears the *powers* of activities (e.g., Paul exists only as man, and as man he is actual only through the powers proper to his human nature—will, reason, sensation, etc.).

***Together**, "nature/essence" and "hypostasis/person" constitute the two most fundamental elements in Maximus's metaphysics—from Trinity to

Christ to human beings to the cosmos. In no case does an abstract nature or hypostasis as such exist, though each bears a principle as such. Every real thing is a tapestry woven with these two ontological threads. Concisely: although separate in principle, nature/essence and hypostasis/person are everywhere *irreducible* to, *inseparable* from, and *indifferent* with respect to each other. Irreducible, since their respective principles differ completely (nature = common; hypostasis = singular). Inseparable, since neither actually exists without the other. Indifferent, since in their real inseparability neither's principle or consequent mode suffers any diminution whatever. All three features surface here as indicated:

> It is plain that a nature could never at any time be without a hypostasis, though nature is not hypostasis: that which is not without hypostasis is not itself contemplated as a hypostasis, since these are not convertible [**irreducible**]. For, on the one hand, the hypostasis *is* in every way also a nature, just as the figure is in every way a body. For a hypostasis cannot be perceived without a nature, just as, again, a figure or color [cannot be perceived] without a body [**inseparable**]. On the other hand, a nature is *not* in every way also a hypostasis. For the nature bears the principle of being common, but the hypostasis has also the principle of being in itself. And the nature bears only the principle of species, but the hypostasis manifests the certain "someone" too [**indifferent**].[24]

Principle (λόγος) and Mode (τρόπος)

General Senses

Both terms carry a broad and plastic conceptual range. *Logos* can mean an "account"[25] or (as in Plato) "definition,"[26] "word," "discourse," "meaning," "reason," "motive," "immanent rationality," "principle."[27] The last of these senses is especially prevalent in Maximus. His famous doctrine that all things are created by and bear their proper *logoi* quite clearly accents the causal or metaphysical sense.[28] Note even here, though, the rather loose sense of "principle." There is a "principle" for everything. Every creature is *what* it is through its essential or natural or formal principle, which is common to every member of that species. But there is also a principle of every hypostasis as such.[29] In both cases an alteration of a thing's principle spells its obliteration.[30] A *logos* in this sense, then, is what grounds the unbroken identity or integrity of that for which it is principle.[31] In this sense too a *logos* is the immanent, logical *structure* that determines what is possible for universal and particular being. Hence it appears in close relation to (or as determinative of) a thing's *power* or even *potency*, that by which an agent first *is* and then *acts*.[32]

Tropos too stretches. It bends flexibly much like the English "way," "manner," or "mode." A thing's *tropos* is the *way* it is, *how* it exists in fact. Yet this "how" does not always refer to a concrete reality or to some dimension of it. Maximus can speak of the "five modes" of contemplation,[33] the "modes" of divine providence and judgment,[34] the "mode" of Christ's union,[35] the "mode of exchange" between his natures (not the same as the "mode of union"), and so on.[36] The latter crystallizes the point well enough: though there is but one "unified mode of the Lord's activities," which itself manifests the hypostatic "mode of union," each of Christ's natures still retains the mode proper to its essential principle.[37] Mode, like principle, receives conceptual determination solely from what it is the mode *of*.

Two Important Relations

(1) *Logos-tropos*. Here we have an axiomatic pair in Maximus's thought. Its likely provenance is Cappadocian-inspired Trinitarian theology.[38] God is one by virtue of his λόγος οὐσίας ("principle of essence"), three by his τρόπος ὑπάρξεως.[39] The former, principle, obviously signifies what is common to divinity. The latter, mode, especially to the extent that it connotes *how* divine person comes to be—its characteristic *origin*[40]—indicates the real distinction of hypostases in God.[41] Notice the link to nature (common, *logos*) and hypostasis (proper, *tropos*). Thus it comes as no surprise that Maximus perceives this pair too, first manifest in God himself, as permeating all creation. A miracle, for instance, does not innovate the natural *principle* of a thing lest that thing desist as *what* it essentially is. Instead, the *mode* corresponding to that nature alters *how* it persists and acts in concrete existence.[42] Water did not mutate into wine. Rather, the water began to behave identically to wine, to take on a wine-mode (i.e., qualities like color and taste). It remained water in *principle*, for God never destroys what he wills to be, and a thing's *logos* is precisely God's will for it.[43] Likewise in Christology: Christ preserves the *principles* proper to each of his natures even as their *modes*, now in hypostatic union with one another, are both natural *and* "supranatural."[44]

(2) *Person-mode*. Although person or hypostasis everywhere corresponds to what Skliris calls "the hypostatical order of particularity,"[45] the order of individual modalities, person and mode are not simply reducible to each other.[46] Especially clear is *Opusculum* 10. Here Maximus criticizes the idea that we should attribute Christ's activity strictly and directly to his hypostasis:

> For he obscured and in a certain sense destroyed the principle for these things [hypostasis/person vs. essence/nature] by assigning to the person *qua* person the activity that characterizes the nature rather than [assigning to the person] the "how" and the "what sort of mode" of its [i.e., nature's] fulfillment [οὐχὶ τὸν πῶς καὶ ὁποῖον τῆς κατ' αὐτὴν ἐκβάσεως τρόπον], according to which one recognizes the difference between those acting and those being acted upon, possessing these with or against nature. For each of us acts principally as *what* we are rather than as *who*—that is, [we act] as man. And as *someone*, say Paul or Peter, he gives expression to the mode of the activity typified by him through impartation, perhaps, or by progress in this way or that according to his dispositive judgment [κατὰ γνώμην]. Hence, on the one hand, we recognize difference among persons in the way of conduct [ἐν μὲν τῷ τρόπῳ . . . κατὰ τὴν πρᾶξιν], and on the other, [we recognize] invariability in the *logos* of the natural activity. For one is not more or less endowed with activity or reason [ἐνεργὴς ἢ λογικός]; we all have the same *logos* and its natural activity.[47]

**Summary.* We can now discern several discrete yet inseparable metaphysical elements of a concrete person.[48] This thumbnail presumes all the features detailed above.

1. A *principle* of person is the immanent cause and ground of
2. the concrete *person* (hypostasis), which itself must possess
3. a universal *essence*/nature/species bearing its proper principle (hence power), and
4. the person imbues this essence with the *individual determination* she is, which
5. instances this universal essence in a *singular mode of activity*, and
6. this activity is simultaneously universal (*qua* natural) and individual (*qua* personal).

Nature and hypostasis, universal and particular, *logos* and *tropos*—these pairs must converge to establish any existent. Nor is it simply that each term of a pair couples like two atoms in a covalent bond; each individual configuration (and indeed the whole cosmos) presupposes a bonding of the bond pairs themselves. It is as if the pairs shared the same "electronegativity" (i.e., divine will and power manifest as each thing's constitutive *logos*) and as if this very sameness just *was* the concrete, hypostatic "whole" of every being and of the cosmos. The final two terms insist upon this interpenetration of metaphysical binaries.

Enhypostasized (τὸ ἐνυπόστατον)
This is an essence or nature or species considered *in* the individual hypostasis as that hypostasis's very own essence. In fact, Maximus openly states that essences *only* exist in this way: you never find an abstract nature floating about. And so he employs a couplet some have claimed never surfaces in the fathers: "The fact that a nature is *not without hypostasis* [τὸ μὴ ἀνυπόστατον] does not make it a hypostasis, but *enhypostasized* [ἐνυπόστατον]."[49] An enhypostasized reality is a nature or essence as it exists singularly in an individual, and, though it retains its universality[50] (all individuals that belong to it possess and perform its common properties), it exists in no other way. A concise definition: "An enhypostasized reality is what is common according to essence or form, which really subsists in the individuals under it and is not contemplated in mere thought. Or again an enhypostasized reality is what, along with another reality that differs according to essence, co-constitutes and co-subsists for the composition and generation of one person and one hypostasis. And it is never recognized by itself."[51]

Enessenced (τὸ ἐνούσιον)
Conversely, no hypostasis really exists except as possessing and therefore actualizing itself through or *in* a nature. This is the "en-natured" or "en-essenced." A hypostasis cannot be the individual instance of some*thing*—a "what" and "how"—unless it is the instance *of* a universal essence. Peter is not at all if he is not human by nature, while, to juxtapose the previous term, there is no real "human nature" that is not actually a Peter or Paul or Mary (or really, the sum total of all human beings). If a nature manifests itself only in and through its immanent

presence in individuals, a person subsists only as the subject that determines and expresses her nature in her proper, unrepeatable way.[52] Another concise definition: "An en-essenced reality is not only what is contemplated as possessing in itself the assemblage of idioms according to which it is known as something [distinguished] from another—but also as what really possesses the common of the essence."[53]

NOTES

Notes to Foreword

1. Hans-Georg Gadamer, *Truth and Method*, 2nd rev. ed., revised translation by Joel Weinsheimer and Donald G. Marshall (London: Continuum, 2004), 305–6.

2. Mikhail M. Bakhtin, "Response to a Question from the *Novy Mir* Editorial Staff," in *Speech Genres and Other Late Essays*, trans. Vern W. McGee (Austin: University of Texas Press, 2013), 4.

Notes to Preface

1. Eriugena, *Joannis Scoti Versio Ambiguorum S. Maximi*, praef., ed. E. Jeauneau, CCSG 18 (Turnhout: Brepols, 1988), 3–4, lines 25–37; my translation.

2. Eriugena, *Periphyseon* III.17, trans. John J. O'Meara, *Periphyseon (The Division of Nature)* (Montreal: Bellarmin, 1987), 161–63: "Proinde non duo a se ipsis distantia debemus intelligere deum et creaturam sed unum et id ipsum."

3. Eriugena, *Periphyseon* III.7, trans. O'Meara, 76–77: "Omnia in verbo dei non solum aeterna verum etiam ipsum {verbum} esse." It is surely significant that Eriugena overtly credits this precise insight to Maximus's *Amb.* 7.

4. Eriugena, *Periphyseon* III.7, trans. O'Meara, 70–71.

5. Eriugena, *Periphyseon* III.16, trans. O'Meara, 144–45.

6. Cf. *Amb. ad Ioh.*, prol., PG 91, 1061A. On Maximus's use of this genre, see Paul M. Blowers, *Exegesis and Spiritual Pedagogy in Maximus the Confessor: An Investigation of the "Questiones ad Thalassium"* (Notre Dame, IN: University of Notre Dame Press, 1991), and Peter van Deun, "Maximus the Confessor's Use of Literary Genres," in *The Oxford Handbook of Maximus the Confessor*, ed. Pauline Allen and Bronwen Neil (Oxford: Oxford University Press, 2015), 275.

7. Already in 1915 Sergei Leontevich Epifanovich, the first major modern scholar of Maximus, identified Maximus's unique genius in his application of the Incarnation to virtually every other dimension of existence; see the discussion in Joshua Lollar, "Reception of Maximian Thought in the Modern Era," in Allen and Neil, *Oxford Handbook*, 565–67.

8. *Amb.* 7.22, PG 91, 1084CD: "Βούλεται γὰρ ἀεὶ καὶ ἐν πᾶσιν ὁ τοῦ Θεοῦ Λόγος καὶ Θεὸς τῆς αὐτοῦ ἐνσωματώσεως ἐνεργεῖσθαι τὸ μυστήριον."

9. Eric D. Perl, "Metaphysics and Christology in Maximus Confessor and Eriugena," in *Eriugena: East and West—Papers of the Eighth International Colloquium of the Society for the Promotion of Eriugenian Studies*, ed. Bernard McGinn and Willemien Otten (Notre Dame, IN: University of Notre Dame Press, 1994), 253–79. Eriugena openly denies the equation of creation and the historical Incarnation (*Periphyseon* III.17, trans. O'Meara, 162–63).

10. Bernard Lonergan, *Method in Theology* (1971; repr., Toronto: University of Toronto Press, 1990), 168.

11. Whether you move within the discipline of history from experience (research), to understanding (interpretation), to judging (history), to deciding (dialectics); or go back within theology proper from deciding (foundations), to judging (doctrines), to understanding (systematics), and again to experience (communications)—you are always taken up into the "spiral" of a "self-correcting process" spurred on by our natural desire to know. That is, when we try to understand *anything*, whether "texts" in history or their "objects" in theology, we are often spinning round the hermeneutical circle of parts to whole to parts to whole again; see Lonergan, *Method in Theology*, 159, 191–94, 208, passim.

12. See the concise summary of Elizabeth A. Clark, *History, Theory, Text: Historians and the Linguistic Turn* (Cambridge, MA: Harvard University Press, 2004), 1–2.

13. John Lukacs, "History and Physics, or the End of the Modern Age," in *Historical Consciousness: The Remembered Past* (1994; repr., New York: Routledge, 2017), 273–315.

14. Lukacs, "History and Physics," 287; Heisenberg's emphasis.

15. This is why Thomas Kuhn's book has become a classic in the humanities; see his *The Structure of Scientific Revolutions*, 3rd ed. (1962; repr., Chicago: University of Chicago Press, 1996).

16. See the meditation, largely on *Amb.* 71, of Paul M. Blowers, "On the 'Play' of Divine Providence in Gregory Nazianzen and Maximus the Confessor," in *Re-reading Gregory of Nazianzus: Essays on History, Theology, and Culture*, ed. Christopher Beeley (Washington, DC: Catholic University of America Press, 2012), 183–201.

17. Cf. George MacDonald, "The Fantastic Imagination," in *The Complete Fairy Tales* (1893; repr., New York: Penguin Books, 1999), 1–15.

18. The advocacy of a strict historicism is a common if natural tendency re-hearsed, for instance, in many introductions to translations of Maximus's work—namely, to lament that this or that theme in Maximus's writings has been unduly privileged above other important themes so that we are left with something less than the whole portrait of the man. But of course there is no reason to think pre-senting a portrait of any truly inspired thinker must always be the goal of any study of him or her, and still less that a whole "historical" portrait actually delivers the whole potency of the thinker's thought. This would even betray Maximus's own approach to prior significant authorities.

19. *Amb. ad Ioh.*, prol., PG 91, 1065A.

20. *Q. Thal.* 1.2.8, ed. Carlos Laga and Carlos Steel, *Quaestiones ad Thalas-sium I*, CCSG 7 (Turnhout: Brepols, 1980), 23: "For the divine word could never be circumscribed by a single individual interpretation, nor does it suffer confinement in a single meaning, on account of its natural infinity." Hence it is because Maximus deems Gregory's words divinely inspired that he can easily confront a literal contra-diction in Gregory (here confusing John the Evangelist with John the Baptist) in the same way that he would an absurdity in scripture itself: it "cannot be resolved by any means other than spiritual contemplation"; cf. *Amb.* 21.3, PG 91, 1244B.

21. Cyril O'Regan, "Von Balthasar and Thick Retrieval: Post-Chalcedonian Symphonic Theology," *Gregorianum* 77.2 (1996): 237 and 258.

22. Here I am influenced by Marc Bloch's "observe" versus "relay" distinc-tion; see his *The Historian's Craft: Reflections on the Nature and Uses of History and the Techniques and Methods of Those Who Write It* (1944; repr., Toronto: Random House, 1953), esp. 141f.

23. Paul M. Blowers, *Maximus the Confessor: Jesus Christ and the Trans-figuration of the World* (Oxford: Oxford University Press, 2016).

24. Élie Ayroulet, "La réception de Maxime le Confesseur à l'époque con-temporaine," *Théophilyon* 21.1 (2016): 74, my translation.

25. Lollar, "Reception," 570.

26. Ayroulet, "Réception," 89, my translation.

INTRODUCTION. The God-World Relation in
Modern Maximus Scholarship

1. This survey unfolds strictly in light of my own question and thesis. It is no generic survey of modern scholarship, of which there are several adequate re-ports. In chronological order: Polycarp Sherwood, "Survey of Recent Work on St. Maximus the Confessor," *Traditio* 20 (1964): 428–37; a tendentious one by Marcel Doucet, "Vues récentes sur les 'métamorphoses' de la pensée de saint Maxime le Confesseur," *Science et Esprit* 31.3 (1979): 269–302; Aidan Nichols,

O.P., *Byzantine Gospel: Maximus the Confessor in Modern Scholarship* (Edinburgh: T. & T. Clark, 1993), esp. the "Appendix: The Rediscovery of Maximus: A Brief History of Maximian Scholarship," 221–52; Andrew Louth, "Recent Research on St Maximus the Confessor: A Survey," *St Vladimir's Theological Quarterly* 42 (1998): 67–84; Peter van Deun, "Maxime le Confesseur: État de la question et bibliographie exhaustive," *Sacris Erudiri* 38 (1999): 485–573, and "Développements récents des recherches sur Maxime le Confesseur (1998–2009)," *Sacris Erudiri* 48 (2009): 97–167; Lollar, "Reception"; Ayroulet, "Réception."

2. Eric D. Perl, "Methexis: Creation, Incarnation, and Deification in Saint Maximus Confessor," (PhD diss., Yale University, 1991). See Louth's cautious but eager anticipation of Perl's doctoral thesis (Louth, "Recent Research," 81–82).

3. Perl, "Metaphysics and Christology."

4. Perl, "Methexis," chap. 6, "Participation and Incarnation" (esp. 184ff.).

5. Perl, "Methexis," 205.

6. Perl, "Methexis," 210–11.

7. Hans Urs von Balthasar, *Cosmic Liturgy: The Universe According to Maximus the Confessor*, 3rd ed., trans. Brian Daley, S.J. (1941; repr., San Francisco: Ignatius Press, 2003), 70.

8. See Balthasar, *Cosmic Liturgy*, 64, 113, and esp. 153f.

9. Nor do scholars who cite Perl do so mainly in demurral. The only monograph in the past several decades to treat my specific topic agrees that Perl's dissertation "represents a major contribution to the Maximus literature"; see Torstein Theodore Tollefsen, *The Christocentric Cosmology of St Maximus the Confessor* (Oxford: Oxford University Press, 2008), 17.

10. Melchisedec Törönen, *Union and Distinction in the Thought of St Maximus the Confessor* (Oxford: Oxford University Press, 2007), 1–6; Andrew Louth, "St Maximos' Doctrine of the *Logoi* of Creation," *Studia Patristica* 48 (2010): 80.

11. Brian Daley, "Translator's Foreword," in Balthasar, *Cosmic Liturgy*, 15; cf. Ayroulet, "Réception," 72–73.

12. So O'Regan, "Von Balthasar," 237: "Balthasar remains perfectly clear that Maximus is without equal. Maximus does not simply repeat; he fundamentally exceeds, both in the specific historical domain of post-Chalcedonian theology, as well as in his potential as a contemporary critical resource." See too Mark A. MacIntosh, *Christology from Within: Spirituality and the Incarnation in Hans Urs von Balthasar* (Notre Dame, IN: University of Notre Dame Press, 1996).

13. It is now generally acknowledged that Barth's rejection was of a piece with his wider repudiation of natural theology, which explains the accompanying vehemence in both the rejection of analogy in the *Dogmatics* and the acerbic contrapuntal tract against Brunner's natural theology called *Nein!*. That Barth was chiefly exercised about theological epistemology (faith and reason) also explains his acceptance of both Balthasar's and Söhngen's concession that the *analogia entis*

must find final epistemic justification in an *analogia fidei*; see Hans Urs von Balthasar, *The Theology of Karl Barth: Exposition and Interpretation.* trans. Edward T. Oakes (1951; repr., San Francisco: Ignatius Press, 1992), 31, 37, passim; and Gottlieb Söhngen, "Analogia fidei: Gottähnlichkeit allein aus Glauben?" *Catholica* 3 (1934): 113–36, and "Analogia fidei: Die Einheit in der Glaubenswissenschaft," *Catholica* 4 (1934): 176–208. For Barth's acceptance of these proposals, see his "Gespräche in Princeton I," 499, cited in Kenneth Oakes, "The Question of Nature and Grace in Karl Barth: Humanity as Creature and as Covenant-Partner," *Modern Theology* 23.4 (2007): 615. And for an updated and expansive account of these and related matters, see John R. Betz, "Translator's Introduction," in *Analogia Entis: Metaphysics: Original Structure and Universal Rhythm*, trans. John R. Betz and David Bentley Hart (1932; repr., Grand Rapids, MI: Eerdmans, 2014), 74f.

14. Balthasar, *Cosmic Liturgy*, 29.

15. Balthasar, *Cosmic Liturgy*, 207. Already in a letter from 1937, Balthasar can write to Emil Lerch: "This morning I put the finishing touches on a new two-hundred-page book about Maximus Confessor, the 'Hegel' of the Greek fathers and 'father' of Eriugena." Quoted in Manfred Lochbrunnner, *Hans Urs von Balthasar (1905–1988): Die Biographie eines Jahrhunderttheologen* (Würzburg: Echter, 2020), 178 (my translation). My thanks to Taylor Ross for the reference.

16. Balthasar, *Cosmic Liturgy*, 49, 63, 126, passim.

17. Hans Urs von Balthasar, *Theo-Drama: Theological Dramatic Theory*, vol. 3, *Dramatis Personae: Persons in Christ*, trans. Graham Harrison (1978; repr., San Francisco: Ignatius Press, 1992), 221–22.

18. Hans Urs von Balthasar, "Retrieving the Tradition: The Fathers, the Scholastics and Ourselves," trans. Edward T. Oakes, S.J., 1939, republished in *Communio* 24 (1997): 354.

19. Hans Urs von Balthasar, *Theo-Logic: Theological Logical Theory*, vol. 2, *Truth of God*, trans. Adrian J. Walker (1985; repr., San Francisco: Ignatius Press, 2004), 315–16.

20. I have not included here the important work of Lars Thunberg, whose basic vantage is Balthasar's. See his *Microcosm and Mediator: The Theological Anthropology of Maximus the Confessor*, 2nd ed. (Chicago: Open Court, 1995).

21. Sherwood, "Survey of Recent Work," 428.

22. Sherwood, "Survey of Recent Work," 435.

23. Sherwood, "Survey of Recent Work," 436, citing I.-H. Dalmais's review of Balthasar's second edition of *Cosmic Liturgy*, "Saint Maxime le Confesseur: Une synthèse théologique," *Vie Spirituelle* 107 (1962): 318.

24. Douglas Hedley, "Pantheism, Trinitarian Theism and the Idea of Unity: Reflections on the Christian Concept of God," *Religious Studies* 32.1 (1996): 61–77. It is striking to recall, though Hedley does not here, that Schelling had diagnosed and lamented this tendency already in 1809; see F. W. J. Schelling, *Philosophical*

Investigations into the Essence of Human Freedom, trans. and introd. Jeff Love and Johannes Schmidt (1809; repr., New York: State University of New York Press, 2006), 11: "It is an undeniably excellent invention that with such labels [as 'pantheism'] entire viewpoints are described all at once. If one has found the right label for a system, the rest falls into place of itself, and one is spared the effort of examining what is characteristic about it more meticulously. As soon as such labels are given, with their help even one who is ignorant can pass judgment on the most thought-through matters."

25. Torstein Tollefsen, "Did St Maximus the Confessor Have a Concept of Participation?" *Studia Patristica* 37 (2001): 618–25, which is a retort to Jean-Claude Larchet's view that Maximus lacks a proper concept of "participation"; see his *La divinisation de l'homme selon saint Maxime le Confesseur* (Paris: Cerf, 1996), 601f.

26. Carlos Steel, "Beyond the Principle of Contradiction? Proclus' 'Parmenides' and the Origin of Negative Theology," in *Die Logik des Transzendentalen: Festschrift für Jan A. Aertsen*, ed. Martin Pickavé (Berlin: De Gruyter, 2003), 594–99.

27. See Norman Russell, *The Doctrine of Deification in the Greek Patristic Tradition* (Oxford: Oxford University Press, 2004).

28. Balthasar himself often flags these developments; see *Cosmic Liturgy*, 64, 113, 153, passim. Some of the most interesting recent work in this vein comes from Johannes Zachhuber; see his "Christology after Chalcedon and the Transformation of the Philosophical Tradition: Reflections on a Neglected Topic," in *The Ways of Byzantine Theology*, ed. Mikonja Knezevic (Alhambra: Sebastian Press, 2015), 89–110, and *The Rise of Christian Theology and the End of Ancient Metaphysics: Patristic Philosophy from the Cappadocian Fathers to John of Damascus* (Oxford: Oxford University Press, 2020).

29. Tollefsen, *Christocentric Cosmology*, 216, is therefore right to say that in Christology proper the hypostatic identification of human and divine natures "makes participation possible." That is, "participation" is *not* the sufficient or whole description of created and uncreated natures in the domain of technical Christology.

30. Origen, *Comm. in Jo.* 2.17–18; see David L. Balas, "The Idea of Participation in the Structure of Origen's Thought: Christian Transposition of a Theme of the Platonic Tradition," in *Origeniana: Premier colloque international des études origéniennes*, ed. Henri Crouzel, Gennaro Lomiento, and Josep Rius-Camps (Bari: Istituto di letteratura cristiana antica, 1975), 263–65; see also Jordan Daniel Wood, "That and How *Perichoresis* Differs from Participation: The Case of Maximus Confessor," in *Platonism and Christian Thought in Late Antiquity*, ed. Panagiotis G. Pavlos et al. (London: Routledge, 2019), 220–36.

31. Tollefsen, *Christocentric Cosmology*, 191. Blowers, *Maximus the Confessor*, 136, has now also sided with these commentators against Törönen on this point.

32. Tollefsen, *Christocentric Cosmology*, 205.

33. Tollefsen, *Christocentric Cosmology*, 216.

34. Balthasar and Tollefsen represent the general current nearly all have followed, often expressing this current in the clearest ways. For instance, the final parts of Felix Heinzer's important work bind Maximus's Christology and cosmology under the concept of "Exemplarität." This indicates the same logic as analogy or participation. See Felix Heinzer, *Gottes Sohn als Mensch: Die Struktur des Menschseins Christi bei Maximus Confessor* (Freiburg: Universitätsverlag Freiburg/Schweiz, 1980), esp. 171ff.

35. Perl, "Metaphysics and Christology," esp. 260–61. So he rightly characterizes deification as the "enhypostatization" of the creature in the Word, as when "the creature receives God the Word as its hypostasis" (260). He also calls this "perfect participation in God" (260). Since participation is the natural relation between effect and cause, here creature and Creator, we would seem to be precisely where Maximus sees an annihilation of hypostasis: two beings with the same nature, say, by "perfect participation," could never become identical in hypostasis and remain two (cf. *Ep.* 15, PG 91, 549B).

36. That Maximus emphasizes the deification of human *persons* or hypostases rather than just human *nature* was a point pressed by W. Völker, *Maximus Confessor als Meister des geistlichen Lebens* (Wiesbaden: Fisteiner, 1965); see Lollar, "Reception," 573, and Ayroulet, "Réception," 78.

37. Evagrius, *Ep. fidei* (the *Great Letter to Melania*) 5, on which see sec. 3.4 below.

38. H. Straubinger, "Die Lehre des Patriarchen Sophronius von Jerusalem über die Trinität, die Inkarnation und die Person Christi: Mit besonderer Berücksichtigung in ihren Hauptpunkten zugleich verglichen mit den Sätzen des hl. Thomas," *Der Katholik*, 3rd ser., 35 (1907): 81–109, 175–98, 251–65. Nichols, *Byzantine Gospel*, 224, thence concludes that Dominican interest in Maximus is "by no means a merely formalistic *démarche* of the Thomistic revival, for real parallels exist."

39. See esp. the very useful Alain Riou, *Le monde et l'Église selon Maxime le Confesseur* (Paris: Beauchesne, 1973).

40. Juan-Miguel Garrigues, *Maxime le Confesseur: La charité, avenir divin de l'homme* (Paris: Beauchesne, 1976), 7, my translation.

41. Larchet, *Divinisation de l'homme*, 73–80 (and passim); see Ayroulet, "Réception," 81f., for a concise account of the controversy since the seventies.

42. Antoine Lévy, O.P., *Le créé et l'incréé: Maxime le Confesseur et Thomas d'Aquin* (Paris: Vrin, 2006). He later edited a volume dedicated to similar themes: *The Architecture of the Cosmos: St Maximus the Confessor, New Perspectives*, ed. Antoine Lévy et al., Schriften der Luther-Agricola-Gesellschaft 69 (Helsinki: Luther-Agricola, 2015).

43. This is the tack taken by Anna N. Williams, *The Ground of Union: Deification in Aquinas and Palamas.* Oxford: Oxford University Press, 1999.

44. This alludes to another important advance Lévy makes on his predecessors: he does not think, as Garrigues did, that Thomas had any meaningful exposure to Maximus's thought. John of Damascus is no substitute for Maximus. Indeed, the frequent Dominican fancy that John sufficiently mediates Maximus to Thomas and the West only betrays a palpable unfamiliarity with Maximus's own spirit and genius. See Lévy, *Créé et l'incréé*, 120–23.

45. Lévy, *Créé et l'incréé*, 422.

46. Lévy, *Créé et l'incréé*, 280.

47. Lévy, *Créé et l'incréé*, 422. He even goes as far as denying, with Garrigues, that Maximus thinks the historical Incarnation was predestined regardless of sin (430–31). In other words, just where Maximus seems most original—when he claims Incarnation is the ground and goal of the world (e.g., *Q. Thal.* 2, 22, and 60)—he really just agrees with Thomas, who permits and prefers the contrary (*ST* III, a. 1, q. 3, *resp*).

48. Lévy, *Créé et l'incréé*, 181. The immediate context is deification by grace, but Lévy's whole argument is that there is but one logic in the "three unions"—in creation (protology), in virtue (being-in-act), in deification (eschatology).

49. For the classic statement of Neoplatonic "double act," see Plotinus, *Enn.* V.4 [7] 2; cf. Eyjólfur Kjalar Emilsson, "Remarks on the Relation between the One and Intellect in Plotinus," in *Traditions of Platonism: Essays in Honour of John Dillon* (Aldershot: Ashgate, 1999), esp. 278–81; and Christian Rutten, "La doctrine des deux actes dans la philosophie de Plotin," *Revue Philosophique de la France et de l'Étranger* 146 (1956): 100–106.

50. Torstein Theodore Tollefsen, *Activity and Participation in Late Antique and Early Christian Thought* (Oxford: Oxford University Press, 2012), appears to adopt the much more philosophically problematic view (one not even Neoplatonists would permit) that God's creative activity might be conceived as following Aristotle's logic of first and second *energeia*. That is, the divine ideas are in God from eternity as "God's capacity to create" and then are actualized "in the creative act itself. . . . This would be Aristotle's second *energeia*" (96, on Gregory of Nyssa here but applied to Maximian *logoi* at 125). Despite Tollefsen's assurances (e.g., 101), I cannot see how this position avoids either horn of the following dilemma: (1) either the Aristotelian first/second act does really describe God's act of bringing creatures into participation in God's own activity, but then we have something like an unactualized potency in the essential power of the simple God—which seems absurd; (2) or God's act of creation—of sharing the divine *energeia* with participants—is *not* unqualifiedly Aristotelian exactly because it implies no inner perfection of the divine power as such, but then we remain with the Neoplatonic doctrine of double activity—which renders the technical application of the Aristotelian first/second act unnecessary and even inappropriate here.

51. See above, Preface, note 9.

52. O'Regan, "Von Balthasar," 241.

53. Tollefsen, *Christocentric Cosmology*, 67, 80, 135, and *Activity and Participation in Late Antique and Early Christian Thought* (Oxford: Oxford University Press, 2012), 122.

54. An instructive example: Ian A. McFarland, "'Always and Everywhere': Divine Presence and the Incarnation," in *The Gift of Theology*, ed. Rosemary P. Carbine and Hilda P. Koster (Minneapolis, MN: Fortress, 2015), 59–79, claims that we should understand Maximus's axiom about the Word's universal Incarnation (*Amb.* 7.22) in a way that conforms entirely to creaturely participatory metaphysics: "Even though Jesus lives a human life, the way in which other humans participate in God's life is crucially different from the way Jesus does. The Word may seek to effect the mystery of embodiment . . . everywhere, but the mode of that embodiment is unique. For while we are called to conform our created *logos* to the Creator Logos, Jesus *is* that Logos, having 'united our [human] nature to Himself according to hypostasis'" (73, original emphasis). For McFarland Maximus conceives this "new mode" of incarnation along the lines of the nature-person distinction. God's nature is universally immanent to creation, but the Word's person becomes immanent in the historical Incarnation. Thus the historical Incarnation effects no "increase" in God's universal presence. Rather, it effects a new mode of that same presence. And these two modes are "distinctively different" from each other (75). McFarland even suggests that while divine immanence (by nature) means that "creation has always been present to God, through the incarnation God now becomes present to the creature," that is, God becomes personally present in a way he never was hitherto (78).

Four major problems arise in this attempt to mitigate the plain sense of Maximus's words. First, presumably the Son participates God only insofar as he becomes and is human by nature. But then if Jesus's way of participating God "is crucially different" from our own, this would seem to imply that he is human in a way we are not. And that of course is something Maximus explicitly rejects (e.g., *Amb.* 5.2). Second, Maximus himself never says that Jesus's "mode" of being human differs from our proper mode. He does say that the historical Incarnation realizes "another, newer mode" (*Amb.* 7.37). But that mode's uniqueness is relative to the sinful, imperfect, Adamic mode of existence, which is *not* humanity's God-willed mode at all. Hence Maximus notes carefully in this same passage that the new mode wrought in Christ was itself God's "purpose" for us "from before the ages, a purpose that underwent no innovation in its own logos." In other words, as Maximus makes very clear elsewhere (*Amb.* 41.5, *Q. Thal.* 60.3–4, etc.), what the historical Incarnation actualized was the very thing Adam was to actualize in himself, since this is the unalterable intention of the divine and eternal counsel for all humanity. Thus McFarland adds qualifications to this text that both this text and Maximus's broader vision actually oppose. Third, McFarland locates Jesus's difference from us in that we merely conform to our "created *logos*" while Jesus is the Logos. For one thing, Maximus never calls any *logos* "created." If "being created" is what differentiates us from Christ, then this cannot obtain on the level of the *logoi*. But then not even "being created" can distinguish us from Christ, since Christ too was created (ἑαυτὸν . . . δημιουργήσας ἐποίησεν ἄνθρωπον) by his own will; cf. *Amb.* 42.11, PG 91, 1325AB). Fourth and finally, it is completely foreign to Maximus's thought to separate the divine nature from its enhypostatization in the three persons. Yet this seems necessary to make sense of McFarland's operative distinction, namely that God's "nature" is universally present in creation while his new, personal mode occurs only in Christ. How could the divine nature be present anywhere the persons are not? And how could the addition of this personal mode of immanence now make God present to us in a way his nature on its own never could? And even if we restrict ourselves to contemplating the absolute transcendence of divinity, McFarland's schema runs exactly backwards. Dionysius, for instance, holds precisely the opposite thesis based on McFarland's same starting point: "For though the Trinity is present to all things, not all things are present to the Trinity" (*DN* 3.11, my translation). When we recall that for Maximus the Logos *is* the *logoi* of all creatures regardless of whether they have actualized the potential that the Logos himself becomes and is in creating all things (chapter 2), it becomes clear that Maximus ventures far closer to Dionysius (with important modifications) than to McFarland here. The latter's schema creates considerably more exegetical and systematic problems than the alternative— taking Maximus at his word and seeing where it leads.

55. Williams, *Ground of Union*, 89.

56. Louth, "Recent Research," 82: "something I find utterly incredible."

57. *Amb.* 41.5, PG 91, 1308B, and *Amb.* 7.37, PG 91, 1097B.

58. *Amb.* 7. 22, PG 91, 1084C.

59. *CT* 2.25, ed. Luis Salés, *Two Hundred Chapters on Theology: St. Maximus the Confessor* (Yonkers, NY: St. Vladimir's Seminary Press, 2015), 122–23.

60. *Amb.* 7.27, PG 91, 1088C.

61. *Amb.* 10.42, PG 91, 1137CD.

62. *Amb.* 10.44, PG 91, 1140D.

63. *Amb.* 10.44, PG 91, 1140D.

64. *Amb.* 10.41, PG 91, 1137C.

65. *Amb.* 21.15, PG, 91, 1253D, slight modification: "καὶ ταὐτὸν αὐτῷ μᾶλλον κατὰ τὴν χάριν ἢ ἀφομοίωμα, τυχὸν δὲ καὶ αὐτὸς ὁ Κύριος, εἰ μὴ φορτικὸς ὁ λόγος τισὶν εἶναι δοκεῖ."

66. On all this, see chapter 3, the section "Perichoresis, the Logic of Deified Creation."

67. *Amb.* 10.9, PG 91, 1113B.

68. *Q. Thal.* 60.4, ed. Carlos Laga and Carlos Steel, *Quaestiones ad Thalassium II*, CCSG 22 (Turnhout: Brepols, 1990), 75, my translation (which accords

with both Blowers's and Constas's): "ἐν Χριστῷ τὴν ἀρχὴν τοῦ εἶναι τὸ τέλος εἰλήφασιν"; cf. *Amb.* 41.9.

69. *Amb.* 33.2, PG 91, 1288A, my translation: "τοσοῦτον ἡμᾶς δι' ἑαυτὸν πρὸς ἕνωσιν ἑαυτοῦ συστείλας, ὅσον αὐτὸς δι' ἡμᾶς ἑαυτὸν συγκαταβάσεως λόγῳ διέστειλεν."

70. My point here does not rest upon a general account (theological or otherwise) of metaphor. I would be quite happy to join those trends in philosophical hermeneutics and literary theory that conceive the boundary between literal and metaphorical senses more fluidly. Perhaps it is true that, as Janet Soskice and others have reminded us, what begins as a metaphorical expression often evolves into a literal one, which then creates new possibilities for both. My aim is rather more modest: to the degree Maximus scholars have labeled his more suggestive statements about creation and Incarnation "metaphor," and have done so precisely to distinguish the logic of the God-world relation from the logic of the historical Incarnation—to just this degree I insist on reading Maximus "literally."

71. Polycarp Sherwood, O.S.B., *The Earlier Ambigua of Saint Maximus the Confessor and His Refutation of Origenism* (Rome: Orbis Catholicus, Herder, 1955), and "Maximus and Origenism: ΑΡΧΗ ΚΑΙ ΤΕΛΟΣ," in *Berichte zum XI: Internationalen Byzantinisten Kongreß* (Munich: C. H. Beck, 1958), 8–16; Pascal Mueller-Jordan, "The Foundation of Origenist Metaphysics," in Allen and Neil, *Oxford Handbook*, 149–63.

72. *Amb.* 7.2, PG 91, 1069A.

73. *Amb.* 41.5; *Q. Thal.* 22, ed. Jean-Claude Larchet, vol. 1, SC 529 (Paris: Cerf, 2010), 264–65, passim.

74. *Amb.* 7.31, PG 91, 1092C. Perl, "Metaphysics and Christology," 260–61, and "Methexis," 209, rightly emphasizes the striking usage here of the technical *enhypostasia* in an expansive metaphysical context. Louth, "Recent Research," 82, hesitates to take this passage very seriously.

75. *Amb.* 5.5.

76. *Q. Thal.* 22.2. With Dionysius he calls God the "beginning, middle, and end" of creation (*DN* 5.8; *CT* 1.10), but he also attributes this specifically to "our Lord Jesus Christ" (*Q. Thal.* 22.6).

77. *Q. Thal.* 60.2–4, ed. Laga and Steel, CCSG 22, 73–77. Other instances where Maximus uses *mystery* to mean specifically the deed wrought in the historical Incarnation: *Amb.* 7.36–38; *Amb.* 10.52; *Amb.* 31.9 (also our deification); *Amb.* 41.2 (also the primordial plan for humanity); *Amb.* 42.5 (explicitly mixed with our origin and end), 17, 25, 29; *Amb.* 71.3; *Q. Thal.* 22.3, ed. Laga and Steel, CCSG 7, 137, and 22.8, ed. Laga and Steel, CCSG 7, 143 (also our deification); *Q. Thal.* 42.4, ed. Laga and Steel, CCSG 7, 289 (also a mystery "about me"); *Q. Thal.* 59.6, ed. Laga and Steel, CCSG 22, 51; *Q. Thal.* 61.11, ed. Laga and Steel, CCSG 22, 101 (also our baptism); *Myst.* 5, ed. Christian Boudignon, *Mystagogia*, CCSG 69 (Turnhout: Brepols, 2011), 23–24, passim.

ONE. The Middle: Christo-Logic

1. So Alois Grillmeier, S.J., "Der Neu-Chalkedonismus: Um die Berechtigung eines neuen Kapitels in der Dogmengeschichte," in *Mit ihm und in ihm: Christologische Forschungen und Perspektiven* (Freiburg: Herder, 1975), 374 (cf. 382): there are "so viele unterscheidende Merkmale" that prove "Neo-Chalcedonianism" designates a distinct reality; so too Brian Daley's introduction to Leontius of Byzantium, *Complete Works*, ed. and trans. Brian E. Daley, S.J. (Oxford: Oxford University Press, 2017), 2–3.

2. Joseph Lebon, *Le monophysisme sévérien* (Louvain: J. Van Linthout, 1909), 522.

3. Marcel Richard, "Le néochalcédonisme," *Mélanges de Sciences Religieuses* 3 (1946): 156–61, intervened to question the utility of these overly broad criteria. He observed, for instance, that recourse to Cyril was possible for known "strict Chalcedonians" such as Hypatia at the Synod of 532 (159), and partly because Cyril's own thought was mediated through Chalcedon's judicious sanctioning of certain less stringent Cyrillian texts, many of which floated about in various post-Chalcedon florilegia (158). These criteria-boundaries fall so wide that they demarcate nothing more than simple "Chalcedonianism" (160). Richard's own proposed criterion was that a Neo-Chalcedonian insists on the dialectical use of both "miaphysite" and "diphysite" formulas as the only secure method to express Chalcedon's true meaning. This too has been qualified: Grillmeier assigns Richard's criterion only to "extreme neo-Chalcedonians," while "moderate neo-Chalcedonians" such as Leontius of Jerusalem and the Emperor Justinian seek only to "supplement" Chalcedon's Definition with Cyril's uncompromising statements (esp. the twelfth anathema appended to his *Third Letter to Nestorius*) without making an absolute injunction to use his *mia physis* formula; cf. Grillmeier, *Christ in Christian Tradition*, vol. 2, pt. 2, *The Church of Constantinople in the Sixth Century*, trans. John Bowden (1989; repr., Louisville, KY: John Knox Press, 1995), 434.

4. Cyril Hovorun, "Maximus, a Cautious Neo-Chalcedonian," in Allen and Neil, *Oxford Handbook*, 106–24; Demetrios Bathrellos, *The Byzantine Christ: Person, Nature, and Will in the Christology of Saint Maximus the Confessor* (Oxford: Oxford University Press, 2004), 112–14, invokes Grillmeier's "extreme Neochalcedonianism" for Maximus, which seems nearer the mark.

5. See esp. Siegried Helmer, "Der Neuchalkedonismus: Geschichte, Berechtigung, und Bedeutung eines dogmengeschichtlichen Begriffes" (PhD diss., University of Bonn, 1962).

6. Thunberg, *Microcosm and Mediator*, 36–48.

7. Helmer, "Neuchalkedonismus," 69.

8. Cyril of Alexandria, third anathema of his *Third Letter to Nestorius* ("two hypostases")—though Grillmeier thinks this wrongly interpreted by John Grammaticus (*Christ in Christian Tradition*, vol. 2, pt. 2, 59).

9. Norman P. Tanner, *Decrees of the Ecumenical Councils* (London: Sheed and Ward, 1990), 85–86, slightly modified.

10. So Basil the Great's *Ep.* 214 (*Ad Terentium Comitem* 4, PG 32, 789AB), a favorite among Neo-Chalcedonians: "If we must also say what seems right to us, we will say this: essence has the same relationship to hypostasis that the universal has to the particular [ὅτι ὃν ἔχει λόγον τὸ κοινὸν πρὸς τὸ ἴδιον, τοῦτον ἔχει ἡ οὐσία πρὸς τὴν ὑπόστασιν]. For each of us participates being through the common principle of essence, and is this or that particular being by the characteristics that cling to it [τοῖς περὶ αὐτὸν ἰδιώμασιν ὁ δεῖνά ἐστιν καὶ ὁ δεῖνα]"; cited (for instance) at Leontius of Byzantium, *CNE* (florilegium), Test. 1, ed. Daley, *Complete Works*, , 180–81, translation modified. Grillmeier, *Christ in Christian Tradition*, vol. 2, pt. 2, 54–61, discusses the use of this and other Cappadocian texts by John Grammaticus. For the successes and problems consequent upon the development of the Cappadocian "classical theory" of how to relate universal and particular being, see Johannes Zachhuber, *Human Nature in Gregory of Nyssa: Philosophical Background and Theological Significance* (Leiden: Brill, 1999). And for a nice overview of the philosophical issues animating the patristic reception of Porphyry's understanding of "individual" and "essence," see Christophe Erismann, "L'individualité expliquée par les accidents: Remarques sur la destinée 'chrétienne' de Porphyre," in *Compléments de substance: Etudes sur les propriétés accidentelles offertes à Alain de Libera*, ed. C. Erismann and A. Schniewind (Paris: Vrin, 2008), 51–66.

11. So Leontius of Byzantium, *CNE*, prol., PG 86, 1276CD, ed. Daley, *Complete Works*, 128–31; *Epil.* 3, PG 86, 1921C–1925B, ed. Daley, *Complete Works*, 276–83; passim. For Severus this distinction is illicit only in Christology. He was perfectly content to deploy it in theology proper (Trinity); cf. Grillmeier, *Christ in Christian Tradition*, vol. 2, pt. 2, 146.

12. The following narration owes much to Zachhuber, "Christology after Chalcedon," 98–106; see also Charles Moeller, "Le Chalcédonisme et le néo-chalcédonisme en Orient de 451 à la fin du VIe siècle," in *Das Konzil von Chalkedon: Geschichte und Gegenwart*, vol. 1, ed. Alois Grillmeier, S.J., and Heinrich Bacht (Würzburg: Echter, 1951), 642, 694–99.

13. Leontius's Severan opponent states it thus: "When the Logos assumed human nature, did he assume it as understood generically, or as in an individual?" (PG 86, 1916B–1917A, ed. Daley, *Complete Works*, 270–71); and later: "Did he assume an individual nature, then?" (Τὴν τινὰ οὖν ἀνέλαβε φύσιν;) (PG 86, 1917B, ed. Daley, *Complete Works*, 272–73).

14. Severus of Antioch, quoted in John Grammaticus, *Apol.* 14.8, in *Iohannis Caesariensis presbyteri et grammatici opera quae supersunt*, ed. M. Richard, CCSG 1 (Turnhout: Brepols, 1977) .

15. Hence Leontius of Byzantium, *CNE*, prol., PG 86, 1276A, ed. Daley, *Complete Works*, 128–29, quotes Nonnus, who calls both Nestorians and miaphysites

"opposite kinds of docetist ['Εναντιοδοκήτας]" (which is also a part of the fuller title of Leontius's *CNE*).

16. Leontius of Byzantium, *CNE* 1, PG 86, 1277B, ed. Daley, *Complete Works*, 132; cf. Maximus, *Opusc.* 16, PG 91, 205AC.

17. Zachhuber, "Christology after Chalcedon," 102–3, notes (following John Grammaticus) how Severus's stress on the particular-pole of the ontological continuum of (abstract) universal to (concrete) particular implied that Christ's *divinity* along with his humanity might be so particularized that it led to tri-theism on the side of divinity—a move the later miaphysite John Philoponus might have made.

18. Leontius of Byzantium, *Epil.* 1, PG 86, 1917AD, does not appear to grasp the fundamental issue. He is content to reply that the human nature "in" Christ "is the same as the species" and so presents no special difficulty as regards his individual distinction from other human beings. This simply assumes that hypostasis is different from species (or the universal essence) rather than argues for it. The point ignores, for instance, whether the universal species is somehow changed or qualified *as* that particular individual. Zachhuber, "Christology after Chalcedon," 99, flags other pro-Chalcedonians who take a similar line (John Grammaticus and Anastasius of Antioch).

Leontius of Jerusalem proves a more provocative case: he uses the very same objection *against* Severan miaphysites (*Contra Mon.* [*Aporiae*] 53 [cf. 61], PG 86, 1797D; ed. and trans. Patrick Gray, *Against the Monophysites: Testimonies of the Saints and Aporiae*, Oxford Early Christian Texts (Oxford: Oxford University Press, 2006), 212–13), and yet quite clearly affirms—as Maximus will too—that Christ's two natures were both universal ("from two natures") and particular or individual ("in two natures")—though he never explains how this is so; cf. *Contra. Mon.* [*Aporiae*] 58, PG 86, 1800D–1801C, ed. Gray, 216–19. His polemic underscores the Severans' indulgence of the phrase "out of two natures" and then turns their own attack back on them: Are these two "prior" natures universal or particular? If the former, then (at least) the humanity whence Christ came was merely conceptual, not actual; if the latter, the miaphysites themselves become Nestorians!

19. For an early implementation of Cappadocian Trinitarian definitions in Christology, cf. (a text attributed to) Eulogius of Alexandria, *Frag. dogm.*, 2944D–2945A; Charles Moeller, "Textes 'monophysites' de Léonce de Jérusalem," *Ephemerides Theologicae Lovanienses* 27 (1951): 470, assigns this fragment to John Grammaticus.

20. Cf. Grillmeier, *Christ in Christian Tradition*, vol. 2. pt. 2, 203. Consider Plotinus's Three Hypostases (*Enn.* V.1). We might see the second definition, therefore, as one viable development of the Cappadocian rejection of (Neo)Platonic "particular natures"; see Gregory of Nyssa, *Ad Graecos* III/1, 23 (cited in Zachhuber, "Christology after Chalcedon," 96); cf. too Leontius of Jerusalem, *Contra Mon.* [*Aporiae*] 53, PG 86, 1797D, ed. Gray, 212–13, whose commitment to the

idea that "particular natures" are achieved or perfected only in concrete existence makes him scoff at the thought of Christ's natures "as vainly having in potentiality what they will never achieve in actuality."

21. Leontius of Jerusalem, *Adv. Nest.* II, PG 86, 1529D, my emphasis and translation.

22. Erismann, "L'Individualité expliquée par les accidents," 51–66.

23. Erismann, "L'Individualité expliqué par les accidents," 57, of Gregory of Nyssa: "Il est donc nécessaire que leur [the divine hypostases'] individualité s'explique par un élément non essentiel, en l'occurence des propriétés. Le modèle porphyrien offre un explication valable. . . . L'adoption du modèle porphyrien est la contrepartie nécessaire et fondamentale de l'interprétation de l'*ousia* comme une entité commune. La fameuse distinction *ousia/hypostasis* requiert un élément exogène."

24. Leontius of Byzantium, *Epil.* 8, PG 86, 1945A, ed. Daley, *Complete Works*, 308–9.

25. Leontius of Byzantium, *Epil.* 8, PG 86, 1944C, slightly modified: "ἀλλ᾽ ἐν τῷ Λόγῳ ὑποστῆναι." This is ultimately why I think Richard Cross's proposal, though certainly correct that Leontius supports something like the concept of in-subsistence, does not account for the precise principle of individuation in the Incarnation; see his "Individual Natures in the Christology of Leontius of Byzantium," *Journal of Early Christian Studies* 10.2 (2002): 245–65, esp. 256–58. Of course for Leontius (as for most) the Son's singular property comes already and only through his eternal generation from the Father rather than through any set of accidents; see, e.g., *CNE* 4, PG 86, 1285D, ed. Daley, *Complete Works*, 144. I do not mean to deny that Christ's humanity had accidents in the proper sense (time, place, skin color, bodily figure, even style of human thinking and communicating), only that these caused or achieved his individuality. They *expressed* it.

26. Leontius of Byzantium, *Epil.* 8, PG 86, 1940B, ed. Daley, *Complete Works*, 300–301: "I am so far from saying that God the Word is united to our [manhood] by the law of nature, that I am not even prepared to say that the union of the human soul with its own body is experienced naturally [τὴν πρὸς τὸ ἑαυτῆς σῶμα συνάφειαν φυσικῶς]." Then follows a striking declaration still about every human soul: in all cases "The mode of union [which is the same as the Word's with his own humanity] rather than the principle of nature [οὐκ ὁ λόγος τῆς φύσεως] contains the great mystery of religion." I discuss this development at some length in Jordan Daniel Wood, "A Novel Use of the Body-Soul Comparison Emerges in Neochalcedonian Christology," *Review of Ecumenical Studies* 11.3 (2019): 263–90.

27. Already at Moeller, "Chalcédonisme," 644, 676, but cf. esp. his "Textes 'monophysites' de Léonce de Jérusalem," *Ephemerides Theologicae Lovanienses* 27 (1951): 467–82, which blames the "monophysite contamination" on Leontius of Jerusalem; see Grillmeier, "Neu-Chalkedonismus," 377–78. Prestige had already decried an "exaggerated assimilation of the theory of the Trinity

to that of the Incarnation" (226), but for reasons quite different from Moeller's and Grillmeier's. However, Prestige too took the mistake to lie in sixth-century thinkers such as the two Leontii. He regarded Maximus as subsequently and similarly errant (233); see G. L. Prestige, *God in Patristic Thought* (London: Society for Promoting Christian Knowledge, 1952).

28. Moeller, "Textes 'monophysites,'" 468n3.

29. Moeller, "Textes 'monophysites,'" 470, identifies John Grammaticus as the first offender.

30. Moeller, "Textes 'monophysites,'" 470–71.

31. Moeller, "Textes 'monophysites,'" 471–74, takes special issue with Leontius's precision that it was the Word's *property* and not just his *hypostasis* that became "most composed" in the historical Incarnation.

32. Moeller, "Chalcédonisme," 701: "On a l'impression que les propriétés concrètes de la nature humaine de Jésus se combinent avec les propriétés concrètes de l'hypostase du Verbe au sein de la Trinité."

33. Moeller, "Textes 'monophysites,'" 475, his emphasis, my translation; cf. his "Chalcédonisme," 703.

34. So Grillmeier, "Neu-Chalkedonismus," 378n34: "Dieser Monophysitismus ist freilich mehr aus der Hilflosigkeit in dem Gebrauch der Definition des Gregor von Nyssa als aus wirklich monophysitischer Tendenz zu erklären."

35. Karl Rahner, "Jesus Christ—The Meaning of Life," *Theological Investigations*, vol. 21, *Science and Christian Faith*, trans. Hugh M. Riley (New York: Crossroad, 1988), 214: "Pure Chalcedonism was always suspicious that the other soteriology [Neo-Chalcedonianism's] would covertly evolve from a communication of properties (of the two natures) into an identity of properties (of both)." Neo-Chalcedonian Christology has borne its most bitter fruit in modern soteriology, where the proposition that "God suffers" is taken "in such a way that this affirmation forges an identity between subject and predicate, the eternity of the divinity and the suffering of the humanity" (214). Death and finitude, Rahner reminds us, "belong only to the created reality of Jesus; they are located on *this side of the infinite distance* between God and what is created" (214, my emphasis). Rahner's critique fails to distinguish properly between the logic of nature as opposed to that of hypostasis. Perhaps some modern theologians say what Rahner styles the Neo-Chalcedonian "interpretation" of Christ's work—that suffering and death apply "to the divinity itself." But no actual Neo-Chalcedonian said that. The innovation demanded by the fact of Christ is precisely one of conceiving new relations between subject and predicate, since in Christology the "subject" is not primarily logical; *he* is rather the most fundamental ontological fact of both sets of predicates, the very positivity that enables that dual and otherwise contradictory predication. See Leontius of Byzantium, *Epil.* 8, PG 86, 1944B, ed. Daley, *Complete Works*, 306–7: "For the one hypostasis and one persona can receive opposite

and contradictory predicates [τὰ ἐναντία καὶ τὰ ἀντικείμενα κατηγορήματα δέχεσθαι] together and in the same subject; but the one nature, as we have said, which can produce contraries [τὰ ἐναντία], cannot at one time come to be contradictory to itself [τὰ ἀντικείμενα ἑαυτῇ]"; cf. too Maximus, *Amb.* 2.4. Mere talk about "this side" of an "infinite distance" between Christ's two natures does not yet register what makes the mystery of Christ mysterious: the fact that Christ's own singular subjectivity not only is indifferent to such "distance" but is its very condition. Rahner's own articulations in his book on the Trinity seem actually to trend Neo-Chalcedonian.

36. Balthasar often reads Maximus's Christology as anticipating but never quite attaining Thomas's "real distinction." He detects some troubling ambivalence just where Moeller and Grillmeier did: when Maximus retains the Trinitarian definition of hypostasis alongside the more appropriate one, "subsistence." See Balthasar, *Cosmic Liturgy*, 64, 113. Aaron Riches, *Ecce Homo: On the Divine Unity of Christ* (Grand Rapids, MI: Eerdmans, 2016), 13, also suggestively links the twentieth-century longing for an "orthodox Nestorianism" in some circles (e.g., Rahner) with the "modern Latin doctrine of *natura pura*" (e.g., Steven A. Long, Lawrence Feingold): "The integrity of nature, on this latter view, is safeguarded by its natural perfectibility *in se*, and so in a manner essentially separable from the order of grace. The convertibility of the doctrine of *natura pura* with a quasi-Nestorian logic of *separatio* lies in the way proponents of *natura pura* insist on deriving the 'species' of the human creature wholly from the 'proximate, proportionate, natural end' of a 'purely natural' human nature, *fully divested from the history of salvation*" (my emphasis). That is, the desire to conceive the entirety of human nature apart from any *fact*—even in Christology—formally parallels broader conceptions of a strict two-tiered God-world relation.

37. See below, "An Analytic Appendix of Key Concepts," for a more concise schematic.

38. *Pyr.* 201–2; *Opusc.* 13, PG 91, 145A–149B.

39. *Ep.* 15, PG 91, 545A (cf. 548D). Maximus then cites Basil three times and Gregory of Nazianzus twice as justification—all explicitly Trinitarian passages.

40. *Ep.* 15, PG 91, 549CD. The Three differ by the idioms ingenerate (Father), generated (Son), and procession (Spirit).

41. This point will be evident across Maximus's texts, but consider one of his more condensed formulations (though some doubt its authenticity) at *Opusc.* 26, PG 91, 264D: "Ὅτι ἡ μὲν φύσις εἴδους λόγον μόνον ἐπέχει, ἡ δὲ ὑπόστασις καὶ τοῦ τινός ἐστι δηλωτική."

42. *Amb.* 1.3; cf. *CC* 2.29. So Pierre Piret, S.J., *Le Christ et la Trinité selon Maxime le Confesseur* (Paris: Beauchesne, 1983), 45–46: "La pensée de Maxime le Confesseur, concernant le Christ Jésus et la Sainte Trinité, s'exerce selon les rapports logiques de l'union et de la différence comme de l'identité et de l'altérité,

qu'elle se réfère aux réalités de l'hypostase et de l'ousie, comprenant la volonté raisonnable et l'opération volontaire, et qu'elle témoigne de la correspondance des dogmes trinitaire et christologique de l'Eglise."

43. *Opusc.* 21, PG 91, 249C.

44. *Amb.* 1.3: "For the Monad is truly a Monad: it is not the origin of the things that come after it, as if it had expanded after a state of contraction, like something naturally poured out and proliferating into a multitude, but is rather the *enhypostasized* being of the consubstantial Trinity [ἀλλ' ἐνυπόστατος ὀντότης ὁμοουσίου Τριάδος]."

45. *Amb.* 17.12; *Opusc.* 21, PG 91, 249A, passim.

46. *Opusc.* 16, PG 91, 204A. Jean-Claude Larchet, "Hypostase, personne, et individu selon saint Maxime le Confesseur," *Revue d'Histoire Ecclésiastique* 109 (2014): 52, while right to deny that this text implies any absolute opposition between "individual" and "person," nevertheless wrongly infers that "il est question de l'*hypostase composée* du Christ qui constitue un cas unique d'une hypostase qui unit deux natures. En tant que Dieu-homme, le Christ n'est pas un membre d'une essence ou d'une nature, ou encore un genre uniques qui comporteraient une multiplicité d'individus." But for Maximus the fact that Christ's composed person is not properly an individual derives from the way he is *person* rather than, as Larchet claims, "du fait précisément qu'elle est composée" (55). If the fact of being a composed hypostasis excludes that hypostasis from individuality, then every human person, which is also a composed hypostasis (since body and soul are "homo-hypostatic" essences in man; cf. *Opusc.* 14, PG 91, 152AB), would likewise not be an individual. The point is rather that when Christ makes himself the identity of natural extremes, he *is individual* in a more fundamental manner than any logical determination of species and differentiae could countenance—for he was a hypostasis already "before" he was human (and divinity is neither genus nor species, so being a divine hypostasis is a determination that moves necessarily beyond the logic of nature). In fact, every hypostasis is in itself more fundamental than the way it is individual, since individuality (in a Porphyrian schema) properly "refers back" to the species it is by nature, as Maximus indicates here. This is why he can define hypostasis or person as what possesses "the delimitation of individuality in themselves [i.e., hypostasis and person] but not [possessing] by nature the predication among many [i.e., hypostasis and person do not have the 'common idioms' of nature or essence]"; *Opusc.* 14, PG 91, 152A, my translation.

47. Nature and hypostasis are so clearly irreducible to each other that Maximus can even say that *each* of Christ's natures *qua* natures "lacks its own proper hypostasis"; *Opusc.* 13.7.

48. *Ep.* 12, PG 91, 493C.

49. Grillmeier, *Christ in Christian Tradition*, vol. 2, pt. 2, 200–211; Balthasar, *Cosmic Liturgy*, 209, 245–46.

50. *Ep.* 13, PG 91, 529C.

51. *Ep.* 13, PG 91, 517C.

52. *Opusc.* 21, PG 91, 256AB; *Ep.* 13, PG 91, 516D–524B.

53. All from *Ep.* 13, PG 91, 516C sq.

54. *Ep.* 13, PG 91, 517B, my translation: "Οὗτος γὰρ πάσης συνθέτου φύσεως ὅρος τε καὶ λόγος καὶ νόμος."

55. First proposed by Leontius of Jerusalem; see Nicholas Madden, O.C.D., "Composite Hypostasis in Maximus Confessor," *Studia Patristica* 28 (1993): 186.

56. Cf. Bathrellos, *Byzantine Christ*, 105.

57. *Ep.* 12, PG 91, 484B, my translation: "For [this one rightly] confesses with the Fathers that the unconfused [natures] from which Christ is composed remained on account of the difference preserved. Apart from the one hypostasis these realities which differ from each other in their natural principle could never exist, and you could never in any way know them separately [from the hypostasis]."

58. Cf. *Ep.* 15, PG 91, 552C, where Maximus claims that even the body-soul analogy supports the point that the hypostatic "idiom," the individuality of a particular *instance* of something, is exactly where and how essentially different realities attain "mutual identity."

59. *Ep.* 13, PG 91, 517C, my translation.

60. *Ep.* 15, PG 91, 557C, my translation: "Hence Christ possessed both the common and the particular of those parts from which he was composed" (Οὐκοῦν ἑκατέρου τῶν ἐξ ὧν συνετέθη μερῶν ὁ Χριστὸς εἶχε, τό τε κοινὸν καὶ τὸ ἰδικόν).

61. *Ep.* 15, PG 91, 557D–560A.

62. *Ep.* 15, PG 91, 553D: "He made Himself a perfect man, assuming a rational and noetic flesh that took nature and hypostasis in Him, that is, being and subsistence, accordingly simultaneous with the Word's very conception"; *Ep.* 12, PG 91, 468A: "From her [i.e., Mary] He united flesh to Himself according to hypostasis, consubstantial with us, animated by a rational and noetic soul, not pre-hypostasized for even the twinkling of an eye, but in Himself, God and Word, that flesh received both 'to be' and 'to subsist' [ἀλλ᾽ ἐν αὐτῷ τῷ Θεῷ καὶ Λόγῳ, καὶ τὸ εἶναι καὶ τὸ ὑποστῆναι λαβοῦσαν]."

63. *Ep.* 15, PG 91, 556B, my translation: "He revealed himself in the unicity of his person absolutely without difference, unified to the supreme degree by the personal identity of His own parts among them [ἐν τῇ πρὸς ἄλληλα κατ᾽ ἄκρον προσωπικῇ ταυτότητι τῶν οἰκείων μερῶν διαπαντὸς ἑνιζόμενον]." Notice that the "personal identity" is not some third thing, as if the "parts" were identical by the law of transference. It is *their* identity, where they are completely and invariably one reality.

64. *Ep.* 15, PG 91, 560AB; my translation.

65. Leontius of Byzantium, *Epil.* 25, PG 86, 1909CD, ed. Daley, *Complete Works*, 327–29: "For by the distinguishing characteristics which divides him from the Father, he is joined to the flesh, just as by the natural property which joins him

to the Father he experiences difference from the flesh; and as he is one nature with the Father because of the sameness of nature, so he is *not* one nature with the flesh, because of its natural and unchanging character, even in union with the Word."

66. Perl, "Metaphysics and Christology," 258–59.

67. *Opusc.* 21, PG 91, 248C–249A.

68. Bathrellos, *Byzantine Christ*, 102–3, observes that "the personal" and "mode" are crucially linked but not identical. Maximus's resolution of the universal-versus-particular flesh dilemma intimates his broader metaphysical view, inspired by Nemesius and perhaps Theophrastus, that both particulars *and universals* are created in time (*Amb.* 7.16; 10.83, 101, ed. Nicholas Constas, *On Difficulties in the Church Fathers: The Ambigua*, 2 vols. (Cambridge, MA: Harvard University Press, 2014), 1:489n57)—a view Tollefsen notes "seems strange" against "the background of Neoplatonic thought" (*Christocentric Cosmology*, 87). I think this strange view finds its more immediate background in Christology proper. It also chimes well with aspects of Stoic cosmology, on which see Jordan Daniel Wood, "Stoic Motifs in the Cosmology of Maximus Confessor," *Dionysius* 37 (2019): 47–61.

69. *Opusc.* 10; PG 91, 136D–137A; my translation.

70. Madden, "Composite Hypostasis," 188: "This gives us an astonishing insight into the mystery of the Incarnation; the flesh is truly the flesh of the only-begotten son of God; all its individual traits are determined by his eternal personality and they reveal it. This extends to every dimension of his being and life as man. It marks his style. . . . The subsistence of the Logos is the principle of individuation of his humanity as well as of its union with him." See too Heinzer, *Gottes Sohn als Mensch*, 133–39.

71. See Richard Sorabji, *The Philosophy of the Commentators, 200-600 AD: A Sourcebook: Volume 3: Logic and Metaphysics* (Ithaca, NY: Cornell University Press, 2005), 128–63.

72. Cf. *Opusc.* 21, PG 91, 248BC, my translation: Here Maximus argues that "for the divine Fathers" the concepts of "quality," "property," and "difference" do "not rest upon being received by a certain substrate [οὐκ ἐπί τινος ὑποκειμένου λαμβανομένη], that is, by an essence or nature but upon those things contemplated in the essence and indeed really those things in the hypostasis [καὶ μέντοι γε τῶν τῇ ὑποστάσει θεωρουμένων]." Just prior to this he ascribes such a view to "those outside," an allusion that, along with the vague description of the position, is sufficiently broad to encompass the whole Porphyrian-inspired tradition.

73. *Opusc.* 21, PG 91, 256AB, my translation; cf. too *Ep.* 15, PG 91, 569D–572A, where Maximus makes a similar point by attributing Severus's conception of "union" to "the aleatoric 'chance' of Epicurus."

74. Or else, if "quality" works differently, as Maximus agrees "nature" does as it relates to hypostasis, he awaits to be stupefied by the explanation! Cf. *Opusc.* 21, PG 91, 256B.

75. This becomes in Maximus a general metaphysical rule for every concrete, individual existence; cf. *Amb.* 17.5 and below at sec. 2.2.

76. If one were to posit another principle of individuation alongside the Son's very self—say, individuation by accidents or a particular nature (or some combination of both)—that principle would be just as constitutive or causal of Christ's flesh as Christ himself. This co-causal principle would codetermine not only the *esse reale* of Christ's flesh but its particularity too. It would therefore cease to be true that the Son *alone* determines his own real and individual flesh. And if his flesh derives from elsewhere, be it ever so slightly, then we might rightly wonder whether it at least partially "subsists" as or attains subsistence by another reality—that is, hastily put, in a sense derives from another hypostasis. We intimate here a major reason Neo-Chalcedonians in general and Maximus in particular saw any attempt even to "conceive" of Christ's flesh *apart from Christ himself* as capitulating to Nestorian "scission"; cf. *Opusc.* 14, PG 91, 80AD.

77. *Ep.* 12, PG 91, 488A: "Being [concretely] one in hypostasis applies both to Christ and to our being human." For more extensive treatment of the pertinent background here, see especially Karl-Heinz Uthemann, "Das anthropologische Modell der hypostatischen Union: Ein Beitrag zu den philosophischen Voraussetzungen und zur innerchalkedonischen Transformation eines Paradigmas," *Kleronomia* 14.2 (1982): 215–312, and my "Novel Use."

78. Severus of Antioch, *Ep.* 10, PO XII, 202–3.

79. Madden, "Composite Hypostasis," 176–77, though he misses that the "achievement" was not just Maximus's. It had already been advanced, for instance, by Leontius of Byzantium, *CNE* 4, PG 86, 1285D–1288A; see Brian Daley, S.J., "'A Richer Union': Leontius of Byzantium and the Relationship of Human and Divine in Christ," *Studia Patristica* 24 (1993): 250–58, 262.

80. *Ep.* 12, PG 91, 488BC; e.g., the soul's nature comprises invisibility, incorporeality, relative transcendence of space, even (perhaps) everlastingness—none of which belongs in principle to the body. Likewise the reverse: corruptibility, mortality, visibility, material complexity, irreducible spatiality—these are natural to body, not soul.

81. Soul acts through body as through "an instrument," e.g., to perceive and receive sensations (*Pyr.* 187); soul unifies body (*Amb.* 7.37); soul partially mediates virtue to body (*Amb.* 10.2); body can restrain soul (*Opusc.* 5, PG 91, 64C).

82. *Ep.* 12, PG 91, 488BC: again, body and soul together constitute one nature, "human." Though this names a genus marked by "a constitutive difference" from other species, it nowhere exists *as such*. It comes only in its individuals, only in instances that themselves presuppose a prior subject, a hypostasis.

83. *Opusc.* 17, PG 91, 212CD. We might say they are analogous.

84. *Amb.* 7.40, 10.57; *Opusc.* 5, PG 91, 64C.

85. *Amb.* 7.43: because the "whole" of a human individual is the hypostasis alone, the latter "reveals that both come into being simultaneously, and demonstrates their essential difference from each other, without violating in any way whatsoever the principles [*logoi*] of their respective substances."

86. Cf. Karl-Heinz Uthemann, "Das anthropologische Modell der hypostatischen Union bei Maximus Confessor," in *Maximus Confessor: Actes du symposium sur Maxime le Confesseur: Fribourg, 2–5 septembre 1980*, ed. Felix Heinzer and Christoph Schönborn (Fribourg: Editions Universitaires, 1982), 223–33.

87. *Ep.* 15, PG 91, 552C: "ἡ πρὸς ἄλληλα θεωρεῖται ταυτότης." Cf. note 58 above for full quotation. This insight into hypostasis as nature's sole concrete identity is for Maximus a general law of metaphysics derived, I think, from Christologic. Hypostasis (again: not a material substrate or an assemblage of properties as such) alone names the concrete identity of differing natures. Maximus often formulates this as a principle: "homo-hypostatic" realities (e.g., body and soul) *must* differ in essence/nature, while "hetero-hypostatic" realities (e.g., individual humans) *can* be united in essence/nature (*Opusc.* 14, PG 91, 152A; *Ep.* 15, PG 91, 552BC); or "union according to hypostasis" applies to "realities of differing essences," while "union according to essence" applies to "realities of differing hypostases" (*Opusc.* 18, PG 91, 216A).

88. *Opusc.* 16, PG 91, 204A; my translation; cf. *Ep.* 12, PG 91, 488A–489C.

89. *Amb.* 10.58; *Pyr.* 29.

90. A subtle point Maximus makes, for instance, to Pyrrhus, who was himself quite stunned by it: "PYRRHUS: There is nothing, then, which the natures and natural properties have in common [κοινόν]? MAXIMUS: Nothing, save only the hypostasis of these same natures. For, just in this way a hypostasis was the very same, unconfusedly, of these same natural properties ['Ωσπερ γὰρ ὑπόστασις ἦν ὁ αὐτὸς ἀσυγχύτως τῶν αὐτῶν φυσικῶν]"; see too *Amb.* 4.8.

91. *Ep.* 15, PG 91, 561B, my translation.

92. Balthasar, *Cosmic Liturgy*, 234–35, and Thunberg, *Microcosm and Mediator*, 36, hesitate to translate ταυτότης as an unqualified "identity." But Perl, "Methexis," 190–91, rightly insists on doing so: "Maximus is not content to speak of hypostatic 'union' (ἕνωσις) in Christ, which could suggest a mere co-presence of two natures 'in' a single hypostasis, but rather insists on the hypostatic and personal *identity* (ταυτότης) of the two natures. . . . True union demands not a mere juxtaposition or joining of two things; rather, in a union there must actually be *one* of something, one same thing which each of the terms united is."

93. Cyril, cf. the eleventh with twelfth anathema; cf. sec. 1.4 below.

94. *Ep.* 15, PG 91, 556A, my translation and emphasis. The acute eye accustomed to reading Gregory of Nyssa will notice the striking use of *diastasis* here, though its Christological use appears already in Leontius of Jerusalem, *Adv. Nest.* II.14, PG 98, 1568B.

95. Georges Florovsky, *Collected Works*, vol. 9, *The Byzantine Fathers of the Sixth to the Eighth Century*, ed. Richard S. Haugh, trans. Raymond Miller, Anne-Marie Döllinger-Labriolle, and Helmut Wilhelm Schmiedel (Vaduz: Büchervertriebsanstalt, 1987), 231.

96. Bathrellos, *Byzantine Christ*, 115. He thinks this a problem endemic to Neo-Chalcedonianism itself. His worries are those of Moeller, Grillmeier, et al. (cf. sec. 1.1), as is especially evident in his hesitations over and criticisms of the Neo-Chalcedonian identification of Christ himself as the individuating principle of his own flesh (51).

97. Bathrellos, *Byzantine Christ*, 105–7. He also speaks of the "formal" aspect. This aspect indicates that the hypostasis grants its particular idioms to both natures and so makes them, as it were, the same *qua* particular. Bathrellos claims inspiration for these categories from Heinzer (*Gottes Sohn als Mensch*, 81–82) though he admits altering them. A major and I think significant difference is that Heinzer alleges no special aspect for "the personal" in Christ.

98. Bathrellos, *Byzantine Christ*, 106: "Maximus integrates successfully the asymmetry on the level of 'personal' hypostasis (which is divine) with the symmetry on the level of the two (divine *and* human) natures, whose unity constitutes the 'material' hypostasis."

99. Bathrellos, *Byzantine Christ*, 105, my emphasis.

100. Bathrellos, *Byzantine Christ*, 106–7, my emphasis.

101. See, for instance, Richard Cross, "*Homo Assumptus* in the Christology of Hugh of St Victor: Some Historical and Theological Revisions," *Journal of Theological Studies* 65.1 (2014): 62–77, esp. 74–77, for Duns Scotus's criticisms of Hugh's strong emphasis on the "identity" (not just sameness) of the Word with his flesh: since Christ came to be and the Word did not, "Christ and the Word are not identical" (77).

102. *Ep.* 12, PG 91, 493BC, my translation; cf. *Opusc.* 24, PG 91, 268AC, which makes the same point.

103. Bathrellos, *Byzantine Christ*, 106, my emphasis.

104. More properly: the Son's own hypostasis is both mode and product. A supernatural mode of union (hypostatic union) generates a product, in and as *concrete reality*, which is nothing other than the mode that generated it. Again, this is possible only because the hypostasis, though *positive* (irreducible to nature), is still not, as some conceive it, "something alongside its own proper parts [ἄλλο τι τὸ ὅλον εἶναι παρὰ τὰ αὐτοῦ οἰκεῖα μέρη], from which and in which it consists" (*Opusc.* 9, PG 91, 117C, my translation).

105. *Ep.* 12, PG 91, 468C; *Opusc.* 21, PG 91, 252B; *Amb.* 5.24; 10.57.

106. *Ep* 12, PG 91, 468AC, my translation: "The same is consubstantial with the Father according to divinity, and the same is consubstantial with us according to humanity, double in nature or essence. Thus He is mediator of God and human

beings, and so it is necessary for Him to preserve the natural properties of the things mediated, to exist as both [τῷ ὑπάρχειν ἀμφότερα]."

107. *Opusc.* 9, PG 91, 117D, my translation.

108. Pierre Piret, S.J., "Christologie et théologie trinitaire chez Maxime le Confesseur, d'après sa formule des natures 'desquelles, en lesquelle et lesquelles est le Christ,'" in Heinzer and Schönborn, *Maximus Confesso*, 215–22. Madden, "Composite Hypostasis," 183, notes its Antiochene provenance; Bathrellos, *Byzantine Christ*, 108, corrects Piret's claim that Maximus was the first to formulate these three together into one phrase—it was Leontius of Byzantium—but notes too that Maximus was the first to make this "formula an oft-repeated way of referring to Christ."

109. Cf. note 104.

110. *Ep.* 15, PG 91, 573A, my translation: "For we recognize Him after the union as a whole of the parts that compose Him. For Christ has nothing else to show that He is than what He preserves and what we call Him—than the perdurance after the union of the parts that compose Him in His being. For not only is Christ *out of* these, but He is also *in* these, and what's still more proper to say, He *is* these [Οὐ μόνον γὰρ ἐκ τούτων, ἀλλὰ καὶ ἐν τούτοις, καὶ κυριώτερον εἰπεῖν, ταῦτά ἐστιν ὁ Χριστός]."

111. *Opusc.* 7, PG 91, 73BC, my translation: "Again, he is twofold by becoming flesh. On the one hand, in this duality of nature he is essentially connatural with the extremes and preserves the natural difference of his parts one from the other. On the other hand, in the unicity of the person he possesses a perfect identity in his parts, as well as the hypostatic difference for his parts as single and unique. And, finally, he is perfect in both respects by natural and essential invariance, flawless regarding those parts that make up the extremes: he himself, the very same, is at once God and man."

112. *Opusc.* 8, PG 91, 97A, my translation.

113. Balthasar, *Cosmic Liturgy*, 122.

114. Benjamin Gleede, *The Development of the Term* ἐνυπόστατος *from Origen to John of Damascus* (Leiden: Brill, 2012), 183.

115. Gleede, *Development*, 17–19, who also observes that these earlier sources (esp. Origen) tend to link *enhypostatos* with certain Christological passages in the New Testament (1 Cor. 1:24, 30; John 1, 14:6; Heb. 1:3) in order to combat modalism. U. M. Lang, "Anhypostatos-Enhypostatos: Church Fathers, Protestant Orthodoxy and Karl Barth," *Journal of Theological Studies* 49.2 (1998): 635, sees that *enhypostatos* (as later in John Damascene), while never predicated of the Father, could be of both Son and Spirit (e.g., the spurious epistle of Pope Felix, *Collectio Sabbaitica VIII, Ep Felicis altera*, in *ACO* III, 21.12–16). Hence he wonders if even here a "locative" sense to the prefix intimated that Son and Spirit originate from Father—subsist "in" the Father, as it were—whereas the Father subsists in no other.

116. Gleede, *Development*, 41. E.g., Athanasius, *Ep. ad Afros*. 4.3 (*Athanasius Werke*, vol. 2, *Historische Schriften*, pt. 8, ed. H. C. Brennecke, U. Heil, and A. von Stockhausen [Berlin: De Gruyter, 2006], 329): "Ἡ δὲ ὑπόστασις οὐσία ἐστὶ, καὶ οὐδὲν ἄλλο σημαινόμενον ἔχει ἢ αὐτὸ τὸ ὄν"—later an important passage for those denouncing the Chalcedonian discretion of *hypostasis* and *ousia*; cf. Gleede, *Development*, 54.

117. E.g., Socrates, *HE* II.19; cf. Gleede, *Development*, 26–41.

118. For the Severan use of this polemic, see Severus of Antioch, *Or. 2 ad Nephalium*, CSCO 119 [120], 16.11–15 [13.1–5], and Lang, "Anhypostatos-Enhypostatos," 636. A Nestorian can wield it the same way: cf. Leontius of Jerusalem, *Adv. Nest.* II.14, PG 86, 1568A.

119. John Grammaticus, *Apol.* IV.3–6, ed. Richard, CCSG 1, 55.

120. Justinian, *Edictum rectae fidei*, in *Drei dogmatische Schriften Iustinians*, ed. M. Amelotti et al. (Milan: Giuffre, 1973), 144.29–146.12, and *Adv. Tria Capitula*, PG 86, 997B; and esp. the remarkable passage from Leontius of Jerusalem, *Adv. Nest.* II.14, PG 86, 1568AC, for instance, lines 3–7: "καὶ γὰρ οὐκ ἐν ἰδιαζούσῃ ὑποστῆναι, ἀλλ᾽ ἐν τῇ τοῦ Λόγου ὑποστάσει ὑφεστηκέναι τὸ ἀνθρώπινόν φαμεν τοῦ Σωτῆρος ἐξ ἀρχῆς· οὔτε μὴν ἁπλῶς τὴν τοῦ Λόγου νῦν ὑπόστασιν, ὡς Λόγου μόνον οὖσαν ὑπόστασιν νῦν οἴδαμεν· ἐπειδὴ σὺν τῷ ἀνθρωπίνῳ συνυφέστηκεν ἐν αὐτῇ τῶν ὁμουσίων ὁ Λόγος μετὰ τὴν ἄφραστον αὐτοῦ ἕνωσιν." Cf. too Grillmeier, *Christ in Christian Tradition*, vol. 2, pt. 2, 436. These texts do not explicitly link ἐνυπόστατος with the idea that Christ's humanity subsisted only in his hypostasis: That is, the in-subsistence principle that Loofs ascribes to Leontius of Byzantium is present here but not described with the precise term ἐνυπόστατος (cf. Gleede, *Development*, 1).

121. The locus classicus is Leontius of Byzantium, *CNE* 1, especially as (uncritically) paired with *Epil.* 8.

122. Friedrich Loofs, *Leontius von Byzanz und die gleichnamigen Schriftsteller der griechischen Kirche* (Leipzig: Hinrichs, 1887), 68.

123. Loofs, *Leontius von Byzanz*, 68: "So wird hier offenbar, dass schon bei Aristoteles die ποιότητες οὐσιώδεις eine Mittelstellung einnehmen zwischen den Substanzen und Qualitäten. . . . An diesen Fehler [of judging essential qualities as still quasi-Platonic, self-subsisting "essences" only partially present in an individual] knüpft die Theologie unserers Verfassers an."

124. Cf. Loofs, *Leontius von Byzanz*, 67, who, though unable to detect in Leontius's own illustrations which of Christ's two natures is ἐνυπόστατον, seems nevertheless to expect that one must be and that this one would therefore be absorbed by the other.

125. Grillmeier, *Christ in Christian Tradition*, vol. 2, pt. 2, 198.

126. Grillmeier, *Christ in Christian Tradition*, vol. 2, pt. 2, 194–95. Daley presented a paper on the topic in 1979, which he has yet to publish. He has, though,

offered the thesis in " 'Richer Union,' " 241–43, and recently in his introduction to *Leontius of Byzantium*, 73–75.

127. An awkward aspect of Grillmeier's and Daley's position surfaces in precisely this contrast, though, especially as it relates to Leontius: per earlier usage, *anhypostatos* names realities not subsistent *in themselves*, e.g., accidents, while *enhypostatos* names those that do subsist *in themselves*, e.g., the Son and Spirit. But Leontius explicitly denies that an enhypostatic nature—here Christ's humanity—subsists *in itself*, and he instead reserves this definition exclusively for hypostasis as opposed to enhypostatic nature (*CNE* 1, PG 86, 1277D, ed. Daley, *Complete Works*, 132; *Epil.* 8, PG 86, 1945AB, ed. Daley, *Complete Works*, 308). In other words, as already with the long philosophical tradition debating the in-subsistence of accidents and species in individuals, it seems difficult here to imagine that Leontius is not also intimating modes of subsistence; so Gleede, *Development*, 69–99. In fact, it is not entirely without warrant to read this very passage from Leontius as at least implying some sort of in-subsistence theory, since the major parallel evoked just afterward is the relation of figure to body: body is never "without figure," but that does not make it reducible to figure; it means only that figure is found always "*in* the body" (*CNE* 1, PG 86, 1280A, ed. Daley, *Complete Works*, 134–35). The obvious implication is that Christ's human nature, the *enhypostatos*, likewise occurs only *in* his hypostasis. Thus it might be significant that Leontius selects *figure* (τὸ σχῆμα): unlike "forms," which Platonists conceived as self-subsistent apart from finite individuals, figures, precisely as essential properties of bodies alone (not, say, of intelligible ideas), must subsist only and ever *in* bodies.

128. Lang, "Anhypostatos-Enhypostatos," 633. Lang's article shows that Loofs's in-subsistence theory as well as its explicit linkage to *enhypostatos* is definitely assumed by John of Damascus; see esp. *Dialectica fus.* 45, 17–22, discussed by Lang, "Anhypostatos-Enhypostatos," 649–50. Riches, *Ecce Homo*, 107–18, offers an overview of this debate in the context of modern theology. He is sympathetic to Lang's (and Barth's) understanding of it (though Maximus does not feature in the discussion). Another reason Daley and Grillmeier's thesis remains unpersuasive, one not often noted, is that it would have us believe Leontius and his pro-Chalcedonian successors failed to muster a convincing or even relevant argument against their immediate opponents. After all, the Nestorian second "hypostasis" that bore a human nature and even the Severan "human quality" that perdured after the union—both of these could just as easily be "real" and "subsistent." The whole point of distinguishing *hypostasis* from *enhypostatos* was to specify the *mode* of union and its concrete product, not to make the simple (and earlier) assertion *that* Christ's humanity possessed bare reality; cf. Leontius, *CNE* 1, and Maximus, *Ep.* 15, PG 91, 557D–560A.

129. Gleede, *Development*, 185. Lang, despite his own bid for John of Damascus's originality here, already noticed that Maximus conceives the *enhypo-*

static nature of Christ's humanity as precisely its singular in-subsistence in the Word and therefore declared (operating under the Daley-Grillmeier thesis about Leontius) that Maximus could "even be said to have anticipated the Loofsian misreading" (Lang, "Anhypostatos-Enhypostatos," 643n60). Lang's and especially Gleede's work validates earlier Maximus scholarship (Perl, Larchet, Riou) against Törönen's uncritical acceptance of Daley's thesis, which Törönen held as "conclusively argued" (*Union and Distinction*, 101). I find Törönen's candor refreshing: he perceives that if the in-subsistence theory prevails in Maximus's Christology it would imply, as Perl claimed, that the mode of Christ's self-identification with his own flesh also describes "a universal ontology"—a view Törönen's whole book rejects. See his *Union and Distinction*, 101–4.

130. *Amb.* 7.15: "Would he not also know that the many logoi are the one Logos, seeing that all things are related to Him without being confused with Him, who is the essential and personally distinct Logos of God the Father." There may be some resonances here of Lang's point about the possibility intra-Trinitarian origin implied in the prefix (cf. note 115), but certainly of the older sense, "personally distinct *from/of* the Father." An exhaustive list of references is in Gleede, *Development*, 141n497.

131. *Amb.* 1.3, modified.

132. *Opusc.* 23, PG 91, 264AB.

133. Cf. *Opusc.* 16, PG 91, 205BC, where in a Christological context Maximus says, "The *enhypostasized* is clearly the *en-existenced*, and the *en-existenced* is what participates essential and natural existence." He here refutes those who would take Christ's two activities to imply two actors. No: the power to act is inherent in nature, not in the hypostasis as such. Again, nature and hypostasis are inseparable, yet distinct. Because these differ even in their inseparable and indifferent identity as *one*, it is yet possible for one hypostasis to possess two natures—and with these two powers prescriptive of two activities. In the case of the Trinity the quantities are reversed but the principle remains unchanged: there we have three hypostases that possess (in a unique manner, yes) one nature, and so three actors perform one act. In Christ one actor performs two acts. In both cases no actor acts except through nature and no nature subsists except in hypostasis.

134. Gleede, *Development*, 142: "This enables Maximus to apply the distinction between ὑπόστασις and ἐνυπόστατος also to trinitarian theology and to establish a univocal technical use of it in trinitarian and Christological contexts."

135. *Ep.* 15, PG 91, 553D; so too *Ep.* 12, PG 91, 468AB; cf. Gleede, *Development*, 151.

136. *Amb.* 2.2: "The Word of God is whole, complete essence (for He is God), and He is whole, undiminished hypostasis (for He is the Son). Having *emptied Himself*, He became the *seed* of His own *flesh*, and being thus compounded by means of His ineffable conception, He became the hypostasis of the flesh He assumed"; cf. *Ep.* 15, PG 91, 553D; *Ep.* 19, PG 91, 592CD.

137. *Amb.* 5.13, modified.

138. Gleede, *Development*, 154: "In reinterpreting the 'property of sonship' as a mode of existence, the identity between Christ qua second hypostasis and qua hypostasis of the two natures becomes much more plausible, as it is not so much a second generation, clearly different from the first, which marks off Christ's hypostasis, but the formally divine actualisation of the human natural properties—the very same way of actualisation which also applies to the divine ones. . . . Maximus makes it absolutely clear that individuality cannot be constituted by one or several accidents . . . but only by a biographical process in its entirety constituted— according to Cappadocian premises—primarily by its origin."

139. *Amb.* 5.14.

140. It is even true, though scandalous to some (Gleede, *Development*, 188; Lang, "Anhypostatos-Enhypostatos," 646), that the divine nature itself is *anhypostatos*. So *Opusc.* 13.7, PG 91, 148C, my translation and emphasis: "Just as you say one sole essence because of the consubstantiality of the Holy Trinity, and because of hypostatic difference you say three hypostases, in the same way because of the essential difference of the Word and the flesh, you say two essences, and by the fact that *each lacks its own proper hypostasis*, you say one sole hypostasis [καὶ τὸ μὴ ἰδιοϋπόστατον, μίαν ὑπόστασιν λέγε]." In *Ep.* 15, PG 91, 557D, Maximus explicitly notes that both natures or "parts" of the "whole" hypostasis, Christ, are themselves "enhypostasized, not a hypostasis" (ἐνυπόστατον, ἀλλ' οὐχ ὑπόστασιν). Lang thinks the "damaging consequence" of this view (found too in the earlier *De sectis*, VII.2, PG 86, 1241B) is the implication that even the divine nature did not subsist on its own from all eternity. But given the Neo-Chalcedonian commitment to the univocity of Trinitarian and Christological concepts, that is precisely the point: there is no tetrad in the Trinity, therefore the Trinity itself grounds and exemplifies the logics of nature and hypostasis. Not even divine nature *qua* nature subsists in itself. Why then would any other nature?

141. *Ep.* 13, PG 91, 546BC, where Maximus admits that "certainly according to a certain principle and mode, because of the hypostatic identity, that is, the one hypostasis according to which there is no possible difference, Christ is one" (πάντως κατά τινα λόγον τε καὶ τρόπον, διὰ τὴν ὑποστατικὴν ταυτότητα, ἤγουν τὴν μίαν ὑπόστασιν, καθ' ἣν διαφορὰν οὐ δύναται, ἐν ἐστιν ὁ Χριστός). But the *logos* and *tropos* of this oneness are themselves *one* principle and mode—the Logos's own hypostasis (which is also a filial mode from eternity)—not, against Severans, one *natural* principle; in Christ abide two natural principles (546CD); cf. *Ep.* 15, PG 91, 572B; *Amb.* 5.11; *Amb.* 10.3; *Pyr.* 35, PG 91, 297D–300A, passim.

142. *Amb.* 5.2. Hence the sense of a thing's *logos* as the natural potential of its actualization, as when λόγος responds to ἐνέργεια; cf. *Amb.* 10.90.

143. Karl-Heinz Uthemann, "Der Neuchalkedonismus als Vorbereitung des Monotheletismus: Ein Beitrag zum eigentlichen Anliegen des Neuchalkedonis-

mus," *Studia Patristica* 29 (1997): 408, my emphasis: "Hier wird das eigentliche Anliegen der Monenergeten deutlich; sie wollen mit dem Begriff der ἕνωσις und darum der μία ὑπόστασις *mehr als nur einen formalen, unanschaulichen Sinn verbinden.* Damit stehen sie in der Wirkungsgeschichte des Neuchalkedonismus und seines Ringens um das Auffüllen des chalkedonischen Hypostasebegriffs." Bathrellos, *Byzantine Christ*, 53, disagrees with Uthemann because "there is no necessary connection between accepting that Christ has a divine hypostasis, on the one hand, and monothelitism [with monenergism implied] on the other." But Uthemann claims only a real and conceivable (not a necessary) connection between Neo-Chalcedonian one-hypostasis Christology and these later heresies, with, as he argues, Maximus's dyothelite Christology representing still another (413).

144. An important inspiration for Maximus derives, of course, from the Christological use of the term at Gregory of Nazianzus, *Ep.* 101, in *Lettres théologiques*, rev. ed., ed. Paul Gallay, SC 208, 48 (translation from Verna Harrison, "Perichoresis in the Greek Fathers," *St. Vladimir's Theological Quarterly* 35 [1991]: 55, slightly modified): "Just as the natures are mixed, so also the names pass reciprocally (περιχωρουσῶν) into each other by the principle of natural co-affinity (συμφυίας)." But see Peter Stemmer, "PERICHORESE: Zur Geschichte eines Begriffs," *Archiv für Begriffsgeschichte* 27 (1983): 17: "Zu einem tragenden theologischen Terminus wird περιχωρεῖν erst bei Maximus Confessor im 7. Jahrhundert."

145. Thunberg, *Microcosm and Mediator*, 23–36; Garrigues, *Maxime le Confesseur*, 136–37; Stemmer, "PERICHORESE," 17–19; Harrison, "Perichoresis," 57–59.

146. *Pyr.* 162.

147. Something unthinkable after Gregory of Nyssa's *Ad Ablabium*.

148. *Pyr.* 170, PG 91, 337C–340A; cf. *Ep.* 19, PG 91, 593BC; *Opusc.* 16, PG 91, 189D. Origen had already likened the "red-hot sword" to the Word's Incarnation; cf. *Princ.* 2.6.6.

149. *Pyr.* 177, PG 91, 340BC.

150. *Pyr.* 182, PG 91, 341A, trans. Joseph P. Farrell, *The Disputation with Pyrrhus of Our Father among the Saints Maximus the Confessor* (Waymart, PA: St. Tikhon's Monastery Press, 2014), 114, slightly modified: "ἐπειδὴ μέσον κτιστῆς καὶ ἀκτίστου οὐδεμία ὑπάρχει τὸ σύνολον."

151. *Pyr.* 183, PG 91, 341B, my emphasis.

152. Karl-Heinz Uthemann, "Der Neuchalkedonismus als Vorbereitung des Monotheletismus: Ein Beitrag zum eigentlichen Anliegen des Neuchalkedonismus," *Studia Patristica* 29 (1997): 399, notes that Anastasius of Antioch preferred to conceive Christ's *energeiai* in terms of their "effect," and that this slips toward a monenergist emphasis on the (pre)dominance of divine activity in Christ. See too Leontius of Byzantium, *CNE* 7, PG 86, 1297C, ed. Daley, *Complete Works*,

162–63: "Our dispute is rather about the product of union [τοῦ ἀποτελέσματος τοῦ ἐκ τῆς ἐνώσεώς], and whether it is about things themselves [τῶν πραγμάτων αὐτῶν] or simply about the words referring to them."

153. *Pyr.* 184, PG 91, 341BC, trans. Farrell modified.

154. Cf. Plotinus, *Enn.* V.4 [7] 2. The walking-to-footprint analogy comes from Emilsson, "Remarks on the Relation," 283.

155. *Pyr.* 186–89; cf. *Opusc.* 7, PG 91, 85D–88A; *Opusc.* 8; *Amb.* 5.19. Cf. Dionysius, *Ep.* 4 (*ad Gaium*), in *Corpus Dionysiacum*, vol. 2, ed. G. Heil and A. M. Ritter (1991; repr., Berlin: De Gruyter, 2014), 161.

156. *Pyr.* 192, PG 91, 345D–348A, trans. Farrell modified: "Εἰδὲ ποιότης ἐστὶν ἡ καινότης, οὐ μίαν δηλοῖ ἐνέργειαν, ἀλλὰ τὸν καινὸν καὶ ἀπόρρητον τρόπον τῆς τῶν φυσικῶν τοῦ Χριστοῦ ἐνεργειῶν ἐκφάνσεως, τῷ ἀπορρήτῳ τρόπῳ τῆς εἰς ἀλλήλας τῶν Χριστοῦ φύσεων περιχωρήσεως προσφόρως, καὶ τὴν κατὰ ἄνθρωπον αὐτοῦ πολιτείαν, ξένην οὖσαν καὶ παράδοξον, καὶ τῇ φύσει τῶν ὄντων ἄγνωστον, καὶ τὸν τρόπον τῆς κατὰ τὴν ἀπόρρητον ἕνωσιν ἀντιδόσεως."

157. Marek Jankowiak and Phil Booth, "A New Date-List of the Works of Maximus the Confessor," in Allen and Neil, *Oxford Handbook*, 64.

158. *Opusc.* 5, PG 91, 64D–65A.

159. *Opusc.* 5, PG 91, 64C: "Then we ourselves would call divine nature created or the body uncreated."

160. *Opusc.* 5, PG 91, 64C.

161. *Opusc.* 5, PG 91, 64A.

162. Aristotle, *Cat.* VII, 6b29.

163. Aristotle, *Cat.* VII, 7b15: "τὰ πρός τι ἅμα τῇ φύσει εἶναι." Cf. Mossman Roueché, "A Middle Byzantine Handbook of Logical Terminology," *Jahrbuch der österreichischen Byzantanistik* 29 (1980): 96 (= 262, lines 178–79).

164. Hence the passive sense of ἀντιδιαιρέω, here "τὰ ἀντιδιαιρούμενα" or "mutually implicative," which means "to be opposed as the members of a *natural* classification" (LSJ, s.v.); see Aristotle, *Cat.* XIV, b34.

165. *Opusc.* 5, PG 91, 64AB, my translation.

166. See Wood, "That and How *Perichoresis* Differs," 220–36.

167. Cf. Stephen Gersh, *From Iamblichus to Eriugena: An Investigation into the Prehistory and Evolution of the Pseudo-Dionysian Tradition* (Leiden: Brill, 1978), 27–44.

168. Plato, *Parm.* 131b–c (the problem of the Sail Cloth); Plotinus, *Enn.* VI.4–5 (basically a commentary on the *Parm.*, on the One's undiminished omnipresence to all things, even to body). Cf. A. C. Lloyd, *The Anatomy of Neoplatonism* (Oxford: Oxford University Press, 1998), 98–110; and Gary M. Gurtler, "Plotinus and the Platonic *Parmenides*," *International Philosophical Quarterly* 32.4 (1992): 443–57.

169. Proclus, *El. Theol.*, prop. 2, ed. and trans. E. R. Dodds, *The Elements of Theology* (1963; repr., Oxford: Clarendon Press, 2004), 3.

170. Proclus, *El. Theol.*, prop. 9, ed. Dodds, 10–11: "Πᾶν τὸ αὔταρκες ἢ κατ' οὐσίαν ἢ ἐνέργειαν κρεῖττόν ἐστι τοῦ μὴ αὐτάρκους ἀλλ' εἰς ἄλλην οὐσίαν ἀνηρτημένου τὴν τῆς τελειότητος αἰτίαν."

171. Proclus, *El. Theol.*, prop. 18, ed. Dodds, 20–21. So arise Proclus's famous three moments of participation: τὸ ἀμέθεκτον ("the unparticipated," the superior cause in its proper mode), τὸ μετεχόμενον ("the participated," the whole presence of the superior cause in the effect according to the effect's proper mode), τὸ μετέχον ("the participating," the effect *qua* distinct/proceeding from what it has identical to its superior cause); cf. Proclus, *El. Theol.*, props. 23–24, ed. Dodds, 26–29. See too Gersh, *From Iamblichus to Eriugena*, 150–51, for the necessary "vertical" and "horizontal" orders of existence (hypostases).

172. Proclus, *El. Theol.*, props. 75, 77, 78; cf. Iamblichus, *De myst.* I.18; Dionysius, *DN* 5.2. I refer here to an idea already developed in Plotinus, that vertical causation consists in the limitation of a higher, interior act by (or in the mode of) a lower power. See Gary M. Gurtler, "Plotinus on the Limitation of Act by Potency," *Saint Anselm Journal* 7 (2009): 1–15.

173. Iamblichus, *De myst.* I.19; Proclus, *El. Theol.*, props. 66–74.

174. Iamblichus, *De myst.* I.9, trans. John M. Dillon, *De mysteriis*, annot. Emma C. Clarke (Atlanta, GA: Society of Biblical Literature, 2003), 40–41: "εἰ γὰρ οὐδείς ἐστι λόγος οὐδὲ σχέσις συμμετρίας οὐδὲ οὐσίας τις κοινωνία οὐδὲ κατὰ δύναμιν ἢ ἐνέργειαν συμπλοκὴ πρὸς τὸ διακοσμοῦν τοῦ διακοσμουμένου."

175. Iamblichus, *De myst.* I.9, trans. Dillon, 40–41; cf. too the quotation from Plato, *Tim.* 52c–d, at note 61 of chapter 2.

176. Christians of course were drawn to the Stoic notion of "interpenetration" or "mixture," which with Stoics was but a strange bit of physics: two bodies can occupy one another in the same space and time and still preserve their proper characteristics; so Stemmer, "PERICHORESE," 10–13. Neoplatonists, though, appropriated this term for purely intelligible realities that enjoy an incorporeal indivisibility; so L. Abramowski, "συνάφεια und ἀσύγχυτος ἕνωσις als Bezeichnung für trinitarische und christologische Einheit," in *Drei christologische Untersuchungen*, Beihefte zur Zeitschrift für die neutestamentliche Wissenschaft (Berlin: De Gruyter, 1981), 70: "Dies ist also die 'geziemende' Weise, von Einheit auf der Ebene des Geistigen zu sprechen." Cf. Proclus, *In Parm.*, ed. Victor Cousin, *Procli philosophi Platonici: Opera inedita continens Procli commentarium in Platonis Parmenidem* (Hildesheim: Olms, 2002), 754, and *El. Theol.*, prop. 176 (on intellectual forms in intellect), ed. Dodds, 154–55: "All interpenetrates all [φοιτᾷ πάντα διὰ πάντων]," are "mutually implicit, interpenetrating one another in their entirety [ὁμοῦ ἐστι καὶ ἐν ἀλλήλοις, ὅλα δι' ὅλων φοιτῶντα ἀδιαστάτως]." So Stoics and Neoplatonists alike conceive the logic of *perichoresis* as applying only among entities on the same horizontal metaphysical plane; they simply pick different planes. When therefore Maximus (following Nazianzen) applies *perichoresis* to Christ's two natures, he does something unparalleled: he makes *perichoresis* a

vertical relation between the cause and the effect, the divine and the human, the superior and the inferior, God and man.

177. Dionysius, *Ep.* 4.

178. *Amb.* 5.2.

179. *Amb.* 5.20, slightly modified: "If, then, the mode of union [ὁ τῆς ἑνώσεως τρόπος] preserves the principle of distinction, the expression of the saint is a circumlocution . . . since in nature and in quality the essential principle of the united natures is in no way diminished [μεμείωται] by the union. Nonetheless it is not, as some would have it, 'by the negation of the two extremes that we arrive at an affirmation' of something in the middle, for there is no kind of intermediary in Christ that could be the positive remainder after the negation of two extremes." Constas, in vol. 1 of *On Difficulties in the Church Fathers*, 476n18, provides the citation, which comes from Pyrrhus's *Dogmatic Tome*, in *ACO*, vol. 2, pt. 2, 608.

180. See *Ep.* 12, PG 91, 472D–473B, my translation. Here Maximus openly rejects "the mere mention of difference" exactly because it can imply, as vertical causality often does, a simple *modal* contraction or difference of *one* essence. This passage is worth quoting in full: "Necessarily, however certain things differ, there lies every [sort of] difference. And where the possibility of difference is perceived there certainly exist the things that differ. For there are such things that in a certain way indicate one another. Thus causes and effects [τὰ αἴτια καὶ τὰ αἰτιατὰ] refer to one another as they are perceived to have the same essence. For if the differing essence *qua* cause produces in Christ the difference of the natures from which He is constituted, then certainly the difference emerges clearly as an effect of the natural otherness of the things united, that is, as [if] from a particular cause. Indeed it is natural, as I said, for such things to indicate one another, such that if one is referenced, this always confesses by necessity the other as well; or if one is denied, the other does not appear either. Therefore it is necessary to say 'two,' lest we introduce a shallow difference [ἵνα μὴ ψιλὴν τὴν διαφορὰν εἰσάγωμεν]. And it is for this reason alone that we use number: the manifest difference of the things concurring remained preserved after the union, though not [a difference] of things divided. In this way [we have] an easier and truer semantic expression for disclosing the difference of the concrete realities rather than 'confirming' these realities by the mere mention of 'a difference.'"

181. This explains the subtle but profound way Maximus modifies the comparison of the two activities of body and soul to Christ's divine and human activities. Unlike the monenergist proposal where the soul's act instrumentalizes the body's, Maximus specifies that the Son first *becomes* the power of the inferior nature and *then* actualizes it in its own right. Again the point is to remove any natural mediation. So *Amb.* 5.8 (slightly modified): "And He did these things . . . moving willingly the assumed nature that truly had become and is called His own, in the way that the soul independently and naturally moves the body that is native

to it, or to speak more precisely, He Himself, without change, truly became what human nature is, and in actual fact fulfilled the economy on our behalf."

182. *Amb.* 5.17, slightly modified.

183. Daley, "'Richer Union,'" 261 and 245. Cf. Leontius of Byzantium, *CNE* 7, PG 86, 1297C, ed. Daley, *Complete Works*, 162; *Epil.* 8, PG 86, 1940BC, ed. Daley, *Complete Works*, 300–301. In both texts "product" translates ἀποτέλεσμα—the very thing Pyrrhus sought to force into a monenergist framework during his dispute with Maximus.

184. A major difference between them emerges in the degree to which each thinker applies reflection on the fact of Christ to the fact of the whole world. I address this in the next chapter.

185. Blowers, *Maximus the Confessor*, 136–37; see too his "The Transfiguration of Jesus Christ as 'Saturated Phenomenon' and as Key to the Dynamics of Biblical Revelation in St. Maximus the Confessor," in *What Is the Bible? The Patristic Doctrine of Scripture*, ed. Matthew Baker and Mark Mourachian (Minneapolis, MN: Fortress Press, 2016), 83–101.

186. *Amb.* 5.13; *Amb.* 7.37; *Pyr.* 192, PG 91, 345D–348A.

187. *Amb.* 10.82; cf. *Amb.* 7.37, *Amb.* 10.49, *Q. Thal.* 22 and 60.

188. *Amb.* 4.8.

189. Faith, I note, is not ultimately separate from intellectual insight, since for Maximus perfected faith is "the true knowledge" (γνῶσις ἀληθὴς); cf. *CT* 1.9, PG 90, 1085CD (cf. *Amb.* 10.2). See Jordan Daniel Wood, "Both Mere Man and Naked God: The Incarnational Logic of Apophasis of St. Maximus the Confessor," in *Maximus the Confessor as a European Philosopher*, ed. Sotiris Mitralexis, Georgios Steiris, and Sebastian Lalla (Eugene, OR: Cascade Books, 2017), 125–26.

190. *Ep.* 15, PG 91, 556B, my translation: "ἐν τῇ πρὸς ἄλληλα κατ᾽ ἄκρον προσωπικῇ ταυτότητι τῶν οἰκείων μερῶν διαπαντὸς ἑνιζόμενον." See too *Ep.* 12, PG 91, 501A: "We know that he is through his parts"; *Opusc.* 8, PG 91, 49.

191. *Amb.* 5.12, slightly modified.

192. *Opusc.* 16, PG 91, 201AB, my translation: "For it is not possible, divine or human nature, to perceive a difference outside of their essential activity. For that which defines a reality is properly the principle of its essential power. This latter removed, so too vanishes the subject. That is why we recognize them naturally preserved in the Incarnate Word. One shows itself through the projection [προσβολῇ] of divine [traits] into the flesh, the other [by the projection of the flesh] into his sovereign power. In this way we also recognize the natures from which the essential activities exist—namely through these very [activities]."

193. *Amb.* 5.24; *Pyr.* 28–31, 192.

194. *Exp. Orat. Dom.* 4, in *Opuscula exegetica duo*, ed. Peter Van Deun, CCSG 23 (Turnhout: Brepols, 1991), 54.

195. *Exp. Orat. Dom.* 1, in *Opuscula exegetica duo*, ed. Van Deun, CCSG 23, 28–29, identifies the divine "counsel of the Father" with "the mysterious self-emptying of the only-begotten Son with a view to the deification of our nature, a self-emptying in which he holds enclosed the limit of all the ages." Maximus immediately continues: "If then the accomplished work of the divine counsel is the deification of our nature [δὲ θείας ὑπάρχει βουλῆς ἔργον ἡ τῆς ἡμετέρας φύσεως θέωσις]" (CCSG 23, 29). The Incarnation reveals the whole of God because it realizes the essential power and counsel of the Three. Cf. too *Q. Thal.* 22.2 and 60.7.

196. *Amb.* 2.4.

197. Thunberg, *Microcosm and Mediator*, 21.

198. Tollefsen, *Christocentric Cosmology*, 67, 80, 135; for Balthasar, see Cyril O'Regan, "Von Balthasar," 241.

T W O . The Beginning: Word Becomes World

1. *Amb.* 7.22, PG 91, 1084CD.

2. Andrew Louth, "The Reception of Dionysius in the Byzantine World," in *Re-thinking Dionysius the Areopagite*, ed. Sarah Coakley and Charles M. Stang (Hoboken, NJ: Wiley-Blackwell, 2009), 63. Not that Maximus lacked any precedent for the *logoi* doctrine: Thunberg, *Microcosm and Mediator*, 73n157, mentions the Stoics, Origen, Augustine (*rationes seminales*; e.g., *De div. quaest.* 83), Evagrius, and Dionysius (and his commentator John of Scythopolis), from whom "Maximus has received a more positive influence." Louth knows these too, but he rightly doubts that any of them really approximate to the sort of metastructural principle this doctrine becomes in Maximus. Indeed, none, I think, evinces Maximus's peculiar emphases as detailed in this chapter and the next.

3. On the *logoi* doctrine's application to Porphyry's tree in Maximus, see *Amb.* 41.10; Tollefsen, *Christocentric Cosmology*, 81–92; Törönen, *Union and Distinction*, 140. That the *logoi* in a thing bear its efficient, formal, and final cause is clear from texts like *Amb.* 21.5, but see secs. 2.3–4 below.

4. Sherwood, "Survey of Recent Work," 435, simply solicited studies of "participation" in Maximus's thought; Balthasar preferred to stress *analogy* and often equated this to some version of participation. Some recent commentators have tried to answer Sherwood's call, sometimes with slight provisos: Lévy, *Créé et l'incréé*, 129–32 and esp. 158–91, summons Simplicius's idea of *sunergeia* by relation (a refined version of Plotinus's theory of double act); Tollefsen, "Did St Maximus the Confessor" and *Activity and Participation*; Marius Portaru, "Gradual Participation According to St Maximus the Confessor," *Studia Patristica* 54 (2012): 281–94; Clement Yung Wen, "Maximus the Confessor and the Problem of

Participation," *Heythrop Journal* 58 (2017): 3–16; Stephen Clarke, "'Christ Plays in Ten Thousand Places': The Relationship of *Logoi* and *Logos* in Plotinus, Maximus, and Beyond," unpublished paper, n.d., 1–18; Jonathan Greig, "Proclus' Doctrine of Participation in Maximus the Confessor's *Centuries of Theology* I.48-50," *Studia Patristica* 75 (2017): 137–48.

I say "nearly all" due to three exceptions: (1) Perl, in "Methexis," 195–97 and 205, and "Metaphysics and Christology," wants to speak of Maximus's distinctly Christological understanding of the God-world relation as "perfect participation." Clearly I share many of Perl's intuitions. But as I also say in the Introduction, I think his commitment to a prior *philosophically* defined idea of "participation" prevents him from seeing his brilliant intuitions through. (2) Larchet, *Divinisation de l'homme*, 600, doubts that Maximus had a clear "doctrine" of participation at all. (3) Marius Portaru, "The Vocabulary of Participation in the Works of Saint Maximus the Confessor," in *Naboth's Vineyard*, ed. Octavian Gordon and Alexandru Mihaila (Cluj-Napoca: Presa Universitara Clujeana, 2012), 295–317, offers an "anthropological lecture" of Maximian participation that tries to avoid either a denial of participation (Larchet) or a basically Neoplatonic view of it (Perl, Tollefsen—though, again, I think Perl's view is more complicated). Now, many of these scholars do recognize important differences between Maximus and Neoplatonists on the God-world relation. In general, however, I confess sympathies with the brief remarks of Stephen Clarke, whose proximate interlocutor is Balthasar: "I don't deny that there may be differences. The problem is to locate them. I have similar qualms even about Tollefsen's much better informed account: in saying that Maximus manages a Christian *alternative* to Neo-Platonist metaphysics, he leaves me very uncertain what exactly the *alternative* consists in" ("Christ Plays," 5).

5. Again *mystery* in Maximus always refers at least to the historical Incarnation; for references in Maximus's corpus, see the introduction to *Q. Thal.* in Fr. Maximos [Nicholas] Constas's translation, *On Difficulties in Sacred Scripture: Responses to Thalassios*, Fathers of the Church 136 (Washington, DC: Catholic University of America Press, 2018), 49n157.

6. See the more hesitant discussion of Paul M. Blowers, *Exegesis and Spiritual Pedagogy*, 120–22; and *Drama of the Divine Economy: Creator and Creation in Early Christian Theology and Piety* (Oxford: Oxford University Press, 2012), 166 and 166n15.

7. Tollefsen, *Christocentric Cosmology*, 67, and *Activity and Participation*, 122.

8. Gregory of Nazianzus, *Or.* 38.2, "On the Nativity," cited at *Amb.* 33.1.

9. *Amb.* 33.2, PG 91, 1285C, slight modification.

10. *Amb.* 33.2, PG 91, 1285D–1288A. I treat this aspect more fully and especially as it relates to speech about God in Wood, "Both Mere Man."

11. *Amb.* 33.2, PG 91, 1285D, my translation.

12. See sec. 1.4

13. See sec. 3.3.

14. As in Plotinus, *Enn.* VI. 9 [9] 8.

15. This point reappears below in sec. 2.3. Here I notice that of Maximus's many modern commentators, Paul Blowers conveys Maximus's own insistence most lucidly: "The Confessor's primary analogy to convey the condescension of the Word into the *logoi* of creatures (*and* of Scripture, *and* of the virtues) is the incarnation in Jesus of Nazareth. In reality this is *not an 'analogy' at all since it is precisely the Logos* 'destined . . . before the foundation of the world' to become the incarnate and sacrificial Lamb (1 Peter 1:19–20) who originally contained the *logoi* and *willingly* communicated his presence to creatures through them" (Blowers, *Drama*, 166, my emphasis; cf. similarly his "From Nonbeing to Eternal Well-Being: Creation ex Nihilo in the Cosmology and Soteriology of Maximus the Confessor," in *Light on Creation: Ancient Commentators in Dialogue and Debate on the Origin of the World*, ed. Geert Roskam and Joseph Verheyden [Tübingen: Mohr Siebeck, 2017], 177). This remarkable observation—that the "analogy" between historical and cosmic Incarnation is no mere analogy—commits Blowers to the thesis that for Maximus the Word's condescension in the *logoi* of creation, in Jesus, in scripture, and in the deified are "eschatologically simultaneous" (cf. Blowers, *Drama*, 163, and his *Maximus the Confessor*, 137–40). Yet analogy, particularly its denial, says much less about simultaneity and much more about the *mode* of Christ's presence in these incarnations. Anyone who believed in divine omnipresence should not have had a problem with the idea that divinity dwelled in the man Jesus, even to a peculiarly concentrated degree, in the same mode that the One cause of all things dwells in all its effects. Indeed, Athanasius tendered that exact argument (*De incarnatione verbi dei* 42), which others after him such as Gregory of Nyssa would have the keen sense to qualify: Gregory reprises Athanasius's argument that moves from divine omnipresence in creation to his presence in the man Jesus but also admits that "the manner in which God is present in us is not the same as it was in that case," namely in Jesus's (*Or. cat.* 25). Christological controversies from Nicaea to Chalcedon (and beyond, really) were rather concerned to *differentiate* the way God was present in Jesus Christ from the way he is present elsewhere. And so the truly astounding insight, one Blowers seems to intimate, is not just that Maximus rethinks how God is present in Jesus in order to distinguish this presence from God's presence in the cosmos but that he then reintroduces *this mode* of presence as the potential mode in which the Word might be present in the entirety of the cosmos itself.

16. *Synkatabasis* often describes the historical Incarnation, both in Maximus and in the Cappadocians. Cf. *Amb.* 4.4, 7.22, 42.3.

17. *Amb.* 33.2, PG 91, 1288A: "τοσοῦτον ἡμᾶς δι' ἑαυτον πρὸς ἕνωσιν ἑαυτοῦ συστείλας, ὅσον αὐτὸς δι' ἡμᾶς ἑαυτὸν συγκαταβάσεως λόγῳ διέστειλεν."

18. Quoted at *Q. Thal.* 60, ed. Laga and Steel, CCSG 7, 73, from the translation of Paul M. Blowers and Robert Louis Wilken in their *On the Cosmic Mystery of Jesus Christ: Selected Writings from St. Maximus the Confessor* (Yonkers, NY: St. Vladimir's Seminary Press, 2003), 123.

19. *Q. Thal.* 60.7, ed. Laga and Steel, CCSG 7, 79.

20. *Q.Thal.* 60.2, ed. Laga and Steel, CCSG 7, 73. Blowers and Wilken translate this as "the whole mystery of Christ," which is also apt. And notice that Col. 1:27 goes on to state explicitly what this "mystery" is: "Christ in you" (ὅ ἐστιν Χριστὸς ἐν ὑμῖν). Maximus never quotes this second half of the sentence. Still I suggest that the rest of his response essentially explicates this very idea.

21. *Q. Thal.* 60.2, ed. Laga and Steel, CCSG 7, 73, my translation.

22. *Q. Thal.* 60.3, ed. Laga and Steel, CCSG 7, 73–75.

23. *Pace* Tollefsen, *Activity and Participation*, 122: "Why should we speak of the embodiment of divine Forms as an incarnation or embodiment of the *Logos*? According to Maximus we should understand it this way because the creation and salvation of the world is knit together in one single divine purpose, exclusively bound up with the great mystery. The creation of the world is the first step towards the fulfilment of God's plan. Even though the *Logos* Himself is not hypostatically present in created essences or natures, the *logoi* defining them and delimiting their natural capacity represent Him in relation to them. They are His patterns for creatures." I take issue below with equating the *logoi* and forms (secs. 2.3–4). Here the problem comes with the qualification—one Maximus never makes—that the Word is not "hypostatically present in created essences." Tollefsen appears to mean that when Maximus first identifies the "mystery according to Christ" with the historical hypostatic union *and then* applies this to the very principle (ἀρχή) and purpose (τέλος) of all creation, he must have surreptitiously modified the meaning of "mystery according to Christ" in the latter case. On this reading there is something like a gradual immanence of the Word in creation: creation from nothing is "the first step" and so an initial and lesser degree of immanence, the historical Incarnation the perfection (or indeed a qualitatively different mode) of that immanence.

24. *Q. Thal.* 60.3, ed. Laga and Steel, CCSG 7, 75: the "mystery according to Christ," the hypostatic identity of humanity and divinity, is "the preconceived divine purpose of the beginning of beings [τῆς ἀρχῆς τῶν ὄντων], which, were we to define it, we would say it is the preconceived *telos* for the sake of which all things are, which itself is for the sake of nothing else. In view of this end, God introduced the essences of beings." Elsewhere Maximus specifies that "had man united created nature with the uncreated through love . . . he would have shown them to be *one and the same* by the state of grace" (*Amb.* 41.5, PG 91, 1308B, my emphasis), and that the "power" to effect this union "was given to us from the beginning by nature for this purpose" (τὴν ἐξ ἀρχῆς φυσικῶς ἡμῖν πρὸς τοῦτο δοθεῖσαν δύναμιν) (*Amb.* 41.9, PG 91, 1309D); on all this, see sec. 3.1.

25. *Q. Thal.* 60.4, ed. Laga and Steel, CCSG 7, 75, my translation: "Διὰ γὰρ τὸν Χριστόν, ἤγουν τὸ κατὰ Χριστὸν μυστήριον, πάντες οἱ αἰῶνες καὶ τὰ ἐν αὐτοῖς αἰῶσιν ἐν Χριστῷ τὴν ἀρχὴν τοῦ εἶναι καὶ τὸ τέλος εἰλήφασιν."

26. Origen's Περὶ Ἀρχῶν, of course, constitutes the most obvious patristic example (see citations in next note too). Maximus frequently uses ἀρχή in just this sense: e.g., *Amb.* 5.12; *Amb.* 10.37, 57, 73, 96; *Amb.* 23.2; *Amb.* 40.3, PG 91, 1304B; *Amb.* 46.4, PG 91, 1357B; *Amb.* 65.2, PG 91, 1392C; *Amb.* 67.4; *Q. Thal.* 59, ed. Laga and Steel, CCSG 7, 61–63; *CT* 1.48–50, passim.

27. Origen, *Hom. in Gen.* 1.1 and *Comm. in Jo.* 1.17–19, 22. Cf. Blowers, *Drama*, 141, for Origen, and 146–53 for Gregory of Nyssa.

28. See sec. 4.3.

29. The date and habit of composition confirm that these supposedly more "spiritual" texts are at least as relevant for understanding Maximus's more "speculative" theology. The *Centuries on Theology and Economy* (*CT*) were likely composed soon after the *Ambigua to John* and (or at least in tandem with) the *Questions to Thalassius*, perhaps between 632 and the summer of 633; see Jankowiak and Booth, "New Date-List," 30; Sherwood, *Earlier Ambigua*, 106–9; and Luis Salés, introduction to *Two Hundred Chapters on Theology: St. Maximus the Confessor* (Yonkers, NY: St. Vladimir's Seminary Press, 2015), 24. Maximus seems to have had a peculiar talent for transposing content he had worked out in a more dialectical, question-answer context (*erotapokriseis*) into the more contemplative mood of the chapters or centuries genre; see Salés, introduction, 25–26, where he signals an especially relevant example: the *tantum-quantum* principle (where human deification and divine Incarnation describe two aspects of the same reality) codified in *Q.Thal.* 22, for instance, undergirds all of Maximus's works, *CT* included.

30. *CT* 1.66, PG 90, 1108AB, my translation.

31. Maximus earlier treated the activities of Christ's life, identifying them with the "rectification [or righteousness] of the commandments" that he enacted and that the human soul must enact too through virtue, the sine qua non of knowledge (and then deified knowledge); cf. *CT* 1.59.

32. *CT* 1.47; *Q. Thal.* 22, ed. Laga and Steel, CCSG 7, 141; *Opusc.* 1, PG 91, 33B.

33. *CT* 1.67, my translation.

34. Cf. sec. 3.1. I quote here a key passage I take up there: it was Adam's vocation from the outset to realize in himself the identity between created and uncreated nature, to show them "to be one and the same by the state of grace" (ἓν καὶ ταὐτὸν δείξειε κατὰ τὴν ἕξιν τῆς χάριτος) (*Amb.* 41.5, PG 91, 1308B). What exactly "by grace" indicates is, of course, the really pressing question, which I reserve for next chapter.

35. For its role in Christo-logic, see sec. 1.3; for its relation to divine creation, see below at sec. 2.2. The denial of any sort of natural "familiarity" holds particular interest, since both Origen and Gregory of Nyssa sought to "Christianize" this Stoic doctrine—which is, I add, yet another way of speaking about ratio-

nal beings' participation in the divine Logos; cf. Ilaria Ramelli, "The Stoic Doctrine of Oikeiosis and its Transformation in Christian Platonism," *Apeiron* 47.1 (2014): 116–40, esp. Origen's claim that those who are "familiar with God" might be called "parts of the Father" (οἰκεῖοί τε ἄνθρωποι οἱ μὲν τῷ πατρί, μερίδες ὄντες αὐτοῦ) at *Comm. in Jo.* 2.3.32 (cited in Ramelli, "Stoic Doctrine of Oikeiosis," 124). Maximus's *logoi* doctrine addresses exactly this sort of claim, found too in Gregory of Nazianzus. So that doctrine *must* explain how we are "portions of God" in a completely non-natural and yet no less actual way; see *Amb.* 7.1, and sec. 2.3 below. For Maximus the way such "familiarity" between created and uncreated comes about is precisely in the hypostatic union; see *Amb.* 41.9, PG 91, 1312A: "οἷς ὡς μέρεσι καθ᾽ ἕκαστον τὸ ἑκάστῳ καθόλου συγγενὲς οἰκειωσάμενος ἄκρον κατὰ τὸν προαποδοθέντα τρόπον"—which is then realized in us through sacrament and liturgy, as in *Myst.* 17, PG 91, 696A, where "those who are worthy will receive intimate familiarity with the Word of God [τὴν πρὸς τὸν Λόγον καὶ Θεὸν οἰκείωσιν]," and *Myst.* 24, PG 91, 709C.

36. So very dear, for instance, to Eriugena, *Periphyseon* III.1–17.

37. *Amb.* 41.2, PG 91, 1304D.

38. *Amb.* 41.2, PG 91, 1305A: "For they say that whereas God in His goodness created the splendid orderly arrangement of all beings, it is not immediately self-evident to this orderly arrangement who and what God is, and they call 'division' the ignorance of what it is that distinguishes God from creation. For to that which naturally divides these realities from each other, and which excludes their union in a single essence (since it cannot admit of one and the same definition), they did not give a name."

39. *Amb.* 41.5, PG 91, 1308B.

40. Eph. 1:10, cited in *Amb.* 41.6, PG 91, 1309A; see esp. *Amb.* 7.37, which showcases many of the same points as our text here.

41. *Amb.* 41.7, PG 91, 1309A.

42. *Amb.* 41.2 (introduction of five divisions), 3–5 (human vocation to unite all five), 6 (Fall), 7–9 (Christ's success).

43. *Amb.* 41.9, PG 91, 1312AB, slightly modified.

44. For Maximus's "Neo-Irenaean" approach to protology, see Blowers, *Maximus the Confessor*, 102–8.

45. *Amb.* 71.2–4 (historical Incarnation as an instance of the Word's "play"), 6 (citing Dionysius, *DN* 4.13). See below, sec. 2.3.

46. *Amb.* 35.2, where Maximus interprets Gregory of Nazianzus's claim that creation "was necessary" and the "effusion of the Good" as God's "impartation" of himself, a word often used to describe the distribution of the eucharistic bread (cf. Lampe, μεταδίδωμι, s.v.): God "uniquely possesses within Himself an inconceivable, eternal, infinite, and incomprehensible permanence, from which, by virtue of an 'ever-giving effusion' of goodness, He brought forth beings out of nothing and endowed them with existence, and also willed to impart Himself without

defilement to them in a manner proportionate to wholes and to each, bestowing upon each the power to exist and to remain in existence"; and again: "Perhaps, then, this, as far as my foolishness allows me to see, is what is meant by the 'effusion of the Good' and its 'progress,' namely, that the one God is multiplied in the impartation of good things proportionately to the recipients]." Cf. too *Q. Thal.* 35. Dionysius also uses these terms to describe the One-Being's "self-impartation" and "self-multiplication" to participating beings or effects (*DN* 2.11) and yet does not obviously intend a sacramental meaning; cf. chapter 3.

47. *Amb.* 6.5, PG 91, 1068C.

48. *Amb.* 6.3, PG 91, 1068AB, modified.

49. *Amb.* 38.2, PG 91, 1300A: "ἐν ἡμῖν νηπιάζοντος θειοτάτου λόγου," which he also identifies with "the form of Christ" (τὴν χριστοειδῆ κατάστασιν) that is our "state."

50. *Amb.* 7.21.

51. *Amb.* 47.2, PG 91, 1360D.

52. *Amb.* 48.2, PG 91, 1361A, modified, emphasis mine: "Ὁ πᾶσαν μετὰ σοφίας φύσιν ὑποστήσας Θεὸς καὶ πρώτην ἑκάστῃ τῶν λογικῶν οὐσιῶν δύναμιν τὴν αὐτοῦ γνῶσιν κρυφίως ἐνθέμενος." That the "God" here specifically refers to the Word is clear from the rest of the *ambiguum*, which grapples with the sense in which the Word was a "slain Lamb from before the foundation of the world."

53. *Amb.* 10.25, PG 91, 1125A, modified: "For to those in whom He is born, the Word of God [Πέφυκε γὰρ ὁ τοῦ Θεοῦ λόγος οἷς ἂν ἐγγένηται] naturally nullifies the movements of the flesh, and restrains the soul from inclining toward them, filling it with the whole power of true discernment."

54. Note that I've not here included any passage that contains the *tantumquantum* principle, i.e., that human deification is just as much and simultaneously a divine incarnation—even though I think those texts comprise some of the most compelling instances of creation as Incarnation (viewed from its perfection). On that pervasive principle in Maximus, see Larchet, *Divinisation de l'homme*, 376–82, and below at sec. 3.3.

55. See sec. 1.4.

56. See note 4 above.

57. E.g., Nicholaos Loudovikos, "Being and Essence Revisited: Reciprocal Logoi and Energies in Maximus the Confessor and Thomas Aquinas, and the Genesis of the Self-Referring Subject," *Revista Portuguesa de Filosofia* 72.1 (2016): 129, too glibly accuses Aquinas (as opposed to Maximus) of a "non-biblical metaphysics of participation." For a relevant critique of the modern (and indeed Enlightenment Protestant) tendency to conceive the history of Christian thought as "a series of accommodations" between "self-enclosed philosophies and the Gospel," see Lewis Ayres, *Nicaea and Its Legacy: An Approach to Fourth-Century Trinitarian Theology* (Oxford: Oxford University Press, 2004), 390–92.

58. Stobaeus, I.136, 31–137, 6, in *SVF* 1.65 and in *The Hellenistic Philosophers*, ed. A. A. Long and D. N. Sedley (Cambridge: Cambridge University Press, 1987), sec. 30A, summarizes how Stoics rejected the self-subsistence of universals or "common concepts," as they called them, and repurposed Platonic "participation" to make the point: "What we 'participate in' is the concepts" (καὶ τῶν μὲν ἐννοημάτων μετέχειν ἡμᾶς). And Stoic "participation" was not merely nominal. So Plutarch, *Comm. not.* 1085C–D, in *SVF* 2.444 and in Long and Sedley, *Hellenistic Philosophers*, sec. 47G: "They say that earth and water sustain neither themselves nor other things, but preserve their unity by participation in a breathy and fiery power [πνευματικῆς δὲ μετοχῇ καὶ πυρώδους τὴν ἑνότητα διαφυλάττειν]; but air and fire because of their tensility can sustain themselves, and by blending with the other two provide them with tension and also stability and substantiality." For early Stoics, then, what is "participated" is the divine principle *within* all things rather than some prior self-subsisting realm of paradigms.

59. Cf. chapter 1, note 176.

60. If you posit several gods or metaphysical first principles for the diversity of things, then you sense far less the problem of the One and the Many. But if, as Eriugena later brilliantly exposes (*Periphyseon* III.14), you reject a Manichaean dualism (or any absolute dualism) and yet hold to *creatio ex nihilo*, it becomes eminently difficult to grasp how real "otherness" can emerge from a single source—particularly if you are Christian and you believe this otherness is meant to endure *even in the final union of all things, where God is "all in all"* (1 Cor. 15:28), for example, if true union with the one God occurs through the resurrection of the body. In this sense the God-world problem proves considerably more difficult for Christians and Jews than, say, for Neoplatonists such as Plotinus, who, though similarly mystified about how any modal otherness might have emerged from the One (*Enn.* V.1.1–2), nevertheless does not have to confront the problem of how this finite (and bodily) otherness could possibly endure in the return to the immaterial, simple One. These kinds of observations rightly lead to the conviction that monotheistic "creation" and Neoplatonic "emanation" as typically conceived do not differ significantly from one another and indeed share many of the same seemingly insurmountable problems. Perhaps their main difference lies in their respective eschatologies. Cf. the excellent discussion in Fernand Brunner, "Création et émanation: Fragment de philosophie comparée," *Studia Philosophica* 33 (1973): 33–63, esp. 43–47.

61. Plato, *Parm.* 129b–c: "ἀλλ᾽ εἰ ὅ ἐστιν ἕν, αὐτὸ τοῦτο πολλὰ ἀποδείξει καὶ αὖ τὰ πολλὰ δὴ ἕν, τοῦτο ἤδη θαυμάσομαι"; cf. too the more general remark about the obscure nature of the world's "receptacle" (the "place" where the icon, Becoming, comes to be and be like the model, Being) at *Tim.* 52d: "So long as one thing is one thing, and another something different, neither of the two will ever come to exist in the other so that the same thing becomes simultaneously both one and

two" (ὡς ἕως ἄν τι τὸ μὲν ἄλλο ᾖ, τὸ δὲ ἄλλο, οὐδετέρῳ ποτὲ γεγενημένον ἐν ἅμα ταὐτὸν καὶ δύο γενήσεσθον).

62. Portaru, "Vocabulary of Participation," 296, notes (against Larchet) that the vast range of "participation" language occurs in all but two of Maximus's works.

63. Here I think we can appreciate Larchet's earlier (and unique) judgment about "participation" in Maximus: "Maxime parle parfoix assez clairement d'une divinisation par participation, avec des expressions diverses et sans développer à ces occasions une doctrine précise de la participation, ou du moins sans indiquer comment précisement il conçoit cette notion"; cf. Larchet, *Divinisation de l'homme*, 600. Tollefsen has challenged this characterization, e.g., at "Did St. Maximus," 624, and yet, outside a few minor additions, I do not see how Tollefsen differs significantly from what Larchet already emphasized as the import of Maximus's participation-talk—that it insists on "la distance qui subsiste entre la nature de l'homme divinisé et la nature divine elle-même" (600).

64. We could say with Wittgenstein: "The meaning of a word is its use." This approach has already been fruitfully performed in an adjacent context: so C. Kavin Rowe, *One True Life: The Stoics and Early Christians as Rival Traditions* (New Haven, CT: Yale University Press, 2016), 2: "To study the Christians and the Stoics is thus to realize that relating their traditions must take account of the fact that difference in the meaning of words is tied to difference in life." Or later at 249: "To recognize that the meaning of words changes with the changes in the wider grammar in which they occur is simultaneously to see that the reembedding of words from one interpretative framework into another is not the translation and appropriation of insights but transformation or transfiguration. As Wittgenstein might have said, 'See how high the seas of language run here!'" And later at 260–61: "Christians have been treasure hunting. The treasures they find are the words in the Stoic texts, not the 'thoughts' that are somehow independent from the Stoic grammar in which thoughts have their shape and meaning—and that can somehow be transported from one grammar to the other without a change in meaning. I am committed, that is, to the view that we cannot think about language in the same way after Wittgenstein. There is no such thing as a word-meaning or language 'as such.'"

65. *Pyr.* 28-31; *Amb.* 5.20; see sec. 2.4–5.

66. *CC* 4.2, ed. Aldo Ceresa-Gastaldo, *Capitoli sulla carita* (Rome: Editrice Studium, 1963), 194: "children [or disciples] of the Greeks" (Ἑλλήνων παῖδες). In his translation of *CC*, Balthasar glosses that the "Greek" views that Maximus refutes here might be found in the philosopher Ammonius Hermeiou (ca. 500), whose "Lehre von der Gleichewigkeit der Weltsubstanz mit Gott war nochmals . . . in Alexandrien aufgebracht," and "von seinen christlichen Schülern Zacharias Rhetor (PG 85, 1011–1144) und Johannes Philoponus . . . widerlegt worden." Balthasar also notes that Evagrius begins his *Kephalaia Gnostica* (1.1, 4) with the

assertion that nothing stands in opposition to God. See his *Kosmische Liturgie: Das Weltbild Maximus' des Bekenners*, 2nd ed. (Freiburg: Johannes Verlag, 1961), 452–53n2.

67. *CC* 3.28, ed. Ceresa-Gastaldo, 156.

68. *CC* 3.27, ed. Ceresa-Gastaldo, 156, cf. *The Ascetic Life; The Four Centuries on Charity*, trans. Polycarp Sherwood (Westminster, MD: Newman Press, 1955), 178: "Ὁ μὲν Θεὸς ὡς αὐτούπαρξις ὢν [note the paradox of juxtaposing those two concepts] καὶ αὐτοαγαθότης καὶ αὐτοσοφία, μᾶλλον δὲ ἀληθέστερον εἰπεῖν καὶ ὑπὲρ ταῦτα πάντα."

69. *CC* 3.27.

70. See "An Analytic Appendix of Key Concepts" below for a brief survey of Maximus's use of this term, especially its Christological transformation.

71. *CC* 3.29, ed. Ceresa-Gastaldo, 156–58, my translation.

72. *CC* 3.28, ed. Ceresa-Gastaldo, 156; trans. Sherwood, *Ascetic Life*, 178, modified: "Οἱ μὲν Ἕλληνες ἐξ ἀϊδίου λέγοντες συνυπάρχειν τῷ Θεῷ τὴν τῶν ὄντων οὐσίαν, τὰς δὲ περὶ αὐτὴν ποιότητας μόνον ἐξ αὐτοῦ ἐσχηκέναι, τῇ μὲν οὐσίᾳ οὐδὲν λέγουσιν ἐναντίον, ἐν δὲ ταῖς μόναις τὴν ἐναντίωσιν εἶναι."

73. *CC* 3.29, ed. Ceresa-Gastaldo, 158, trans. Sherwood, *Ascetic Life*, 178, lightly altered: "It depends on the power of Him who truly is whether the essence of things should ever be or not be; and *His gifts are without repentance* [Rom. 11:29]. Therefore it both ever is [ἔστιν ἀεὶ] and will be sustained by His all-powerful might, even though, as was said, it has non-being as contrary." Cf. *Amb.* 42.15; see below, sec. 2.5.

74. This term *coexist* (used at both *CC* 3.28 and 4.6) signifies a metaphysically simultaneous relation of two parts that together constitute a greater whole. When the parts relate naturally, the consequent whole is a form. Maximus often wields this point against Origenist "preexistence of souls," namely that since the soul and body of a concrete individual together constitute the individual whole or nature of that individual, then they must share the same origin lest they be subject to essential change and destruction (i.e., not really *be* the parts of *that* whole)—they must "coexist"; cf. *Ep.* 15, PG 91, 557D; *Amb.* 7.40–43, 42.9–13 and 25.

75. *CC* 4.6, ed. Ceresa-Gastaldo, 196, trans. Sherwood, *Ascetic Life*, 193, slight modification.

76. Maximus makes the same point when he says God is essentially "without relation" (ἄσχετος); cf. *Amb.* 10.58, 15.9, 20.2, 41.10.

77. *CC* 4.2, trans. Sherwood, *Ascetic Life*, 192.

78. *CC* 4.1, trans. Sherwood, *Ascetic Life*, 192.

79. *CC* 4.3, trans. Sherwood, *Ascetic Life*, 192.

80. *CC* 4.4, ed. Ceresa-Gastaldo, 194, trans. Sherwood, *Ascetic Life*, 192–93.

81. Sherwood, *Earlier Ambigua*, 92–102.

82. That is a summary of how Maximus seems to have viewed (contemporary versions of) Origenism, as evinced at *Amb.* 7.2–7, 15.10–11, 42.13–14. For a sympathetic survey of the good reasons Origen might have adopted some form of a preexistent henad of rational beings—mostly to do with Christian theodicy rather than Platonic poisoning—see Peter W. Martens, "Embodiment, Heresy, and the Hellenization of Christianity: The Descent of the Soul in Origen and Plato," *Harvard Theological Review* 108.4 (2015): 594–620. But see now the suggestive discussion in John Behr's introduction to his edition and translation *Origen: On First Principles: A Reader's Edition* (Oxford: Oxford University Press, 2019), lxxix–lxxxviii.

83. Cf. esp. *Amb.* 7.5. Maximus repeatedly affirms our natural desire for God: *Amb.* 48.2, *Pyr.* 33, passim.

84. Origen, *Princ.* 2.9.2, ed. H. Görgemanns and H. Karpp, *Origenes vier Bücher von den Prinzipien* (Darmstadt: WBG, 1976), 402–4, and trans. G. W. Butterworth, *On First Principles* (New York: Harper and Row, 1966), 130: "But since these rational beings, which as we said above were made in the beginning, were made when before they did not exist, by this very fact that they did not exist and then began to exist they are of necessity subject to change and alteration. For whatever may have been the goodness that existed in their being, it existed in them not by nature but as a result of their Creator's beneficence. What they are, therefore, is something neither their own nor eternal, but given by God." See too Mueller-Jourdan, "Foundation of Origenist Metaphysics," 159.

85. Hence the logical structure of *Ambiguum* 7, which runs as follows. It turns on Maximus's identification of two distinct (though related) features of Origenist protology (*Amb.* 7.2): (1) that it posits a "connatural" relation to God, and (2) that it places "becoming" (*genesis*) after both the primordial unity (*stasis*) and fall from God (*kinesis*). Most, we observed, focus on the second feature, which does arrive first in Maximus's response (*Amb.* 7.3–14). But just after this disquisition on the metaphysics of motion comes Maximus's *logoi* doctrine (*Amb.* 7.15ff.), which is no mere repitition in a different idiom of the earlier points about genesis and motion. Rather, it responds most directly to the first and distinct feature of Origenist protology—namely the precise relation between God and the world—in such a way that it avoids positing a natural relation and yet still retains a relation of *identity* between them (*Amb.* 7.21 and 7.31).

86. *Amb.* 7.1 = *Or.* 14.7.

87. *Amb.* 7.2.

88. Cf. the note of Constas, *On Difficulties in the Church Fathers*, 1:478n2.

89. *Amb.* 15.10.

90. *Amb.* 15.8, PG 91, 1220A: the potential and perfection of a creature's *natural* movement is already given, and so already delimited, in its concrete nature (what Maximus called "qualified substances" at *CC* 4.6). Therefore the actualiza-

tion of every created nature necessarily terminates in a concrete, finite, limited *fact* or thing done. Take the soul. "Its potentiality [δύναμιν] is the intellect, its motion [κίνησιν] is the process of thinking, and its actuality [ἐνέργειαν] is thought [τὸ νόημα], as well as of the thinker and the thing thought about, since it [i.e., the concrete fact of the thought] limits and defines the relationship of the two poles that frame the entire process." This describes the "form of motion that obtains among all beings." And yet created motion's necessarily dynamic, polarized, and diachronic realization does not finally mean that creaturely motion has as its end something other than God. It means that though creaturely motion "will come to an end in the infinity that is around God," this end is not the divine essence (that would imply, once again, *some* sort of natural relation between soul and God), for "infinity is around God, but it is not God Himself, for He incomparably transcends even this" (*Amb.* 15.9).

91. Cf. *Amb.* 20.2, 65.2. The keen reader senses here an unresolved tension in Maximus: he seems to maintain that the rational creature simultaneously possesses God as its natural and ultimate object of desire, and yet lacks a primordial, natural relation that would ground such a desire; on this see sec. 3.2.

92. Blowers, *Drama*, 54–58.

93. So Mueller-Jourdan, "Foundation of Origenist Metaphysics," 160: Maximus "radically differs from the Origenian system in regard to the conception of created substance (οὐσία). . . . For Maximus the concept of substance depends on this Aristotelian background which radically rejects any form of pre-existence for rational beings, a characteristic of Platonism." But Maximus also departs from Aristotle because he insists on "the simultaneity of creation of soul and body" (rather than Aristotle's postexistence of soul), so that for Maximus "There is one unique world" (161). Is this fair to Origenism? A thorny issue, to be sure, especially while scholars such as Augustine Casiday and Ramelli attempt to salvage Evagrius's thought from the wreckage wrought by Constantinople II (553). However that comes out, I note here that Origenist thought suffered similar accusations long before Maximus. Pope Theophilus of Alexandria, in *Festal Letter of 402*, alleged that Origenists teach that "our soul is thus of the same nature with God"; cf. Antoine Guillaumont, *Les "Kephalaia Gnostica" d'Évagre le Pontique et l'histoire de l'origénisme chez les Grecs et chez les Syriens* (Paris: Éditions du Seuil, 1962), 100–101. Canons 13–15, associated with Constantinople II, similarly target so-called isochrist Origenism; cf. Richard Price, ed. and trans., *Canons of the Quinisext Council (691/2)* (Liverpool: Liverpool University Press, 2020), 2:286.

94. *Ep.* 15, PG 91, 565D, my translation.

95. Proclus, *El. Theol.*, props. 18, ed. Dodds, 20–21 and 30.

96. Proclus, *El. Theol.*, props. 32, 78–79 (Plotinus's double-act theory), passim. See Johannes Hirschberger, "Ähnlichkeit und Seinsanalogie vom platonischen Parmenides bis Proklos," in *Philomates: Studies in the Humanities in*

Memory of Philip Merlan, ed. Robert B. Palmer and Robert G. Hamerton-Kelly (The Hague: Nijhoff, 1971), 57–74.

97. Proclus, *El. Theol.*, prop. 97. This is why even Proclus (prop. 114) will not speak of the henads' "participation" in the One: you cannot say, strictly speaking, that the One has anything in common with lower realities (even the henads or Intellect) because, as Plotinus already claimed, the One has nothing at all (*Enn.* VI.8 [39] 7); so Christian Guérard, "La théorie des hénades et la mystique de Proclus," *Dionysius* 6 (1982): 77. Thus Neoplatonism too arrives at its own qualification of participation-talk. But of course that only exacerbates the problem participation meant to resolve and indeed explains nothing about how the One's very mode (of not "being" any mode at all) comes to produce *other* modes of being that, unlike the One, do possess their own proper and determinate modes (and therefore could never, for instance, cause all that the One causes; cf. *El. Theol.*, props. 1–2, 78).

98. Balthasar, *Cosmic Liturgy*, 152–53, though he errs in his additional claim that Maximus's "predominantly Western style of thought"—an extreme emphasis on *ex nihilo*—means he "can only conceive of final divinization as a perfecting of what has been created finite." The next chapter shows that deification involves far more than finitude's perfection, and the subsequent chapter demonstrates that and how cleaving to finitude as such constitutes the Fall itself—and, oddly, these conclusions follow precisely from Balthasar's correct observation that "it is Christology that will decide the issue" (153).

99. Georges Florovsky, "Creation and Creaturehood," in *Collected Works*, vol. 3, *Creation and Redemption* (Belmont, MA: Nordland, 1976), 46–48.

100. Gregory of Nazianzus, *Or.* 41.12 (= *Amb.* 71.6, PG 91, 1413A).

101. Dionysius, *DN* 4.13 (= *Amb.* 71.6, PG 91, 1413AB), my emphasis.

102. *Amb.* 7.6, my emphasis.

103. Proclus, *El. Theol.*, props. 1–2, 78–79, passim.

104. *Amb.* 7.15, PG 91, 1077C: "τῇ πρὸς αὐτὸν τῶν πάντων ἀναφορᾷ." It is hard to miss the eucharistic tones of ἡ ἀναφορά; see Lampe, *s.v.* Hearing them already begins to intimate that there is something more profound going on in the divine procession into and as the world than, say, a cascading chain of ever more determinate modes of essential power.

105. Balthasar, in *Cosmic Liturgy* (the appendix "The Problem of the Scholia to Pseudo-Dionysius"), 376, notices this, though he routinely elides the *logoi* with "ideas"; see, e.g., Balthasar, *Cosmic Liturgy*, 116–21. Maximus does not even retain the language of "paradigm," even when he (twice) cites a Dionysian text that does; cf. *Amb.* 7.24 (cp. *DN* 5.8) and *Q. Thal.* 13—in both instances Maximus prefers Dionysius's "divine wills." It might matter too that Gregory of Nazianzus had openly maligned "Plato's Ideas" at *Or.* 27.10. This section and the next (2.3–4) have appeared in distilled form in Jordan Daniel Wood, "Creation Is Incarnation: The Metaphysical Peculiarity of the *Logoi* in Maximus Confessor," *Modern Theology* 34.1 (2018): 85–92.

106. Translation in Paul Rorem and John C. Lamoureaux's *John of Scythopolis and the Dionysian Corpus: Annotating the Areopagite* (Oxford: Clarendon Press, 1998). Sergius of Resha'ina, though, likely composed his sizable introduction before John's more comprehensive edition; see Istvan Perczel, "The Earliest Syriac Reception of Dionysius," *Modern Theology* 24.4 (2008): 557–71.

107. This tale of concealment was exposed only last century, principally by Balthasar, "The Problem of the Scholia to Pseudo-Dionysius," translated as an appendix in *Cosmic Liturgy*. Beate Regina Suchla is still in the process of sorting out all the details. See her "Das Scholienwerke des Johannes von Skythopolis zu den Areopagitischen Traktaten in seiner Philosophie—und theologiegeschichtlichen Bedeutung," in *Denys l'Aréopagite et sa postérité en Orient et en Occident: Actes du Colloque International Paris, 21–24 septembre 1994*, ed. Ysabel de Andia (Paris: Institut d'Études Augustiniennes, 1997), 155–65, and her edition of *Corpus Dionysiacum*, vol. 4, pt. 1, *Ioannis Scythopolitani prologus et scholia in Dionysii Areopagitae librum "De divinis nominibus" cum additamentis interpretum aliorum*, Patristische Texte und Studien 62 (Berlin: De Gruyter, 2011); and Rorem and Lamoureaux, *John of Scythopolis*, 2.

108. Rorem and Lamoureaux speak of "John's obsessive linkage of the two words 'idea' and 'paradigm'" about fourteen times in ten different scholia (88). Only once does John specify that these ideas are found in Logos (*SchDN* 353.3), and this because the text at hand concerns why God is called "Logos" (*DN* 7.4). John indicates nothing special about it being the Word who contains these ideas.

109. John of Scythopolis, *SchDN* 329.1 (on *DN* 5.8), trans. Rorem and Lamoureaux, *John of Scythopolis*, 222 (PG 4, 329A).

110. John of Scythopolis, *SchDN* 329.1 and 332.1.

111. John of Scythopolis, *SchDN* 320.3 (on *DN* 5.6), trans. Rorem and Lamoureaux, 220.

112. John of Scythopolis, *SchDN* 316.4, trans. Rorem and Lamoureaux, 219.

113. John even says that the *logoi* are "a [single] nature" that together have one *logos* and cause, though still in God (*SchDN* 353.3, trans. Rorem and Lamoureaux, 230). They are like the most common nature of which particular creatures are but more determined and circumscribed instances. This is strikingly similar to the Plotinian Intellect. It again confirms that John's *logoi* are overwritten by the logic of formal causality.

114. *Amb.* 7.15, PG 91, 1077C.

115. *Amb.* 7.16.

116. *Amb.* 7.19; *Q. Thal.* 13.2.

117. *Amb.* 7.16.

118. *Amb.* 7.20.

119. Two reasons for introducing Plotinus's *logoi*. First, the few scholars open to putting Maximus in conversation with Neoplatonic philosophers (a good idea in my view) tend not to discern important differences between Maximus and

Plotinus, especially their versions of the *logoi*; see Tollefsen's remark at note 135 below. Second, as others have noticed, there's relatively little to compare when it comes to say, Evagrius's *logoi*, which already function (at least in "second contemplation" of visible realities) less as the primordial and creative foundation of the single world and more as God's providential means for intellects in a given age (*aeon*) to ascend from number and bodily division and reidentify with the "substantial knowledge" that the Trinity is; cf., e.g., Evagrius, *KG* 1.27, 5.16 and 27, 6.75, and Guillaumont, *"Kephalaia Gnostica,"* 110. For a brief survey of Evagrian *logoi*, see Luke Dysinger, O.S.B, "The *Logoi* of Providence and Judgment in the Exegetical Writings of Evagrius Ponticus," *Studia Patristica* 37 (2001): 462–71.

120. Plotinus, *Enn.* V.1.

121. Plotinus, *Enn.* VI.2 [43] 21. That the Intellect "wills" these *logoi* suffices to undermine any facile claim that Maximus's (and Dionysius's) *logoi* differ from Plotinus's because the former are voluntarily elected principles (*pace* Tollefsen, *Activity and Participation*, 114). Plotinus actually has an entire treatise on the One's free will in making all things, wherein he depicts the One (as did Plato himself at *Tim.* 29e–30a) generating intellectual causes "as he himself willed" (*Enn.* VI.8 [39] 18). The hackneyed contrast between voluntary creation and necessary emanation, unfortunately widespread in its acceptance among contemporary Christian thinkers, requires comprehensive reappraisal. Gregory of Nyssa, for instance, had no qualms identifying the two: see Harry Wolfson, "The Identification of *Ex Nihilo* with Emanation in Gregory of Nyssa," *Harvard Theological Review* 63 (1970): 53–60. See too the helpful remarks of Jean Trouillard, "Procession néoplatonicienne et création judéo-chrétienne," in *Néoplatonisme: Mélanges offerts à Jean Trouillard*, Cahiers de Fontenay, nos. 19–22 (Fontenay-aux-Roses: École Normale Supérieure, 1981), 79–108, esp. 83–89. Real differences do obtain. But from the Maximian vantage the differences emerge in other, less perceived ways, such as in the fact that the God-world relation involves no natural but rather a hypostatic relation (more precisely: it involves an identity-relation generative of a modal/actual symmetry).

122. Aristotle, *De an.* III.4–5.

123. *Enn.* III.8 [30] 6–7.

124. *Enn.* VI.2 [43] 21. The διάφορα of magnitudes, figures, qualities, and material division are specified in this text.

125. This short review of Plotinus's notion of the *logoi* as Intellect reveals the limitations of Larchet's narration of how Maximus's *logoi* differ from Plato's ideas: "Selon Maxime, le Verbe, qui a créé le monde, s'est référé aux *logoi* qui étaient contenus Lui [*sic*]; tandis que selon Platon, les Idées que le Démiurge a pris comme modèles pour produire le cosmos étaient extérieures à lui"; Jean-Claude Larchet, "La conception maximienne des énergies divines et des *logoi* et la théorie platonicienne des Idées," *Philotheos* 4 (2004): 282.

126. Plotinus, *Enn.* V.3 [49] 15, slightly modified. See Asger Ousager, "Sufficient Reason, Identities and Discernibles in Plotinus," *Dionysius* 21 (2003): 232.

127. Clement of Alexandria, *Strom.* IV.25; Origen, *Princ.* 1.2.2 and *Comm. in Jo.* 1.22.

128. Proclus, *El. Theol.*, props. 113–16. Neoplatonists after Proclus largely returned to Plotinus's simpler threefold schema; see Cristina D'Ancona, "Plotinus and Later Platonic Philosophers on the Causality of the First Principle," in *The Cambridge Companion to Plotinus*, ed. Lloyd P. Gerson (Cambridge: Cambridge University Press, 1996), 377–78.

129. Dionysius, *DN* 5.2, trans. John Parker, *The Works of Dionysius the Areopagite* (London: James Parker, 1897), 74, slightly modified; ed. Suchla, *Corpus Dionysiacum*, vol. 4, pt. 1, 181.

130. Gersh, *From Iamblichus to Eriugena*, argues that Maximus "is perhaps the first thinker in the Neoplatonic tradition to tackle the problem [of procession] head-on," though he doesn't seem to think Maximus offers anything more than does Dionysius.

131. *Amb.* 7.20.

132. The first instance in *Amb.* 7 of the Logos-*logoi* copula appears *along with* a declaration of the consubstantiality of Logos and Father (*Amb.* 7.15). Cp. Proclus, *El. Theol.*, prop. 18: "Thus the character as it pre-exists in the original giver has a higher reality than the character bestowed: it is what the bestowed character is, but is not identical with it, since it exists primitively and the other only by derivation [ἀλλ' οὐ ταὐτὸν ἐκείνῳ· πρώτως γὰρ ἔστι, τὸ δὲ δευτέρως]. For it must be that either the two are identical and have a common definition [ἕνα λόγον ἀμφοτέρων]; or there is nothing common or identical in both; or the one exists primitively and the other by derivation. . . . It remains, then, that where one thing receives bestowal from another in virtue of that other's mere existence, the giver possesses primitively the character which it gives, while the recipient is by derivation what the giver is [τὸ μὲν εἶναι πρώτως ὃ δίδωσι, τὸ δὲ δευτέρως ὃ τὸ διδόν ἐστιν]" (ed. Dodds, 20–21). Only an identity by derivation is possible where participation among stratified levels of nature—a metaphysics of "more or less" like in kind (cf. prop. 9)—is the only conceivable relation. Maximus too knows that in this way we are "not the same" (*Ep.* 6; ταὐτόν).

133. *Pace* Törönen, *Union and Distinction*, 132, who perceives in the "creation song" of C. S. Lewis's Aslan an apt analogy for Maximus's *logoi*: "The connection between the creatures and the creator is presented in this figure as different musical notes. With the notes everything seems to proceed, as the young observer puts it, 'out of the Lion's head.' Yet, it is clear that this is not a process of emanation but an act of creation. It is *not* the Lion, as it were, unfolding into creatures." But for Maximus it is *precisely* the Lion-Logos who unfolds in the "creative and sustaining procession of the One to individual beings" as their *logoi*

(*Amb.* 7.20), who, as he says elsewhere, "expanded himself" into all multiplicity (*Amb.* 33.2, PG 91, 1288A: "ἑαυτὸν . . . διέστειλεν"; cf. *Amb.* 22.3). The same observation applies to Maximus's use of the Neoplatonic center-radii-circle image (*Amb.* 7.20; *CT* 2.4; *Myst.* 1). Some take this is a straightforward adaptation of Neoplatonic procession, which Maximus received from Dionysius (*DN* 5.5–9); so Perl, "Methexis," 171, and Torstein T. Tollefsen, "Christocentric Cosmology," in Allen and Neil, *Oxford Handbook*, 310–11. But Maximus's use *must* differ to the extent that the hypostasis of the Logos, unlike, say of the Plotinian One, does not itself simply remain when proceeding, as the center-point in the expanding circle. The Word himself expands.

134. Not only does Maximus specify this at *Amb.* 7.15 ("ἐνούσιόν καὶ ἐνυπόστατον τοῦ Θεοῦ καὶ Πατρὸς Θεὸν Λόγον"), but he later adds that this procession is emphatically *not* that of the ineffable divine nature (*Amb.* 7.20: "ὡς ὑπερούσιος, οὐδὲ ὑπό τινος οὐδαμῶς καθ' ὁτιοῦν μετέχεται"). Again consider *Amb.* 61.3, PG 91, 1385D–1388A: "But the tent is also an image of the totality of creation, intelligible and sensible, which God the Father as Intellect (*Nous*) conceived, and which the Son as Word created, and which the Holy Spirit brought to completion." Not only is the Father Intellect here (rather than the Son, as required by a Son = Intellect view), but it is distinctively the Son/Word who executes the creative act—a notion that, whatever potential problems, must at least mean that creation "in the Word" is really linked to his *distinctive* personhood.

135. I therefore cannot agree with Tollefsen, *Christocentric Cosmology*, 88, who sees little substantive difference between Plotinian and Maximian *logoi*: "The Plotinian Intellect contemplates the Forms as its thoughts, and there is unity because what contemplates (subject) and what is contemplated (object) are the same. Of course, this is the case with God and His divine wisdom expressed in the [Maximian] *logoi* as well." That for Maximus the *logoi* in no way complete or actualize the one nature of the Logos distinguishes his doctrine quite clearly from Neoplatonic *logoi*. Again contrast Syrianus, *In Metaph.* 106, 26–107, 1 (quoted in Sorabji, *Philosophy of the Commentators,* 3:146): "And, being complete, [Intellect] thinks everything. So nothing that has real being is left out of the essence of the Intellect, but it always situates the Forms (*eide*) in itself. They are not different in it and in its essence, but complete its being and bring to everything productive (*poietike*), paradigmatic and final cause. For it creates as Intellect, and the paradigms exist as Forms and are productive through themselves and their own goodness."

136. Aetius, *Plac.* I.7, in *SVF* 2.1027 and in Long and Sedley, *Hellenistic Philosophers*, sec. 46A; cf. *Amb.* 10.52. For more convergences between Maximus and ancient Stoicism, see Wood, "Stoic Motifs."

137. Diogenes Laertius, 7.135–36, in *SVF* 1.102 and 2.580 and in Long and Sedley *Hellenistic Philosophers*, sec. 46B; cf. the discussion of *Amb.* 6 above, sec. 2.1.

138. Diogenes Laertius, 7.137: "ἐξ ἑαυτοῦ γεννῶν."

139. Origen, *Cels.* IV.41, in *SVF* 2.1052. I have rendered "ἐπὶ μέρους" in the plural, partly because the immediate context implies it: Origen's critique of the idea that God has a body. For Origen this must mean the Stoic god is, among other absurdities, composed of parts.

140. Plotinus, *Enn.* V.1 [10] 6, for instance, teaches that Intellect's *logos* is not Intellect itself but the hypostasis of Soul that derives from Intellect. Plotinus evinces a conspicuous tendency to separate and stratify a hypostasis and its *logos*, so that the *logos* appears "always as an expression of the preceding level respectively." Indeed, "It would seem that Plotinus is concerned to avoid any expression that might be taken as a step" in the direction of equating them; so Andreas Graeser, *Plotinus and the Stoics: A Preliminary Study* (Leiden: Brill, 1972), 35 (cf. 41).

141. David Sedley, "The Stoic Theory of Universals," *Southern Journal of Philosophy* 23.1 (1985): 89.

142. Cf. Tollefsen, *Christocentric Cosmology*, 78.

143. *Amb.* 10.89, PG 91, 1177BC: "κατὰ διαστολὴν καὶ συστολὴν λόγῳ τε καὶ τρόπῳ."

144. Cp. Galen, *Nat. fac.* 106.13–17, in *SVF* 2.406 and in Long and Sedley, *Hellenistic Philosophers*, sec. 47E; and Philo, *Quod deus sit immut.* 35–36, in *SVF* 2.458 and in Long and Sedley, *Hellenistic Philosophers*, sec. 47Q.

145. *Amb.* 33.2, discussed above in sec. 2.1.

146. Maximus notes two wrong ways to understand the expansion of Word into world. (1) It is a real multiplication of hypostases *and* essences, a real "other," as it were, from God. Thus the Word's expansion "through the principle of condescension" (*Amb.* 33.2) differs from the intra-Trinitarian generation of the Son, which motion does not imply a different *essence* from the Father's. The "Monad," he says, "is not like the origin of the things that come after it, as if it had expanded after a state of contraction, like something naturally poured out and proliferating into a multitude" (*Amb.* 1.3, PG 91, 1036B). And this of course is one way Maximus's creative Word-expansion diverges from Stoicism. (2) It is not a fragmentation of the Word (either in person or in essence): the Word proceeds "without expanding disparately into the infinite differences of the beings in which He exists as Being." And yet, Maximus marvels, the Word truly becomes wholly, indivisibly, and personally present as the *logos* of what is "common" and "individual" in every single thing and in the whole of all things—"truly *all things in all* [1 Cor. 12:6, 15:20; Eph. 1:23]" (*Amb.* 22.3).

147. Here we must exercise due care and precision when predicating "preexistence" of the Word. To say the Creator Word "preexisted" obviously cannot refer to an existence *prior* to creation in some sort of sequential sense, since creation is the generation of temporal sequence itself. Better to distinguish two uses of the suffix *pre-* in talk of the "preexistent" or "pre-Incarnate Word"—a phrase John Behr confesses he has "yet to encounter in the Fathers" (cf. his *John the Theologian and His Pascal Gospel: A Prologue to Theology* [Oxford: Oxford University

Press, 2019], Pref.). First, there is the straightforward, serial, temporal sense that would signify the Word's presence and activity "before" the first century CE. The Word has indeed "existed" prior to that century; it is not as if he had to wait until his conception in Mary in order to be at all. But this sense immediately implicates and indeed gives way to a second, less heeded one: the "beyond," "transcendent," or simply "non-" existent nature of the Word's divinity. In this sense the "pre-" in the affirmation, "the Word preexists the world," in no way indicates an episode (or infinite episodes) that preceded his human existence. It means rather that the Word's divine nature is without origin or beginning and is therefore not subject to temporal existence as such (Maximus often simply refers to this as divine "eternity," or even his being prior to eternity itself; e.g., *CC* 3.28). But both of these predications, note well, are (necessarily) *of Christ's natures*. He himself, his person or hypostasis, supposes both by nature. Therefore it is more correct to say: the Word, God by nature, exists in every temporal moment (including those before the first century) as the God who does not properly "exist" at all; and yet the selfsame Word, man by nature, exists *only* from the first century forward. Still more proper, given the deification of the Word's humanity that renders even creatures "without origin" (*Amb.* 10.48), we must eventually say: the *very same Word* born in the "middle" of time and thus marked by the properties acquired in that birth (his Jewishness, his biological DNA inherited from Mary, etc.)—through the interpenetration of human and divine nature in himself—that very Word is present and "exists" in every age *and "there" too bears the existence of his earthly life*. For more on the necessarily odd relation between time and the Incarnation, see below at sec. 4.3.

148. *Pace* Balthasar, *Cosmic Liturgy*, 120–21, though he is correct in his immediate point that there exist no "unrealized possibilities" in Maximus's Word; cf. Tollefsen, *Christocentric Cosmology*, 76, 88, passim.

149. See above, sec. 2.1, text 4.

150. Thomas Bénatouïl, "How Industrious Can Zeus Be? The Extent and Objects of Divine Activity in Stoicism," in *God and Cosmos in Stoicism*, ed. Ricardo Salles (Oxford: Oxford University Press, 2009), 33.

151. Plutarch, *St. rep.* 1054B, in *SVF* 2.449 and Long and Sedley, *Hellenistic Philosophers*, sec. 47M, slightly modified; cf. Alexander of Aphrodisias, *De mixt.* 18–27, in *SVF* 2.1044.

152. *Amb.* 17.7, PG 91, 1228AB, slightly modified: "Τίνες οἱ ἑκάστῳ τῶν ὄντων τῇ ὑπάρξει πρώτως ἐγκαταβληθέντες λόγοι, καθ' οὓς καὶ ἔστι καὶ πέφυκε τῶν ὄντων ἕκαστον, καὶ εἰδοπεποίηται, καὶ ἐσχημάτισται, καὶ συντέθειται, καὶ δύναται, καὶ ἐνεργεῖ, καὶ πάσχει"; see too *Ep.* 15, PG 91, 561D, where Maximus specifies that the divine power causes each being by "emplacing" (ἐνθεμένης) "a *logos* in each creature which is constitutive of being [τοῦ εἶναι συστατικὸν]."

153. No contradiction arises, therefore, between the fact that the *logoi* are not themselves forms and yet perform the task of formal causality: they are indeed

"archetypical *logoi*" (*Q. Thal.* 55, ed. Jean-Claude Larchet, *Questions à Thalassios*, vol. 2, SC 554 [Paris: Cerf, 2012], 234), but the fully subsistent "archetype of divine and true life" is also "still to come" (*Amb.* 71.10, PG 91, 1416C: "τὴν μέλλουσαν . . . ἀρχετυπίαν).

154. *Amb.* 65.2.

155. Thunberg, *Microcosm and Mediator*, 77, correctly observes that the *logoi* "are not identical either with the essence of God or with the existence of things in the created world" but sees in this principally (and vaguely) "an apophatic tendency" allied to "an anti-pantheistic tendency." I suggest more: the *logoi* are both uncreated and the foundation of creation because, as we saw with the historical body of Jesus Christ, the Logos himself in his ineffable economy proves to be both uncreated and created *by nature*—indeed, he becomes the concrete *identity* of both (sec. 1.2). Again the basic distinction (not separation) between the logics of hypostasis and essence, even and especially in the Trinity's case, ought to hold in protology as well, lest it be utter nonsense to speak of the *Word*'s personal role in creating all things (as at *Amb.* 7.15).

156. Tollefsen, *Activity and Participation*, 129; cf. 29–30 (on Plotinus) and 117 (on Dionysius).

157. This is not a problem for Neoplatonists, at least not with respect to participation in Intellect by its lower participants. Lower hypostases are nothing but modified or qualified permutations of Intellect's own essential activity. So Neoplatonists have a perfectly reasonable way of explaining the movement from Intellect's hypostasis to lower participations in it: participants in Intellect were never *separate* from the "sphere" of Intellect's activity, since they essentially *are* Intellect. Their departure or procession from Intellect is actually a move into *lesser* activity, not a move from nonactivity to activity. Lower hypostases = participations. Cf. too Proclus, *El. Theol.*, props. 1–2.

158. Again see sec. 1.2.

159. *Amb.* 15.5; cf. *CT* 1.3.

160. *Amb.* 7.16: through the Word God creates and continues to create "universals as well as particulars" (τὰ καθόλου τε καὶ τὰ καθ' ἕκαστον). Maximus is clear that an individual's *logos* establishes its simultaneous participation in many levels of being, from its species to its highest genera ("common being"): within the concrete individual are wrought "many and sundry unifications of things separated," like many "angles" converging upon a single point (*Q. Thal.* 48.17, ed. Laga and Steel, CCSG 7, 341).

161. *Amb.* 41.10–11.

162. *Amb.* 7.22; *Amb.* 41.10, passim. For "being" (οὐσία) as the most universal genus of creatures, as well as how this diverges from Aristotelian-Porphyrian conceptions, see Tollefsen, *Christocentric Cosmology*, 97, and Törönen, *Union and Distinction*, 140.

163. Cf. Porphyry, *Isag.* (CAG 4.1.7) with *Amb.* 17.5–6; cf. *Amb.* 7.15, 19 and *Amb.* 22.2. The differentiating role of *logos* is especially clear in Christological discussions; cf. *Amb.* 36.2, and below.

164. *Amb.* 17.5: "ἀλλὰ δεῖ πάντως καὶ τὸ ὑποκείμενον τούτοις, θεμελίου τρόπον ἐφ᾽ ᾧ ταῦτα βέβηκε."

165. *Amb.* 17.6.

166. *Opusc.* 26, PG 91, 264A (some doubt authenticity).

167. Perl, "Methexis," 148n2. This appears to be assumed by Tollefsen, *Christocentric Cosmology*, 88; Balthasar, *Cosmic Liturgy*, 116–17.

168. Sorabji, *Philosophy of the Commentators,* 3:362. For what follows, see 362–67.

169. Plotinus, *Enn.* V.7 [18] 1, ed. A. H. Armstrong, *Ennead IV*, Loeb Classical Library (Harvard, MA: Cambridge University Press, 1984), 223.

170. Plotinus, *Enn.* V.7 [18] 1, ed. Armstrong, 225.

171. Plotinus, *Enn.* V.7 [18] 2, V.9 [5] 12; cf. Proclus, *El. Theol.*, prop. 206.

172. Plotinus, *Enn.* V.7 [18] 3, ed. Armstrong, 229: "συνεζεῦχθαι δεῖ τῷ εἴδει τὸ διάφορον"; cf. Proclus, *El. Theol.*, prop. 194.

173. Proclus, *PT* 1.21, 98, 16–19, ed. H. D. Saffrey and L. G. Westerink, *Theologie Platonicienne* (Paris: Belles Lettres, 1968). Proclus adds two arguments against the preexistent potency of an individual *qua* individual: (1) if an individual's own preexistent idea is also its cause, and if that idea is eternal, then this would imply the eternal fixity of the individual—a manifest absurdity (*In Parm.* 824, 12 f.); (2) if an individual's own preexistent idea is precisely its *paradigm*, then this entails it to be always a paradigm *of* the individual. But then the individual must always exist so that its idea is always a paradigm. But the individual is obviously not eternal, *ergo etc.* (*In Parm.* 824, 23ff.).

174. *Opusc.* 26, PG 91, 264B: "Ὅτι ἡ μὲν φύσις εἴδους λόγον μόνον ἐπέχει, ἡ δὲ ὑπόστασις καὶ τοῦ τινός ἐστι δηλωτική."

175. *Amb.* 22.3, modified.

176. Larchet, "Conception maximienne," 281, rightly remarks that the fact that each existent has its own individual *logos* "fonde en Dieu même la diversité du monde créé et la singularité de chaque être."

177. Balthasar too notices in Maximus this play of the "negative identity" and "positive identity" of the individual. But as far as I can see he does not expressly link these aspects to the *causation* of a created hypostasis as such: he says only that the "negativity" means every creature comes from nothing and is not God, and the "positivity" that all creatures are yet held in being by God "through his relationship to them" (*Cosmic Liturgy*, 68). My point here is that the very negative positivity of a hypostasis evades every metaphysical relation and that this relation, whatever it is, must "keep" a thing in being in an utterly unique and mysterious way. Maximus thinks that that way—not just that *fact*—has indeed been revealed in Christ, in all its manifest mysteriousness.

178. *Q. Thal.* 2.2, ed. Larchet, SC 529, 158; cf. *Amb.* 7.19.

179. *Amb.* 17.10. I think this is why Maximus tends to transition straightaway from the creation of *hypostases* to amazement at God's "power" and "wisdom"; cf. *Ep.* 13, PG 91, 521AD; *Ep.* 15, PG 91, 561D; *Amb.* 7.19 (cited below at note 183); *Amb.* 35.2 (here he cites Dionysius in support; *DN* 9.2); *Amb.* 48.2.

180. *Amb.* 15.5. So too Perl, "Methexis," 52–59; followed by Tollefsen, *Christocentric Cosmology*, 174.

181. *Amb.* 7.21, PG 91, 1084A; cf. *Myst.* 24, PG 91, 704D.

182. *Pace* Perl, "Methexis," 153: "A logos is no more than the presence of the participated in the participant"; and 163: "Because the hierarchy is continuous from Being down to the logoi of particulars, there is no difference between a creature's having a logos and its participating in the perfections." The presence of the participated, if what is participated is an energy or perfection (*CT* 1.48–50) or even a created universal (*Amb.* 7.16), can be present only as that creature's particular *form* (cf. Proclus's "whole-in-part" at *El. Theol.*, props. 72–74). A Maximian hypostasis and its *logos* cannot be present as form. However the *logos* of hypostasis may be immanent, it is not simply through the transcendence-immanence dialectic of participated and participating forms.

183. *Amb.* 7.19: "In the wisdom of the Creator, individual things [ἕκαστα] were created at the appropriate moment in time, in a manner consistent with their *logoi*, and thus they received in themselves actual existence as beings [τὸ εἶναι τῇ ἐνεργείᾳ λαμβάνῃ]. For God is eternally an active creator, but creatures exist first in potential, and only later in actuality [Ἐπειδὴ ὁ μὲν ἀεὶ κατ' ἐνέργειάν ἐστι Δημιουργός, τὰ δὲ δυνάμει μέν ἐστιν, ἐνεργείᾳ δὲ οὐκ ἔτι], since it is not possible for the infinite and the finite to exist simultaneously on the same level of being."

184. John 5:17 (as cited at *Q. Thal.* 2.2, ed. Larchet, SC 529, 158).

185. *Q. Thal.* 2.2, ed. Larchet, SC 529, 158.

186. *Amb.* 7.19, 10.90, 42.14, 65.2.

187. *Amb.* 46.4, PG 91, 1357AB, where, once again, this act of creation comes by the Word's condescension to become the very power of each and all: "He deigned to vary the modes of His presence so that the good things He planted in beings might ripen to full maturity, until the ages will have reached their appointed limit. At that point He will *gather together* the fruits of His own *sowing*"; cf. too *Amb.* 7.16.

188. *Amb.* 10.37, modified.

189. *Q. Thal.* 2, ed. Larchet, SC 529, 160.

190. *Q. Thal.* 60, ed. Larchet, SC 569, 88; *Exp. orat. dom.*, in *Opuscula exegetica duo*, ed. Van Deun, CCSG 7, 51.

191. Florovsky, "Creation and Creaturehood," 45, 51; starkly put at 57: "In a sense, it would be 'indifferent' to God whether the world exists or not—herein consists the absolute 'all-sufficiency' of God, the Divine autarchy. . . . The might of God and the freedom of God must be defined not only as the power to create and

to produce but also as the absolute freedom *not to create.*" His main case rests on creation's inherent instability and lack of self-sufficiency. But to deduce pure contingency from instability is to think creation apart from the nature of the Creator. The issue is not whether creation *depends* on God but whether God is the sort of God who could not but give himself as the source of what wholly depends on him. Even the strictest emanationist, after all, admits that finite beings depend on higher principles.

192. Florovsky, "Creation and Creaturehood," 56.

193. *Amb.* 42.16. This association was made in a general way at Constantinople II; cf. Evagrius Scholasticus, *HE* IV.38.

194. *Amb.* 42.15, PG 91, 1329C.

195. *Q. Thal.* 60.8, ed. Larchet, SC 569, 90: "For it was truly necessary that He who is by nature the Creator of the essence of beings should have also been, through Himself, the Author of the deification of beings by grace. In this way the Giver of well-being might also show Himself the Dispenser of the grace of eternal well-being."

196. Blowers, *Drama*, 173–78. He cites Irenaeus, *Haer.* 3.22.3; Athanasius, *Contra gent.* 35; Gregory of Nyssa, *Or. cat.* (*GNO* 3/4:17, lines 5–18, line 4). I add Gregory of Nazianzus, *Or.* 38.9, cited at *Amb.* 35.1, PG 91, 1288D: "But since this did not suffice to Goodness—to move solely within self-contemplation—it was necessary that the Good should overflow and make progress, so that a greater number of beings would benefit." Maximus comments with no fuss over the talk of necessity and even adds Dionysius's "ever-giving effusion" of divine goodness that proceeds from an "incomprehensible permanence" within God himself; *Amb.* 35.2, cf. *DN* 9.2.

197. Sergius Bulgakov, *The Lamb of God*, trans. Boris Jakim (1933; repr., Grand Rapids, MI: Eerdmans, 2008), 120: "God needs the world, and it could not have remained uncreated. But God needs the world not for himself but for the world itself. God is love, and it is proper for love to love and to expand in love. . . . Otherwise, absoluteness itself becomes a limit for the Absolute, a limit of self-love or self-affirmation, and that would attest to the limitedness of the Absolute's omnipotence—to its impotence, as it were. . . . And if it is in general possible for God's omnipotence to create the world, it would be improper for God's love not to actualize this possibility, inasmuch as, for love, it is natural to love, exhausting to the end all the possibilities of love. . . . God-Love needs the creation of the world in order to love, no longer only in his own life, but also outside himself, in creation." Cf. Maximus's remark at *Amb.* 10.119: "For it was on the highest logoi of God accessible by man, namely, His goodness and love, that they rightly concentrated their vision, and it was from these that they learned that God was moved to give being to all the things that exist."

198. *CT* 1.49, ed. Salés, *Two Hundred Chapters*, 70: "Πᾶν τὰρ εἴ τι τὸν τοῦ εἶναι λόγον ἔχει κατηγορούμενον, ἔργον Θεοῦ τυγχάνει."

199. *CT* 1.48, ed. Salés, *Two Hundred Chapters*, 70–71, slightly modified.

200. *CT* 1.48, ed. Salés, *Two Hundred Chapters*, 70–71.

201. *CT* 1.48, ed. Salés, *Two Hundred Chapters*, 70–71: "πᾶσα ζωὴ καὶ ἀναθανασία καὶ ἁπλότης καὶ ἀτρεψία καὶ ἀπειρία," and *CT* 1.50, ed. Salés, *Two Hundred Chapters*, 72: "αὐτὴ ἡ ὀντότης."

202. *CT* 1.49, ed. Salés, *Two Hundred Chapters*, 70–71.

203. Cf. *Amb.* 42.15.

204. Proclus, *El. Theol.*, esp. prop. 63, ed. Dodds, 60–61: "Every unparticipated term gives rise to two orders of participated terms, the one in contingent participants, the other in things which participate at all times and in virtue of their nature."

205. Proclus, *El. Theol.*, prop. 64, ed. Dodds, 60: "αἱ . . . αὐτοτελεῖς ὑποστάσεις." See Greig, "Proclus' Doctrine of Participation," 12–13.

206. If eternal works of God were neither Trinitarian nor created hypostases (in time), they would seem to form a middle term that would mediate by possessing qualities from both extremes. As we saw at sec. 2.2, though, Maximus faults "the Greeks" for exactly this—that they conceive difference as gradual qualification of one primal essence or reality.

207. Tollefsen, *Christocentric Cosmology*, 164.

208. *CC* 1.50, ed. Salés, *Two Hundred Chapters*, 72. Tollefsen, *Christocentric Cosmology*, 164, seems to sense the tension but remarks only that this passage (1.50) does not mention the "being" of this list of "works." But surely, as he goes on to assume, they belong to the same class as those in *CT* 1.47–48; three (Goodness, Immortality, Life) appear in both lists. They are therefore also participated *beings*, and so "Being itself" is a participated *being*.

209. Mentioned even here at *CC* 1.49 and at 1.50, ed. Salés, *Two Hundred Chapters*, 72.

210. Greig, "Proclus' Doctrine of Participation," 14n35, seems right to say that the "being" of God's eternal works constitutes "a new ontological category for the partcipated entities, insofar as their ontological status is modified from Proclus while still yet distinct from God himself."

211. Tollefsen, *Christocentric Cosmology*, 161, observes: "If we read *Cap. gnost.* 1.47 in connection with 1.48 it seems a quite reasonable interpretation to hold that the divine works without beginning (1.48) are collectively identified as the divine activity (ἡ θεία ἐνέργεια, 1.47)."

212. *CT* 1.49, ed. Salés, *Two Hundred Chapters*, 70–71: "τὸ δὲ κατὰ χάριν τοῖς γεγονόσιν ἐμπέφυκεν, οἷα τις δύναμις ἔμφυτος, τὸν ἐν πᾶσι ὄντα Θεὸν διαπρυσίως κηρύττουσα." It's obvious from later passages that such "implanted powers" are the *logoi* of beings; see esp. *Amb.* 17.7 and 21.8.

213. Proclus, *El. Theol.*, prop. 81, ed. Dodds, 76–77.

214. Proclus, *El. Theol.*, prop. 81, ed. Dodds, 76–77. That is a very compact way of describing the Neoplatonic principle of the limitation of (higher) act by (lower) power, though the isolation of a "medium" is Proclus's touch.

215. Proclus, *El. Theol.*, esp. props. 77–78.

216. Cf. too *Amb.* 10.102.

217. *Amb.* 7.20, PG 91, 1081BC.

218. *Amb.* 17.8.

219. *Amb.* 22.2.

220. *Amb.* 5.19, slightly modified.

221. *Amb.* 5.20.

222. *Amb.* 36.2, my emphasis: "It was not so amazing . . . for God to bring into communion with Himself, through the *infusion of breath*, the first formation of human nature . . . granting to that *likeness* a share of the divine beauty *according to His image*—as it was for Him to deign to draw near to it after it had been stained, and ran from Him . . . and to enter into intimate communion with it, and to partake of what was inferior [καὶ τοῦ χείρονος μετασχεῖν], and to heighten the miracle by means of a paradoxical union with things utterly beyond mixture with Him."

223. Proclus, *El. Theol.*, prop. 18.

224. *Amb.* 1.2–3.

225. So "virtue," which Maximus numbers among the "eternal works," is, a scholiast (unlikely Maximus) says in one place, "enhypostasized" in the deified, which is how Maximus can say "God continually becomes man" in all the deified; cf. *Q. Thal.* 22, schol. 8. This gloss also helps elucidate why Maximus appeals to the role of virtue in deification to illustrate his *logoi* doctrine at *Amb.* 7.21–23: because the Word (with the Father and Spirit) enhypostasizes God's "eternal works" (e.g., virtue) and because the Word makes himself identical to our *logoi*, so that the actualization of our *logoi* is simultaneously the Word's actualization of his works—indeed himself—in us. See too *Amb.* 10.41, modified, where the Word is the "is" of creatures: "Through this act of contemplation the saints gathered up the aforementioned modes into one, and they shaped within themselves, to the extent possible, the absolutely unique principles, which, with the different forms of virtues, totally fills the substance of the world of the willing mind, having passed beyond not simply the *logoi* of beings, but also the *logoi* of the virtues themselves, or rather with these *logoi* they arrived at the One who is beyond them all . . . to the Word who is beyond being and beyond goodness, out of Whom and Who *is* being for these [being and goodness] [καὶ εἰς ὃν οὗτοι καὶ ἐξ οὗ τὸ εἶναι τούτοις ἐστὶν ὑπερούσιον καὶ ὑπεράγαθον Λόγον]."

226. *Amb.* 54.2, PG 91, 1376C, lightly altered: "The 'body' of Christ is either the soul, or its powers, or sensations, or the body of each human being, or the members of the body, or the commandments, or the virtues, or the *logoi* of created

beings, or, to put it simply and more truthfully, each and all of these things, both individually and collectively, are the body of Christ [ἰδίᾳ τε καὶ κοινῇ, ταῦτα πάντα καὶ τούτων ἕκαστόν ἐστι τὸ σῶμα τοῦ Χριστοῦ]." On Maximus's theology of Christ's Body, see sec. 3.4.

227. *Q. Thal.* 35.2, ed. Larchet, SC 529, 374–75.

228. *Amb.* 48.7, PG 91, 1365BC, my modifications and emphasis.

229. *Amb.* 7.31, modified, my emphasis.

THREE. The End: World Becomes Trinity

1. Russell, *Doctrine of Deification*, 8.

2. Especially Völker, *Maximus Confessor*; Larchet, *Divinisation de l'homme*; Elie Ayroulet, *De l'image à l'Image: Réflexions sur un concept clef de la doctrine de la divinization de saint Maxime le Confesseur* (Rome: Institutum patristicum Augustinianum, 2013); and also Russell, *Doctrine of Deification*, 262–95.

3. Thus I assume and do not linger over the concrete means of human deification—both subjective (ascetical discipline, virtuous deeds) and objective (sacraments, especially the Eucharist). I do not neglect them entirely. They emerge when directly pertinent to the task at hand. That task is to trace the "architecture" or ontological structure, as it were, of the fact or eventuation of creaturely deification. Doing so proves that creation's end bears the logic of Christ. For the subjective and objective means of human deification, see mainly Thunberg, *Microcosm and Mediator*, 231–432; Larchet, *Divinisation de l'homme*, 399–436 (sacraments) and 437–94 (asceticism); Ayroulet, *De l'image à l'Image*, 286–92.

4. Cf. sec. 1.4. Recall that Christo-logic's "fourth" element is really no discrete element but the character of the whole logic: such logic derives from and applies to only the peculiar event of the Incarnation.

5. Remember that this "actuality"—the "composite hypostasis" of Christ that is itself the *result* of the economic processs—cannot in principle indicate an actuality in any way natural. It is neither a mere Aristotelian reduction of natural potency to act nor a mere Neoplatonic declension of higher act to lower act in accordance with the lower natural power. The composite Christ's concrete, historical, positive existence includes and exceeds both kinds of activity.

6. On Dionysius's language of the One's self-distribution in creating (or emanating) all things, see the remarks of Eric D. Perl, "Hierarchy and Participation," *American Catholic Philosophical Quarterly* 68.1 (1994): 17–20, and his *Theophany: The Neoplatonic Philosophy of Dionysius the Areopagite* (Albany: State University of New York Press, 2007), 17–34. I discussed similar expressions in Maximus in sec. 2.3.

7. Dionysius, *DN* 2.11, in *Corpus Dionysiacum*, vol. 4, pt. 1, ed. Suchla, 136, my translation. As Ysabel De Andia notes in her edition, *Les Noms divins: Chapitres I–IV*, SC 578 (Paris: Cerf, 2016), 404n2 (following Hadot especially), "Les commentateurs néoplatoniciens du *Parménide* identifient le τὸ ἓν ὄν au νοῦς." This recalls how Dionysius, even while hewing quite closely to Neoplatonic forms here, yet applies Christian pressure by insisting that it is *the very same God* who is at once the superessential One, the "Being-One" (typically "Nous" for Neoplatonism), and the oneness of derived/emanated being (ἓν ὤν)—an equation that seems indeed "paradoxale," as De Andia says (405n6).

8. Russell, *Doctrine of Deification*, 256, applies the following feature of Neoplatonic participation to Dionysius too: "For participation (μέθεξις) emphasizes that an inferior cannot possess a superior entire." From Lucas Siovanes, *Proclus: Neo-Platonic Philosophy and Science* (Edinburgh: Edinburgh University Press, 1996), 72.

9. Dionysius, *DN* 2.8, in *Corpus Dionysiacum*, vol. 4, pt. 1, ed. Suchla, 132, my translation and emphasis: "Οὐδὲ γὰρ ἔστιν ἀκριβὴς ἐμφέρεια τοῖς αἰτιατοῖς καὶ τοῖς αἰτίοις, ἀλλ'ἔχει μὲν τὰ αἰτιατὰ τὰς τῶν αἰτίων ἐνδεχομένας εἰκόνας, αὐτὰ δὲ τὰ αἴτια τῶν αἰτιατῶν ἐξήρηται κὰ ὑπερίδρυται κατὰ τὸν τῆς οἰκείας ἀρχῆς λόγον."

10. Dionysius, *DN* 3.11, in *Corpus Dionysiacum*, vol. 4, pt. 1, ed. Suchla, 138, my translation: "Καὶ γὰρ αὐτὴ [i.e., the Trinity] μὲν ἅπασι πάρεστιν, οὐ πάντα δὲ αὐτῇ πάρεστι." In context Dionysius is commending the necessity of "pure prayer," which, if rightly executed, "then we are present to the Trinity" (ed. Suchla, 138). But the *character* of that mutual presence is what concerns us. Dionysius does not here elaborate on that state, but he does appear to proscribe one possibility: "But to say that [the Trinity or the Good] is in all beings is to stand removed from the infinity above and embracing all things." Finite and infinite modes remain separate even in prayerful "union."

11. Plotinus, *Enn.* 1.2 [19] 2, identifies two senses of metaphysical "likeness" (ἡ ὁμοίωσις). First, there is a "likeness" between two things that "derive their likeness equally from the same principle [ὅσα ἐπίσης ὡμοίωται ἀπὸ τοῦ αὐτοῦ]." Call this the likeness of metaphysically similar effects. Second, there is the "likeness" where "one thing is like the other, but the other is primary, not reciprocally related to the thing in its likeness and not said to be like it" (τὸ μὲν ὡμοίωται πρὸς ἕτερον, τὸ δὲ ἕτερόν ἐστι πρῶτον, οὐκ ἀντιστρέφον πρὸς ἐκεῖνο οὐδὲ ὅμοιον αὐτοῦ λεγόμενον). Call this the likeness of metaphysically nonreciprocal cause and its effect. In this latter sense Plotinus warns against understanding "likeness" as sharing the same form. Rather, the cause differs (and is not symmetrically related) because the cause possesses "another" form than the effect. And as context makes plain (e.g., the "extended" vs. "intelligible" house of the paragraph before this one), this form exists with different properties, less determinate qualities, that

is, in a different essential mode. Vertical "likeness" between cause and effect therefore comes about "in a different way" (κατὰ τὸν ἕτερον τρόπον), namely in a *nonreciprocal* way.

12. Dionysius, *DN* 2.6, in *Corpus Dionysiacum*, vol. 4, pt. 1, ed. Suchla, 129, my translation: "Τούτου δὲ οὐχ ἡ σφραγὶς αἰτία, πᾶσαν γὰρ ἑαυτὴν ἐκείνη καὶ ταὐτὴν καὶ ἑκάστῳ ἐπιδίδωσιν, ἡ δὲ τῶν μετεχόντων διαφορότης ἀνόμοια ποιεῖ τὰ ἀπομόργματα τῆς μιᾶς καὶ ὅλης καὶ ταὐτῆς ἀρχετυπίας." The trope derives from Plato himself: *Theat.* 191c–d, 194c–e, 196a–b; *Tim.* 50c. For the law of "all in all, each according to its own mode," see Proclus, *El. Theol.*, prop. 103, and the remarks of Trouillard, "Procession néoplatonicienne," 91.

13. Dionysius, *DN* 2.6, in *Corpus Dionysiacum*, vol. 4, pt. 1, ed. Suchla, 130, my translation: "Διακέκριται δὲ τῆς ἀγαθοπρεποῦς εἰς ἡμᾶς θεουργίας τὸ καθ' ἡμᾶς ἐξ ἡμῶν ὁλικῶς καὶ ἀληθῶς οὐσιωθῆναι τὸν ὑπερούσιον λόγον καὶ δρᾶσαι καὶ παθεῖν, ὅσα τῆς ἀνθρωπικῆς αὐτοῦ θεουργίας ἐστὶν ἔκκριτα κὰ ἐξαίρετα."

14. So Dionysius, *Ep.* 4, in *Corpus Dionysiacum*, vol. 2, ed. Heil and Ritter, 161—discussed at *Amb.* 5.19. De Andia, in her edition *Noms divins*, SC 578, 388n1, suggests that even in the exceptional case of the Word's Incarnation Dionysius tends to conceive the divine activity according to the more familiar logic of the limitation of (higher) act by the modality of (lower) power, and that this might differ from Maximus's later Christological concerns: "Les *acta et passa Christi* relèvent, selon Denys, de son action divine (théurgie) en tant qu'elle s'exerce d'une manière humaine. Denys ne distingue pas deux volontés dans le Christ, comme Maxime le Confesseur, mais, comme dans la *Lettre* 4 à propos de la θεανδρικὴ ἐνέργεια . . . il *qualifie* son action divine d'une *modalité* humaine."

15. *Amb.* 7.31, modified.

16. One obviously senses Cappadocian "mixture" language here (e.g., *Amb.* 10.35, 41, etc.).

17. Williams, *Ground of Union*, 89.

18. Blowers, *Exegesis and Spiritual Pedagogy*, 118: "In Maximus' thought, however, the transcendent Logos is never conceptually separate from the *historical* Incarnate Christ." Juan-Miguel Garrigues, "Le dessein d'adoption du Créateur dans son rapport au Fils d'après s. Maxime le Confesseur," in Heinzer and Schönborn, *Maximus Confessor*, esp. 178–79, tried to argue that Maximus held to a basically scholastic view of God's "antecedent will" that did *not* include the historical Incarnation (or indeed the divine economy entire), since Maximus supposedly assigns the latter to God's "consequent will" in response to human sin. This view has been disproved, for instance, in the lovely essay by Artemije Radosavljevic, "Le problème du 'présupposé' ou du 'non-présupposé' de l'incarnation de dieu le Verbe," in Heinzer and Schönborn, *Maximus Confessor*, 193–206, who correctly insists that Maximus makes our deification depend specifically on the hypostatic identity between created and uncreated nature achieved in the

historical Incarnation (200, 204–5), which means that no posterior human action (sinful or not) could serve as the presupposition for Christ—quite the reverse. See too Larchet, *Divinisation de l'homme*, 221–24; Ayroulet, *De l'image à l'Image*, 162.

19. *Exp. Orat. Dom.* Prol., in *Opuscula exegetica duo*, ed. Van Deun, CCSG 23, 28–29; *Amb.* 7.37; *Amb.* 41.2, 6; *Amb.* 42.29; *Q. Thal.* 22.2–4, ed. Laga and Steel, CCSG 7, 137–9; *Q. Thal.* 60.3, ed. Laga and Steel, CCSG 22, 75, etc.

20. *Q. Thal.* 60.2, ed. Laga and Steel, CCSG 22, 73: "Τοῦτο προδήλως ἐστὶν ἄρρητός τε καὶ ἀπερινόητος θεότητός τε καὶ ἀνθρωπότητος καθ' ὑπόστασιν ἕνωσις, εἰς ταὐτὸν ἄγουσα τῇ θεότητι κατὰ πάντα τρόπον τῷ τῆς ὑποστάσεως λόγῳ τὴν ἀνθρωπότητα."

21. *Q. Thal.* 60.4, ed. Laga and Steel, CCSG 22, 75: "Διὰ γὰρ τὸν Χριστόν, ἤγουν τὸ κατὰ Χριστὸν μυστήριον, πάντες οἱ αἰῶνες καὶ τὰ ἐν αὐτοῖς τοῖς αἰῶσιν ἐν Χριστῷ τὴν ἀρχὴν τοῦ εἶναι καὶ τὸ τέλος εἰλήφασιν." I do not find in Maximus any grounds for a final union of creation with God that somehow circumvents—or ever could have circumvented—the precise *historical* identity achieved in Jesus of Nazareth. Indeed, the scriptural passage under discussion appears to proscribe this: it is "the pure and spotless lamb" who is foreknown (1 Pet. 1:20), the lamb slain since before the foundation of the world (Rev. 13:10). Where and when else is the Lord slain if not *in that time and place*, upon first-century Golgotha? Striking here is that Maximus claims this particular event, "Christ" in whom every conceivable polarity attains hypostatic identity, is "the fulfillment of God's foreknowledge" (*Q. Thal.* 60.4, ed. Laga and Steel, CCSG 22, 77: "ἥτις ἐν Χριστῷ ἐπ' ἐσχάτων τῶν χρόνων φανερωθεῖσα γέγονεν, πλήρωσιν δοῦσα τῇ προγνώσει τοῦ θεοῦ δι' ἑαυτῆς"; and esp. 60.8: God did not "foreknow" Christ "as what He was in Himself by nature, but as what He manifested when, in the economy of salvation, He later became man on our behalf"). Hence arises the possibility—one that has grounds, I think, in parts of Maximus's corpus—of a fundamental or primordial reciprocity between God's eternal self-knowledge (cf. *Q. Thal.* 56.7) and the particularities of historical events, yet not in such a way that the former simply *determines* the latter (lest there be no true reciprocity at all). From this vantage the Word himself, through his creative condescension as the *logoi* of creation (cf. *CT* 1.66–67—historical and cosmic at once!), would be the identity that grounds such a reciprocity. Then creation would prove an inevitable "result" of God's self-knowledge even while it does not possess any "simultaneous" or "co-eternal" (i.e., natural) relation to the divine essence itself (as ruled out by texts like *Q. Thal.* 60.9, ed. Laga and Steel, CCSG 22, 81; *Amb.* 15.9 and 11; *Ep.* 13, PG 91, 532AB). See secs. 4.2–3.

22. *Q. Thal.* 60.3, ed. Laga and Steel, CCSG 22, 75, slightly modified. For the meaning of predicating "preexistence" of the Word, see chapter 2, note 147.

23. *Amb.* 41.2, PG 91, 1305AC: "πᾶσαν ἔχων δηλαδὴ φυσικῶς ταῖς τῶν ἄκρων πάντων μεσότησι διὰ τῆς πρὸς τὰ ἄκρα πάντα τῶν ἰδίων μερῶν σχετικῆς ἰδιότητος τὴν πρὸς ἕνωσιν δύναμιν."

24. Hence Basil Studer, O.S.B., "Zur Soteriologie des Maximus Confessor," in Heinzer and Schönborn, *Maximus Confessor*, 242, rightly comments: "In ähnlicher Weise versteht Maximus die in der Menschwerdung Gottes erfolgte Erneuerung der Naturen als Aufhebung von Gegensätzen."

25. *Amb.* 41.2, PG 91, 1305B, slight modification and my emphasis: "δι' ἧς [ref. δύναμις] ὁ κατὰ τὴν αἰτίαν τῆς τῶν διηρημένων γενέσεως συμπληρούμενος τρόπος ἔμελλε τοῦ θείου σκοποῦ τὸ μέγα μυστήριον ἔκδηλον δι' ἑαυτοῦ καταστῆσαι."

26. *Amb.* 41.5, PG 91, 1308BC, my emphasis.

27. *Amb.* 7.9; *Q. Thal.* 22.4, ed. Laga and Steel, CCSG 7, 139; *Opusc.* 1, PG 91, 57AD; *Ep.* 6, PG 91, 429A; *Ep.* 15, PG 91, 565D.

28. See secs. 1.2 and 2.2.

29. *Pyr.* 139, PG 91, 325A, states that "nature" is predicated of God only "super-essentially" (ὑπερουσίως).

30. I add here two more vocation statements from this *Ambiguum*, loose bookends of our passage: (1) *Amb.* 41.3, PG 91, 1305BC, slightly modified: God introduced man "last among beings—like a kind of natural bond mediating between the universal extremes through his parts, and bringing into one reality through himself things that by nature are separated from each other by a great distance [οἱονεὶ σύνδεσμός τις φυσικὸς τοῖς καθόλου διὰ τῶν οἰκείων μερῶν μεσιτεύων ἄκροις, καὶ εἰς ἓν ἄγων ἐν ἑαυτῷ τὰ πολλῷ κατὰ τὴν φύσιν ἀλλήλων διεστηκότα τῷ διαστήματι]"; (2) *Amb.* 41. 9, PG 91, 1309CD: Christ, in the historical Incarnation, accomplished what Adam was originally meant to, namely "having completed the whole plan of God the Father for us, who through our misuse had rendered ineffective the power that was given to us from the beginning by nature for this purpose" (καὶ τελειώσας πᾶσαν βουλὴν τοῦ Θεοῦ καὶ Πατρὸς ὑπὲρ ἡμῶν τῶν ἀχρειωσάντων τῇ παραχρήσει τὴν ἐξ ἀρχῆς φυσικῶς ἡμῖν πρὸς τοῦτο δοθεῖσαν δύναμιν).

31. *Opusc.* 1, PG 91, 36AB.

32. *Amb.* 3.3; *Amb.* 42.25.

33. So *Q. Thal.* 22, schol. 1, ed. Laga and Steel, CCSG 7, 143 (likely of Maximus's hand): "The union according to hypostasis of the Word with the flesh revealed the ineffable purpose of the divine counsel in that it did not mix the divine essence with the flesh, but rather showed forth one hypostasis of the Word even in His becoming flesh, so that the flesh might both remain flesh according to its essence and become divine according to the hypostasis" (Ἡ πρὸς τὴν σάρκα τοῦ λόγου καθ' ὑπόστασιν ἕνωσις τὸν ἀπόρρητον τῆς θείας βουλῆς ἐφανέρωσε σκοπὸν ἐν τῷ μὴ φῦραι τῇ ἑνώσει τῆς σαρκὸς τὴν οὐσίαν, μίαν δὲ δεῖξαι κἂν τῇ σαρκώσει τοῦ λόγου τὴν ὑπόστασιν, ἵνα καὶ μείνῃ σὰρξ κατὰ τὴν οὐσίαν ἡ σὰρξ καὶ γένηται θεία κατὰ τὴν ὑπόστασιν); so too *Q. Thal.* 40, schol. 2, ed. Laga and Steel, CCSG 7, 275 (again Maximus's gloss).

34. *Pyr.* 182, PG 91, 341A.

35. See István Perczel, "St Maximus on the Lord's Prayer: An Inquiry into His Relationship to the Origenist Tradition," in Lévy et al., *Architecture of the Cosmos*, 221–78, who convincingly argues that Maximus's *Exp. Orat. Dom.* evinces structural similarities to the so-called isochrist strand of Origenism—legitimate similarities that Maximus's later Syriac (Maronite) opponents would interpret (illegitimately) as indices of a dogmatic or theological isomorphism between Maximus and condemned Origenism.

36. Guillaumont, *"Kephalaia Gnostica,"* 155, thinks Evagrian Origenism led naturally to isochristist eschatology: "L'expression 'égaux du Christ' ne se rencontre pas dans Evagre, mais l'idée correspondante est bien présente" (he cites Evagrius, *KG* 3.72, 4.51, 5.81). Recent scholars have questioned the adequacy of this line; e.g., Augustine M. C. Casiday, "Deification in Origen, Evagrius, and Cassian," in *Origeniana Octava: Origen and the Alexandrian Tradition / Origene e la tradizione alessandrina: Papers of the 8th International Origen Congress, Pisa, 27–31 August 2001*, ed. Lorenzo Perrone, P. Bernardino, and D. Marchini (Leuven: Leuven University Press, 2003), 995–1001 (esp. 999); and his *Reconstructing the Theology of Evagrius Ponticus: Beyond Heresy* (Cambridge: Cambridge University Press, 2013), esp. chaps. 7 and 8; consult too the scattered remarks of Ilaria L. E. Ramelli in her commentary and translation, *Evagrius's Kephalaia Gnostika: A New Translation of the Unreformed Text from the Syriac* (Atlanta, GA: SBL Press, 2015), esp. the introduction, lxv, and the comments on *KG* 6.14, where she inserts quotation marks around one statement to make it the position of a phantom interlocutor rather than Evagrius's own. Ramelli and Casiday's recovery efforts, laudable in places, are often wrong to the extent that they do not appreciate what "catechrestic" predication allows Evagrius to say and not say—that is, the sort of "improper" predication that results from standard Platonic participation according to which what is proper to the participated (the Logos, say) can improperly be said of the participant (Christ, say). Such predication preserves a two-subjects Christology while indulging a certain elision on occasion (*KG* 3.1–3). This seems to be exactly the claim at *KG* 4.18, 6.14, 6.16, 6.18, and 6.79 especially, and so I think Constantinople II got it right in the eighth canon, which identifies and condemns this practice. The main point here is that if Origen (esp. at *Princ.* 2.6.4) and Evagrius *can* be and indeed were read as dividing "Christ" (a separate soul or intellect) from the Word (who is, particularly in Evagrius's theology, consubstantial with Father and Spirit), then isochrist eschatology becomes at once more palatable and more extreme. Palatable, since our equality with Christ in deification is simply an equality with (the highest, true) fellow creature. Extreme, since the final fusion of Christ's intellect with the numberless Trinity implies the dissolution of all hypostases along with that one (e.g., *KG* 2.17; see too can. 14 of Constantinople II, ed. Price, *Canons*, 2:286).

37. Guillaumont, *"Kephalaia Gnostica,"* 151n91, mentions another Origenist faction called "the Protoctists" who, in an effort "conserver au Christ une certaine supériorité," believed that Christ was "created" (*ktistos*) before all other intellects (*protos*); this helped them reject an original henad destined for restoration in a final apokatastasis.

38. Evagrius Scholasticus (6th cent.), *HE* IV.38, PG 86, 2780A (my translation), cites from a collection of "blasphemous statements" made by Origenists of the New Laura, not far south of Jerusalem. It quotes the bishop of Caesarea and erstwhile confidant of Emperor Justinian, Theodore of Ascidas, as saying: "If even now the Apostles and martyrs work wonders and enjoy such high honor, what restoration remains for them in the [coming] restoration except to become equal to Christ?" (Εἰ νῦν οἱ ἀπόστολοι καὶ οἱ μάρτυρες θαυματουργοῦσι, καὶ ἐν τῇ τοσαύτῃ τιμῇ ὑπάρχουσιν, ἐν τῇ ἀποκαταστάσει εἰ μὴ ἴσοι γένοιντο Χριστῷ, ποία ἀποκατάστασις αὐτοῖς ἐστιν); cf. Cyril of Scythopolis, *Vita Cyriacus* 12, 229.32–230.10.

39. Guillaumont, *"Kephalaia Gnostica,"* 119, 147ff.

40. Theodore of Scythopolis, *Libel*, Cap. 11, PG 86, 236A, my translation: "Εἴ τις λέγει, ἢ φρονεῖ, ἢ διδάσκει ἐξισοῦσθαι ἡμᾶς τῷ Σωτῆρι ἡμῶν Χριστῷ τῷ Θεῷ ἡμῶν τῷ τεχθέντι ἐκ τῆς ἁγίας Θεοτόκου καὶ ἀεὶ παρθένου Μαρίας, καὶ μέλλειν καὶ ἡμῖν ἐνοῦσθαι τὸν Θεὸν Λόγον, ὡς τῇ Μαρίας προσληφθείσῃ ἐμψυχωμένῃ σαρκὶ κατ' οὐσίαν καὶ καθ' ὑπόστασιν· ἀνάθεμα ἔστω." Cf. Guillaumont, *"Kephalaia Gnostica,"* 151n91.

41. Justinian, *Ep. ad conc.* (553), in Price, *Canons*, 2:282–83; Greek text is from Georgius Monachus, *Chron.* II, ed. Carolus de Boor, *Georgii Monachi chronicon* (1904; repr., Stuttgart: Teubner, 2012), 631: "ἀποκαθισταμένου δηλονότι καὶ αὐτοῦ τοῦ διαβόλου καὶ τῶν λοιπῶν δαιμόνων εἰς τὴν αὐτὴν ἐνάδα καὶ τῶν ἀσεβῶν καὶ ἀθέων ἀνθρώπων μετὰ τῶν θείων καὶ θεοφόρων ἀνδρῶν καὶ τῶν οὐρανίων δυνάμεων καὶ τὴν αὐτὴν ἐξόντων ἕνωσιν πρὸς τὸν θεόν, ὁποίαν ἔχει καὶ ὁ Χριστός, καθὼς καὶ προϋπῆρχον, ὡς μηδεμίαν εἶναι διαφορὰν τῷ Χριστῷ πρὸς τὰ λοιπὰ λογικὰ παντελῶς οὔτε τῇ οὐσίᾳ οὔτε τῇ γνώσει οὔτε τῇ δυνάμει οὔτε τῇ ἐνεργείᾳ."

42. *ACO* IV.1, 248–49; Price, *Canons*, 2:286.

43. Even Leontius of Byzantium, a notorious "Origenist" to detractors like Cyril of Scythopolis (*Vita Sabae* 72, 74, 83–86), strove to maintain Christ's uniqueness, as did many "protoctist" Origenists; see Brian Daley, "The Origenism of Leontius of Byzantium," *Journal of Theological Studies* 27.2 (1976): 343.

44. See Guillaumont, *"Kephalaia Gnostica,"* 176–82, for more on Simeon of Kennesrin's anti-Maximus polemic; and Perczel, "St Maximus," esp. 234, where a passage from Michael the Syrian's *Chronicle* (12th cent.) reads: "[And these monks of the New Laura said that] Christ will not be superior to us in anything and, just as he is God, so also we will be transformed to become gods" (Perczel's translation).

45. The last two forbidden "identities"—in power or activity—seem to pose the greatest prima facie challenge to Maximian deification, since Maximus openly asserts that the "activity" of deification is solely divine. He later had to clarify that and how this does not mean eschatological monenergism. See *Amb.* 7.12 and *Opusc.* 1, PG 91, 33A–36A.

46. Gregory of Nazianzus, *Or.* 28.20 = *Amb.* 21.1.

47. *Amb.* 21.2.

48. *Amb.* 21.3: "ὅτιπερ καὶ Ἰωάννης ὁ μέγας εὐαγγελιστὴς ἐν τῷ κατ' Εὐαγγελίῳ πρόδρομός ἐστι τοῦ δι' αὐτοῦ μηνυομένου μυστικωτέρου καὶ μείζονος Λόγου."

49. *Amb.* 21.5–8.

50. *Amb.* 21.8, my emphasis: "Moreover, [the soul] will unite the four general virtues like elements in a synthesis, and by means of the intellect will frame a world that will be completed by the spirit, since *the soul endows each virtue with subsistence through the actualization of its own inner potentials in relation to the senses* [κατὰ συμπλοκὴν μέντοι τῆς πρὸς τὰς αἰσθήσεις τῶν αὐτῆς δυνάμεων ἐνεργείας ἑκάστην ἀρετὴν ὑποστήσασα]"; cf. too *Amb.* 10.3. Stunning, because Maximus defines creation itself in very similar terms—*Q. Thal.* 22.2, ed. Laga and Steel, CCSG 7, 137: "He who brought all visible and invisible creation into being solely through the momentum of His will" (Ὁ πάσης κτίσεως, ὁρατῆς τε καὶ ἀοράτου, κατὰ μόνην τοῦ θελήματος τὴν ῥοπὴν ὑποστήσας τὴν γένεσιν); or *Q. Thal.* 51.2, ed. Laga and Steel, CCSG 7, 395: "Having granted existence to the entire visible creation" (Τὴν ὁρωμένην ἅπασαν φύσιν ὁ θεὸς ὑποστήσας). The point here is that lower modes of existence—the circumscribed, finite modes of created effects—are valorized *in themselves* to such a degree that Maximus can view their "completion" and participation in virtue as some sort of positive actualization of virtue itself. It is as if virtue *gains* something in some sense (not in any natural sense, clearly) by its realization in our finite, personal mode of life.

51. *Amb.* 21.9. For more on these intervening passages, especially as they touch on analogy and perichoresis, cf. below, sec. 3.4.

52. Gen. 1:26–27. So Clement of Alexandria, *Protr.* 9.87; Evagrius, *Letter to Melania* 62 and *Letter to Anatolius* 18, 61; Diodochus of Photice, *De perf.* 89.

53. *CC* 3.25; *Amb.* 7.21; cf. *Q. Thal.* 53.3 and 6.

54. *Amb.* 21.15, PG 91, 1253D, my modifications and emphasis.

55. Some of Maximus's key predecessors who were not obviously "Origenists" after the manner of Evagrius appear noticably reticent about overstating the character of our deification. Gregory of Nazianzus, as noted by Russell, *Doctrine of Deification*, 224, nowhere quotes 2 Pet. 1:4. Even if Russell overstates the matter when he says, "For the Cappadocians, deification never went beyond a figure of speech" (13), his basic view that the Cappadocian anti-Eunomian polemic put peculiar pressure on how and to what degree they spoke of our *theosis* seems right, at least for Basil and Gregory of Nazianzus (Gregory of Nyssa is more complicated).

Those pressures are much less urgent in Maximus, and this in part explains why his "realistic" view of deification seems in several respects like a return to Origen's.

56. *Amb.* 7.12 ("if I may put it this way," after saying God perichoretically penetrates the deified); *Amb.* 10.9 ("if it be permitted thus" (εἰ θέμις τοῦτο εἰπεῖν), in the midst of stating the *tantum-quantum* principle); *Q. Thal.* 53.3 ("if one may be permitted to put it this way," while saying we become God's "mirror" in deification); etc.

57. Aristotle, *Po.* 1453b11, for instance, which Ayroulet correlates with the metaphysics of first and second *ousia* at *Cat.* 2a 11–23; Ayroulet, *De l'image à l'Image*, 42: "Dans le platonisme, les Idées archétypales existent en soi et précèdent dans l'existence les images qui en sont les copies, que ce soit dans le monde sensible ou dans l'art qui imite le sensible. Chez Aristote, au contraire, il semble que le prototype n'existe pas en tant que les mais seulement dans la μίμησις actualisée dans l'image." He says Aristotle's view implies "une simultanéité existentielle entre le modèle et l'image" (77) and applies this insight to Maximus (148, 296).

58. *Amb.* 21.16, PG 91, 1256B.

59. Although "by its nature the uncreated cannot be contained by any created thing" (*Amb.* 10.78), Maximus also says, "For He knows how to be contained by creation" (*Amb.* 10.59). Both affirmations come in the course of Maximus's meditation on the Transfiguration, which revealed that God's power means he can "become a type and symbol of Himself, presenting Himself symbolically by means of His own self" (*Amb.* 10.77); see too *Myst.* 5, ed. Boudignon, CCSG 69, 23–24, discussed below (sec. 3.2), where the mutual interpenetration with Christ we enjoy in deification means that "Jesus my God and Savior," "is completed through me who am saved" (Ἰησοῦν μὲν τὸν ἐμὸν Θεὸν καὶ Σωτῆρα συμπληρωθέντα δι' ἐμοῦ σωζομένου).

60. *Amb.* 5.5. See Wood, "Both Mere Man," 110–30.

61. Constas's rendering of *Amb.* 21.16 (*On Difficulties in the Church Fathers*, 1:445, my emphasis), "and are made ready by the Word through the hope that they will be spiritually vivified *by their union with the archetype*," is imprecise since it does not indicate the directionality of the union itself. Maximus can employ the Platonic, vertical direction of image to archetype (*Amb.* 7.25). Here he reverses it: the Word prepares the deified for "the reception of the archetype [i.e., the Word himself]," where "reception" (ἡ παραδοχή) can mean the "reception of a seed/sperm" (LSJ, s.v.; ref. Oribasius, *Coll. medic.* 22.7.1) or even the "reception of a person" (Lampe, s.v., IV)—both highly relevant senses.

62. Proclus, *PT* VI.3.

63. Dionysius, *EH* 1.3, in *Corpus Dionysiacum*, vol. 2, ed. Heil and Ritter, 66, lines 12–13, my translation: "ἡ δὲ θέωσις ἐστιν ἡ πρὸς θεὸν ὡς ἐφικτὸν ἀφομοίωσίς τε καὶ ἕνωσις."

64. Gregory of Nazianzus, *Or.* 40.2 = *Amb.* 42.1.

65. Gregory of Nazianzus, *Or.* 40.2 = *Amb.* 42.1: "τὴν δέ, τῇ σαρκώσει καὶ τῷ βαπτίσματι, ὅπερ αὐτὸς ἐβαπτίσατο."

66. *Amb.* 42.31, slightly modified.

67. Cf. esp. *Q. Thal.* 61.11. I treat this in detail in sec. 4.1.

68. Irenaeus, *Haer.* 4.38.4, ed. A. Rousseau et al., *Contre les hérésies, Livre IV*, SC 100/2 (1965; repr., Paris: Cerf, 2006), my translation: "quamvis secundum simplicitatem bonitatis suae hoc fecerit, ne quis eum putet invidiosum aut impraestantem" (lines 98–100), and "Secundum enim benignitatem suam bene dedit bonum et similes sibi suae potestatis homines fecit" (lines 105–7).

69. Irenaeus, *Haer.* 5.21.3. On Irenaeus's idea of recapitulation, see Eric Osborn, *Irenaeus of Lyons* (Cambridge: Cambridge University Press, 2001), 97–116. On Maximus's programmatic or methodological debt to Irenaeus, see Blowers, *Maximus the Confessor*, 102–8.

70. *Amb.* 42.31.

71. *Amb.* 42.32, my modification and emphasis.

72. *Q. Thal.* 6.2; *Q. Thal.* 61.11.

73. Blowers, *Maximus the Confessor*, 191–93.

74. See *Myst.* 21, and the note in *Maximus Confessor: Selected Writings*, Classics of Western Spirituality, ed. and trans. George C. Berthold (Mahwah, NJ: Paulist Press, 1985), 223n112.

75. *Myst.* 13, ed. Boudignon, CCSG 69, 42, slightly modified: "τῇ χάριτι θεωθέντας, καὶ κατὰ μέθεξιν πρὸς αὐτὴν ὁμοιωθέντας τῇ κατὰ δύναμιν ἀδιαιρέτῳ ταυτότητι." On analogy or, here, "according to each one's power," see sec. 3.4.

76. *Myst.* 24, ed. Boudignon, CCSG 69, 55–56.

77. *Myst.* 24, ed. Boudignon, CCSG 69, 58, slight change: "διὰ δὲ τῆς ἁγίας μεταλήψεως τῶν ἀχράντων καὶ ζωοποιῶν μυστηρίων, τὴν πρὸς αὐτὸν κατὰ μέθεξιν ἐνδεχομένην δι' ὁμοιότητος κοινωνίαν τε καὶ ταυτότητα· δι' ἧς γενέσθαι θεὸς ἐξ ἀνθρώπου καταξιοῦται ὁ ἄνθρωπος."

78. *Myst.* 24, ed. Boudignon, CCSG 69, 59, slightly modified. Cf. too *Amb.* 50.3, where the Eucharist is also celebrated "in the future age of the divine promises." Then "Without any mediation we will eat the most sublime Word of Wisdom—and being transformed with respect to Him, we will become Gods by grace" (τὸν ἀκρότατον ἀμέσως ἐσθίοντες τῆς Σοφίας Λόγον, πρὸς ὃν μεταποιηθέντες κατὰ χάριν θεούμεθα). Portaru, "Vocabulary of Participation," 303, glosses Maximus's language in these texts: "A term that should be noted is the verb μεταποιέω, which designates a profound transformation of human being by grace. . . . Since the context is the receiving of Eucharist, I believe these images *must be understood literally, not metaphorically*" (my emphasis). He doesn't elaborate.

79. *Exp. Orat. Dom.* 3 (cf. 1), in *Opuscula exegetica duo*, ed. Van Deun, CCSG 23, 40, slightly modified.

80. *Exp. Orat. Dom.* 1: (1) theology (i.e., knowing God as Trinity); (2) adoption in grace; (3) equality of honor with the angels; (4) participation in eternal life; (5) the restoration of nature; (6) the abolition of sin; (7) the overthrow of evil's

tyranny and deception. The order seems to bear the logic of the "two ages" of Incarnation and deification in *Q. Thal.* 22: phenomenologically, both history and individual biographies unfold from 7 to 1; eschatologically, from 1 to 7; Christologically, in both directions at once.

81. *Exp. Orat. Dom.* 2, in *Opuscula exegetica duo*, ed. Van Deun, CCSG 23, 33: "Ἰσοτίμους δὲ τοῖς ἀγγέλοις τοὺς ἀνθρώπους πεποίηκεν." An idea precious to Evagrius, *De orat.* 113; Russell, *Doctrine of Deification*, 239.

82. *Exp. Orat. Dom.* 2, in *Opuscula exegetica duo*, ed. Van Deun, CCSG 23, 34, greatly modified. Fuller quotation: "Ζωῆς δὲ θείας ποιεῖται μετάδοσιν, ἐδώδιμον ἑαυτὸν ἐργαζόμενος, ὡς οἶδεν αὐτὸς καὶ οἱ παρ᾽ αὐτοῦ τοιαύτην αἴσθησιν νοερὰν εἰληφότες, ὥστε τῇ γεύσει ταύτης τῆς βρώσεως εἰδέναι κατ᾽ ἐπίγνωσιν ἀληθῶς ὅτι χρηστὸς ὁ κύριος, ποιότητι θείᾳ πρὸς θέωσιν μετακιρνῶν τοὺς ἐσθίοντας, οἷα δὴ σαφῶς ζωῆς καὶ δυνάμεως ἄρτος καὶ ὢν καὶ καλούμενος." Cf. Origen, *Hom. in Lev.* 16.5; *Comm. in Jo.* 20.35, passim.

83. *Exp. Orat. Dom.* 5, in *Opuscula exegetica duo*, ed. Van Deun, CCSG 23, 70, my modifications and emphasis. In fact, the logic emerges if you simply trace the order of Maximus's scriptural allusions as they appear:

1. The Middle: The Word becomes incarnate.
   i. Christ gives himself as "the Bread of Life" (John 6:35, 48)
   ii. and descends from the "Father of lights" (James 1:17).
2. The End: The Word's Incarnation induces our deification.
   iii. Therefore we're empowered to become "sharers in the divine nature" itself (2 Pet. 1:4),
   iv. and this takes the specific form of filiation, of receiving the Son through the Spirit as "children of God" (John 1:12, 11:52; Rom. 8:16, 12, 9:8; Phil. 2:15; 1 John 3:1–2, 10, 5:2).
3. The Beginning: The Word *Incarnate* is therefore shown to become the very principles of creation,
   v. since Maximus here substitutes "Christ" and "Son" for the vaguer "in Him" of Acts 17:28.
   vi. Hence too Maximus claimed earlier that "the same divine food" wrought in Christ was available to Adam (*Exp. Orat. Dom.* 4, in *Opuscula exegetica duo*, ed. Van Deun, CCSG 23, 60).

84. *Exp. Orat. Dom.* 4, in *Opuscula exegetica duo*, ed. Van Deun, CCSG 23, 50, slightly modified. I favor the rendering, "according to this hypostasis," as implied below in sec. 3.2.

85. *Q. Thal.* 59.8, ed. Laga and Steel, CCSG 22, 53, explicitly defines the "likeness" of the fully deified as "the received [and] actualized identity to the very one who is participated by participants through likeness [ἡ κατ᾽ ἐνέργειαν πρὸς αὐτὸ τὸ μετεχόμενον τῶν μετεχόντων δι᾽ ὁμοιότητος ἐνδεχομένη ταυτότης]"

(modified)—on which consult Portaru, "Vocabulary of Participation," 316; *Q. Thal.* 25.5, ed. Laga and Steel, CCSG 7, 163, says the human intellect attains "identity with God by grace" (τῆς πρὸς θεὸν κατὰ χάριν ταὐτότητος), and indeed identity with "the Divine Intellect," the Father himself; *Amb.* 20.7 claims that in the state of grace we are "like and equal to God" (ὅμοιον Θεῷ καὶ ἴσον, ὡς ἐφικτόν, τῇ χάριτι κατὰ τὴν ἕξιν); *Amb.* 31.4 says the gift of grace makes us "equal in honor to the Father" (ἰσότιμον τῷ Πατρὶ κατὰ τὴν ἐκ χάριτος δωρεάν); and *Q. Thal.* 29.5, especially schol. 4, ed. Laga and Steel, CCSG 7, 217, which, though probably not by Maximus himself, dares to say the very thing Theophilus of Scythopolis condemned: that Paul, because he "became another Christ," was indeed "united to Him according to hypostasis" (ἑνωθῆναι σπεύδων τῷ Χριστῷ κατὰ τὴν ἐν εἴδει τῶν ἀγαθῶν ὑπόστασιν)!

86. For the Macarian legacy in Maximus, see Marcus Plested, *The Macarian Legacy: The Place of Macarius-Symeon in the Eastern Christian Tradition* (Oxford: Oxford University Press, 2004), 213–54; and Russell, *Doctrine of Deification*, 241–45.

87. Pseudo-Macarius, *Hom.* 2.5, PG 34, 468A.

88. Pseudo-Macarius, *Hom.* 17.1, PG 34, 624C: "Οὗτοί εἰσι καὶ υἱοὶ, καὶ κύριοι, καὶ θεοὶ, δεδεμένοι, ἠχμαλωτισμένοι, βεβυθισμένοι, ἐσταυρωμένοι, ἀφιερωμένοι"; cf. the *Great Letter*, in *The Fifty Spiritual Homilies and The Great Letter*, ed. and trans. George A. Maloney (New York: Paulist Press, 1992), 258–59.

89. Pseudo-Macarius, *Hom.* 43.1, PG 34, 772BC, my translation and slight modification: "ἵνα τῷ αὐτῷ ἐλαίῳ, ᾧ αὐτὸς ἐχρίσθη, καὶ ἡμεῖς χρισθέντες γενώμεθα Χριστοί, τῆς αὐτῆς, ὡς εἰπεῖν, οὐσίας καὶ ἑνὸς σώματος."

90. Pseudo-Macarius, *Hom.* 34.2, PG 34, 745B, my translation.

91. Pseudo-Macarius, *Hom.* 39.1, PG 34, 761CD, my translation: "λάβωσι δωρεὰν οὐράνιον ἐκ τῆς ὑποστάσεως τῆς θεότητος αὐτοῦ . . . ἧς ἄνευ ἀδύνατόν ἐστι ζωῆς ἀθανάτου τυχεῖν, ἥτις ἐστὶν ὁ Χριστός." Cf. *Exp. Orat. Dom.* 4, quoted at note 84.

92. On these Origenist influences, see Balthasar, *Cosmic Liturgy*, 115–36; Sherwood, *Earlier Ambigua*; and Blowers, *Maximus the Confessor*, 1–3, 67–68, and 222–23. On the Cappadocian influence, see George Berthold, "The Cappadocian Roots of Maximus the Confessor," in Heinzer and Schönborn, *Maximus Confessor*, 51–59.

93. Perczel, "St Maximus," 239–40, 271.

94. Larchet, *Divinisation de l'homme*, 376–82; Thunberg, *Microcosm and Mediator*, 32–33.

95. Irenaeus, *Haer.* 5.pref.; Athanasius, *De incarn. Verb.* 54.3. Of course, Maximus began here (cf. *Lib. ascet.* 43) and so maintained it throughout his corpus; see Larchet, *Divinisation de l'homme*, 376.

96. Gregory of Nazianzus, *Or.* 29.19 = *Amb.* 3.1: "because He deigned to take on your thick corporeality, consorting with the flesh through the medium of the

intellect—and God on earth became man, for it (i.e., the flesh) was blended with God, and He became one, because the stronger predominated, so that I might be made God to the same extent that He was made man [ἵνα γένωμαι τοσοῦτον Θεὸς ὅσον ἐκαῖνος ἄνθρωπος]." Though not cast in the same technical formula, the central idea that *tantum-quantum* expresses—a fundamental reciprocity between creaturely *ascent* to (and as) God and God's *descent* to (and as) creature—finds precedent in lesser-known byways of the Alexandrian tradition. Clement of Alexandria wrote: "For the Word of God is intelligible [νοερός], according to which the image of the mind [νοῦς] is seen in the human being alone, by which also the good man is deiform and dei-similar [θεοειδὴς καὶ θεοείκελος] in his soul, *and God, in turn, is anthropoform* [ἀνθρωποειδής]. For the form of both is the mind [ὁ νοῦς], by which we are fashioned"; *Strom.* 6.9.72.2, my emphasis, but translation taken from David I. Litwa, "'I Will Become Him': Homology and Deification in the Gospel of Thomas," *Journal of Biblical Literature* 133.2 (2015): 446. Maximus could never brook a natural relation between God and the deified mind after the manner of Clement here and Origen at times (*Princ.* 4.4.9), though some of his influences appear to have held that view; cf. Dirk Krausmüller, "Human Souls as Consubstantial Sons of God: The Heterodox Anthropology of Leontius of Jerusalem," *Journal for Late Antique Religion and Culture* 4 (2010): 43–67. This further substantiates my principal point: Maximus's Neo-Chalcedonian Christology allowed him to eschew and replace the *dogmatic* content of these parts of the tradition while retaining and even intensifying (since hypostatic identity is stronger than the formal identity among stratified levels of nature) their *structure* or *thought-forms*.

97. Larchet, *Divinisation de l'homme*, 381, quoting François Brune, *Pour que l'homme devienne Dieu*, 2nd ed. (Saint-Jean-de-Braye: Dangles, 1992), 332.

98. *Exp. Orat. Dom.* 2, in *Opuscula exegetica duo*, ed. Van Deun, CCSG 23, 32–33, my modifications and emphasis.

99. See Larchet, *Divinisation de l'homme*, 376–77 for others, esp. *Q. Thal.* 64.33, ed. Laga and Steel, CCSG 22, 237.

100. *Amb.* 3.3, my emphasis (quoting Gregory of Nazianzus, *Or.* 29.19): "Through the flesh, which by nature is passible, He manifested His infinitely immeasurable power, for 'it'—obviously the flesh—was 'blended with God and He became one, the strong side predominating,' precisely because it was assumed by the Word, *who deified it by identifying it with His own hypostasis* [ὑποστατικῇ ταυτότητι κυρίως αὐτὴν τοῦ προσλαβόντος Λόγου θεώσαντος]."

101. So Perczel, "St Maximus," 241: "The measure of appropriation of the godhead by men equals the measure of the acquisition of human nature through the self-emptying of the Word of God; in fact there is no quantitative difference; men through grace, acquired through their acts of free will, become just as much God as God the Word through the free act of his self-emptying had become entirely man." Perczel prefers to explain this by invoking Aristotle's principle of "substance," which prescribes that "substance does not admit the concept of more or less" (*Cat.* 5,

3b33-4a9) (240, 247). In that case Maximian deification requires the Word to dwell within the deified "substantially and not only operatively or energetically" (241). This edges very close to my own interpretation (see sec. 3.2): since the Word's hypostasis is the very principle for created hypostases (and their natures), then the Word is personally present as a supranatural power in every creature (as their *logoi*).

102. *Amb.* 7.22.

103. *Q. Thal.* 22.4, ed. Laga and Steel, CCSG 7, 137–39.

104. Larchet, *Divinisation de l'homme*, 381–82, my translation.

105. *Amb.* 42.17, 29.

106. *Amb.* 10.9, modified.

107. *Amb.* 20.7, slightly modified: "ἔργον . . . τῆς δὲ θεολογικῆς μυσταγωγίας ὅμοιον Θεῷ καὶ ἴσον, ὡς ἐφικτόν, τῇ χάριτι κατὰ τὴν ἕξιν ποιῆσαι."

108. *Amb.* 41.5. Even the great Larchet, *Divinisation de l'homme*, 487, tends to give this sense: "Il y bien alors, appropriées par la personne, communication à la nature qu'elle hypostasie, par le biais des vertus, non pas des propriétés essentielles de Dieu . . . non pas de la nature même de Dieu (de sorte que l'homme ne devient pas Dieu Lui-Même, n'acquiert pas avec Dieu l'identité d'essence), mais des énergies divines, le fidèle devenant ainsi dieu par participation, par position et par grâce."

109. *Q. Thal.* 59.8, quoted at note 85.

110. *CC* 3.25, ed. Ceresa-Gastaldo, 154: God, because he is extremely good, communicates four "divine properties" to rational creatures: "being and ever-being, goodness and wisdom" (τὸ ὄν, τὸ ἀεὶ ὄν, τὴν ἀγαθότητα καὶ τὴν σοφίαν). The first two God allots "to the essence" (τῇ οὐσίᾳ), the last two "to the gnomic receptivity" (τῇ δὲ γνωμικῇ ἐπιτηδειότητι), i.e., to human progress in freely appropriating the virtues. The first two correspond to "to the image" of God in us from the beginning, the last two "to the likeness" achieved unto eternity. And these three pair-sets reduce neatly to the most general one: "The one [i.e., image/essence/being] is by nature, the other [i.e., likeness/freedom/goodness-wisdom] by grace" (τοῦ κατὰ φύσιν, ὁ κατὰ χάριν).

111. *Q. Thal.* 19.2, 64.34, passim; see Blowers, *Exegesis and Spiritual Pedagogy*, 117–21; Vasilios Karayiannis, *Maxime le Confesseur: Essence et énergies de Dieu* (Paris: Beauchesne, 1993), 290–340; and see the still very good discussion of the natural and scriptural laws in Balthasar, *Cosmic Liturgy*, 291–314.

112. Much discussed, but see especially the discussion in Riou, *Monde et l'Église*, 89. Clearly this schema is a protracted version of the one at *CC* 3.25; cf. too *Amb.* 7.10.

113. *Amb.* 65.2, my slight modifications and emphasis.

114. Cf. *CC* 1.100.

115. On "ecstasy," see Sherwood, *Earlier Ambigua*, 128–54; on "experience," see Pierre Miquel, "Πεῖρα: Contribution à l'étude du vocabulaire de l'expérience religieuse dans l'oeuvre de Maxime le Confesseur," *Studia Patristica* 7 (1966): 355–61.

116. *Amb.* 20.2.

117. *Amb.* 7.40–43. In sec. 1.5 I noted that monenergists proposed something similar for the divine-human activity in Christ and that Maximus rejected it because it would introduce a "mutual conditioning" even among inferior and superior modes of existence such that the consequent activity would imply a composed power from a composed nature (*Opusc.* 5).

118. Even in *Opusc.* 1, where Maximus clarifies what he meant by saying that "the grace of the Spirit" conquers the deified soul to the point that "it has God alone acting within it" with "only one sole energy, that of God and of those worthy of God, or rather of God alone"—even then he doubles down on his denial of any natural power on our part in the work of deification: "But deification does not come about from our natural powers; it is not in our control. For there exists in nature no *logos* of the things above nature" (*Opusc.* 1, PG 91, 33C, my translation).

119. *Q. Thal.* 60.6, ed. Laga and Steel, CCSG 22, 77; here Maximus defines "reasoning about God" (λόγος περὶ θεοῦ) as "the use of the analogy of beings in the cognitive contemplation of God" (τὴν ἐκ τῶν ὄντων ἀναλογίαν τῆς περὶ αὐτοῦ γνωστικῆς θεωρίας).

120. *Q. Thal.* 60.5, ed. Laga and Steel, CCSG 22, 77.

121. *Myst.* 5, ed. Boudignon, CCSG 69, 29; cf. *DN* 2.9, in *Corpus Dionysiacum*, vol. 4, pt. 1, ed. Suchla, 134.

122. *Amb.* 15.9: "κατὰ τὴν ἁπλῆν ὡς ἄσχετον καὶ ὑπὲρ νόησιν ἕνωσιν, καί τινα λόγον ἄρρητόν τε καὶ ἀνερμήνευτον, ὃν μόνος οἶδεν ὁ τὴν ἄφατον ταύτην χάριν τοῖς ἀξίοις δωρούμενος Θεός, καὶ οἱ ταύτην ὕστερον πείσεσθαι μέλλοντες."

123. *Q. Thal.* 22.7, ed. Laga and Steel, CCSG 7, 141: "For then passivity will transcend nature, having no principle (*logos*) limiting the infinite divinization of those who passively experience it" (Ὑπὲρ φύσιν γὰρ τότε τὸ πάθος ἐστὶ καὶ μηδένα λόγον ἔχον ὁριστικὸν τῆς ἐπ᾽ ἄπειρον τῶν τοῦτο πασχόντων θεουργίας).

124. *Q. Thal.* 22.7, ed. Laga and Steel, CCSG 7, 141: "ἐκεῖνο γινόμενοι ὅπερ τῆς κατὰ φύσιν δυνάμεως οὐδαμῶς ὑπάρχει κατόρθωμα."

125. *Q. Thal.* 22.7, ed. Laga and Steel, CCSG 7, 141, modified: "Θεώσεως γὰρ οὐδὲν γενητὸν κατὰ φύσιν ἐστὶ ποιητικόν, ἐπειδὴ μηδὲ θεοῦ καταληπτικόν. Μόνης γὰρ τῆς θείας χάριτος ἴδιον τοῦτο πέφυκεν εἶναι τὸ ἀναλόγως τοῖς οὖσι χαρίζεσθαι θέωσιν, καὶ λαμπρυνούσης τὴν φύσιν τῷ ὑπὲρ φύσιν φωτὶ καὶ τῶν οἰκείων ὅρων αὐτὴν ὑπεράνω κατὰ τὴν ὑπερβολὴν τῆς δόξης ποιουμένης."

126. "Proportionately" or "analogously" (ἀναλόγως) here carries a peculiar sense; cf. below, sec. 3.4.

127. So *Amb.* 5.11, PG 91, 1052B, modified, where Maximus interprets Dionysius's Christological sense of "super-nature" in explicitly Neo-Chalcedonian terms: "The coming together of these two natures constitutes the great mystery 'of Jesus' natural logic, which is supra-natural' [*DN* 2.9], and shows that both the difference of the activities and their union are preserved intact, the former understood

to be 'without division' in the natural principle of what has been united, while the latter are 'known without confusion' in the unified mode of the Lord's activities" (ἡ σύνοδος τὸ μέγα 'τῆς ὑπερφυοῦς Ἰησοῦ φυσιολογίας' ποιησαμένη μυστήριον, σωζομένην ἔδειξεν ἐν ταυτῷ τὴν διαφορὰν τῶν ἐνεργειῶν καὶ τὴν ἕνωσιν, τὴν μὲν 'ἀδιαιρέτως' ἐν τῷ φυσικῷ θεωρουμένην λόγῳ τῶν ἡνωμένων, τὴν δὲ 'ἀσυγχύτως' ἐν τῷ μοναδικῷ 'γνωριζομένην' τρόπῳ τῶν γινομένων). Christ's "singular mode" is the actualized supernatural state, which includes three elements at once: (1) a single hypostasis as the ground of identity; (2) two distinct natural principles; (3) two wholly interpenetrating activities of those natures (cf. *Amb.* 5.14). There is no need of a supernatural habit or mode in Christ's humanity. His own person—no modal hybrid—mediates, identifies, and preserves distinct his two infinitely different natures, both in principle and in activity.

128. *Ep.* 13, PG 91, 532BC, my translation and emphasis: "But the Word of God did not possess the activities and powers proper to the nature he assumed by any principle or mode corresponding to that [i.e., to the principle naturally binding body and soul at birth]. For the supra-natural is not measured out to nature, nor does there exist in beings any natural capacity at all receptive of it [i.e., the supra-natural]. Therefore he is most singular in his assumption of a rationally and intellectually animated flesh, ineffably willing to become man; and, *qua* being and pre-being, possessing the power [to do] all things, he renovated the natures *by a supra-natural mode* so that he might save [preserve] man." The entire logic runs just so: (1) the *process* (in either principle or mode) of Incarnation is in no sense natural; (2) yet the Word himself, in hypostasis, became human and *in that way* possessed powers and activities natural to human nature; (3) since he possessed them thus, in that "supranatural mode" of assumption, *therefore* their modalities have been preserved and renewed—i.e., they assume an existential modality that need not pass through their own proper (natural) modality. Christo-logic conceives a supranatural process where "supranatural" means that nature—*either human or divine* (created or uncreated)—is completely relieved of having to achieve the result (i.e., hypostatic identity) by its own principles or modes. Cf. too *Ep.* 19, PG 91, 593A.

129. Thus I agree with Lars Thunberg, "Spirit, Grace, and Human Receptivity," *Studia Patristica* 37 (2001): 612, that the deified *hexis* or "state" in Maximus "should not at all be identified with supernatural *habitus* in a Thomistic sense," since this state comprises no modal hybrid but rather the total, simultaneous actualization of both divine and human modes in the deified person. Again, nature never shoulders the burden of accounting for deification. See too Larchet, *Divinisation de l'homme*, 604.

130. *Amb.* 37.8, PG 91, 1296CD, slightly modified. The whole statement: "Therefore the Word in whom the universe is gathered transcends the truth, and also, insofar as He is man and God, He truly transcends all humanity and divinity"

(Ὑπὲρ ἀλήθειαν ἄρα ὁ πρὸς ὃν τὰ πάντα συνάγεται Λόγος, καὶ αὖθις, ὡς ἄνθρωπος καὶ Θεὸς ὑπάρχων, καὶ ὑπὲρ πᾶσαν ὢν ἀληθῶς ἀνθρωπότητα τε καὶ θεότητα).

131. Here we've returned to the critiques of Neo-Chalcedonian Christology, namely that it lacks "created grace" as a mediator between the person and flesh of Christ; see sec. 1.1.

132. *Pyr.* 33, PG 91, 297D–300A: "Καὶ καθόλου φάναι, πᾶν φυσικὸν ἐπὶ Χριστοῦ, συνημμένον ἔχει τῷ κατ' αὐτὸ λόγῳ καὶ τὸν ὑπὲρ φύσιν τρόπον· ἵνα καὶ ἡ φύσις διὰ τοῦ λόγου πιστωθῇ, καὶ ἡ οἰκονομία διὰ τοῦ τρόπου." This is why Maximus conceives the historical Incarnation as the *means* for every miracle and sacrament; see *Amb.* 42.17 and 29.

133. *Ep.* 15, PG 91, 565B, where Maximus concludes from the fact that the essential principles of both Christ's natures remained totally untouched (ἀναλλοίωτος) "after the union" that this means neither "transgressed the limit of its own essence with respect to its other."

134. Miquel, "Πεῖρα," 358, rightly notes that because Maximus clearly distinguishes his sense of "experience" or experiential "knowledge" from both typically Aristotelian (*episteme, aisthesis*) and Platonic (*logos, noesis*) unitive modes, Maximian experience "est donc un mode de connaissance tout à fait original." I suggest the originality derives from Christo-logic, which uniquely furnishes an immediate identity beyond and preservative of natural potencies and acts.

135. *Opusc.* 1, PG 91, 33CD: "Οὐκ ἀνεῖλον. . . ."

136. *Opusc.* 1, PG 91, 33D–36A.

137. *Amb.* 5.14; cf. below, sec. 4.4.

138. Maximus never qualifies grace as "created." Indeed, he explicitly calls grace "uncreated" at *Amb.* 10.44 when commending Melchizedek's supranatural birth through grace as the great paradigm of human deification: "Therefore the great Melchizedek is said to be *without father or mother or genealogy, having neither beginning of days nor end of life*, just as our God-bearing fathers have truly said, that is, not on account of his human nature, which was created out of nothing, and by virtue of which he had both a beginning and an end, but on account of divine and uncreated grace [τὴν χάριν τὴν θείαν καὶ ἄκτιστον], which exists eternally and is beyond all nature and time, for it is the grace of the eternal God, and it was solely by this that he was begotten—wholly and willingly [καθ' ἣν δι' ὅλου μόνην ὅλος γνωμικῶς γεννηθείς]—and solely from this that he can now be known" (slightly modified).

139. Ayroulet, *De l'image à l'Image*, 261, my translation.

140. *Amb.* 10.46.

141. *Q. Thal.* 1.1.2, ed. Laga and Steel, CCSG, 7, 9–11, slight modification: "ὃν [i.e., 'reason,' *logon*] καὶ τὸ πνεῦμα τοῦ θεοῦ τὸ ἅγιον, καλῶς ταῖς ἀρεταῖς διαπλασθέντα, πρὸς συμβίωσιν πέφυκεν ἄγεσθαι καὶ θεῖον ἄγαλμα τῆς καθ'

ὁμοίωσιν ὡραιότητος αὐτοῦ κατασκευάζειν μηδενὶ τῶν προςόντων φυσικῶς τῇ θεότητι κατὰ τὴν χάριν λειπόμενον."

142. *Q. Thal.* 61.11.

143. *Q. Thal.* 6.2.

144. *Q. Thal.* 15.4, ed. Laga and Steel, CCSG 7, 101–3: "καὶ ἐν πᾶσι τοῖς τὸ θεῖον καὶ θεοποιὸν ὄντως ὄνομα τοῦ Χριστοῦ κληρωσαμένοις διὰ τῆς πίστεως . . . ἀλλὰ καὶ ὡς δημιουργικὸν τῆς κατὰ χάριν διὰ τῆς πίστεως δοθείσης υἱοθεσίας."

145. *Q. Thal.* 15.4.

146. *Q. Thal.* 15.3.

147. *Q. Thal.* 15.2, ed. Laga and Steel, CCSG 7, 101. Cf. Constas, *On Difficulties in Sacred Scripture*, 127n3, who notes that *anakinein* ("to stir") "in the Platonic tradition describes the awakening or arousing required for the soul to grasp or recollect innate knowledge. The word is employed extensively by Proclus and Dionysius the Areopagite."

148. *Q. Thal.* 15.5, ed. Laga and Steel, CCSG 7, 103, modified: "Ἔστιν οὖν ἐν πᾶσι μὲν ἁπλῶς, καθ' ὃ πάντων ἐστὶ συνεκτικὸν καὶ προνοητικὸν καὶ τῶν φυσικῶν σπερμάτων ἀνακινητικόν."

149. This is one reason he completely rejects the idea that faith alone can save, namely that faith must be actualized in and *as* works; cf. *Lib. ascet.* 34, *CC* 1.39, etc.

150. *Q. Thal.* 59.8.

151. *Q. Thal.* 33.3, 54.22–23.

152. *Q. Thal.* 33.2; cf. 51, schol. 4.

153. *Q. Thal.* 51.7 (cf. schol. 7), 59.4; *Myst.* 5 and 24; *CC* 3.99.

154. *Q. Thal.* 33.2, ed. Laga and Steel, CCSG 7, 229, slightly modified.

155. *Q. Thal.* 51, schol. 5: "For faith is the beginning of good things among human beings, before which we have nothing to offer."

156. *CC* 1.32.

157. *CT* 1.50.

158. *Pyr.* 89, PG 91, 309C.

159. *Amb.* 10.3: "λόγους, καθ' οὓς πᾶσα ἀρετὴ καὶ γνῶσίς ἐστι καὶ ὑφέστηκεν, ὡς δυνάμεις ὄντας ψυχῆς λογικῆς."

160. *Amb.* 10.42 (Τῇ φύσει γὰρ ἡ ἀρετὴ μάχεσθαι πέφυκε), 44; cf. *Amb.* 20.4. Quote from Irénée Hausherr, *Philautie: De la tendresse pour soi à la charité selon Saint Maxime le Confesseur*, Orientalia Christiana Analecta 137 (Rome: Pont. Institutum Orientalium Studiorum, 1952), 141.

161. *Amb.* 10.102; *Amb.* 21.5 (they bear the "cause of all" in themselves) or 21.8 (the *logoi* are the principles "in which God is concealed and silently proclaimed").

162. *Pyr.* 214, PG 91, 352AB: "τὸν δημιουργικῶς αὐτοῖς ἐντεθέντα παρὰ τῆς τὸ πᾶν συστησαμένης αἰτίας λόγον"; *Amb.* 17.7: "Τίνες οἱ ἑκάστῳ τῶν ὄντων τῇ ὑπάρξει πρώτως ἐγκαταβληθέντες λόγοι."

163. *Q. Thal.* 35.3, ed. Laga and Steel, CCSG 7, 239–41.

164. See sec. 2.5.

165. E.g., *Amb.* 41.6.

166. *Amb.* 7.22.

167. *Exp. Orat. Dom.* 4, in *Opuscula exegetica duo*, ed. Van Deun, CCSG 23, 65–66.

168. *Q. Thal.* 61.6, ed. Laga and Steel, CCSG 22, 91, modified: "τὴν δὲ τῆς ὑπερβαλλούσης δυνάμεως ἰσχὺν δήλην κατέστησεν, τῶν οἷς αὐτὸς ἔπασχεν ἐναντίων ὑποστήσας τῇ φύσει τὴν γένεσιν ἄτρεπτον· διὰ πάθους γὰρ τὴν ἀπάθειαν καὶ διὰ πόνων τὴν ἄνεσιν καὶ διὰ θανάτου τὴν ἀΐδιον ζωὴν τῇ φύσει δούς, πάλιν ἀποκατέστησεν, ταῖς ἑαυτοῦ κατὰ σάρκα στερήσεσι τὰς ἕξεις ἀνακαινίσας τῆς φύσεως καὶ διὰ τῆς ἰδίας σαρκώσεως τὴν ὑπὲρ φύσιν χάριν δωρησάμενος τῇ φύσει, τὴν θέωσιν."

169. Ayroulet, *De l'image à l'Image*, 282–84.

170. See Thunberg, *Microcosm and Mediator*, 323–30, for a classic overview of Maximus's statements in this vein.

171. Quoted at note 158.

172. *Amb.* 7.21; cf. too *In psal.*, in Blowers, "A Psalm 'Unto the End,'" 278.

173. Cf. *Amb.* 10.8; *Amb.* 42.5; *Q. Thal.* 53.3. An idea especially dear to Athanasius, of course; cf. *De incarn. Verb.* 41–43.

174. Origen, *Princ.* 1.6.1.

175. Sherwood, "Maximus and Origenism," 5–7, though surely there's more to say than that Maximus rejects "cosmogonic" speculation about a primordial henad and instead favors "participations in the Word" (7). After all, Maximus has no qualms speaking of the Logos-*logoi* procession in a properly protological sense; cf. sec. 2.3.

176. So Larchet, *Divinisation de l'homme*, 485, describes the saint's actualization of virtue in direct connection with that virtue as hypostasized in Christ's flesh: "une véritable appropriation ontologique des vertus qu'Il manifeste en plénitude dans Son humanité et qui sont elles-même les propriétés divines dont Il a rendu participante, par toute l'oeuvre de Son économie, la nature qu'Il a assumée."

177. *Amb.* 7.20: "When, however, we exclude the highest form of negative theology concerning the Logos—according to which the Logos is neither called, nor considered, nor is, in His entirety anything that can be attributed to anything else, since He is beyond all being, and is not participated in by any being whatsoever—when, I say, we set this way of thinking aside, *the one Logos is many logoi and the many are One*" (my emphasis). See sec. 2.2.

178. *Amb.* 7.21. Maximus uses the term προσδιωρισμένως to indicate a qualified, particular kind or case; cf. Aristotle, *De an.* II.2, 414a23.

179. *Amb.* 48.6, my emphasis: "καὶ παντάπασιν ἀμόλυντον μετὰ τῆς ψυχῆς τὴν σάρκα διατηρῶν, καὶ ὅλον ἀπαραλείπτως αὐτῇ τὸν Λόγον ταῖς ἀρεταῖς διαμορφῶν σάρκα γενόμενον."

180. *Amb.* 10.41.

181. *Opusc.* 10, PG 91, 136D–137A; cf. sec. 1.2.2 ("Indifference").

182. *Amb. ad Thom.*, prol. 2, slight modification: "πολυτελῶς τῇ καλῇ μίξει τῶν ἐναντίων ἐν σεαυτῷ δεικνὺς τὸν Θεὸν ταῖς ἀρεταῖς σωματούμενον"; cf. esp. *Amb.* 47.2 (proper to Paul), discussed below at sec. 3.3.

183. *Amb.* 10.42, 44.

184. *Amb.* 10.42, slight modifications: "χρόνου καὶ φύσεως ὑπεράνω γενέσθαι καὶ ὁμοιωθῆναι τῷ Υἱῷ τοῦ Θεοῦ κατηξιώθη," and "οἷος αὐτὸς ὁ δοτὴρ τῆς χάριτος κατὰ τὴν οὐσίαν ὑπάρχων πιστεύεται."

185. *Amb.* 10.44: "καθ' ἣν δι' ὅλου μόνην ὅλος γνωμικῶς γεννηθείς."

186. *Amb.* 10.45.

187. Cf. *Amb.* 7.38, where being created "similar" to God (ἑαυτῷ ὁμοίους) means we are imbued with "the exact characteristics" (ἀκριβῆ γνωρίσματα) of divine goodness.

188. *Amb.* 10.44, slightly modified.

189. *Amb* 10.48.

190. *Amb.* 7.7; *Amb.* 10.97–98; *Pyr.* 182, PG 91, 341A.

191. Cf. *Q. Thal.* 15.5, ed. Laga and Steel, CCSG 7, 103, where the Spirit's "deifying indwelling" (τῆς αὐτοῦ θεωτικῆς ἐνοικήσεως) depends explicitly on those who are "in Christ." The Spirit is in the deified soul because the Spirit is wholly in the Son, and the Son is in that soul. Cf. below, sec. 3.4.

192. Origen, *Hom. in Jer.* 9.4, *Hom. in Luc.* 22.3, *Hom. in Num.* 23; Evagrius, *KG* 6.39; cf. A. K. Squire, "The Idea of the Soul as Virgin and Mother in Maximus the Confessor," *Studia Patristica* 8 (1966): 456–61, esp. 460.

193. *Exp. Orat. Dom.* 4, in *Opuscula exegetica duo*, ed. Van Deun, CCSG 23, 50, slightly modified.

194. *Q. Thal.* 22.6, ed. Laga and Steel, CCSG 7, 139.

195. As created and finite by nature, this must be so: every created thing *must* move from potency to act, as Maximus's famous metaphysics of motion dictates; cf. *Amb.* 7.3–14; Sherwood, *Early Ambigua*, 96–102.

196. *Exp. Orat. Dom.* 4, in *Opuscula exegetica duo*, ed. Van Deun, CCSG 23, 50; quoted above at note 84.

197. *Q. Thal.* 15.4, ed. Laga and Steel, CCSG 7, 101–3: "καὶ ἐν πᾶσι τοῖς τὸ θεῖον καὶ θεοποιὸν ὄντως ὄνομα τοῦ Χριστοῦ κληρωσαμένοις διὰ τῆς πίστεως . . . ἀλλὰ καὶ ὡς δημιουργικὸν τῆς κατὰ χάριν διὰ πίστεως δοθείσης υἱοθεσίας."

198. *Q. Thal.* 40.8, ed. Laga and Steel, CCSG 7, 273. See too *Q. Thal.* 53.4, ed. Laga and Steel, CCSG 7, 435, where he speaks of *our* birth from Christ in the Spirit. Deification is simultaneously our birth from Christ and his from us, a veritable Chalcedonian symmetry of two births now predicated of us.

199. *CT* 2.37, ed. Salés, *Two Hundred Chapters*, 132–33: "Ἐν μὲν πρακτικῷ τοῖς τῶν ἀρετῶν τρόποις παχυνόμενος ὁ Λόγος γίνεται σάρξ"; cf. *Q. Thal.* 1.2.2.

200. *Ep.* 19, PG 91, 592AB, my translation.

201. *Ep.* 19, PG 91, 592CD (he became his own seed); recall the description of the *logoi* as the Word's insemination into the womb of the world at *Amb.* 6, discussed in sec. 2.1.

202. *Amb.* 21.8.

203. *Myst.* 5, ed. Boudignon, CCSG 69, 23–24, my slight modification and emphasis: "Ἰησοῦν μὲν τὸν ἐμὸν θεὸν καὶ σωτῆρα συμπληρωθέντα δι' ἐμοῦ σωζομένου πρὸς ἑαυτὸν ἐπανάγει, τὸν ἀεὶ πληρέστατόν τε καὶ ὑπερπληρέστατον μηδέποτε ἑαυτοῦ ἐκστῆναι δυνάμενον, ἐμὲ δὲ τὸν ἄνθρωπον ἐμαυτῷ θαυμαστῶς ἀποκαθίστησιν, μᾶλλον δὲ θεῷ, παρ' οὗ τὸ εἶναι λαβὼν ἔχω, καὶ πρὸς ὃν ἐπείγομαι, πόρρωθεν, τὸ εὖ εἶναι προσλαβεῖν ἐφιέμενος· ὅπερ ὁ γνῶναι δυνηθεὶς ἐκ τοῦ παθεῖν, τὰ λεγόμενα εἴσεται πάντως, γνωρίσας ἤδη κατὰ τὴν πεῖραν ἐναρχῶς τὸ οἰκεῖον ἀξίωμα, πῶς ἀποδίδοται τῇ εἰκόνι τὸ κατ'εἰκόνα, καὶ πῶς τιμᾶται τὸ ἀρχέτυπον, καὶ τίς τοῦ μυστηρίου τῆς ἡμῶν σωτηρίας ἡ δύναμις, καὶ ὑπὲρ τίνος Χριστὸς ἀπέθανε, πῶς τε πάλιν ἐν αὐτῷ μεῖναι δυνάμεθα καὶ αὐτος ἐν ἡμῖν, καθὼς εἶπεν"; the image and archetype phrases come from Gregory of Nazianzus, *Or.* 1 and 4.

204. *Myst.* 5, PG 91, 677; 21, PG 91, 697A; 24, PG 91, 712A; *Ep.* 9, PG 91, 445C; *Opusc.* 1, PG 91, 33C; *Amb.* 20.2, PG 91, 1237A; cf. Larchet, *Divinisation de l'homme*, 601–3.

205. LSJ, ἡ θέσις, s.v., III; Lampe, s.v., IV.

206. Larchet, *Divinisation de l'homme*, 602n308: "Certains traducteurs rendent ce terme par adoption: mais cette traduction n'est acceptable que pour le composé υἱοθεσία que Maxime utilise par ailleurs et qui se réfère à une filialité non pas possédée par nature, mais acquise ou conférée par institution, autrement dit qui désigne proprement l'adoption filiale."

207. Larchet, *Divinisation de l'homme*, 601–2.

208. *CT* 2.21, ed. Salés, *Two Hundred Chapters*, 120, my translation.

209. LSJ, ἡ θέσις, s.v., VII.

210. Davidson, "The Grammar of Dionysios Thrax," *Journal of Speculative Philosophy* 8.4 (1874): 326.

211. Dionysius Thrax, *Ars gramm.* VIII, ed. Gustavus Uhlig, *Dionysii Thracis Ars Grammatica* (Leipzig: Teubner Verlagsgesellschaft, 1883), 17, l.4; Davidson, "Grammar of Dionysios Thrax," 330.

212. Dionysius Thrax, *Ars. gramm.* II, ed. Uhlig, 6, l.7–8; Davidson, "Grammar of Dionysios Thrax," 327: "ἐκ δὲ τῆς προσῳδίας τὴν τέχνην."

213. *Myst.* 21, PG 91, 697A, slightly modified.

214. *Amb.* 20.2.

215. *Amb.* 21.16; see too *In psal.*, in Blowers, "A Psalm 'Unto the End,'" 274: the Christ shows "the principles of his deeds to be living principles, more sonorous than any audible voice" (i.e., in the deeds of the deified).

216. *Myst.* 24, ed. Boudignon, CCSG 69, 65–66, modified. Here Maximus applies the words of the father from the Parable of the Prodigal Son—"Son, you are always with me, and everything I have is yours" (Luke 15:31)—directly to the deified soul and concludes: "According to each's ability, they have become by position in grace what God is and is believed [to be] by nature and by cause" (Τοῦτο κατὰ τὴν ἐν χάριτι θέσιν ἐνδεχομένως ὑπάρχοντες ὅπερ ὁ θεὸς κατὰ τὴν φύσιν καὶ αἰτίαν καὶ ἔστι καὶ πιστεύεται).

217. *Amb.* 10.31; *Amb.* 21.7; *Amb.* 33.2.

218. Blowers, *Maximus the Confessor*, 113.

219. *Q. Thal.* 22.8, ed. Laga and Steel, CCSG 7, 143: "Μακάριος οὖν ὁ μετὰ τὸ ποιῆσαι διὰ σοφίας ἐν ἑαυτῷ τὸν θεὸν ἄνθρωπον καὶ τοῦ τοιούτου μυστηρίου πληρώσας τὴν γένεσιν, πάσχων τὸ γενέσθαι τῇ χάριτι θεός, ὅτι τοῦ ἀεὶ τοῦτο γίνεσθαι πέρας οὐ λήψεται."

220. *Amb.* 10.42, slightly modified.

221. *Amb.* 10.41, PG 91, 1137BC, modified.

222. Diogenes Laertius, 7.151, in *SVF* 2.479; Stemmer, "PERICHORESE," 13.

223. *CT* 2.1; *Exp. Orat. Dom.* 2, in *Opuscula exegetica duo*, ed. Van Deun, CCSG 23, 31–32.

224. August Deneffe, "Perichoresis, circumincessio, circuminsessio: Eine terminologisches Untersuchung," *Zeitschrift für katholische Theologie* 47.4 (1923): 501–2.

225. I treat this at some length in sec. 1.4, but see too Maximus's diagnosis of Greek metaphysics in sec. 2.2.

226. As others rightly notice, Maximus could readily discover the initial steps of this move in Gregory of Nazianzus, who waxes Stoic in both Christology and soteriology; cf. *Or.* 29.20 and esp. *Or.* 30 (esp. 6), which Maximus cites at *Amb.* 2.3 and 3.5; see too Harrison, "Perichoresis," 57. I court my own suspicions that Maximus derived much from Gregory of Nyssa's Christological polemics against Apollinarianism, but that would require another study.

227. So Guido Bausenhart, *"In allem uns gleich außer der Sünde": Studien zum Beitrag Maximos' des Bekenners zur altkirchlichen Christologie mit einer kommentierten Übersetzung der "Disputatio cum Pyrrho"* (Mainz: Matthias-Grünewald-Verlag, 1992), 180–81, who describes the actual "identity" achieved in the perichoretic state thus: "Sie ist keine abstrakt zusammengefügte, sondern eine nur in der konkreten Vermittlung als Beziehung vollzogene. So wird der Mensch—in einem wahren geschichtlichen Werden—er selbst im Selbig-werden mit dem, was er glaubt."

228. According to Deneffe, "Perichoresis," 502, Maximus's very use of the noun seems original: "Es ist hier [at *Pyr.*, PG 91, 336D] seit 11 Jahrhunderten wohl das erstemal, daß das Hauptwort περιχώρησις wieder bei einem griechischen Schriftsteller erscheint"; cf. *Q. Thal.* 59.8, ed. Laga and Steel, CCSG 22, 53, for another use of the nominal form.

229. *Amb.* 7.12.

230. E.g., Balthasar, *Cosmic Liturgy*, 63–64, who makes perichoresis into the *analogia entis* with its emphasis on the "ever-greater difference" between and similarity of Creator and creature.

231. *Amb.* 42.5, PG 91, 1320AB, slight modification.

232. *Pyr.* 128, PG 91, 320D: "ἡ δι' ὅλου περιχωρήσασα αὐτοῖς χάρις τοῦ Πνεύματος"; *Amb.* 7.10: "γένηται ὅλον ἐν ὅλῳ τῷ ἐραστῷ καὶ ὑφ' ὅλου περιληφθῇ, ἑκουσίως ὅλον . . . ἵν' ὅλον ὅλῳ ποιωθῇ τῷ περιγραφόντι . . . ὡς ἀὴρ δι' ὅλου πεφωτισμένος φωτὶ καὶ πυρὶ σίδηρος ὅλος ὅλῳ πεπυρακτωμένος"; *Amb.* 7.26 (become wholly God in whole body and whole soul); *Amb.* 21.10 (whole soul in whole God); *Amb.* 22.3 (whole God in common and individual realities); *Amb.* 31.8 (whole God assumes the whole deified man); *Amb.* 48.7, PG 91, 1365C (Word in "the essence of concrete wholes"); *Amb.* 65.3, PG 91, 1392CD (whole God abides in whole being of the worthy); *Q. Thal.* 2.2 (whole God contemplated in whole of the worthy); *Myst.* 21, PG 91, 697A (whole God wholly fills those who consume the Eucharist, "leaves no part of them empty of his presence"); *Myst.* 23, PG 91, 701BC (God penetrates the soul completely, transforms it into himself); passim.

233. In other words, the deific condition presumes and actualizes the aporia of grace, which the *tantum-quantum* principle entails as well.

234. Proclus, *El. Theol.*, prop. 18; cf. sec. 1.4.

235. An absolutely essential issue of Maximian *ex nihilo*; cf. sec. 2.2.

236. *Q. Thal.* 8.2, ed. Laga and Steel, CCSG 7, 77, modified.

237. The whole verse: "Ἐὰν δὲ ἐν τῷ φωτὶ περιπατῶμεν ὡς αὐτὸς ἐστιν ἐν τῷ φωτὶ, κοινωνίαν ἔχομεν μετ' ἀλλήλων καὶ τὸ αἷμα Ἰησοῦ τοῦ υἱοῦ αὐτοῦ καθαρίζει ἡμᾶς ἀπὸ πάσης ἁμαρτίας" (1 John 1:7; SBL Greek New Testament).

238. *Amb.* 41.5; *Amb.* 48.7; *Amb.* 53.3; *Q. Thal.* 40.8; etc.

239. *Q. Thal.* 55.18, ed. Laga and Steel, CCSG 7, 499, my emphasis: "ἕως ἂν καταποθῇ τῷ νόμῳ τοῦ πνεύματος τελείως ὁ τῆς φύσεως νόμος, καθάπερ ὑπὸ ζωῆς ἀπείρου σαρκὸς δυστήνου θάνατος, καὶ πᾶσα δειχθῇ καθαρῶς ἡ τῆς ἀνάρχου βασιλείας εἰκών, πᾶσαν ἔχουσα τοῦ ἀρχετύπου διὰ μιμήσεως τὴν μορφήν." Ayroulet, *De l'image à l'Image*, 239, rightly notes that *morphe* here recalls Phil. 2, and so "L'idée principale est que le Christ a pris notre 'forme' pour nous puissions prendre la sienne." Once more Christo-logic alone permits the extreme claim about the descent (and perichoresis) of the divine mode in the deified; cf. also *CT* 2.21.

240. *Exp. Orat. Dom.* 4, in *Opuscula exegetica duo*, ed. Van Deun, CCSG 23, 46–47, modified; cf. too *Exp. Orat. Dom.* 5, in *Opuscula exegetica duo*, ed. Van Deun, CCSG 23, 70, and *Amb.* 10.41, cited at this section's outset. The qualifier "as much as possible for man" might seem to contradict my claim about modal limitation. But given Maximus's fairly constant insistence on the *wholeness* of the divine mode and activity in deified persons, we should not take this qualification to mean that divine activity is *limited* to the natural human mode as such. Instead

I offer two interpretations: (1) given this text's anarticular construction, we could easily read it as referring to the *individual* human person, "as much as is possible for *a* human person." This then would refer to the individual *expression* of the wholly present divinity—how, I mean, that deified hypostasis uniquely modalizes (excuse the barbarism) *both* the natures it bears (human and divine). I discuss this a bit more below as "analogy" (sec. 3.4). (2) It could refer simply to the limits of human modality as concerns *expressing* the divine activity. Christ's human deeds, for instance, do not always and in all ways *express* (to a rational onlooker) what is yet present entirely. This is not only because divinity is infinite in itself (and so not obviously expressible to a finite degree) but also because what it means to "express" is itself relative to the one perceiving what is expressed. It may well be, for instance, that there is another way of perceiving divinity's infinite modality as it is really present in deified creation. But that perception would have to transcend every notion of perceiving, knowing, and therefore "expressing," precisely to the extent that the perception transcends subject/object limitations. I think Maximian "ecstasy" and "experience" aim at exactly this. If so, then such a state would prove necessarily inexplicable (as at *Q. Thal.* 9.2).

241. *Amb.* 41.5, PG 91, 1308BC.

242. *Q. Thal.* 59.8, ed. Laga and Steel, CCSG 22, 53, modified: "ἀληθὴς δὲ τοῦ πιστευθέντος ἐστὶν ἀποκάλυψις ἡ κατὰ ἀναλογίαν τῆς ἐν ἑκάστῳ πίστεως ἄρρητος τοῦ πεπιστευμένου περιχώρησις."

243. So Harrison, "Perichoresis," 58: "Notice how created beings are said to penetrate into the divine, as it were, from below, even though it is brought about from above by God's activity."

244. *Amb.* 7.21–22.

245. *Amb.* 5.14, slightly modified and emphasized.

246. It is clear enough here that "union" and "being united" happens according to hypostasis, but see *Amb.* 5.7, where it is explicitly stated in a similar context (perichoresis of Christ's modes).

247. *Amb.* 5.11, modified.

248. *Q. Thal.* 28.5, ed. Laga and Steel, CCSG 7, 205–7; *Amb.* 67.10, PG 91, 1400D–1401A.

249. *Exp. Orat. Dom.* 4, in *Opuscula exegetica duo*, ed. Van Deun, CCSG 23, 40–41 and esp. 54, where he refers to this revelation as "the understanding of God in the light of Christ" and "the new proclamation of truth" (ἅπερ φεύγων ὁ κατὰ Χριστὸν λαμπρύνεται λόγος, λέγω δὲ Χριστοῦ λόγον, τὸ καινὸν κήρυγμα τῆς ἀληθείας).

250. See canon 14 of Canstantinople II, in Price, *Canons*, 2:286.

251. Evagrius, *Ep. fidei* (or *Great Letter to Melania*) 5: "Just as the nature of the human mind will be united to the nature of the Father, as it is his body, thus the names 'soul' and 'body' will be absorbed in the persons of the Son and the Spirit,

and remain continually one nature and three persons of God and his image, as it was before the Incarnation and as it will be again, also after the Incarnation, because of the unanimity of wills." Ramelli, *Evagrius's Kephalaia Gnostika*, xxxix, denies that Evagrius intends here the obliteration of individuals. She interprets the "unanimity of wills" as indicative of the final state, which would seem to suggest individual wills in concert with the Trinity's. The problem is that Evagrius sees volitional union as the *means* rather than the *end* of eschatological union, as he states in the very next section: "But in time the body, the soul and the mind, because of the changes of their wills, will become one entity" (*Ep. fidei* 6). Cf. too Timothy of Constantinople (against the Messalians), no. 11, PG 86, 49C; cf. Russell, *Doctrine of Deification*, 245.

252. Diadochus of Photice, *De perf.* 78, PG 65, 1195D (Latin); cf. Russell, *Doctrine of Deification*, 246.

253. Pseudo-Macarius, *Hom.* 15.10, PG 34, 481CD, slightly modified: "καὶ ὅλα γίγνονται φωτοειδῆ, ὅλα εἰς φῶς καὶ πῦρ βάπτονται, καὶ μεταβάλλονται, ἀλλ' οὐχ, ὡς τινες λέγουσιν, ἀναλύεται καὶ γίνεται πῦρ, καὶ οὐκέτι ὑφέστηκεν ἡ φύσις. Πέτρος γὰρ Πέτρος ἐστὶ, καὶ Παῦλος Παῦλος, καὶ Φίλιππος Φίλιππος· ἕκαστος ἐν τῇ ἰδίᾳ φύσει καὶ ὑποστάσει μένει πεπληρωμένος τοῦ Πνεύματος."

254. See esp. *Opusc* 1, PG 91, 25A–28A, and *CT* 2.83–84.

255. *Amb.* 10.41, quoted at note 229.

256. *Amb. ad Thom.*, prol. 3, slightly modified; cf. Gal. 2:20 and Eph 3:17 (as Constas, *On Difficulties in the Church Fathers*, indicates), and *Pyr.* 128, PG 91, 320D.

257. *Ep.* 44, PG 91, 644B, my translation: "Behold the most mysterious of all mysteries: very God, because of love, really became a man according to the assumption of rationally and noetically living flesh, unchangeably receiving into himself the passions of nature so that he might save man and give himself as a pattern of virtue for us human beings—he, a living icon of benevolence and love for himself and among others, capable of baffling everyone with respect to the owed exchange." The stronger sense of "characterized" for ὑποτύπωσιν comes from and is defended by Ayroulet, *De l'image à l'Image*, 282–84.

258. *Amb.* 7.11: "Καὶ μετ' αὐτὸν [i.e. Christ in Gesthemane] ὁ θεσπέσιος Παῦλος, ὥσπερ ἑαυτὸν ἀρνησέμενος καὶ ἰδίαν ἔχειν ἔτι ζωὴν μὴ εἰδώς· ζῶ δὲ οὐκ ἔτι ἐγώ· ζῇ δὲ ἐν ἐμοὶ Χριστός."

259. *Amb.* 47.1 = Gregory of Nazianzus, *Or.* 45.14.

260. *Amb.* 47.2, PG 91, 1360d–1361A.

261. Recall the first definition of *hypostasis* in Neo-Chalcedonian Christology, derived from Basil the Great, *Ep.* 214: "Essence has the same relationship to hypostasis that the universal has to the particular" (ὅτι ὃν ἔχει λόγον τὸ κοινὸν πρὸς τὸ ἴδιον, τοῦτον ἔχει ἡ οὐσία πρὸς τὴν ὑπόστασιν); for Maximus's use of this definition, see *Ep.* 15, PG 91, 545A, and "An Analytic Appendix of Key Concepts."

262. See Wood, "Creation Is Incarnation."

263. *Amb.* 7.16 (particulars and universals created); *Q. Thal.* 48.17, ed. Laga and Steel, CCSG 7, 341 (universals united in individual instances as if "at corners" in a grand edifice); *Amb.* 10.83 (universals and particulars mutually causative) and esp. 10.101 (universals "subsist in the particulars," τὰ καθόλου ἐν τοῖς κατὰ μέρος ὑφέστηκεν). Cf. Torstein T. Tollefsen, "The Concept of the Universal in the Philosophy of St Maximus," in Lévy et al., *Architecture of the Cosmos*, 85, 87, 90.

264. Balthasar, *Cosmic Liturgy*, 161, deserves credit for recognizing this fundamental reciprocity between universal and particular being in Maximus, which Balthasar calls "an original philosophical contribution" drawn from Chalcedon. But then Balthasar seems to read this reciprocity as implying the basic contingency of the *logoi* (he calls them "ideas"). However useful this notion might be against Hegel, it cannot be Maximus's meaning here (163).

265. Larchet, *Divinisation de l'homme*, 365–74, e.g., 365: "Bon nombre de passages de l'oeuvre de Maxime indiquent que pour lui la divinisation de la nature humaine du Christ affecte la nature humaine tout entière et atteint immédiatement et concrètement tous les homme." Bathrellos, *Byzantine Christ*, 103n19, disagrees sharply but offers no rationale. Nor does he explain how his own view—that Christ assumed only a particular nature that "laid the foundation" for the rest of humanity's deification—coheres with Maximus's clear articulation of the ontological and existential reciprocity of universals and particulars.

266. *Amb.* 4.4.

267. *Amb.* 31.9–10, quoting Rom. 6:5: "σύμφυτοι γενήσονται καὶ τῆς ἀναστάσεως αὐτοῦ." Cf. Larchet, *Divinisation de l'homme*, 374, on the way Maximus thus subscribes to and enhances the traditional or "physicalist" view of salvation.

268. See sec. 1.2.

269. *Opusc.* 10, PG 91, 136D–137A.

270. *Amb.* 17.10: "When endeavoring to look deeply into these *logoi* of the things mentioned above, or even into one of them, one is left feeling completely debilitated and speechless, for the intellect finds nothing to grasp, except for the divine power"; *Amb.* 22.2: "For it provides the intellect with no means of understanding how God—who is truly none of the things that exist, and who, properly speaking, *is all things*, and at the same time beyond them—is present in the logos of each thing in itself [οὐκ ἔχων νοῆσαι πῶς ἐν ἑκάστῳ τῶν καθ᾽ ἑαυτὸν ἑκάστου λόγῳ], and *in all* the logoi together, according to which *all things* exist."

271. *Exp. Orat. Dom.* 4, in *Opuscula exegetica duo*, ed. Van Deun, CCSG 23, 59: "καὶ δι᾽ ἑκάστου τῶν σωζομένων ποικίλως, ὡς οἶδεν αὐτός, σωματούμενον."

272. *Q. Thal.* 60.7, ed. Laga and Steel, CCSG 22, 79; cf. *CT* 1.66–67.

273. Plato, *Tim.* 30b–d (the world as one Living Creature, "τόνδε τὸν κόσμον ζῷον ἔμψυχον ἔννουν"), which is itself a second god "generated" by the highest God called "Father"; cf. *Tim.* 34b: "θεὸν αὐτὸν ἐγεννήσατο." The Stoic conception is obviously much stronger. There the God whose body the cosmos is, is no second

god but the one divine Logos; see Diogenes Laertius, 7.137, in *SVF* 2.526 and in Long and Sedley, *Hellenistic Philosophers*, sec. 44F. Maximus's *Logos*-cosmology affirms both at once—namely that the one Logos who is himself the *logoi* of the world (Stoic claim) is both a second, generated God (*Timaeus* claim) and yet essentially the one and only God (consubstantial with Father and Spirit).

274. See *Exp. Orat. Dom.* 4, in *Opuscula exegetica duo*, ed. Van Deun, CCSG 23, 55 (slightly modified), where Maximus summons Col. 3:11 in particular even though he's commenting Gal. 3:28: "'But Christ is all things and in all things,' creating by what surpasses nature and the Law, the form of the kingdom which has no beginning, a form characterized, as has been shown, by humility and meekness of heart. Their concurrence shows forth the perfect man created according to Christ" (ἀλλὰ πάντα καὶ ἐν πᾶσι Χριστός, διὰ τῶν ὑπὲρ φύσιν καὶ νόμον τὴν τῆς ἀνάρχου βασιλείας δημιουργῶν ἐν Πνεύματι μόρφωσιν, ἥν, ὡς ἀποδέδεικται, πέφυκε χαρακτηρίζειν καρδίας ταπείνωσις καὶ πραότης, ὧν ἡ σύνοδος τέλειον τὸν κατὰ Χριστὸν κτιζόμενον ἀποδείκνυσιν ἄνθρωπον). Both scriptural passages are similar, and it is true that Col. 3:12 mentions two major themes Maximus wants to treat here, humility and meekness. But the Colossians text also makes a stronger claim about our oneness than Gal. 3:28. And Col. 3:11 more lucidly presents perichoretic logic: Christ is everything and in everything (whole in whole), *therefore* you are one with each and with yourself: "the perfect man created according to Christ."

275. *Amb.* 7.31, modified.

276. So *Amb.* 7.27: "What could be more desirable to those who are worthy of it than deification? For through it God is united with those who have become Gods, and by His goodness makes all things His own." But this assimilation comes in a perichoretic mode: "These examples, drawn from nature, demonstrate persuasively that there is no higher summit or culmination for created beings [τῶν ὄντῶν κεφάλαιον] apart from that in which their natural elements remain inviolate."

277. *Amb.* 6.3; treated in sec. 2.1.

278. *Amb.* 7.36.

279. *Amb.* 7.36 = Eph. 1:17–23.

280. *Amb.* 7.36 = Eph. 4:11–16.

281. *Amb.* 7.37.

282. See above, note 50.

283. Thunberg, *Microcosm and Mediator*, everywhere assumes and celebrates this reciprocity. I've tried to root it firmly and precisely in Christo-logic.

284. *Amb.* 31.9. So too *Amb.* 31.10, slightly modified: "In fact, [the world above] has already been filled in Christ, and will be filled again in those who become according to Christ, when they, who have already *shared in the likeness of His death* through their sufferings, *shall come to be natural outgrowths of His resurrection* [Rom. 6:5: σύμφυτοι γενήσονται καὶ τῆς ἀναστάσεως αὐτοῦ]."

285. *Amb.* 54.2, PG 91, 1376C, slightly modified.

286. *Amb.* 54.2, PG 91, 1376D–1377A, my emphasis. This entire way of conceiving Christ's Body and the type of analogy unique to it is, I think, almost exactly parallel to that of Gregory of Nyssa in *In Illud: Tunc et ipse filius*. Gregory argues, for instance, that the Son's "subjection" to the Father (1 Cor. 15:28) will not occur until the "consummation of the universe"—that it will occur in and as all of us, for we are his members. Gregory even suggests that the perfection of Christ's Body grants to the Son, "as it were, an addition and increase of his own glory, something up to the present time he does not have" (*In Illud* 9–10, trans. Rowan A. Greer, *One Path for All: Gregory of Nyssa on the Christian Life and Human Destiny* [Eugene, OR: Cascade Books, 2015], 121). Since the Son's "subjection . . . takes place through us" (*In Illud* 16) then "Christ builds himself up through those who are always being added to the faith. He will cease building himself up at the same time when the increase and perfection of his body attains its own measure (Eph. 4:13)" (*In Illud* 19). In accordance with "the proportion of each person's faith," Christ's Body, who is also the Son himself, *increases* in "stature." In fact, so completely does the Son identify himself with his Body that Gregory can say of the Body's members—of Paul, for instance—that "everything Paul did and said is rightly attributed to Christ, who lives in him (Gal. 2:20)" (*In Illud* 24). The major lesson here is this: Gregory's pro-Nicene interpretation of the Son's eschatological subjection to the Father hinges entirely on the Son's personal identification with each of his Body's members, with each of us. It's a lesson too little heeded: for Gregory, at least, the more you insist upon the Son's consubstantial divinity with the Father, the more you must *simultaneously* insist upon his personal (and consubstantial) identity with us—for the *Son* is subject in and through and as us. This Christological and eschatological body-logic is an insight Maximus appropriates and develops to its furthest implications.

287. *Amb.* 41.9, slightly modified: "θεοπρεπῶς τὰ πάντα εἰς ἑαυτὸν ἀνεκεθα-λαιώσατο [Eph. 1:10], μίαν ὑπάρχουσαν τὴν ἅπασαν κτίσιν δείξας, καθάπερ ἄνθρωπον ἄλλον, τῇ τῶν μερῶν ἑαυτῆς πρὸς ἄλληλα συνόδῳ συμπληρουμένην καὶ πρὸς ἑαυτὴν νεύουσαν τῇ ὁλότητι τῆς ὑπάρξεως."

288. Adam G. Cooper, *The Body in St. Maximus the Confessor: Holy Flesh, Wholly Deified* (Oxford: Oxford University Press, 2005), 36–48, esp. 48 on the "three human beings" (scripture, cosmos, individual person) of *Myst.* 7.

289. *Amb.* 7.26 (which begins to say God will be to the soul what soul is to body, but finally says God will be wholly throughout soul and body alike); cf. *Amb.* 10.48 and esp. *Q. Thal.* 2.2.

290. Cf. sec. 1.4 for the Christological shape of this anthropology.

291. *Amb.* 7.42; *Amb.* 42.25 (for the Christological justification).

292. *Amb.* 7.42.

293. *Amb.* 42.10 ("Ἡ ψυχὴ τὸ εἶναι λαμβάνουσα κατὰ τὴν σύλληψιν ἅμα τῷ σώματι πρὸς ἑνὸς ἀνθρώπου συμπλήρωσιν ἄγεται"), 13 ("συνύπαρξιν").

294. If we were to pursue this insight further, we would have to say that the Word's birth from Mary, just as much as his generation from the Father, is the "when" and "where" of the entire world.

295. *Amb.* 17.8, slightly modified: "ἡ τῶν ἐναντίων κατὰ τὴν κρᾶσιν διὰ συνθέσεως συμπλοκή."

296. *Amb.* 17.8, slightly modified.

297. Alexander of Aphrodisias, *De mixt.* 216.28–31. And a bit later at 217.32–36 he cites the body-soul "mixture" in a human being to show how even though the soul still "has its own hypostasis" (τὴν ψυχὴν ἰδίαν ὑπόστασιν ἔχουσαν), it "entirely pervades the body" (δι' ὅλου τοῦ σώματος διήκειν). See Stemmer, "PERICHORESE," 11–13. Obviously terms like *hypostasis* do not carry the exact meaning in early Stoics as they do in Maximus. Chrysippus here, in Alexander's report, seems to use it to emphasize the soul's superior existential stability; even though it *receives* the body, it bears its own essence (essence and hypostasis are still more or less equivalent). And yet the degree of terminological and conceptual convergence, especially here in *Amb.* 17, between Maximus and Stoics still impresses; so Harrison, "Perichoresis," 58. It is worth asking why Maximus can repair back (wittingly or not) to more Stoic forms of thought even while denying essential Stoic tenets, such as divine corporeality. My study implies that the careful recognition and distinction of hypostasis from essence under Christological pressures reopens the possibility that another, nonformal dimension of existence (hypostasis) might perform some similar existential functions that Stoics thought only some kind of underlying bodily-yet-divine substance could—which they too could name "Logos."

298. *Myst.* 24, ed. Boudignon, CCSG 69, 59–60, slight modification: "Thus the holy church, as we said, is the figure and image of God inasmuch as through it he effects in his infinite power and wisdom an unconfused union from the various essences of beings, attaching them to himself as creator to their highest point, and this operates according to the grace of faith for the faithful, joining them all to each other in one form according to a single grace and calling of faith." (Ἔστι μὲν οὖν ἡ ἁγία ἐκκλησία τύπος, ὡς εἴρηται, καὶ εἰκὼν τοῦ μὲν θεοῦ, διότι ἣν ἐργάζεται κατὰ τὴν ἄπειρον αὐτοῦ δύναμιν καὶ σοφίαν περὶ τὰς διαφόρους τῶν ὄντων οὐσίας ἀσύγχυτον ἕνωσιν, ὡς δημιουργὸς κατ' ἄκρον ἑαυτῷ συνέχων, καὶ αὐτὴ κατὰ τὴν χάριν τῆς πίστεως εἰς τοὺς πιστοὺς ἀλλήλοις ἑνοειδῶς συνάπτουσα.) See too *Amb.* 21.14, where Maximus intimates that Gregory may have attributed John the Evangelist's words to John the Baptist according "to a more mysterious" reason, namely that any saint can "exchange places" with another because the same Word comes to be in all the saints.

299. E.g., Josef Loosen, *Logos und Pneuma im begnadeten Menschen bei Maximus Confessor* (Munster: Aschendorf, 1941), 50–59.

300. Philip Gabriel Renczes, *Agir de Dieu et liberté de l'homme: Recherches sur l'anthropologie théologique de saint Maxime le Confesseur* (Paris: Cerf, 2003), 349–54; Ayroulet, *De l'image à l'Image*, 285, 293–94.

301. Ayroulet, *De l'image à l'Image*, 285.

302. And to complicate matters, both authors deduce the ontological differ-ence from the *gnomic* mode of a person's natural volition; so Renczes, *Agir de Dieu*, 351: "Nous avons déjà envisagé la γνώμη comme circonstance d'une divergence essentielle de la divinisation de l'homme par rapport à celle de la nature humaine du Christ dans l'union hypostatique." But as a mode destined to give way to the utterly natural and immediate willing of the lover for the beloved, the fact that Christ lacks a *gnome* (*Pyr.* 85–87) indicates only a difference of *process*, not of *essence* (lest Christ not be *personally* human). I therefore follow Larchet, *Divinisation de l'homme*, 239–47, who correctly argues that the absence of a gnomic mode in Christ evinces only the attainment of his humanity's deified state. For a useful summary of the soteriological issues involved, see Blowers, *Maximus the Confessor*, 242–46.

303. Renczes, *Agir de Dieu*, 353–54, speaks of "*l'unité analogique* de la périchorèse dans l'agir," which he claims predominates even in Christ himself: "[Maximus's mention in *Amb.* 7 of] une seule opération 'divine-humaine' ne peut être conçue que de manière analogique: à la manière de la périchorèse de la nature divine et humaine dans le Christ, cette opération unique exprime *le concours des deux opérations vers la même finalité dans la proportion qui convient* sans que l'une signifie l'annihilation de l'autre" (his emphasis). Balthasar, *Cosmic Liturgy*, 63–64, reduces Maximus's great and ultimately costly Christological tenacity to a defense of Christo-logic understood in terms of asymmetrical analogy: "From the moment that Chalcedon, in its sober and holy wisdom, elevated the adverbs 'indi-visibly' (ἀδιαιρέτως) and 'unconfusedly' (ἀσυγχύτως) to a dogmatic formula, the image of a reciprocal indwelling of two distinct poles of being replaced the image of mixture. This mutual ontological presence (περιχώρησις) not only preserves the being particular to each element, to the divine and the human natures, but also brings each of them to its perfection in their very difference, even enhancing that difference. Love, which is the highest level of union, only takes root in the grow-ing independence of the lovers; the union between God and the world reveals, in the very nearness it creates between these two poles of being, the ever-greater difference between created being and the essentially incomparable God. Maximus defended the formula of Chalcedon, even with his blood, out of a deep insight into this difference." Here "analogical" and "perichoretic" seem synonymous. But ei-ther "analogy" bears perichoretic logic—and so cannot be asymmetrical; or else perichoresis analogy's, and so the "newness of modes" putatively achieved in Christ simply follows the standard logic of the relation between a natural cause and its effect (an asymmetrical relation, however greater the difference)—the very thing Maximus consistently denied; so *Pyr.* 192, PG 91, 345D–348A; *Amb.* 5.1–2. So Jonathan Bieler, "Body and Soul Immovably Related: Considering an Aspect of Maximus the Confessor's Concept of Analogy," *Studia Patristica* 75 (2017): 223–35, appears to assume their synonymity in Christology, anthropology, and

Trinitarian theology. He says, for instance, that the Father "expresses himself fully or analogically in the Son" (235). Unlike earlier scholars who also equate pericho-resis and analogy, Bieler differs to the extent that his reading privileges (wittingly or not) the former over or in the latter.

304. *Q. et dub.* 102, ed. J. H. Declerck, CCSG 10 (Turnhout: Brepols, 1982), 77: "κατὰ τὴν ἀναλόγως προσοῦσαν δύναμιν ἑκάστῳ"; *Amb.* 10.85; *Amb.* 21.4; *Q. Thal.* 29.2.

305. Luke Steven, "Deification and the Workings of the Body: The Logic of 'Proportion' in Maximus the Confessor," *Studia Patristica* 75 (2017): 241: "In Maximus' mind, the logic of proportion is not an abstract logic of reciprocity. Rather, it is most fundamentally a description of the mechanisms of a very concrete and lively reality: the body."

306. Cf. *Q. Thal.* 29.2, ed. Laga and Steel, CCSG 7, 211, where Maximus quotes Rom. 12:6: "according to the proportion of one's faith" (κατὰ τὴν ἀναλογίαν τῆς πίστεως); see too Steven, "Deification," 243–46, on the Pauline tradition of "proportion" as it was transmitted through the Christian Alexandrian tradition (Clement, Origen, Gregory of Nyssa), and 249: "For Maximus deifica-tion works 'in proportion,' which, following Paul, means that deification works like a body."

307. So Stefan Dienstbeck, *Die Theologie der Stoa* (Berlin: De Gruyter, 2015), 198–99, cautions against eliding the Stoic stress on the "identity" between individual entities (esp. the human being) and the universal essence into a rela-tion of polarity (fairly common in modern theological versions of analogy): "Missverstanden wäre dieser Komplex, wollte man ihn als ein polares Verhältnis beschreiben, in dem das Eine seinem Teil bzw. insgesamt seinen Teilen ge-genüberstände." He continues: "Kosmisches Sein und Einzelnersein stehen in wesensmäßiger Identität, *nicht weil sie strukturanalog wären*, sondern weil sie tatsächlich als wesensidentisch zu bestimmen sind. Dem tut auch der individu-elle Zuschnitt im Wesen der Einzelentitäten keinen Abbruch. Vielmehr bestätigt die Strukturidentität, dass Wesensidentität *nicht durch Differenz in der Verfass-theit verlustig geht*. Gerade als Einzelnes befindet sich das Einzelne mit der Struktur von allem in Wesensidentität" (my emphasis). Again, Maximus's con-cept of "essence" obviously differs from the earlier Stoic one (and from many others). But the form or shape of the Stoic view of the God-world relation reso-nates rather strongly with Maximus's. Replace "essence" with the Word's "hy-postasis" and this becomes apparent enough. The Stoic Logos pervades every individual entity and thus sustains and unites all *by being the universal, imma-nent bond of all*, through procession. Stoics could even admit that so long as you concede that one Logos runs through all as the sole, concrete identity of the world, then yes, at that point you might admit that each individual thing is per-vaded by (as tenor) and so manifests that Logos "to a greater" or "lesser degree"

(ἀλλ’ ἤδη δι’ ὧν μὲν μᾶλλον, δι’ ὧν δὲ ἧττον)—"just like the soul in us"; Diogenes Laertius, 7.138–39 = *SVF* 2.634. Cf. *Amb.* 35.2 and *Amb.* 48.7, where the Logos "becomes the essence in concrete wholes."

308.   *Q. Thal.* 51.8–15 canvasses an array of creatures—the Sun, eagle, deer, serpent, turtledove—in order to contemplate their own *ways* of exemplifying "the divine wisdom invisibly contained in created beings" (πᾶσαν ἐκκαλύπτων ἐν ἑαυτῷ κατὰ τὸν βίον τῆς ἐμπερομένης ἀοράτως τοῖς οὖσι θείας σοφίας τὴν μεγαλοπρέπειαν); ed. Laga and Steel, CCSG 7, 3; *Amb.* 51.15. So too *Amb.* 33.2, where the Logos "is obliquely signified in proportion to each visible thing [ἀναλόγως δι’ ἑκάστου τῶν ὁρωμένων], as if through certain letters."

309.   *Amb.* 47.2: "ἕκαστος . . . κατὰ τὴν ἑαυτοῦ δύναμιν, καὶ τὴν κατ’ ἀξίαν χορηγουμένην αὐτῷ τοῦ Πνεύματος χάριν τὸν Χριστὸν ἔχων ἀναλόγως ἑαυτῷ τὰς ὑψηλὰς διὰ τῆς πρὸς πάντα νεκρώσεως ἀναβάσεις ποιούμενον"; cf. *Q. Thal.* 59.8, ed. Laga and Steel, CCSG 22, 23; *Amb.* 10.31 and 85; *Myst.* 13, ed. Boudignon, CCSG 69, 42; etc.

310.   *Q. Thal.* 61.14, ed. Laga and Steel, CCSG 22, 103: "πᾶσι πάντα γινόμενος [1 Cor. 9:22] κατὰ τὴν ἀναλογίαν τῆς δικαιοσύνης, μᾶλλον δὲ κατὰ τὸ μέτρον τῶν μετὰ γνώσεως ὑπὲρ δικαιοσύνης ἐνταῦθα παθημάτων ἑαυτὸν ἑκάστῳ δωρούμενος, καθάπερ ψυχὴ σώματος μέλεσι κατὰ τὴν ὑποκειμένην ἑκάστῳ μέλει δύναμιν ἑαυτὴν ἐνεργοῦσαν ἐκφαίνουσα." The Body-cosmos logic can even portray eschatological judgment; see just before this, *Q. Thal.* 61.13, ed. Laga and Steel, CCSG 22, 103.

311.   *Amb.* 21.4: "Since the same Christ is flesh and spirit, He becomes the one or the other analogous to the form of knowledge" (ἐπειδὴ γὰρ σὰρξ καὶ πνεῦμά ἐστιν ὁ αὐτὸς κατὰ τὴν ἑκάστῳ τῆς γνώσεως ἀναλογίαν τοῦτο ἢ ἐκεῖνο γινόμενος); *Amb.* 48.7: "He has made Himself edible and participable to all in proportion to the measure of each" (καθ’ ἃς ἐδώδιμον ἑαυτὸν καὶ μεταληπτὸν ἀναλόγως ἑκάστῳ πεποίηκεν). Even the Spirit (as wholly in the Son) exists in an analogous way in each of his gifts; so *Q. Thal.* 29.2, ed. Laga and Steel, CCSG 7, 211: "[Isa. 11:1–3] used the word 'spirits' to name the activities of one and the same Holy Spirit, because the actuating Holy Spirit exists proportionately in all of its activities whole and without diminishment" (ἀλλ’ τὰς ἐνεργείας τοῦ ἑνὸς καὶ τοῦ αὐτοῦ ἁγίου πνεύματος πνεύματα καλέσας διὰ τὸ πάσῃ ἐνεργείᾳ ὅλον ἀνελλιπῶς ὑπάρχειν ἀναλόγως τὸ ἐνεργοῦν ἅγιον πνεῦμα).

312.   Lop off an appendage—it's still *mine*. It still bears a distinctive relation as being proper to the hypostatic "whole" that *I* am, the relation it bore through the "principle of becoming" at my birth. The fact that I don't need it to endure (i.e., it is not an *essential* attribute) makes it no *less* mine or *less* me. Thinking otherwise is simply still thinking according to the logic of essence, so that "accidental" and "essential" characteristics also name the primary ways wholes relate to parts (and the reverse). But in Maximus's Christology, and I dare say in any Chalcedonian

Christology, Christ's *hypostasis* is itself the "whole" of the parts, which are themselves essential wholes. This part-whole relation—that between the two natures
and their hypostasis—cannot therefore follow any logic restricted to the logic of
essences (as "accidents" and "essences" are). So it is with God and the world, on
my reading.

313. *Amb.* 10.9, quoted in full at note 110.

314. *Exp. Orat. Dom.* 4, in *Opuscula exegetica duo*, ed. Van Deun, CCSG
23, 64–65, slight modification.

315. *Myst.* 24, ed. Boudignon, CCSG 69, 68–69, modified; cf. *Amb.* 4.9,
where Maximus remarks that besides the need to cleanse humanity of sin, another
motive for the Word's Incarnation was that he wanted "to experience" our obedience (cf. *Q. Thal.* 61.6); and *Cap. X*, where Maximus notes the psychological benefit of knowing that God himself suffers with us—on which see Portaru, "Vocabulary of Participation," 307, who knows no ancient precedent for this idea.

316. See sec. 1.5.

317. *Amb.* 53.7, PG 91, 1376B.

318. See the Conclusion.

319. *Q. Thal.* 60.7, ed. Laga and Steel, CCSG 22, 79; *Exp. Orat. Dom.* 2, in
Opuscula exegetica duo, ed. Van Deun, CCSG 23, 31–32; cf. *Amb.* 61.2–3.

320. *Q. Thal.* 2.2, ed. Laga and Steel, CCSG 7, 51, slightly modified.

FOUR. The Whole: Creation as Christ

1. Eriugena, *Periphyseon* III.1–17.

2. *Ep.* 12, PG 91, 488B; *Ep.* 13, PG 91, 528D–529A; *Opusc.* 16, PG 91,
204A; and see the Conclusion.

3. See David S. Yeago, "Jesus of Nazareth and Cosmic Redemption: The
Relevance of St. Maximus the Confessor," *Modern Theology* 12.2 (1996): 163–93,
esp. 163–64, who articulates the dilemma as that of the universal (or symbolic)
meaning of Jesus as opposed to his "particularity." One meets many important
exegetical insights in Yeago's essay, yet I remain unpersuaded that "narrative synthesis" is the main or ultimate synthesis in Maximus's thought. In fact, we'll see in
this chapter, the narrative *qua* narrative demands its own transcendence to make
sense of it even on the narrative level, since the central "character" is himself the
ground of all narratives—of "all the ages and their inhabitants" (*Q. Thal.* 60.4).

4. This forms, I take it, the main (though perhaps implicit) motive underlying the four ways Maximus scholars have effectively attenuated Maximus's more
radical (and unqualified) statements on the God-world relation; see the Introduction.

5. *Amb.* 7.16; *Amb.* 10.83, 101.

6. *Q. Thal.* 64.6, ed. Laga and Steel, CCSG 22, 191.

7. See below, sec. 4.1.

8. Ian A. McFarland, *The Word Made Flesh: A Theology of the Incarnation* (Louisville, KY: Westminster John Knox Press, 2019), 204n41, for example, criticizes my position partly by making the following point: "After all, the claim that the Word *wishes* to effect the mystery of his embodiment in every creature implies that this goal has not yet been effected and so cannot be coeval with creation" (emphasis original). One immediate problem with McFarland's critique here is that it would undermine the realization of the very historical Incarnation whose primacy and uniqueness he seeks to vouchsafe. After all, as Maximus affirms in *Q. Thal.* 60.2–4 and *Exp. Orat. Dom.* 1 (in *Opuscula exegetica duo*, ed. Van Deun, CCSG 23, 29), the mystery known and *willed* by the Trinity from all eternity is exactly the hypostatic union of created and uncreated that Christ achieved. Does the fact that God eternally *wills* this deed imply that the historical Incarnation itself "has not yet been effected"? Surely not. McFarland would have to do more work to explain how the Word's willing to be incarnate in all things relates to the Word's accomplishment of this will. McFarland's main concern must instead be (and his immediate remarks indicate it is) that creation has not yet fully actualized its potential to be whatever it is, whatever God wills it to be. But in that case his objection simply presupposes that "creation" is predicated truly or simply of what "has not yet been effected," as if the act of creation were subject to the phenomenological laws of seriality. And that is an assumption that, I try to show in what follows, Maximus himself does not share.

9. Balthasar, *Cosmic Liturgy*, 186–87. Blowers, *Maximus the Confessor*, 211, judges similarly that Maximus betrays a "relative indifference to abstract theories of human protology" and that this indifference "strongly qualifies his treatment of the events in Eden."

10. *Q. Thal.* 59.12, ed. Laga and Steel, CCSG 22, 61–63.

11. Balthasar, *Cosmic Liturgy*, 187.

12. Gregory of Nyssa, *De hom. opif.* 17–18.

13. *Amb.* 31.3, PG 91, 1276D, my translation. The same idea occurs under many expressions, e.g., "having been born in/by the Spirit" (γεννηθέντα τῷ Πνεύματι) (*Amb.* 42.31, PG 91, 1345D), "birth out of the Spirit unto deification" (τὴν εἰς θέωσιν ἐκ Πνεύματος γέννησιν) (*Amb.* 42.32, PG 91, 1348C), and so forth.

14. The prime example of this is the question of the origin and fate of biological gender among human beings. For some important reflections, see Doru Costache, "Living above Gender: Insights from Saint Maximus the Confessor," *Journal of Early Christian Studies* 21.2 (2013): 261–90; and Adam G. Cooper, "Saint Maximus on the Mystery of Marriage and the Body: A Reconsideration," in *Knowing the Purpose of Creation through the Resurrection: Proceedings of the Symposium on St Maximus the Confessor, Belgrade, October 18–21*, ed. Bishop Maxim Vaslijevic (Belgrade: Sebastian Press, 2013), 195–221.

15. *Amb.* 42.31, PG 91, 1345D, slightly modified.

16. Balthasar, *Cosmic Liturgy*, 204, on Maximus's denial of "a final and ful-filling meaning" for human sexuality: "Metaphysics . . . must systematically take on a monastic character!"

17. *Q. Thal.* 6.2, ed. Laga and Steel, CCSG 7, 69. On the deifying and trans-figurative force of love, see the famous *Ep.* 2, as well as what is likely Eriugena's scholion on this Question, which concludes: "For in this mode the power to sin has not yet been removed by our free will, since all of our love has yet to be united to God by grace" (*Q. Thal.* 6, schol. 1).

18. *Q. Thal.* 6.2, ed. Laga and Steel, CCSG 7, 69: "καὶ τὴν τοῦ γεννωμένου πᾶσαν πρὸς τὸν γεννῶντα θεὸν προαίρεσιν γνωμικῶς μεταπλάττουσαν εἰσάγων." Constas, *On Difficulties in Sacred Scripture*, 108n5, rightly perceives that throughout this Question Maximus "shows a decided preference for the words 'free choice' (προαίρεσις) and 'voluntary intention' (γνώμη), and not 'will' (θέλησις)," because the first two terms express "actual choices and decisions of the will, and not volition as an abstract possibility."

19. *Q. Thal.* 6.2, ed. Laga and Steel, CCSG 7, 69, slightly modified: "Οὐ γὰρ γεννᾷ γνώμην τὸ πνεῦμα μὴ θέλουσαν, ἀλλὰ βουλομένην μεταπλάττει πρὸς θέωσιν."

20. *Q. Thal.* 6.2, ed. Laga and Steel, CCSG 7, 71: "Λείπει τοιγαροῦν ἑκάστῳ ἡμῶν τῶν ἁμαρτεῖν ἔτι δυναμένων τὸ καθαρῶς ἑαυτοὺς ὅλους κατὰ τὴν γνώμην ἐμπαρέχειν βουληθῆναι τῷ πνεύματι."

21. *Exp. Orat. Dom.* 2, in *Opuscula exegetica duo*, ed. Van Deun, CCSG 23, 32–33: "Υἱοθεσίαν δὲ δίδωμι, τὴν ὑπὲρ φύσιν ἄνωθεν διὰ Πνεύματος ἐν χάριτι δωρούμενος γέννησιν, ἧς σὺν θεῷ φυλακή τε καὶ τήρησις ἐστὶν ἡ τῶν γεννωμένων προαίρεσις"; cf. too *Exp. Orat. Dom.* 4, in *Opuscula exegetica duo*, ed. Van Deun, CCSG 23, 50: "The holiness of the divine image has been naturally included to persuade the soul to transform itself by its free will to the likeness of God."

22. *Amb.* 42.31, PG 91, 1348A. Again, this passage is clearly indebted to Greg-ory of Nyssa, *De hom. opif.* 17.2–18.5, though, unlike Gregory (17.2), Maximus al-lows that marriage was intended by God as a good and natural law (*Amb.* 42.24).

23. *Amb.* 42.31, PG 91, 1348B, my emphasis: "εἰς ἀθέτησιν τῆς ἐκ σωμάτων γεννήσεως."

24. *Amb.* 42.32, PG 91, 1348C.

25. Worth recalling here is that Maximus believes (*Q. Thal.* 15) that the Holy Spirit is *universally* present in all creatures, "stirring up" their natural principles (*logoi*) unto spiritual generation. And the Spirit's universal presence is an actual potency precisely because of the historical Incarnation: the Word conceived in Mary by the Spirit, the Word who was baptized and born in the Spirit, the Word who was raised from the dead by the Spirit's power—that Word, the Logos, is himself all the *logoi*, the very potency of all things (chapter 2). This Word makes

himself the sole mediator of the Spirit *in* all things, such that spiritual birth (i.e., deification "without origin"; *Q. Thal.* 61.12, ed. Laga and Steel, CCSG 22, 101) reduces to act by a power immanent in all created nature even as that power is in no way anticipated by created nature (chapter 3). On the Christological ground of baptismal grace, see Jean-Claude Larchet, "Le baptême selon saint Maxime le Confesseur," *Revue des Sciences Religieuses* 65.1–2 (1991): 51–70, esp. 54–60.

26. *Q. Thal.* 61.11, ed. Laga and Steel, CCSG 22, 97: "πάντες οἱ ἀπὸ Χριστοῦ κατὰ θέλησιν πνεύματι διὰ λουτροῦ παλιγγενεσίας ἀναγεννηθέντες καὶ τὴν καθ' ἡδονὴν προτέραν τοῦ Ἀδὰμ διὰ τῆς χάριτος ἀποθέμενοι γένεσιν." Here, as at *Q. Thal.* 6, Maximus portrays "baptismal grace" as the power preserved and actualized in "keeping the gospel commandments," which accomplishes "mystical adoption in the Spirit."

27. *Q. Thal.* 61.11, ed. Laga and Steel, CCSG 22, 99, modified.

28. For Maximus (*Q. Thal.* 61.11) this is true whether you consider baptism/ spiritual adoption from a personal or a historical perspective. Personally, spiritual birth begins to be realized at one's baptism and more generally when one begins to enact the power of baptismal grace through obedience and love. Historically, it begins at the Word's historical Incarnation in the first century. But both perspectives might lead one to assume that phenomenological ordering just is the order of creation. First I was born; later on I chose obedience to Christ (personal). First the world begins; later on Christ is born into time (historical). We will see below that Maximus thinks Christ's conception and birth make these various beginnings one and the same reality, separable "only in thought" (*Amb.* 42.4). Thus even the primordial "vital inbreathing" of the Spirit (Gen. 2:7) that constituted Adam is "identical with" Christ's bodily birth from Mary (*Amb.* 42.4).

29. *Amb.* 42.32, PG 91, 1348D–1349A, my emphasis and slight modification.

30. *Q. Thal.* 61.7, ed. Laga and Steel, CCSG 22, 91: "οὕτως καὶ ὁ κύριος, γενόμενος ἄνθρωπος καὶ ἄλλην ἀρχὴν δευτέρας γενέσεως ἐκ πνεύματος ἁγίου τῇ φύσει δημιουργήσας"; cf. also *Amb.* 5.13. Maximus thus intimates that a person receives her true beginning in Christ only by personal assent, and so, phenomenologically, in a moment naturally (or spatiotemporally) separated from Christ himself. But deifying grace, we will see (sec. 4.3), does not simply arrive at a certain moment; it unites all moments into one reality. The very "parts" constitutive of our nature, body and soul (which necessarily bear space-time properties), receive deifying grace only in and as their hypostatic whole. "Holy rebirth," then, unites space-time predicates with the anarchic, deifying activity that uncreated grace is (*Opusc.* 8, PG 91, 104B–C). This would seem to imply that the true creation of a hypostasis as such need not necessarily be confined entirely to a definite space-time event, even if, as seems plausible from Maximus's texts (e.g., *Amb.* 7.40–43), the hypostatic relations inherent in a person's space-time (bodily) birth are never relinquished insofar as they are fundamental to that person's unique identity.

31. I have in mind Kant's portrayal of "radical evil" in *Religion within the Boundaries of Mere Reason*, pt. 2. Notice too that even if Maximus had considered Adam as the individual, historical origin of all humanity, the paradox would not thereby vanish. For Adam's transgression of the divine command "introduced into our nature another beginning of becoming [ἄλλην ἀρχὴν γενέσεως . . . τῇ φύσει]," subjecting "all those who like him were born of the flesh, together with himself, to the just end of death through suffering" (*Q. Thal.* 61.7, ed. Laga and Steel, CCSG 22, 91). So Adam, however defined, freely sinned *and thus* made a new beginning of and for himself. Adam's sin becomes the cause and consequence of historical "Adam." It is as if his act of sin is simultaneous with his concrete becoming, as if his bodily birth is itself a consequence of the very sin of which it is the necessary condition! This insight, as Balthasar, *Cosmic Liturgy*, 187, noted long ago, bears and more deeply engraves the marks of Gregory of Nyssa's idea of the Fall as "the paradox of reciprocal causality"; cf. Gregory of Nyssa, *De hom. opif.* 17.4–18.1, and *Hom. in Cant.* 15, *GNO* 6:458.

32. A nearly ubiquitous leitmotif in all of Maximus's works; e.g., *CT* 2.84; *Amb.* 65.2–3; *Exp. Orat. Dom.* 4.

33. See Blowers, *Maximus the Confessor*, 156–66, for a very useful discussion of the various modalities of freedom in (their proper) Christological and eschatological context.

34. *Opusc.* 1, PG 91, 16C: "Μικτὸν γάρ τι, καὶ πολλοῖς σύγκρατον ἡ προαίρεσις"; or again, at PG 91, 17C: "As I have said several times, free choice is a deliberated desire about things that lie within our practical power." All translations from this work are mine.

35. Blowers, *Maximus the Confessor*, 161; he also calls it "the personal horizon of moral choice" (158).

36. *Opusc.* 1, PG 91, 16C.

37. *Opusc.* 1, PG 91, 16C: "Επειδὴ τότε προαίρεσις, καὶ προαιρετὸν γίνεται, τὸ προκριθὲν ἐκ τῆς βουλῆς, περὶ οὗ ἡ προαίρεσις, ὅταν προσλάβῃ τὴν ὄρεξιν."

38. Literally: "They say that intention is not simply natural but is qualified [Βούλησιν γὰρ εἶναί φασιν, οὐ τὴν ἁπλῶς φυσικήν, ἀλλὰ τὴν ποιάν]." Since the lengthy quotation demonstrates that Maximus's main point here is that every *act* of rational free desire is determined by its particular object of desire—is "qualified" by a definite rather than an abstract object—I render this phrase to underscore that the *enacted* "intention" does not bear a "simple" or merely abstract ("nature-level") aim. It is not, then, that intending is more than natural (a possible misunderstanding from the English literally rendered). Rather, the idea is that a person's natural power of rational desire is only ever concrete as an activity that is more determinate than the natural faculty in itself (for a parallel use and sense of ἁπλῶς vs. πῶς, see *CT* 1.4). This is the way Maximus clarifies an earlier remark (*Amb.* 7.12), which seemed to imply that, in the deified state, only God's single active will would characterize

our own will. Maximus nuances this remark by detailing the various stages of rational desire, so that the "one willing" does not annihilate the deified person's individual activity of willing even as the desired object is utterly one and singular, namely God himself. Since the desired end characterizes the actuality of every aspect of rational desire, all deified persons will manifest the exact same characterization even as they retain their personal distinction—for they will all be characterized by the same desire. Distinguishing from yet intrinsically linking the process to the object of rational desire also allows Maximus to refute monothelitism later in this *Opusculum* (PG 91, 28B–33A) in that every operation of rational desire is an activity of one's natural faculty (so if Christ possesses only one will, this implies only one natural power/nature)—although Christ can very well desire the same end through both natural faculties, divine and human; on the latter, cf. too *Pyr.* 23, PG 91, 293A–B.

39. *Opusc.* 1, PG 91, 21D–24B.

40. Cf. *Amb.* 7.3: "For nothing but the appearance of the ultimate object of desire can bring to rest that which is carried along by the power of its own nature."

41. The precise point here does not concern the formal structure of rational freedom, particularly the idea that the very possibility of our desiring anything already depends upon an innate, transcendental desire for God. Maximus certainly thinks this; see *Pyr.* 33, *Opusc.* 1, *CC* 1.100, 4.1; *Amb.* 7.3–5 and 28, 21.5, 23.3, esp. 48.2 and *Q. Thal.* 59.2. Rather, I stress here the personal character of the concrete process, which, though always occurring within a formal structure whose beginning and end is God alone, yet unfolds within the sphere of an individual's will in an irrepressibly unique manner—indeed, in a manner as unique as the person herself. We could not rationally desire at all without possessing God as our determinate and ultimate end—our "limit," Maximus often says—but that end must be attained in and by a person, a hypostasis, and will thus be accomplished in a myriad of particular manners and by abundant individual courses. That was, recall, the deepest sense of how each of us is destined to become "analogous" to God as unique members of Christ's single Body (sec. 3.4).

42. Cf. *Amb.* 71, on which see just below.

43. *Amb.* 42.31.

44. See Costache, "Living above Gender," 281–83, who observes *inter alia* that Maximus thinks the truth of pleasure lies in its spiritual transfiguration (cf. *Q. Thal.* 61.2). More, for Maximus not only will sensible realities persist in the resurrection and deification of the world (*Amb.* 42.32); the deified will know and delight in sensible creation just as God himself does (*Q. Thal.* 1.2.18)—namely through the unity of knowledge and desire in love (cf. *Amb.* 7.24).

45. Cf. *Amb.* 41.2–5, where multiplication of persons is still very much in view, but by a "spiritual mode"; cf. Gregory of Nyssa's "angelic mode" of propagation at *De hom. opif.* 17–18.

46. Cf. *Amb.* 45.4, PG 91, 1353D: "Thus the first man possessed no barrier between himself and God, which might have veiled his knowledge, or hindered his kinship with God, which was to have been realized as a freely chosen movement to Him in love." See just below (sec. 4.1.2) on the relation between this primordial motion and phenomenological "Adam."

47. The antithesis to "free choice" (προαίρεσις), itself the distinctive mark of birth by Spirit, is "necessity" (ἀνάγκη); see LSJ, s.v., I, but also Maximus's use of κατηναγκασμένην at *Amb.* 42.31.

48. *Q. Thal.* 61.7, ed. Laga and Steel, CCSG 22, 91, slightly modified. Fuller quotation at note 30.

49. Cf. *Q. et dub.* 113, where Maximus says that even Old Testament saints, because they too are born by "sexual intercourse," were not entirely free of the illicit passion that comes from this mindless mode of generation, and *CC* 3.72, where he says our impassioned attachment to sensible realities "from birth" is why we have never truly experienced God. On Maximus's "pessimistic" account of ancestral sin, see Jean-Claude Larchet, *Maxime le Confesseur: Médiateur entre l'Orient et l'Occident* (Paris: Cerf, 1998), 78–124, esp. 93–95.

50. *Q. Thal.* 21.2, ed. Laga and Steel, CCSG 7, 127, modified.

51. *Q. Thal.* 60.4, ed. Laga and Steel, CCSG 22, 75: "πάντες οἱ αἰῶνες καὶ τὰ ἐν αὐτοῖς τοῖς αἰῶσιν ἐν Χριστῷ τὴν ἀρχὴν τοῦ εἶναι καὶ τὸ τέλος εἰλήφασιν."

52. *Amb.* 31.2, PG 91, 1276A–B.

53. E.g., *Ep.* 15, PG 91, 553D.

54. E.g., *Amb.* 5.13.

55. E.g., *Q. Thal.* 60.7.

56. *Amb.* 41.12, PG 91, 1313C–D.

57. *Amb.* 31.3, PG 91, 1276C, slightly modified. Cf. too *Q. Thal.* 61.10: "In Christ our nature has been completely stripped of birth through pleasure," given that sensible pleasure for its own sake curbs the truly spiritual delight and intent that ought to characterize all our intercourse, whether with God or visible creation (*Q. Thal.* 61.2).

58. *Amb.* 31.2, PG 91, 1276B: "καὶ οὕτω τῆς πρώτης καὶ ὄντως θείας δημιουργίας τοὺς νόμους ἀνανεώσασθαι."

59. *Amb.* 31.3, PG 91, 1276C–D; *Q. Thal.* 61.11, ed. Laga and Steel, CCSG 22, 99.

60. *Amb.* 42.3, PG 91, 1317A: "καὶ γέγονε τελείως νέος Ἀδάμ, τὸν πρῶτον τοῖς κατ' ἄμφω μέρεσιν Ἀδὰμ ἐν ἑαυτῷ φέρων ἀμείωτον [cf. 1 Cor. 15:45]." The "parts" are specifically fleshly birth and passible nature. Adam ignorantly misused both and thus made himself another principle for all human beings (e.g., *Q. Thal.* 61.4). That Christ bore "within himself" even the "first Adam" implies that Adam's Fall was itself made possible by Christ's act of overcoming it (see sec. 4.2).

61. *Q. Thal.* 61.7, ed. Laga and Steel, CCSG 22, 91, modified.

62. *Amb.* 5.13, 1052D: "*γενέσεως ἀρχὴν* καὶ γεννήσεως *ἑτέραν* [Wisd. 7:5] τῇ φύσει δημιουργήσας." Cf. below (sec. 4.2) on the "vital inbreathing" simultaneous with Christ's other three births (*Amb.* 42). Again, the true creation Christ achieves in himself comes to individual members of his Body in the spiritual life of ascetic struggle, the process of deification: "Therefore, he is crucified for those who are yet being introduced to piety through the practical life, by divine fear nailing their impassioned activities. But he is raised and ascends into the heavens for those who have stripped off the entirety of old human who is being corrupted by the desires of deceit, and who have put on the entirety of the new one, who *through the Spirit is created* according to the image of God" (*CT* 2.27, PG 90, 1137AB, trans. Salés, *Two Hundred Chapters*, 124–25, my emphasis and slight modifications).

63. *Q. Thal.* 59.12, ed. Laga and Steel, CCSG 22, 61; *Q. Thal.* 61.2, ed. Laga and Steel, CCSG 22, 85: "ἅμα τῷ γενέσθαι"; *Amb.* 42.7, PG 91, 1321A: "ἅμα τῷ γενέσθαι."

64. Balthasar, *Cosmic Liturgy*, 186.

65. Sherwood, "Maximus and Origenism," 8–16. Thunberg, *Microcosm and Mediator*, 153, thinks Maximus differs from Gregory of Nyssa in that the latter conceives Adam as a concrete being providentially constituted in a less-than-ideal state (e.g., the gender distinction appears from the start), whereas for Maximus "the first man [i.e., the *ideal* man] and Adam seem to be identical." But Thunberg too swiftly elides "first" and "ideal": Maximus calls Adam the former but never the latter (however elevated his portrayal of Adam in *Amb.* 45.4; see below). And, really, the main issue is not whether Maximus identifies Adam with the ideal man but whether Adam so construed existed in fact. Paul M. Blowers, "Gentiles of the Soul: Maximus the Confessor on the Substructure and Transformation of Human Passions," *Journal of Early Christian Studies* 4.1 (1996): 66–69, seems to follow Balthasar when he remarks that Maximus's Adam is "more a potency than an actuality." However, in his later work *Maximus the Confessor*, 211n49, he agrees with Larchet that Adam's "original perfection" was "instantiated *in fact*, even if its duration was fleeting" (emphasis original). Still, in both places Blowers edges closer to Balthasar's view by presenting Maximus's Adam as a "proto-ascetic," an ideal type of the monk's struggle against slavery to irrational sensuality.

66. Larchet, *Divinisation de l'homme*, 187.

67. LSJ, ἅμα, s.v., for instance, lists no meaning, primary or secondary, that even intimates Larchet's reading. Not only does Maximus frequently grant the word its common acceptation—e.g., when he says the passions entered human nature "at the very moment of the transgression" (*Q. Thal.* 1.2, ed. Laga and Steel, CCSG 7, 47: "εὐθὺς ἅμα τῇ παραβάσει); or that when God created human nature he "simultaneously gave it being and power of intention" (*Q. Thal.* 40.2, ed. Laga and Steel, CCSG 7, 267: "ἅμα βουλήσει τὸ εἶναι αὐτῇ δέδωκεν"); or that body and soul form a "simultaneous conjunction with each other" in the generation of a hyposta-

sis (*Ep.* 15, PG 91, 552C: "τὴν ἅμα τῷ εἶναι πρὸς ἄλληλα σύνοδον"; cf. *Amb.* 7.40–41). But his Christology yields instances where the term is used explicitly to oppose the sort of meaning Larchet wants to assign it in protology: that Christ's "noetic flesh" received its subsistence solely in his hypostasis means it came to be "simultaneously with the Word's very conception" (*Ep.* 15, PG 91, 553D: "κατ' αὐτὴν ἅμα τοῦ Λόγου τὴν σύλληψιν"), and indeed the "vital inbreathing" constitutive of Adam came about in Christ "not at some moment after His conception, but in the very same moment of His conception, without any suggestion whatsoever of an antecedent temporal interval" (*Amb.* 42.12, PG 91, 1325C: "ἅμα τῇ συλλήψει κατὰ ταὐτόν, χρονικῆς οὐδ' ὅλως ῥοπῆς προεπινοουμένης . . . καὶ οὐ μετὰ τὴν σύλληψιν"). Larchet's "short lapse of time" would prove utterly exceptional. Even Sherwood, "Maximus and Origenism," 10, who postulates that the Fall concerns "real, historic events," concedes that in Maximus's depiction of these events "there is nowhere an indication of a lapse of time." Sherwood then proposes conceiving these historic events "*in instanti*." I confess that I cannot see how events that require rational motion from potency to act (with or against nature) might occur in some uniform instant *without* any measurable duration of time. Time, as Maximus himself defines it, "is circumscribed motion" (*Q. Thal.* 65.23, ed. Laga and Steel, CCSG 22, 283–85). And if "motion is stilled," then "time is the age" (*Amb.* 10.73). But surely we mustn't take Maximus to imply that the Fall is an actual, eternal event, which would thus constitute an element of "the divine life of the age to come" (*Amb.* 10.73; cf. sec. 4.3 below)?

68. Larchet, *Divinisation de l'homme*, 187–88; so too Sherwood, "Maximus and Origenism," 9: "This instantaneity should not be construed in the sense of rendering the additional element co-essential with the being."

69. Since, of course, it is not immediately evident which becoming, Christ's or Adam's, γενέσθαι indicates in *Q. Thal.* 61.2 and *Amb.* 42.7.

70. *Q. Thal.* 21.2, ed. Laga and Steel, CCSG 7, 127; cf. *Q. et dub.* I.3, trans. Despina Prassas, *St. Maximus the Confessor's "Questions and Doubts"* (De Kalb: Northern Illinois University Press, 2021), 142: "All who are born of Adam are 'conceived in iniquity' [Ps. 50:7] and fall under the forefather's sentence of condemnation"; *In psal.*, in *Opuscula exegetica duo*, ed. Van Deun, CCSG 23, 5–6: the devil, having deceived Adam, utterly dissolved "the spiritual force of our nature" so that humanity is now "a slave to nature and time." See Larchet, *Maxime le Confesseur*, 89–95, for good discussion of these and related texts.

71. Larchet, *Maxime le Confesseur*, 95–97.

72. *Amb.* 7.32, PG 91, 1092D; second quotation from *Amb.* 45.4, PG 91, 1353D, on which see below.

73. *Q. Thal.* 21.3, ed. Laga and Steel, CCSG 7, 127.

74. Cf. *Q. Thal.* 61.7, ed. Laga and Steel, CCSG 22, 91, where Christ is said to "destroy" the "beginning and end of human becoming according to Adam."

75. *Q. Thal.* 64.6, ed. Laga and Steel, CCSG 22, 191.

76. See *Amb.* 17.5, and above at secs. 2.2 and 3.5.

77. *Q. Thal.* 64.5; similarly at *Amb.* 10.60, PG 91, 1156D: "It's always the case that through the very things Adam believed to support life [ἀεὶ ἄρα δι' ὧν εἶναι τὴν ζωὴν ἐπίστευσεν], death finds opportunity to flourish, both in him and in us."

78. *Q. Thal.* 62.7, ed. Laga and Steel, CCSG 22, 123.

79. So too *Amb.* 7.11, PG 91, 1076AB: "And this [i.e., our freely willed subjection to the Father in the Son] will take place because that which is within our power, I mean our free will—through which death made its entry among us [ὡς τοῦ ἐρ' ἡμῖν, ἤγουν τοῦ αὐτεξουσίου, δι' οὗ πρὸς ἡμᾶς ποιούμενος], and confirmed at our expense the power of corruption—will have surrendered voluntarily and wholly to God." Here as elsewhere, the critical point is that we must each personally choose God (*Amb.* 7.10, "κατὰ προαίρεσιν," and esp. 7.12) and thus be born by the Spirit exactly because death enters and disfigures the world *through each person's freedom.* The Fall is as universal and personal as salvation itself; for both "births," we saw, revolve around the paradox of created freedom.

80. So Constas, *On Difficulties in the Church Fathers,* 1:362n3, on *Amb.* 42.3 (Christ's four births), writes: "Note that Adam was not born, but created from earth, so that procreation and birth are realities that appear subsequent to Adam's transgression." In this same *Ambiguum* (42.4 and 33), however, Maximus takes care to say that though "becoming is naturally conceived as preceding" bodily birth, they are in fact "identical," and that, at least in Christ's case, we "separate them only in thought." Again, we will see below why Christ's case equates to Adam's too. But it is at least noteworthy that even as Maximus relates the narrative in a straightforward manner he can make these kinds of qualifications in the next breath.

81. *Amb.* 8.2, PG 91, 1104B. Even if Sherwood, "Maximus and Origenism," 18–19, is correct that Maximus prefers the second option he lists in this passage—that matter's essential "instability" was created "from the beginning" (ἐξ ἀρχῆς) in accordance with God's foreknowledge of the Fall—notice that this does not alter my point here at all, since on both views Adam's becoming putatively precedes his corrupt, bodily birth. In fact, I tend to think this *Ambiguum* is less about primordial origins and more about the reason God would create an inherently entropic "essence" (ὑλικῆς οὐσίας) in the first place.

82. E.g., *Amb.* 2.2–3.

83. *Q. Thal.* 65.32, ed. Laga and Steel, CCSG 22, 299, slightly modified.

84. *Amb.* 41.6, PG 91, 1208C, slight modification: "But moving naturally, as he was created to do, around the unmoved, as his own beginning (by which I mean God), is not what man has done [ὁ ἄνθρωπος οὐ κεκίνηται]. Instead, contrary to nature, he willingly and foolishly moved around the things below him [περὶ δὲ τὰ ὑπ' αὐτόν . . . παρὰ φύσιν ἑκὼν ἀνοήτως κεκίνηται]."

85. *Amb.* 8.2, PG 91, 1104A.

86. *Q. Thal.* 1.2.12, ed. Laga and Steel, CCSG 7, 29–31: "τὸ κακὸν τῶν φυσικῶν δυνάμεων κατ' ἐσφαλμένην κρίσιν ἐστὶν ἐπ' ἄλλο παρὰ τὸ τέλος ἀλόγιστος κίνησις."

87. Maximus's account of creaturely motion, especially in his anti-Origenist polemic, has long been known and discussed. See Sherwood, *Earlier Ambigua*, 96–102; and Sotiris Mitralexis, "Maximus' Theory of Motion: Motion κατὰ φύσιν, Returning Motion, Motion παρὰ φύσιν," in *Maximus the Confessor as a European Philosopher*, ed. Sotiris Mitralexis et al. (Eugene, OR: Cascade Books, 2017), 73–91. But the ramifications for Maximus's view of the Fall have attracted far less attention.

88. *Amb.* 7.2, PG 91, 1069AB.

89. *Amb.* 7.14, PG 91, 1077B.

90. *Amb.* 7.6, PG 91, 1072A: "Καὶ πάλιν, τῶν ἐκ Θεοῦ γενομένων νοητῶν τε καὶ αἰσθητῶν ἡ γένεσις τῆς κινήσεως προεπινοεῖται."

91. *Amb.* 7.3, PG 91, 1069B.

92. *Amb.* 7.7, PG 91, 1072B (slight modification) is particularly clear: "Nothing that has come into being is its own proper end, insofar as it is not self-caused, for if it were, it would be ingenerate, without beginning, and without motion, having no way of being moved toward something else."

93. *Amb.* 23.2–4; *Amb.* 41.5 (esp. PG 91, 1308C), passim.

94. *Amb.* 7.4, PG 91, 1069C.

95. *Amb.* 7.5, PG 91, 1069D.

96. *Amb.* 7.5, PG 91, 1069D–1072A; cf. *Ep.* 2.

97. *Amb.* 45.1, PG 91, 1352B = Gregory of Nazianzus, *Or.* 45.8, PG 36, 632C.

98. *Amb.* 45.3, PG 91, 1353A: "πρὸ τοῦ παραπτώματος," here the prelapsarian constitution of the body is the immediate object, but it's clear that every contemplation takes up a different aspect of Adam prior to the transgression.

99. *Amb.* 45.3, PG 91, 1353A.

100. *Amb.* 45.4, PG 91, 1353C.

101. *Amb.* 45.4, PG 91, 1353CD, slight modification.

102. *Amb.* 7.26, PG 91, 1088C, slight change; see too *Amb.* 42.32; *Q. Thal.* 1.2.18; *Q. Thal.* 42.3 and esp. 4 (where Maximus writes that through Christ's death and Resurrection "He granted that I be called back and restored to immortality"— once more "Adam" is at once universal and personal, as if *I* once enjoyed immortality); *Q. Thal.* 54.19; *In psal.* (in Blowers, "A Psalm 'Unto the End,'" 270); *Exp. Orat. Dom.* 4, in *Opuscula exegetica duo*, ed. Van Deun, CCSG 23, 60; *Myst.* 24, PG 91, 709B.

103. *Amb.* 7.7, PG 91, 1072C: "Οὐδ' ἀπαθές, ἐπεὶ καὶ μόνον καὶ ἄπειρον καὶ ἀπερίγραφον."

104. *Amb.* 7.7, PG 91, 1072C.

105. *Amb.* 7.9, PG 91, 1073B.

106. *Amb.* 7.10, PG 91, 1073C–1076A.

107. Cf. *Opusc* 8. If there were Forms, perhaps one could say that a participant's "potency" subsisted actually in an eminent manner in that which it participated. But since this notion is absent from Maximus's vision (chapter 2), there are only ever two essential modes of existence: uncreated or created. If a creature exists, it is essentially in motion, a state of striving after its true beginning and end. To be sure, the Incarnation and concomitant deification (chapter 3) mean precisely to overcome this natural finitude, and clinging to created nature's inherent limits proves thus to be a version of the Fall (see below). But it is also true that the very task of God's act of creation is to make a world that is essentially finite (i.e., not God by essence) into a world that is actually infinite (i.e., by the deifying grace of Incarnation).

108. Cf. Gregory of Nyssa, *Hom. in Cant.* 15, *GNO* 6:458, trans. Richard A. Norris, *Gregory of Nyssa: Homilies on the Song of Songs* (Atlanta, GA: Society of Biblical Literature, 2012), 486–87: "For when at the beginning [κατ' ἀρχὰς] the created order came into existence by God's power, it was the case for each of these that its start and its full actualization were achieved together without any interval, since for all that were brought from nonexistence to existence their perfection coincided with their beginning."

109. *Amb.* 41.5, recall, claims that Adam might have attained in himself the very union of created and uncreated natures Christ achieved in himself. See sec. 2.1.

110. Irenaeus, *Haer.* 4.38.3; see Robert F. Brown, "On the Necessary Imperfection of Creation: Irenaeus' *Adversus Haereses* IV, 38," *Scottish Journal of Theology* 28.1 (1975): 17–25.

111. Irenaeus, *Haer.* 4.38.3.

112. Irenaeus, *Haer.* 5.6.1.

113. Irenaeus, *Haer.* 3.20.2 and 4.38.1–3. See M. C. Steenberg, "Children in Paradise: Adam and Eve as 'Infants' in Irenaeus of Lyons," *Journal of Early Christian Studies* 12.1 (2004): 1–22, esp. 17: "The postulation that 'God created man as imperfect' must be carefully qualified, for on its own it may be construed to imply an arbitrary act or choice of God in His creative work. . . . *AH* 4.38 suggests, in fact, that God created an imperfect Adam not solely because it was His desire at a later time to confer upon him a proper perfection, but because Adam *could not have been created into any other state than the imperfect*, specifically as a consequence of his status as created being" (emphasis original).

114. M. C. Steenberg, *Irenaeus on Creation: The Cosmic Christ and the Saga of Redemption* (Leiden: Brill, 2008), 175–76.

115. *Q. Thal.* 1.2.13, ed. Laga and Steel, CCSG 7, 21.

116. *Q. Thal.* 1.2.11, ed. Laga and Steel, CCSG 7, 29, modified.

117. *Q. Thal.* 1.2.12, ed. Laga and Steel, CCSG 7, 29–31, slight modification.

118. Of course, Maximus's focus here rests upon Adam, with the devil playing the role of an external and alien seducer. In general Maximus says very little

about the provenance of demonic evil, though the reference to the devil's "envy" above recalls Gregory of Nyssa's view that wicked powers become evil from envy (or jealousy) of God's kindness toward humanity (see *Or. cat.* 6). Still I assume that, in Maximus's view, even the devil's wickedness occurred in ignorance of God, since, as he says at *CT* 2.76, not even the angels knew "the essence or hypostasis" of the Word apart from the historical Incarnation; so too *Q. Thal.* 62.10.

119. *Q. Thal.* 1.2.13, ed. Laga and Steel, CCSG 7, 31. So too *Amb.* 10.60, PG 91, 1156D, modified: "It is always the case that through the very things [i.e., death, eating, ingestion, corruption generally] Adam believed to support life, death finds opportunity to flourish."

120. *Q. Thal.* 1.2.13, ed. Laga and Steel, CCSG 7, 31, slight modification.

121. *Q. Thal.* 1.2.14, ed. Laga and Steel, CCSG 7, 31–33.

122. *Ep.* 2, PG 91, 397A, trans. as "Letter 2: On Love," in Alexander Louth, *Maximus the Confessor* (New York: Routledge, 1996), 87: "For out of ignorance concerning God there arises self-love. And out of this comes tyranny towards one's kin: of this there is no doubt." So sure is Maximus that primordial sin immediately involves one's ignorance of oneself *as* self-love, he can describe the reverse motion, one's love of God through virtue, as a motion wherein "one willing frees himself from himself" (*Ep.* 2, PG 91, 400A, trans. Louth, "Letter 2," 88). See the classic study of Hausherr, *Philautie.*

123. Cf. *Q. Thal.* 1.2.15.

124. On all this, see Christoph Schönborn, O.P., "Plaisir et douleur dans l'analyse de S. Maxime, d'après les *Quaestiones ad Thalassium*," in Heinzer and Schönborn, *Maximus Confessor*, 273–84.

125. *Q. Thal.* 1.2.16, ed. Laga and Steel, CCSG 7, 35–37: "ἐσθίων ἀεὶ τὸ ξύλον τῆς παρακοῆς, τὸ καλοῦ τε καὶ κακοῦ κατὰ ταὐτὸν μεμιγμένην κατὰ τὴν αἴσθησιν διὰ τῆς πείρας ἔχον τὴν γνῶσιν."

126. *Q. Thal.* 1.2.17–18, ed. Laga and Steel, CCSG 7, 37, slightly modified.

127. *Q. Thal.* 1.2.18, ed. Laga and Steel, CCSG 7, 37, slight modification. Similarly at *Amb.* 10.60, PG 91, 1156C: Adam attempted "to make his own (as one must not) the things of God without God, and before God, and not according to God, which is, in any case, impossible."

128. *Ep.* 15, PG 91, 549C. See also sec. 2.2.

129. *Q. Thal.* 42.3, ed. Laga and Steel, CCSG 7, 287, slight modification: "And just as in Adam, the individual free choice for evil rescinded the common glory of nature's incorruptibility [τὸ περὶ κακίαν τῆς προαιρέσεως ἴδιον τὸ κοινὸν τῆς ἀφθαρσίας ἀφείλετο κλέος τῆς φύσεως]—since God judged that it was not good for man, who had used his free choice for evil to have an immortal nature— so too, in Christ, the individual free choice for good took away the common disgrace of corruption from the whole of nature [τὸ περὶ τὸ καλὸν τῆς προαιρέσεως ἴδιον τὸ κοινὸν τῆς φθορᾶς αἶσχος τῆς ὅλης ἀφείλετο φύσεως], that nature being

recreated through the resurrection on account of the immutability of the faculty of free will, since God judged that it was good for man again to receive an immortal nature, in that he did not turn away his free will. By 'man' I am referring to the incarnate God the Word [Ἄνθρωπον δὲ λέγω τὸν σαρκωθέντα θεὸν λόγον], on account of the flesh endowed with a rational soul that He united to Himself according to hypostasis. For if the turning away of the faculty of free will in Adam brought about passibility, corruption, and mortality in nature, it follows quite naturally that the immutability of the same [capacity] in Christ brought about, through the resurrection, a return of impassibility, incorruptibility, and immortality."

130. *CT* 1.70 and 2.87. On the perichoretic character of the deified state, see sec. 3.3.

131. See sec. 2.5.

132. *Q. Thal.* 1.2, ed. Laga and Steel, CCSG 7, 47, where Maximus's point, following Gregory of Nyssa, is not that the passive faculty itself is a consequence of the Fall but rather that God has "added extrinsically" the deadly symptoms of the evil passions (grief, anger, merely sensual pleasure, etc.) in preemptive response to our misuse of passionate motion. Many scholars have addressed this, but see the succinct remarks of Sherwood, "Maximus and Origenism," 11–16.

133. *Q. Thal.* 1.2.16, quoted at note 126.

134. *Q. Thal.* 64.4.

135. *Amb.* 19.3, PG 91, 1236A: "Through the mediation of the imagination (which is a relation of two extremes), an image is produced, being the end product both of the activity of the imagining subject and the passivity of the imagined object, in which the two extremes have converged through the relational medium of the imagination."

136. *Q. Thal.* 65.7, ed. Laga and Steel, CCSG 22, 257. Maximus immediately applies this insight to literal or merely "corporeal" interpretations of scripture (65.8).

137. The term rendered here as "conceptual capacity" (ἐπινοητικῆς δυνάμεως) connotes creativity or inventiveness. Hence Constas, *On Difficulties in Sacred Scripture*, translates it as "inventive capacity" at *Q. Thal.* 65.15.

138. *Q. Thal.* 65.20, ed. Laga and Steel, CCSG 22, 279.

139. *Amb.* 10.8, PG 91, 1112CD, and *Amb.* 10.60, PG 91, 1156C.

140. *Amb.* 45.4, PG 91, 1353C: "Κινεῖται γὰρ νῦν ὁ ἄνθρωπος, ἢ περὶ φαντασίας ἀλόλους παθῶν ἐξ ἀπάτης διὰ φιληδονίαν."

141. *Q. Thal.* 64.37, ed. Laga and Steel, CCSG 22, 239–41: "to say nothing of things that do not exist, and which only seem real because of an error in judgment, but which in fact have absolutely no principle of existence, being nothing more than a fantasy deceiving the mind, providing passion with the empty appearance, but not the reality, of things that have no being" (ἤπου γε τῶν οὐκ ὄντων καὶ μόνῃ προλήψει κατ᾽ ἐσφαλμένην κρίσιν εἶναι δοκούντων, ὧν οὐδεὶς τὸ παράπαν ἐστὶ

κατὰ τὴν ὕπαρξιν λόγος, μόνη δὲ φαντασία τὸν νοῦν φενακίζουσα καὶ σχῆμα τοῖς οὐκ οὖσι διάκενον, ἀλλ' οὐχ ὑπόστασιν, τῷ πάθει παρεχομένη).

142. *Q. Thal.* 61.9, ed. Laga and Steel, CCSG 22, 95, slight modification.

143. *Q. Thal.* 61.7, ed. Laga and Steel, CCSG 22, 91.

144. *Amb.* 7.23, and esp. *Amb.* 10.60, PG 91, 1156D.

145. Whereas, of course, the process of deification—of actualizing virtue and knowledge in ever greater degrees in the ascent to God—is just the opposite, namely the Word's true Incarnation in us; see secs. 3.3–4 above.

146. *Q. Thal.* 51.19, ed. Laga and Steel, CCSG 7, 405. Cf. Dionysius, *DN* 4.31. And yet I suggest that this language carries specific gravity in Maximus, given his careful Christological development of *hypostasis*, *ousia*, and related terms such as *enhypostatos*; see sec. 1.2 and the "Analytic Appendix of Key Concepts."

147. *Amb.* 10.60, PG 91, 1156CD, slightly modified.

148. *Q. Thal.* 65.6, ed. Laga and Steel, CCSG 22, 255: "Alternatively, 'anathema on them' signifies the place where nature is now subjected to the prevailing punishment, that is, this world, as the region of death and corruption, which came about on account of sin. It is into this place that the first man fell from paradise after he transgressed the divine commandment. And it is in this world, due to the will's attachment to the love of pleasure (that is, its passionate attachment to the world)"; cf. *Q. Thal.* 65.15.

149. *Q. Thal.* 25.8, esp. *Q. Thal.* 64.6, ed. Laga and Steel, CCSG 22, 193, slight modification: "But later, the nature of human beings became their [the wicked spirits'] very basis, on account of its most wicked disposition, possessing, like eternal bars, innate attachments to material things."

150. *Amb.* 10.60, PG 91, 1156D, slightly modified: "φθορὰ γενέσεως ὑπάρχει ὁ θάνατος."

151. Origen, *Comm. in Jo* 20.182, on which see Behr's remarks in his introduction to *Origen: On First Principles*, 1:lxi–lxii; Gregory of Nyssa, *De virg.* 12, *GNO* 8:298–99, and *De mort.*, *GNO* 9:58; cf. Blowers, "Gentiles of the Soul," 64–65.

152. *Q. Thal.* 42.4, ed. Laga and Steel, CCSG 7, 289; cf. *Q. Thal.* 51.19.

153. *Q. Thal.* 1.1.3, ed. Laga and Steel, CCSG 7, 11, slight modification: "ἀπάγει τῆς κατὰ φύσιν ζωῆς καὶ πείθει τῆς ἀνυποστάτου κακίας αὐτὴν [i.e., the soul] γενέσθαι δημιουργόν"; cf. *Ep.* 2, PG 91, 397A, my translation: "And so humankind . . . has hypostasized in itself the three great and ancient evils, which, to put it simply, are the begetters of every evil [ἀφ' οὗ τὸν ἄνθρωπον . . . καὶ τρία τὰ μέγιστα καὶ ἀρχαῖα κακὰ, παὶ πάσης ἁπλῶς εἰπεῖν κακίας γεννητικὰ ἑαυτῷ ὑποστήσασθαι]: I mean ignorance, self-love, and tyranny, which depend upon and constitute each other." One is tempted to call Maximus's vision here a type of Gnosticism. Really his depiction is far more disconcerting. In many so-called Gnostic myths, the contingent of aeons or the demiurge opposes the true God by crafting this fallen world. For Maximus, *we* become the demiurge.

154. Hence Maximus systematically links purely "corporeal" perceptions of the world and purely literal interpretations of scripture; e.g., *Q. Thal.* 65.19.

155. *Q. Thal.* 1.2.19, ed. Laga and Steel, CCSG 7, 39; cf. *Ep.* 2, PG 91, 396D.

156. *Q. Thal.* 65.6, ed. Laga and Steel, CCSG 22, 255, and 65.15, ed. Laga and Steel, CCSG 22, 269.

157. *Q. Thal.* 65.6, ed. Laga and Steel, CCSG 22, 255.

158. *Q. Thal.* 65.16, ed. Laga and Steel, CCSG 22, 271, modified: "λέγω δὲ τὴν ἐμπαθῆ τε καὶ παρὰ φύσιν πρὸς τὰ αἰσθητὰ τῶν αἰσθήσεων συμπλοκήν, ἤγουν τὰ ὑπὸ χρόνον καὶ ῥεῦσιν."

159. *Q. Thal.* 65.23, ed. Laga and Steel, CCSG 22, 283–85.

160. *Q. Thal.* 65.23, ed. Laga and Steel, CCSG 22, 283–85.

161. Gregory of Nyssa, *Hom. in Cant.* 15, *GNO* 6:458, trans. Norris, 487: "ἐπὶ μὲν οὖν τῆς πρώτης κτίσεως ἀδιαστάτως τῇ ἀρχῇ συνανεφάνη τὸ πέρας καὶ ἀπὸ τῆς τελειότητος ἡ φύσις τοῦ εἶναι ἤρξατο."

162. Gregory of Nyssa, *Hom. in Eccl.* 1, *GNO* 5:296, 19, trans. Stuart G. Hall, *Homilies on Ecclesiastes* (New York: De Gruyter, 1993), modified.

163. Gregory of Nyssa, *Hom. in Eccl.* 1, *GNO* 5:297, 11, trans. Hall. Origen, *Princ.* 1.4.5 and 3.5.3, also interprets these verses in the context of God's act of creation. His chief concern there is to explain how the world began in time even as God was "always" creator, and he does this by locating the primordial "prefigurations" of all things in divine Wisdom. I think Maximus more indebted to Gregory's exegesis, since the latter adds the specific points about this world's nonexistence and its eschatological oblivion.

164. Gregory of Nazianzus, *Carm. Moralia* 2 = *Amb.* 71.1.

165. *Amb.* 71.5, PG 91, 1412BC: "Ὁ καὶ παράδοξον, στάσιν ἀεὶ ῥεῦσιν καὶ φερομένην θεᾶσθαι."

166. *Amb.* 8.4, PG 91, 1105B: "καὶ μόνον τοῦτο κεκτημένη σταθερόν τε καὶ βάσιμον, τό ἄστατον καὶ φερόμενον."

167. A point Maximus makes in both previously cited texts; but see esp. *CT* 1.70, PG 90, 1109.

168. *Amb.* 71.5, PG 91, 1412C, modified; cf. *Amb.* 7.16, 22, *Amb.* 10.34, 41, and esp. *Q. Thal.* 60.3, ed. Laga and Steel, CCSG 22, 75: "The essential Word of God became a messenger of this plan when He became man, and, if I may rightly say so, revealed Himself as the innermost depth of the Father's goodness while also displaying in Himself the very goal for which creatures manifestly received the beginning of their existence."

169. *Amb.* 71.5, PG 91, 1412CD.

170. *Amb.* 71.8, PG 91, 1416A.

171. *In psal.*, in *Opuscula exegetica duo*, ed. Van Deun, CCSG 23, 5–6; cf. too *CT* 1.99.

172. *Q. Thal.* 59.8, ed. Laga and Steel, CCSG 22, 53, partly modified with the translation of Blowers, *Maximus the Confessor*, 96.

173. For one valiant attempt among many, see Blowers (against Zizioulas), *Maximus the Confessor*, 205–6, 317–18.

174. Cf. *Amb.* 10.42; *Amb.* 20.4; *Opusc.* 10, PG 91, 136D–137A; passim.

175. Cf. *Q. Thal.* 59.6; *Q. Thal.* 65. 31; *Amb.* 7.17; *Amb.* 65.3; passim.

176. *Ep.* 9, PG 91, 445C.

177. *Ep.* 9, PG 91, 445C: "κἀκεῖνο ποιοῦν αὐτὸν θέσει, ὅπερ αὐτὸ ὑπάρχον φύσει γνωρίζεται." On the distinction of "by position" versus "by nature," see sec. 3.2.

178. *Ep.* 9, PG 91, 448A; cf. *Amb.* 15.3.

179. *Ep.* 9, PG 91, 448AD: "τὸν φυσικὸν . . . ἄνθρωπον."

180. *Ep.* 9, PG 91, 448AB.

181. *Ep.* 9, PG 91, 448CD: "Σκοπὸς γὰρ τῷ δοτῆρι τῶν ἐντολῶν, κόσμου καὶ φύσεως ἐλευθερῶσαι τὸν ἄνθρωπον."

182. *Ep.* 13, PG 91, 529D: "μάτην τοῖς ὑπὸ φύσιν θεσμοῖς ὑπαγαγεῖν ἀθέσμως ἐπιχειροῦσιν οἱ ἀμαθεῖς τὴν πάντα φύσεως ὅρον τε καὶ λόγον ἐκβαίνουσαν σύνθεσιν."

183. *Q. Thal.* 54.19, ed. Laga and Steel, CCSG 7, 459, modified.

184. *Q. Thal.* 60.4, ed. Laga and Steel, CCSG 22, 75–77.

185. Origen, *Princ.* 1.6.2, ed. Görgemanns and Karpp, 220 (trans. Behr); cf. too *Princ.* 2.9.8 and 2.11.5. Görgemanns and Karpp cite (221n9) Plato, *Leg.* X, 904AE, and Clement of Alexandria, *Strom.* VII.6.1–15.4, as potential sources for Origen's claim that the world's current distribution is a divine reaction, as it were, to the variously deviant free choices of rational beings.

186. There has been and continues to be much rich debate about these subjects in Origen. For a representative of the regnant position, i.e., that Origen taught a primordially realized state of rational, incorporeal beings (i.e., "paradise"), see Peter W. Martens, "Origen's Doctrine of Pre-existence and the Opening Chapters of Genesis," *Zeitschrift für Antikes Christentum / Journal of Ancient Christianity* 16 (2012): 516–49, "Embodiment, Heresy," and "Response to Mark Edwards," *Zeitschrift für Antikes Christentum / Journal of Ancient Christianity* 23.2 (2019): 186–200. A rather different reading appears in Marguérite Harl, "La préexistence des âmes dans l'oeuvre d'Origène," *Origeniana Quarta: Die Referate des 4. Internationalen Origenskongresses (Innsbruck, 2.–6. September 1985)*, edited by Lothar Lies (Innsbruck: Tyrolia-Verlag, 1987), 238–58; Mark Julian Edwards, *Origen against Plato* (Aldershot: Ashgate, 2002), esp. 87–122; and now John Behr in the introductory essay to his edition and translation, *Origen: On First Principles*, lvi–lxxxviii. Behr moves the protological discussion beyond Origen's conception of the body-soul relation in his attention to the way Origen conceives Christ, the Incarnate Word, as our true beginning, in express opposition to Adam's false beginning. Many convergences between Behr's reinterpretation of Origen and what I independently discovered in Maximus are striking indeed.

187. Hans Urs von Balthasar, "Die Hiera des Evagrius," *Zeitschrift für katholische Theologie* 63 (1939): 90n28, and esp. remark at 104: "Daraus geht

hervor, daß Didymus zwar in der Tat sich sich um πρόνοια und κρίσις bekümmert, daß ihm aber der fixierte, bei Evagrius . . . technisch gewordene Ausdruck ὁ λόγος (οἱ λόγοι) τῆς προνοίας καὶ τῆς κρίσεως völlig unbedannt ist"—which is striking, since Evagrius names and credits Didymus for the doctrine (cf. *Gnost.* 48). Balthasar also notes (98–99) the absence in Origen of that latter phrase as well as another Evagrian signature, "the contemplation of judgment and providence" (ἡ θεωρία τῆς κρίσεως καὶ προνοίας).

188. Evagrius, *Gnost.* 48, ed. Antoine Guillaumont and Claire Guillaumont, *Le Gnostique*, SC 356, 186, trans. in Dysinger, "*Logoi* of Providence," 463.

189. Evagrius, *KG* 1.27.

190. Evagrius, *In Prov.*, schol. 275, ed. Guillaumont and Guillaumont, SC 340, 370, trans. Dysinger, "*Logoi* of Providence," 464): "κρίσις δέ ἐστιν γένεσις αἰῶνος κατ᾽ ἀναλογίαν ἑκάστῳ τῶν λογικῶν σώματα διανέμοντος"; cf. *KG* 3.38 and 41.

191. Cf. Evagrius, *KG* 5.24, and the comments of Ramelli in her translation *Evagrius's Kephalaia Gnostika*, 265f.

192. Evagrius, *KG* 6.59, trans. Ramelli, 353.

193. Cf. Evagrius, *In Prov.*, schol. 3, quoted in Ramelli, *Evagrius's Kephalaia Gnostika*, 124.

194. Evagrius, *KG* 2.59.

195. Evagrius, *KG* 6.43, trans. Ramelli, 341.

196. Evagrius, *KG* 5.4, 7; 6.76, 88. On the *logoi* of providence and judgment as hermeneutical "lenses" by which the true Gnostic reads scripture, oneself, and the world, and then munificently guides others in the same endeavor, see Dysinger, "*Logoi* of Providence."

197. Evagrius, *KG* 4.89, trans. Ramelli, 243; cf. too his *Ep.* 6.4, quoted in Dysinger, "*Logoi* of Providence." 462n3: "[Aidesios, the recipient's son] should concern himself with reading the Scriptures, which not only testify that [Christ] is the redeemer of the world, but also that he is the creator of the ages, and of the judgement and providence in them."

198. Evagrius, *KG* 6.75, trans. Ramelli, 362. Ramelli's major thesis is that Evagrius's "five contemplations" should be taken in narrative fashion: knowledge of the Trinity is absolute and primordial, Trinity first creates incorporeal intellects (the *logika*), then responds to their deviant motion by creating corporeal worlds, all of which are governed by the principles of judgment (order) and providence (individual modes/courses of life eventually culminating in the *apokatastasis* of all things). See Ramelli's introduction to her edition *Evagrius's Kephalaia Gnostika*, lxxxi–lxxxvi, alongside the relevant commentary on *KG* 1.27. Origen too has most often been read this way (notably by Constantinople II)—that is, as telling a grand tale that extends from preexistent, henadic unity to fall, to the generation of this material creation, restored at length (through meticulous education) to primordial

unity. For a classic presentation, see Hal Koch, *Pronoia und Paideusis: Studien über Origenes und sein Verhältnis zum Platonismus* (Berlin: De Gruyter, 1932), esp. 36–96.

199. Gregory of Nyssa, *De hom. opif.* 16.6. My thanks to John Behr for supplying prepublication drafts of his forthcoming edition and translation of this work. I use his translations here.

200. Gregory of Nyssa, *De hom. opif.* 16.7.

201. Gregory of Nyssa, *De hom. opif.* 16.16. For a concise presentation of Gregory's "collective, immanent universal," see Johannes Zachhuber, "Once Again: Gregory of Nyssa on Universals," *Journal of Theological Studies* 56.1 (2005): 75–98; cf. *Amb.* 7.16, 10.101; *Q. Thal.* 48.17, 64.10; and Wood, "Stoic Motifs."

202. Gregory of Nyssa, *De hom. opif.* 17.4.

203. Gregory of Nyssa, *De hom. opif.* 18.2–4 and 22.4.

204. Gregory of Nyssa, *Hex.* 1; Charlotte Köckert, "The Concept of Seed in Christian Cosmology: Gregory of Nyssa, *Apologia in Hexaemeron*," *Studia Patristica* 47 (2010): 27–32, and *Christliche Kosmologie und kaiserzeitliche Philosophie: Die Auslegung des Schöpfungsberichtes bei Origenes, Basilius und Gregor von Nyssa vor dem Hintergrund kaiserzeitlicher Timaeus-Interpretationen* (Tübingen: Mohr-Siebeck, 2009), esp. 461–80.

205. Köckert, "Concept of Seed," 28.

206. Gregory of Nyssa, *Hom. in Cant.* 15, *GNO* 6:458–59, trans. Norris, 487.

207. Gregory of Nyssa, *Hom. in Cant.* 15, *GNO* 6:458, trans. Norris, 487: "ἀπὸ τῆς τελειότητος ἡ φύσις τοῦ εἶναι ἤρξατο."

208. So Gregory of Nyssa, *Hom. in Cant.* 15, *GNO* 6:459, right after the text just cited, attributes the long pedagogy exercised through the very passions that tempt us as "a cunning discipline" (τῆς ἀστειοτέρας ἀγωγῆς) devised by divine foresight.

209. Cf. Richard A. Norris Jr., "Two Trees in the Midst of the Garden (Genesis 2:9b): Gregory of Nyssa and the Puzzle of Human Evil," in *In Dominico Eloquio: In Lordly Eloquence: Essays on Patristic Exegesis in Honor of Robert Louis Wilken*, ed. Paul M. Blowers et al. (Grand Rapids, MI: Eerdmans, 2002), 218–41, who offers an elegant reading of the relevant issues in Gregory.

210. E.g., Gregory of Nyssa, *In Illud, GNO* 3/2:11, trans. Greer, *One Path for All*, 122: "The divine will became the matter and being of the creatures." See Blowers, *Drama*, 180f.

211. So Grigory Benevich, "Maximus Confessor's Teaching on God's Providence," in Lévy et al., *Architecture of the Cosmos*, 123–40, presents a decent summary of Maximus's (mostly Evagrian and Dionysian) view of the metaphysical and moral dimensions of providence and judgment. But he never mentions what is most distinctive of Maximus's view: his equation of these with the historical Incarnation.

212. See esp. *CC* 1.78, 2.98, 2.99; *CT* 2.16. See the classic study of Marcel Viller, "Aux sources de la spiritualité de S. Maxime: Les oeuvres d'Évagre le Pontique," *Revue des Études Byzantines* 162 (1931): 156–84, 239–68.

213. *Amb.* 7.20, PG 91, 1081C; cf. *Amb.* 23.2, *Q. Thal.* 13.2.

214. *Amb.* 10.37, PG 91, 1133D–1136A, last line modified: "Μίαν γὰρ καὶ τὴν αὐτὴν οἶδα κατὰ τὴν δύναμιν, διάφοραν δὲ ὡς πρὸς ἡμᾶς καὶ πολύτροπον τὴν ἐνέργειαν ἔχουσαν."

215. *Amb.* 10.20, 101–4.

216. Cf. too *Amb.* 31.5, and esp. *Q. Thal.* 15.2, where the Holy Spirit is said to work the ways of providence by stirring the universal *logoi* in all particular beings.

217. *Q. Thal.* 1.2, ed. Laga and Steel, CCSG 7, 47; cf. *Q. Thal.* 65.20; cf. Gregory of Nyssa, *De virg.* 12.2; *De anim. et resurr.* 3; *De hom. opif.* 17–18; and *Hom in Cant.* 8. Worth noting is that "introduced" here (verb = ἐπεισάγω; adj. = ἐπείσακτος) means simply "brought in from outside," i.e., it indicates something extrinsic, "alien," or even "adventitious." It need not imply temporal duration. Significant too is Maximus's insistence on the absolute concurrence (he says not just "simultaneous with," ἅμα, but "immediately simultaneous with," εὐθὺς ἅμα) of irrational passions with the transgression. If my earlier interpretation is correct that Adam's transgression really does occur "simultaneously with the becoming" of Adam (and thus this phenomenal world), then Maximus adopts wholesale Gregory's view of the reciprocal causality operative in the generation-Fall.

218. So *Amb.* 8.2–3 lists three providential purposes that God seeks through the elusive flux of material creation: (1) it punishes us for past sins; (2) it purges us in the present (cf. *Amb.* 44.2 and *Q. Thal.* 52.7); and (3) it gives occasion for the more advanced in virtue to become exemplars for the weaker to imitate (cf. *Amb.* 10.12; *CC* 3.99; *CT* 2.17).

219. *Q. Thal.* 61.2, ed. Laga and Steel, CCSG 22, 85: "τὴν ὀδύνην, καθ' ἣν ὁ τοῦ θανάτου μετὰ σοφίας ἐνερριζώθη τῇ τοῦ σώματος φύσει νόμος"; cf. *Q. Thal.* 63.4; *Amb.* 7.32, passim.

220. *Amb.* 10.82, PG 91, 1169A.

221. Cf. *Amb.* 7.7. This is a mostly Aristotelian definition of "end" (cf. *Metaph.* 999B), but see Sherwood, *Earlier Ambigua*, 100: "It is then the more piquant to know that the outside source cited is none other than Evagrius," and "Maximus and Origenism," 22.

222. *Q. Thal.* 60.3, ed. Laga and Steel, CCSG 22, 75; cf. *Q. Thal.* 60, schol. 1. See too *Myst.* 23, where Maximus says the *logoi* of providence and judgment are proclaimed in the Gospel reading during Divine Liturgy "in a single burst of meaning" (trans. Berthold, 205).

223. *Q. Thal.* 63.18, ed. Laga and Steel, CCSG 22, 173, heavily modified.

224. *Q. Thal.* 63.19, ed. Laga and Steel, CCSG 22, 173–75, slightly modified.

225. *Q. Thal.* 61.6, ed. Laga and Steel, CCSG 22, 91, modified.

226. *Ep.* 19, PG 91, 592D; *Amb.* 4.4 and *Amb.* 42.3.

227. So too *Q. Thal.* 61.7, ed. Laga and Steel, CCSG 22, 91: "God, then, truly became man and gave our nature another beginning of a second becoming [δέδωκεν ἄλλην ἀρχὴν τῇ φύσει δευτέρας γενέσεως], which through pain ends in the pleasure of the life to come."

228. *Q. Thal.* 42.3; *Q. Thal.* 59.10, passim.

229. *Q. Thal.* 21.7, ed. Laga and Steel, CCSG 7, 131–33.

230. *Q. Thal.* 61.8, ed. Laga and Steel, CCSG 22, 93; cf. *Q. Thal.* 1.2, ed. Laga and Steel, CCSG 7.

231. *Q. Thal.* 65.22, ed. Laga and Steel, CCSG 22, 283: "ὡς ἀρχὴ καὶ τέλος τῶν ὄντων καὶ λόγος, ᾧ τὰ πάντα φύσει συνέστηκεν."

232. *Q. Thal.* 53.2, ed. Laga and Steel, CCSG 22, 7, 431; cf. *Q. Thal.* 35.4, where Christ's body and blood are contemplated as the *logoi* of providence and judgment, respectively, and his unbroken bones as the ineffable *logoi* of his divinity.

233. *Myst.* 24, CCSG 69, 68–69, trans. Berthold, *Maximus Confessor*, 212, modified. He immediately links this *healing* suffering of the Word in us to the power "of sustaining providence."

234. *Amb.* 53.3, PG 91, 1373A: "The ungrateful thief is one who, suffering ill treatment because of sin, for which he is to blame, fails to recognize, because of his contentious frame of mind, the Word of righteousness, who in His love for mankind is blamelessly suffering together with him [τὸν ἀνευθύνως ὑπὲρ φιλανθρωπίας αὐτῷ συμμπάσχοντα τῆς δικαιοσύνης Λόγον]."

235. So *Amb.* 4.9: "It is in this manner, then, as it seems to me, that He who is Lord by nature 'honors obedience,' and 'experiences it by suffering,' not simply to preserve what is properly His own, by cleansing all nature of the 'meaner element,' but so that He who by nature contains all knowledge might also 'test our own obedience,' and *learn* [see Heb. 5:8] that which concerns us by experiencing what is our own, namely, 'how much could be demanded of us, and how much we are to be excused,' with a view to that perfect submission through which He habitually *leads* [1 Pet. 3:18] to the Father those who are saved in Him, revealed by the power of grace." I suggest that one thing the Word "learns," something he meets that is truly not of his own making, is every actual sin (and its consequences), which is "our own" in the worst sense.

236. *Q. Thal.* 64.36, ed. Laga and Steel, CCSG 22, 239.

237. Cf. *CT* 1.70.

238. *Q. Thal.* 64.33, ed. Laga and Steel, CCSG 22, 237: "καὶ τὴν ἡμετέραν κατάκρισιν οἰκείαν ποιήσασθαι μὴ παραιτήσασθαι καὶ τοσοῦτον ἡμᾶς θεῶσαι κατὰ τὴν χάριν, ὅσον κατ' οἰκονομίαν αὐτὸς φύσει γέγονεν ἄνθρωπος."

239. *Q. Thal.* 64.28, ed. Laga and Steel, CCSG 22, 229–31: "ὡς ἀληθεύει τὴν αὐτὴν καταστρέθων καὶ σῴζων." I do not here address the fraught debate over Maximus's eschatological views, particularly regarding *apokatastasis*. But I do

suggest that much of the debate has not been sufficiently contextualized in the absolute paradox this chapter attempts to describe, that of Adam's false and true beginnings and ends. If our attachment to sheer finitude illicitly creates a "world" unwilled by God, then of course its complete destruction or eternal annihilation would simply be the necessary corollary of the perfection of all creatures. In fact, earlier in this Question Maximus can say both that our "innate attachments to material things" are "like eternal bars" (οἱ μοχλοὶ οἱ αἰώνιοι; cf. Job 10:21) that shackle our wills and make nature "the very basis" of the activity of wicked spirits (*Q. Thal.* 64.6, ed. Laga and Steel, CCSG 22, 193) and also that, because Christ "led up the whole of our captive nature to heaven" and granted us the power to become Gods through spiritual birth, he thus "breaks" those same bars and liberates the whole of humanity (*Q. Thal.* 64.7, ed. Laga and Steel, CCSG 22, 195–97; at 64.10 he defines human nature as the individual human beings "who constitute human nature").

240. *Amb.* 41.6: "The One who is completely immobile according to His nature moved immovably, so to speak, around that which by nature is moved, 'and God became man' in order to save lost man"; cf. *Amb.* 23.3, PG 91, 1260C (citing Gregory of Nazianzus, *Or.* 40.27): "And again, [divinity] moves and is moved, since it 'thirsts to be thirsted for,' desires to be desired, and loves to be loved."

241. *Q. Thal.* 65.24, ed. Laga and Steel, CCSG 22, 285: "ἡ πρὸς τὸν λόγον κατὰ τὴν τῆς προνοίας ἐπίνοιαν τῆς φύσεως ἕνωσις, καθ᾽ ἣν οὐδεμία τὸ παράπαν ἐστὶ χρόνου καὶ γενέσεως ἔμφασις."

242. *Exp. Orat. Dom.*, prol., in *Opuscula exegetica duo*, ed. Van Deun, CCSG 23, 28–29, my translation: "καθ᾽ ἣν [kenosis] ἔχει πάντων τῶν αἰώνων τὸ πέρας περιγραφόμενον."

243. *CT* 1.5.

244. Cf. *CT* 1.6; *Amb.* 10.57–58; see Torstein Theodor Tollefsen, "Proclus, Philoponus, and Maximus: The Paradigm of the World and Temporal Beginning," in *Platonism and Christian Thought in Late Antiquity*, ed. Panagiotis G. Pavlos et al. (New York: Routledge, 2019), 100–114, though my differences from Tollefsen's explanation of why Maximus denies the world's eternity will be clear.

245. *CT* 1.4, PG 90, 1084C–D, ed. Salés, *Two Hundred Chapters*, 45, slightly modified.

246. *CT* 1.5, PG 90, 1085A, ed. Salés, *Two Hundred Chapters*, 45–47, slightly modified.

247. Maximus employs here a very common definition of time; cf. Plato, *Tim.* 38A–C; Aristotle, *Phys.* 218b21–222a9, and the various references at *CT*, trans. Salés, *Two Hundred Chapters*, 45n8; cf. too Sotiris Mitralexis, *Ever-Moving Repose: A Contemporary Reading of Maximus the Confessor's Theory of Time* (Eugene, OR: Cascade Books, 2017), esp. 125–33.

248. Cf. esp. *Amb.* 10.75.

249. Aristotle, *Cat.* 4, 1b26; see esp. Pascal Mueller-Jourdan, "Where and When as Metaphysical Prerequisites for Creation in Ambiguum 10," in *Knowing the Purpose of Creation through the Resurrection: Proceedings of the Symposium on St Maximus the Confessor, Belgrade, October 18–21*, ed. Bishop Maxim Vaslijevic (Belgrade: Sebastian Press, 2013), 287–96.

250. *CT* 1.68; *Q. Thal.* 64.13; *Amb.* 10.58, passim. Constas, in *On Difficulties in Sacred Scripture*, 358n9, observes that this idea extends back as far as Philo, *Dec.* 31.1, and becomes commonplace in later Neoplatonism.

251. *CT* 1.68.

252. *Amb.* 10.92, PG 91, 1180BC; cf. *Amb.* 7.42 and *Opusc.* 5, PG 91, 64A.

253. J. M. McTaggart, *The Nature of Existence* (Cambridge: Cambridge University Press, 1927), vol. 2, chap. 3. For a concise summary of McTaggart's schema, see Richard Sorabji, *Time, Creation, and the Continuum: Theories in Antiquity and the Early Middle Ages* (Chicago: University of Chicago Press, 1983), 33–37.

254. *Q. Thal.* 65.23, ed. Laga and Steel, CCSG 22, 283–85: "Ὁπηνίκα δὲ τὸν τόπον διελθοῦσα καὶ τὸν χρόνον κατ' ἐνέργειάν τε καὶ ἔννοιαν ἡ φύσις."

255. *CT* 1.35, PG 90, 1096AB, ed. Salés, *Two Hundred Chapters*, 62–65.

256. *Amb.* 10.73, PG 91, 1164BC, slightly modified: "χρόνον ἐστερημένον κινήσεως, τὸν δὲ χρόνον αἰῶνα κινήσει μετρούμενον"; cf. Constas, *On Difficulties in the Church Fathers*, 1:488n52, who rightly notes that the age "is an intermediate state between divine eternity and ordinary time, being a kind of synthesis of the two, enabling the divinized creature to exist in divine infinity without obliterating the limits proper to created being." I add that the synthesis is Christ himself, and so the existential or experiential condition of the age is perichoretic. So understood, it is true to say we have no obliteration of creaturely limits. Just as true is that the condition itself is in no sense limited by created nature.

257. Evagrius (e.g., *KG* 2.17) explicitly denies the perdurance of "ages" or aeons in the final restoration.

258. Precisely this insight into the age's creation through Christ, especially against the background of Origenist conceptions of the eschatological suppression of the manifold "aeons" (rather than simply an Aristotelian conception of time and motion), leads me to depart from the threefold schema offered by Mitralexis, *Ever-Moving Repose* (e.g., xv). There he presents deified time (*stasis aeikinetos*) as a separate and pinnacle level of temporality, the first two being *chronos* and the age. To my mind, deified time is the perichoretic mode *of* the age of all ages, which receives its potency and actuality in the historical Incarnation itself. The age, then, is not something separate from deified time, since the latter describes the existential mode of the former.

259. See esp. Paul M. Blowers, "Realized Eschatology in Maximus the Confessor, *Ad Thalassium* 22," *Studia Patristica* 33 (1997): 258–63.

260. *Q. Thal.* 22.2, ed. Laga and Steel, CCSG 7, 137.

261. *Q. Thal.* 22.3, ed. Laga and Steel, CCSG 7, 137, my emphasis: "οὐχ ἁπλῶς παρ' ἡμῶν νοουμένων τῶν αἰώνων, ἀλλὰ τῶν, ἐπ' ἐνεργείᾳ δηλονότι τοῦ τῆς ἐνσωματώσεως μυστηρίου."

262. *Amb.* 7.22, PG 91, 1084CD, my translation.

263. See esp. the description of Melchizedek at *Amb.* 10.42–44.

264. Though he does that too; cf. *CT* 1.10.

265. *Q. Thal.* 22.6, ed. Laga and Steel, CCSG 7, 139, slight modification: "ἐπειδὴ καὶ ἀρχὴ καὶ μεσότης καὶ τέλος ἐστὶ πάντων τῶν αἰώνων τε παρελθόντων καὶ ὄντων καὶ ἐσομένων ὁ κύριος ἡμῶν Ἰησοῦς ὁ Χριστός, εἰκότως εἰς ἡμᾶς κατήντησε δυνάμει πίστεως τὸ κατ' εἶδος ἐνεργείᾳ κατὰ τὴν χάριν ἐσόμενον ἐπὶ θεώσει τῶν ἀξίων τέλος τῶν αἰώνων."

CONCLUSION. The Whole Mystery of Christ

1. Even the qualification that our identity with God comes about "by grace" qualifies the character of our process rather than the actuality of the product, as I labored to demonstrate (sec. 3.2). And even that process is not foreign to the God-man, who in us becomes "a son by grace" (*Q. Thal.* 40.8, ed. Laga and Steel, CCSG 7, 273). He identifies himself with everything that is human, including the very process of becoming God.

2. Against this claim one could adduce *Amb.* 46.4, PG 91, 1357AB: "He deigned to vary the modes of His presence so that the good things He planted in beings might ripen to full maturity, until the ages will have reached their appointed limit. At that point He will *gather together* the fruits of His own *sowing.*" But my claim is that the Word must be fundamentally identical to what he is not by nature in order to vary himself in and through that very nature. Again, Christ's human flesh, considering its natural properties, presented his person in accordance with those properties. Hypostatic identity actually grounds natural expression; the latter presupposes the former.

3. G. W. F. Hegel, *Lectures on the Philosophy of Religion*, vol. 1, *Introduction and the Concept of Religion*, ed. Peter C. Hodgson (1827; repr., Oxford: Clarendon Press, 2007), 171.

4. Hegel, *Lectures*, 171–72.

5. *Opusc.* 16, PG 91, 204A—here Maximus makes both denials; cf. sec. 1.2.

6. Balthasar, *Theo-Logic*, 2:312, after asserting the uniqueness of the Christ event, continues: "Christology is not concerned with the general relationship between God and the creature distinguished by their immeasurable distance from each other"; and O'Regan, "Von Balthasar," 240–41, stipulates that the hypostatic union cannot apply to creatures because they are "constitutionally unable to replicate the hypostatic union" so that "the difference between the

human and the divine remains absolute." The latter point is moot, since, of course, even in the historical Incarnation the difference between the human and the divine remains absolute—indeed, hypostatic union generates this very difference (sec. 1.3). Why exactly being created (a quality of *nature*) makes it constitutionally impossible to be uncreated too—to be God—remains a bare abstract assertion and actually seems beside the point in view of Maximian Christo-logic.

7. *Opusc.* 16, PG 91, 204A; cf. *Ep.* 12, PG 91, 488A–489C.

8. *Amb.* 41.2.

9. *Amb.* 42.11: "τὸ ἑαυτοῦ ἀνθρώπινον ἐδημιούργησεν, ἢ ἑαυτὸν ἀτρέπτως κατὰ πρόσληψιν σαρκὸς νοερῶς τε καὶ λογικῶς ἐψυχωμένης, δι' ἡμᾶς ἑκουσίως, ὡς παντοδύναμος, δημιουργήσας ἐποίησεν ἄνθρωπον." I add here that the Lateran Synod of 649, in which Maximus most likely participated, insists on confessing that Christ is "at once created and uncreated [τὸν αὐτὸν ἄκιστον καὶ κτιστόν / eundem inconditum et conditum]" (can. 4). Heinrich Denzinger and Peter Hünermann, eds., *Enchiridion symbolorum definitionum et declarationum de rebus fidei et morum: Compendium of Creeds, Definitions, and Declarations on Matters of Faith and Morals: Latin-English*, 43rd ed. (San Francisco: Ignatius Press, 2012), 175.

10. *Amb.* 27.3.

11. *Amb.* 27.3. The inner quotations come from Gregory of Nazianzus, *Or.* 30.8, where Gregory discusses John 20:17.

12. *Amb.* 27.4; Maximus can even claim that it is "more proper" to say Christ "is" his two natures than it is to say merely that he exists "out of" or "in" his two natures (*Ep.* 15, PG 91, 573A; cf. chapter 1, note 110). This is because Christ himself is "by nature properly God and by nature properly man" (*Opusc.* 7, PG 91, 96A).

13. Cyril of Alexandria, *Ep.* 46.13, in *Letters 1–50*, trans. John I. McEnerney, Fathers of the Church 76 (Washington, DC: Catholic University of America Press, 1987), 204.

14. So even Erich Przywara, S.J., "The Scope of Analogy as a Fundamental Catholic Form" (1940), in *Analogia Entis: Metaphysics: Original Structure and Universal Rhythm*, trans. John R. Betz and David Bentley Hart (Grand Rapids, MI: Eerdmans, 2014), 361, notes that Lateran IV's famous formulation of what Przywara calls the *analogia entis*—namely that "one cannot note any similarity between creator and creature, however great, without being compelled to observe an ever greater dissimilarity between them"—is a pronouncement given from the vantage of contemplating the creator and creature "as such." Of course in Christo-logic it never suffices to consider creator and creature as such, not, I mean, if one wants to contemplate the deepest real relation between uncreated and created natures. Hence, from a Maximian vantage, analogy so conceived does not even

countenance the possibility of a Christo-logical God-world relation. One observation illustrates the point. For Przywara, e.g., in "Between Metaphysics and Christianity" (1958), in *Analogia Entis*, 526, Aristotle's formulation of the ἄλλο πρὸς ἄλλο relation of proportionality (*Metaph.* IV.1) laid the groundwork for the only possible "metaphysics of 'analogy,'" which Lateran IV took up and universalized. And yet Constantinople II, can. 3, specifically warns against conceiving Christ as *"one* who is the Word of God who does wonders, and then *another* who is the suffering Christ" (ἄλλον εἶναι τοῦ Θεοῦ λόγον τὸν θαυματουργήσαντα, καὶ ἄλλον τὸν Χριστὸν τὸν παθόντα) (Denzinger and Hünermann, *Enchiridion symbolorum*, 148, my translation). Again, this is not to say that one cannot both adhere to analogy and affirm this of Christ. The point rather is that these are not the same logics. Restricting the logic of the God-world relation to analogy, to a proportion of "one toward another," simply assumes from the outset the impossibility of conceiving that relation according to Christo-logic, to "one toward another only *because* these are more fundamentally the very same one."

15. So Robert Sokolowski, *The God of Faith and Reason: Foundations of Christian Theology* (Notre Dame, IN: University of Notre Dame Press, 1982), 18, 33, passim; and Ayres, *Nicaea and Its Legacy*, 286–88. My point is not that individual Nicene theologians emphasized the reverse implication of making the Son very God. Indeed, in the face of Eunomius's theology, it is likely that they didn't, or at least didn't emphasize it too much. But I leave that for others to decide (especially about Gregory of Nyssa; his *In Illud* seems to perform exactly the trend Maximus takes up and perfects). Rather, my claim is that someone like Maximus, who did his thinking on the far side of Nicaea, Chalcedon, and the highly developed Neo-Chalcedonianism he himself perfected, could not avoid perceiving this, especially under Cyril of Alexandria's great weight. My point is also that this perception is systematically right.

16. Robert W. Jenson, "Jesus in the Trinity," *Pro Ecclesia* 8.3 (1999): 308–18.

17. Gregory of Nazianzus, *Or.* 41.12, quoted at *Amb.* 71.6.

18. Dionysius, *DN* 4.13, quoted at *Amb.* 71.6.

19. *Myst.* 24, CCSG 69, 68–69, in *Maximus Confessor*, trans. Berthold, 212, modified.

20. *Amb.* 7.31, PG 91, 1092C.

21. *Amb.* 37.8, PG 91, 1296CD, slightly modified.

Analytic Appendix of Key Concepts

1. *Pyr.* 11.

2. E.g., *Ep.* 12, PG 91, 484A, where Maximus offers a formal definition of "relational union" (σχετικὴ ἕνωσις) as part of his polemical interpretation of Cyril's "one nature of the Word Incarnate"—namely, that *this* sort of union is what

Cyril meant to forfend; cf. too *Ep.* 15, PG 91, 561A, where definitions of "difference" (διαφορά) and "identity" (ταυτότης) conclude a dense section on Christ's assumption of noetic flesh.

3. Mossman Roueché, "Byzantine Philosophical Texts of the Seventh Century," *Jahrbuch der österreichischen Byzantinistik* 23 (1974): 61–76, and "Middle Byzantine Handbook." Roueché doubts that even the two manuscripts explicitly attributed to Maximus are original to him but still thinks it likely that these "were found among his papers after his death" ("Byzantine Philosophical Texts," 63). Tollefsen, *Christocentric Cosmology*, 15, thinks that later editors "considered these logical texts a useful tool in understanding [Maximus]."

4. *Opusc.* 14, PG 91, 149B. All translations from this work are mine.

5. *Opusc.* 14, PG 91, 149B; *Ep.* 15, PG 91, 545A, 548D; *Ep.* 12, PG 91, 447A; *Opusc.* 16, PG 91, 197CD; passim.

6. *Ep.* 13, PG 91, 528AB.

7. *Opusc.* 21, PG 91, 249A; *Opusc.* 23, PG 91, 264B; *Opusc.* 26, PG 91, 264B; *Pyr.* 166–67; *Amb.* 7.42.

8. *Opusc.* 14, PG 91, 149B: "in no degree ever defined by one sole person" (μήποτε καθοτιοῦν ἑνὶ προσώπῳ περιοριζόμενα).

9. Tollefsen, *Christocentric Cosmology*, 104–5.

10. *Opusc.* 14, PG 91, 152A; cf. the wealth of citations in Larchet, "Hypostase, personne," 36–41.

11. *Opusc.* 14, PG 91, 152A; *Ep.* 15, PG 91, 454A.

12. *Amb.* 17.5–6.

13. *Opusc.* 10, PG 91, 137A, quoted at note 47.

14. *Opusc.* 14, PG 91, 152A; *Opusc.* 26, PG 91, 264A.

15. *Opusc.* 26; PG 91, 264A; *Ep.* 15, PG 91, 557D: "For a hypostasis is what subsists distinctively in itself" (Τὸ γὰρ καθ' αὐτὸ διωρισμένως συνεστώς ἐστιν ὑπόστασις).

16. So *Ep.* 12, PG 91, 477A, where "hypostasis" (the topic at hand here) stands synonymous to "underlying subject": "So too every quantitative number of things differing, according to the *logos* of 'how to be' or of 'how to subsist' [κατὰ τὸν τοῦ πῶς εἶναι, ἢ τὸν τοῦ πῶς ὑφεστάναι λόγον], is [a number] that indicates the difference of the underlying subjects [τῶν ὑποκειμένων] and does not introduce relation." As I indicate in sec. 1.2, Maximus also distinguishes "hypostasis" (esp. Christ's) from the Aristotelian "underlying subject": hypostasis replaces the latter in Maximian metaphysics (cf. *Amb.* 17.5).

17. *Ep.* 13, PG 91, 513B: Number does not make an individual; number merely "names" what comes only by "divine wisdom and power"—distinct, idiomatic entities.

18. *Ep.* 12, PG 91, 489D: "The particular [of Christ's composed hypostasis] imparts nothing whatever to the generic" (τοῦ δὲ ἰδίου τὸ σύνολον λόγου τῷ γενικῷ μεταδιδοῦνος οὐδέν); cf. *Amb.* 17.4–5.

19. This point emerges most plainly in Christology, where the flesh of Christ receives both its concrete existence *and* its particular way of being from the Son's very hypostasis (*Ep.* 12, PG 91, 468A); but cf. too the more general pronouncement at *Amb.* 10.91: "I will not address the fact that the very being of beings itself [αὐτὸ τὸ εἶναι τῶν ὄντων] does not exist simply or without qualities, but in a particular way [or: "has a *how* 'to be'"], which constitutes its first form of delimitation." Recall, in relation to this latter passage, that the "how" or mode of being ultimately derives from the hypostasis and its proper principle (cf. "mode" below).

20. *Opusc.* 14, PG 91, 151AB; *Opusc.* 18, PG 91, 216A; passim.

21. *Ep.* 13, PG 91, 528AB; *Ep.* 15, PG 91, 557D.

22. *Opusc.* 21, PG 91, 249C.

23. *Opusc.* 23, PG 91, 264A (probably spurious yet a useful gloss): "ὅτι ἡ μὲν φύσις τὸν τοῦ εἶναι λόγον κοινὸν ἐπέχει, ἡ δὲ ὑπόστασις, καὶ τὸν τοῦ καθ' ἑαυτὸ εἶναι." Tollefsen rightly observes this distinction goes for both universals and particulars (and, I add, for hypostases); cf. Tollefsen, *Christocentric Cosmology*, 81–92, esp. 92.

24. *Opusc.* 23, PG 91, 264AB.

25. *Ep.* 15, PG 91, 549C.

26. Plato, *Ep.* 7, 342B.

27. Lampe, λόγος, s.v.

28. *Amb.* 7.16.

29. *Opusc.* 23 (note 24 above); *Opusc.* 14, PG 91, 152B (my emphasis): "And hypostatic difference hits upon *a principle* according to which the otherness of the assemblage of properties contemplated in the common essence—[an otherness] that divides one from another by number—*makes* the multitude of individuals" (Ὑποστατικὴ δὲ διαφορά, τυγχάνει λόγος, καθ' ὃν ἡ κατὰ τὸ ἄθροισμα τῶν ἐνθεωρουμένων ἰδιωμάτων τῷ κοινῷ τῆς οὐσίας ἑτερότης, τέμνουσα κατ' ἀριθμὸν ἄλλον ἀπ' ἄλλου, τὴν τῶν ἀτόμων ποιεῖται πληθύν).

30. *Amb.* 42.29 (natural principle); *Ep.* 15, PG 91, 549B (hypostatic invariability).

31. *Opusc.* 14, PG 91, 153B: "Identity is indistinguishability, according to which the *principle* of the thing signified possesses utter singularity, [which is] recognized to differ in no sense" (Ταυτότης ἐστὶν ἀπαραλλαξία, καθ' ἣν ὁ τοῦ σημαινομένου λόγος τὸ πάντη κέκτηται μοναδικὸν, μηδενὶ τρόπῳ διαφορᾶς γνωριζόμενον).

32. *Amb.* 2.5 (of Christ's human agency); *Amb.* 7.19 (preexistent *logoi* establish τὰ δυνάμει, which will by divine ordinance come into ἐνεργείᾳ).

33. *Amb.* 10.35–41.

34. *Amb.* 10.20.

35. *Amb.* 5.20; *Ep.* 12, PG 91, 492A ("mode of economy").

36. *Amb.* 5.24; *Pyr.* 28–31, PG 91, 296C–297A; 192, PG 91, 345D–348A.

37. *Amb.* 5.11 (singular "mode"); 5.17 (plural "modes").

38. Sherwood, *Earlier Ambigua*, 155–66.

39. Gregory of Nyssa, *C. Eun.* III.6.14, is a *locus classicus* for this pairing.

40. Sherwood, *Earlier Ambigua*, 161, notes that while Gregory of Nyssa and Basil applied τρόπος ὑπάρξεως only to the Son and Spirit—for these persons, unlike the Father, have origin—subsequent theologians linked it to the Father too in a negative way: the "how" of his existence is precisely that, as "the unoriginated originator," he receives no "how" from another.

41. *Amb.* 1.4; cf. *Amb.* 10.39 and Sherwood, *Earlier Ambigua*, 164. Yet even here *logos* and *tropos* do not simply follow a rigid equation of *logos* = unity, *tropos* = trinity. Maximus calls the "principle" that constitutes the divine Monad "the principle of essence or of 'to be'" (μονάδα μὲν κατὰ τὸν τῆς οὐσίας, ἤτοι τὸν τοῦ εἶναι λόγον) but also names a "principle" for the divine Trinity: "the principle of *how* to exist and subsist" (τριάδα δὲ, κατὰ τὸν τοῦ πῶς ὑπάρχειν καὶ ὑφεστάναι λόγον) (*Myst.* 23, PG 91, 700D–701A; my translation).

42. *Amb.* 42.29.

43. *Amb.* 7.24; *Amb.* 42.13–16.

44. This is very much the operative principle in Maximus's rebuttal of monenergism; cf. *Pyr.* 192, PG 91, 345D–348A; see sec. 1.4.

45. Dionysius Skliris, "'Hypostasis,' 'Person,' 'Individual,' 'Mode': A Comparison between the Terms That Denote Concrete Being in St. Maximus's Theology," in *Knowing the Purpose of Everything through the Resurrection: Proceedings on the Symposium on St Maximus the Confessor, Belgrade, October, 18–21, 2012*, ed. M. Vasiljevic (Belgrade: Sebastian Press, 2013), 445.

46. Bathrellos, *Byzantine Christ*, 103.

47. *Opusc.* 10, PG 91, 136D–137A.

48. I deliberately bracket the controversy over whether there are grounds for detecting a modern "personalist" precedent in Maximus's theological anthropology. This list, I repeat, treats only some important metaphysical principles, not—and I'm convinced this is where the debate should go—the singularity of the concrete human person that results from these principles.

49. *Opusc.* 16, PG 91, 205A: "τὸ μὴ ἀνυπόστατον, οὐχ ὑπόστασιν εἶναι τὴν φύσιν ποιεῖ, ἀλλ᾽ ἐνυπόστατον." For some the alleged absence of the *anhypostasis-enhypostasis* couplet in the fathers or at Constantinople II discredits the pedigree Barth claimed for the doctrine; so F. LeRon Shults, "A Dubious Christological Formula: From Leontius of Byzantium to Karl Barth," *Theological Studies* 57 (1996): 431–46. Riches, *Ecce Homo*, 110, though an adherent of the doctrine, still repeats the thesis that this "couplet appears nowhere in the Fathers." That the noun form, *enhypostasia* or *enhypostasis*, never appears poses no real problem here, especially since the adjectives are frequently (as here) *substantive*; they function grammatically as nouns.

50. So *Opusc.* 16, PG 91, 205B: the "enhypostasized reality," since it is a nature *in concreto* ("the en-existenced reality"), in *this* way alone "participates essential and natural existence."

51. *Opusc.* 14, PG 91, 150BC: "Ἐνυπόστατόν ἐστι, τὸ κατὰ τὴν οὐσίαν κοινόν, ἤγουν τὸ εἶδος, τὸ ἐν τοῖς ὑπ' αὐτὸ ἀτόμοις πραγματικῶς ὑφιστάμενον, καὶ οὐκ ἐπινοίᾳ ψιλῇ θεωρούμενον."

52. *Opusc.* 16, PG, 91, 205B: "In this way too the fact that hypostasis is not without essence does not make it [identical to] an essence but proves it *enessenced*, so that it is not identical to a mere property. Rather we know the property with the one [hypostasis that] is properly in it [i.e., in the nature]." *Opusc.* 23, PG 91, 261C: "For these [i.e., the enhypostasized and enessenced] do not possess existence *in themselves* but are always contemplated around the hypostasis." Cf. *Opusc.* 16, quoted at note 49.

53. *Opusc.* 14, PG 91, 152A: "Ἐνούσιόν ἐστι τὸ μὴ μόνον ἐνθεωρούμενου ἔχον ἐφ' ἑαυτοῦ τὸ τῶν ἰδιωμάτων ἄθροισμα, καθ' ὃ ἄλλο ἀπ' ἄλλο γνωρίζεται, ἀλλὰ καὶ τὸ κοινὸν τῆς οὐσίας πραγματικῶς κεκτημένον."

BIBLIOGRAPHY

Primary Literature

Arnim, H. von, ed. *Stoicorum veterum fragmenta*. 1903–5. Reprint, Stuttgart: Teubner, 1964.

Athanasius. *Athanasius Werke*. Vol. 2. *Historische Schriften*. Pt. 8. Edited by H. C. Brennecke, U. Heil, and A. von Stockhausen. Berlin: De Gruyter, 2006.

Cyril of Alexandria. *Letters 1–50*. Translated by John I. McEnerney. Fathers of the Church 76. Washington, DC: Catholic University of America Press, 1987.

Denzinger, Heinrich, and Peter Hünermann, eds. *Enchiridion symbolorum definitionum et declarationum de rebus fidei et morum: Compendium of Creeds, Definitions, and Declarations on Matters of Faith and Morals: Latin-English*. 43rd ed. San Francisco: Ignatius Press, 2012.

Dionysius. *Corpus Dionysiacum*. Vol. 2. Edited by G. Heil and A. M. Ritter. 1991. Reprint, Berlin: De Gruyter, 2014.

———. *Corpus Dionysiacum*. Vol. 4, pt. 1. *Ioannis Scythopolitani prologus et scholia in Dionysii Areopagitae librum "De divinis nominibus" cum additamentis interpretum aliorum*. Edited by Beate Regina Suchla. Patristische Texte und Studien 62. Berlin: De Gruyter, 2011.

———. *Les Noms divins: Chapitres I–IV*. Edited by Ysabel De Andia. SC 578. Paris: Cerf, 2016.

———. *The Works of Dionysius the Areopagite*. Translated by John Parker. London: James Parker, 1897.

Dionysius Thrax. *Dionysii Thracis Ars grammatica*. Edited by Gustavus Uhlig. Leipzig: Teubner Verlagsgesellschaft, 1883.

Eriugena. *Joannis Scoti Versio Ambiguorum S. Maximi*. Edited by E. Jeauneau. CCSG 18. Turnhout: Brepols, 1988.

———. *Periphyseon (The Division of Nature)*. Translated by John J. O'Meara. Montreal: Bellarmin, 1987.

Evagrius. *Le Gnostique*. Edited by Antoine Guillaumont and Claire Guillaumont. SC 356. Paris: Cerf, 1989.

———. *Evagrius's Kephalaia Gnostika: A New Translation of the Unreformed Text from the Syriac*. Translated by Ilaria L. E. Ramelli. Atlanta, GA: SBL Press, 2015.

Georgius Monachus. *Georgii Monachi chronicon*. Edited by Carolus de Boor. 1904. Reprint, Stuttgart: Teubner, 2012.

Gregory of Nazianzus. *Lettres théologiques*. Rev. ed. Edited by Paul Gallay. SC 208. Paris: Cerf, 2013.

Gregory of Nyssa. *Gregorii Nysseni Opera*. 17 vols. Leiden: Brill, 1960–.

———. *Homilies on Ecclesiastes*. Translated by Stuart G. Hall. New York: De Gruyter, 1993.

———. *Homilies on the Song of Songs*. Translated by Richard A. Norris. Atlanta, GA: Society of Biblical Literature, 2012.

———. *One Path for All: Gregory of Nyssa on the Christian Life and Human Destiny*. Edited by Rowan A. Greer. Eugene, OR: Cascade Books, 2015.

Iamblichus. *De mysteriis*. Édouard Des Places's edition annotated by Emma C. Clarke. Translated by John Dillon. Atlanta, GA: Society of Biblical Literature, 2003.

Iraeneus. *Contre les hérésies, Livre IV*. Vol. 2. Edited by A. Rousseau, B. Hemmerdinger, C. Mercier, and L. Doutreleau. SC 100/2. 1965. Reprint, Paris: Cerf, 2006.

John Grammaticus. *Iohannis Caesariensis presbyteri et grammatici opera quae supersunt*. Edited by M. Richard. CCSG 1. Turnhout: Brepols, 1977.

Justinian. *Drei dogmatische Schriften Iustinians*. Edited by M. Amelotti, R. Albertella, L. Migliardi, and Eduard Schwartz. Milan: Giuffre, 1973.

Leontius of Byzantium. *Complete Works*. Edited and translated by Brian Daley, S.J. Oxford: Oxford University Press, 2017.

Leontius of Jerusalem. *Against the Monophysites: Testimonies of the Saints and Aporiae*. Edited and translated by Patrick T. R. Gray. Oxford Early Christian Texts. Oxford: Oxford University Press, 2006.

Long, A. A., and D. N. Sedley, eds. *The Hellenistic Philosophers*. Cambridge: Cambridge University Press, 1987.

Maximus Confessor. *The Ascetic Life; The Four Centuries on Charity*. Translated by Polycarp Sherwood. Westminster, MD: Newman Press, 1955.

———. *Capitoli sulla carita*. Edited by Aldo Ceresa-Gastaldo. Rome: Editrice Studium, 1963.

———. *The Disputation with Pyrrhus of Our Father among the Saints Maximus the Confessor*. Translated by Joseph P. Farrell. Waymart, PA: St. Tikhon's Monastery Press, 2014.

———. "Letter 2: On Love." Translated by Andrew Louth. In *Maximus the Confessor*, by Andrew Louth. New York: Routledge, 1996.

———. *Liber asceticus.* Edited by Peter Van Deun. CCSG 40. Turnhout: Brepols, 2000.

———. *Maximus Confessor: Selected Writings.* Classics of Western Spirituality. Translated and annotated by George C. Berthold. Mahwah, NJ: Paulist Press, 1985.

———. *Mystagogia.* Edited by Christian Boudignon. CCSG 69. Turnhout: Brepols, 2011.

———. *On Difficulties in Sacred Scripture: Responses to Thalassios.* Translated by Fr. Maximos Constas. Fathers of the Church 136. Washington, DC: Catholic University of America Press, 2018.

———. *On Difficulties in the Church Fathers: The Ambigua.* 2 vols. Translated and edited by Nicholas Constas. Dumbarton Oaks Medieval Library 28–29. Cambridge, MA: Harvard University Press, 2014.

———. *On the Cosmic Mystery of Jesus Christ: Selected Writings from St. Maximus the Confessor.* Translated by Paul M. Blowers and Robert Louis Wilken. Yonkers, NY: St. Vladimir's Seminary Press, 2003.

———. *Opera omnia.* PG 90 and 91.

———. *Opuscula exegetica duo* [*In psal.* and *Exp. Orat. Dom.*]. Edited by Peter Van Deun. CCSG 23. Turnhout: Brepols, 1991.

———. *Quaestiones ad Thalassium I.* Edited by Carlos Laga and Carlos Steel. CCSG 7. Turnhout: Brepols, 1980.

———. *Quaestiones ad Thalassium II.* Edited by Carlos Laga and Carlos Steel. CCSG 22. Turnhout: Brepols, 1990.

———. *Quaestiones et dubia.* Edited by J. H. Declerck. CCSG 10. Turnhout: Brepols, 1982.

———. *Questions à Thalassios.* Edited by Jean-Claude Larchet. Vol. 1. SC 529. Paris: Cerf, 2010.

———. *Questions à Thalassios.* Edited by Jean-Claude Larchet. Vol. 2. SC 554. Paris: Cerf, 2012.

———. *St. Maximus the Confessor's "Questions and Doubts."* Translated by Despina D. Prassas. De Kalb: Northern Illinois University Press, 2021.

———. *Two Hundred Chapters on Theology: St. Maximus the Confessor.* Translated by Luis Salés. Yonkers, NY: St. Vladimir's Seminary Press, 2015.

Origen. *On First Principles.* Translated by G. W. Butterworth. New York: Harper and Row, 1966.

———. *Origenes vier Bücher von den Prinzipien.* Edited by H. Görgemanns and H. Karpp. Darmstadt: WBG, 1976.

Plotinus. *Ennead IV.* Edited by A. H. Armstrong. Loeb Classical Library. Harvard, MA: Cambridge University Press, 1984.

Price, Richard, ed. *Canons of the Quinisext Council (691/2).* Liverpool: Liverpool University Press, 2020.

Proclus. *The Elements of Theology*. Edited and translated by E. R. Dodds. 1963. Reprint, Oxford: Clarendon Press, 2004.

———. *In Parmenides*. In *Procli philosophi Platonici: Opera inedita continens Procli commentarium in Platonis Parmenidem*. Edited by Victor Cousin. Hildesheim: Olms, 2002.

———. *Theologie Platonicienne*. Edited by H. D. Saffrey and L. G. Westerink. Paris: Belles Lettres, 1968.

Pseudo-Macarius. *The Fifty Spiritual Homilies and The Great Letter*. Edited and translated by George A. Maloney. New York: Paulist Press, 1992.

Roosen, Bram, ed. "Epifanovitch Revisited. (Pseudo-) *Maximi Confessoris Opuscula varia*: A Critical Edition with Extensive Notes on Manuscript Tradition and Authenticity." PhD diss., Leuven University, 2001.

Secondary Literature

Abramowski, L. "συνάφεια und ἀσύγχυτος ἕνωσις als Bezeichnung für trinitarische und christologische Einheit." In *Drei christologische Untersuchungen*, 63–109. Beihefte zur Zeitschrift für die neutestamentliche Wissenschaft. Berlin: De Gruyter, 1981.

Ayres, Lewis. *Nicaea and Its Legacy: An Approach to Fourth-Century Trinitarian Theology*. Oxford: Oxford University Press, 2004.

Ayroulet, Élie. *De l'image à l'Image: Réflexions sur un concept clef de la doctrine de la divinization de saint Maxime le Confesseur*. Rome: Institutum patristicum Augustinianum, 2013.

———. "La réception de Maxime le Confesseur à l'époque contemporaine." *Théophilyon* 21.1 (2016): 71–90.

Bakhtin, Mikhail M. "Response to a Question from the *Novy Mir* Editorial Staff." In *Speech Genres and Other Late Essays*, translated by Vern W. McGee, 1–9. Austin: University of Texas Press, 2013.

Balas, David L. "The Idea of Participation in the Structure of Origen's Thought: Christian Transposition of a Theme of the Platonic Tradition." In *Origeniana: Premier colloque international des études origéniennes*, edited by Henri Crouzel, Gennaro Lomiento, and Josep Rius-Camps, 257–75. Bari: Istituto di letteratura cristiana antica, 1975.

Balthasar, Hans Urs von. *Cosmic Liturgy: The Universe According to Maximus the Confessor*. 3rd ed. Translated by Brian Daley, S.J. 1941. Reprint, San Francisco: Ignatius Press, 2003.

———. "Die Hiera des Evagrius." *Zeitschrift für katholische Theologie* 63 (1939): 86–106, 181–206.

———. *Kosmische Liturgie: Das Weltbild Maximus' des Bekenners*. Freiburg: Johannes Verlag, 1961.

————. "Retrieving the Tradition: The Fathers, the Scholastics and Ourselves." Translated by Edward T. Oakes, S.J. 1939. Republished in *Communio* 24 (1997): 347–96.

————. *Theo-Drama: Theological Dramatic Theory*. Vol. 3, *Dramatis Personae: Persons in Christ*. Translated by Graham Harrison. 1978. Reprint, San Francisco: Ignatius Press, 1992.

————. *Theo-Logic: Theological Logical Theory*. Vol. 2, *Truth of God*. Translated by Adrian J. Walker. 1985. Reprint, San Francisco: Ignatius Press, 2004.

————. *The Theology of Karl Barth: Exposition and Interpretation*. Translated by Edward T. Oakes. 1951. Reprint, San Francisco: Ignatius Press, 1992.

Bathrellos, Demetrios. *The Byzantine Christ: Person, Nature, and Will in the Christology of Saint Maximus the Confessor*. Oxford: Oxford University Press, 2004.

Bausenhart, Guido. *"In allem uns gleich außer der Sünde": Studien zum Beitrag Maximos' des Bekenners zur altkirchlichen Christologie mit einer kommentierten Übersetzung der "Disputatio cum Pyrrho."* Mainz: Matthias-Grünewald-Verlag, 1992.

Behr, John. Introduction to *Origen: On First Principles*, edited and translated by John Behr. Vol. 1. Oxford: Oxford University Press, 2017.

————. *John the Theologian and His Pascal Gospel: A Prologue to Theology*. Oxford: Oxford University Press, 2019.

Bénatouïl, Thomas. "How Industrious Can Zeus Be? The Extent and Objects of Divine Activity in Stoicism." In *God and Cosmos in Stoicism*, edited by Ricardo Salles, 23–45. Oxford: Oxford University Press, 2009.

Benevich, Grigory. "Maximus Confessor's Teaching on God's Providence." In *The Architecture of the Cosmos: St Maximus the Confessor, New Perspectives*, edited by Antoine Lévy, Pauli Annala, Olli Hallamaa, and Tuomo Lankila, 123–40. Schriften der Luther-Agricola-Gesellschaft 69. Helsinki: Luther-Agricola, 2015.

Berthold, George. "The Cappadocian Roots of Maximus the Confessor." In *Maximus Confessor: Actes du symposium sur Maxime le Confesseur: Fribourg, 2–5 septembre 1980*, edited by Felix Heinzer and Christoph Schönborn, 51–59. Fribourg: Editions Universitaires, 1982.

Betz, John R. "Translator's Introduction." In *Analogia Entis: Metaphysics: Original Structure and Universal Rhythm*, translated by John R. Betz and David Bentley Hart. 1932. Reprint, Grand Rapids, MI: Eerdmans, 2014.

Bieler, Jonathan. "Body and Soul Immovably Related: Considering an Aspect of Maximus the Confessor's Concept of Analogy." *Studia Patristica* 75 (2017): 223–35.

Bloch, Marc. *The Historian's Craft: Reflections on the Nature and Uses of History and the Techniques and Methods of Those Who Write It*. 1944. Reprint, Toronto: Random House, 1953.

Blowers, Paul M. *Drama of the Divine Economy: Creator and Creation in Early Christian Theology and Piety.* Oxford: Oxford University Press, 2012.

———. *Exegesis and Spiritual Pedagogy in Maximus the Confessor: An Investigation of the "Questiones ad Thalassium."* Notre Dame, IN: University of Notre Dame Press, 1991.

———. "From Nonbeing to Eternal Well-Being: Creation ex Nihilo in the Cosmology and Soteriology of Maximus the Confessor." In *Light on Creation: Ancient Commentators in Dialogue and Debate on the Origin of the World*, edited by Geert Roskam and Joseph Verheyden, 169–85. Tübingen: Mohr Siebeck, 2017.

———. "Gentiles of the Soul: Maximus the Confessor on the Substructure and Transformation of Human Passions." *Journal of Early Christian Studies* 4.1 (1996): 57–85.

———. *Maximus the Confessor: Jesus Christ and the Transfiguration of the World.* Oxford: Oxford University Press, 2016.

———. "On the 'Play' of Divine Providence in Gregory Nazianzen and Maximus the Confessor." In *Re-reading Gregory of Nazianzus: Essays on History, Theology, and Culture*, edited by Christopher Beeley, 183–201. Washington, DC: Catholic University of America Press, 2012.

———. "A Psalm 'Unto the End': Eschatology and Anthropology in Maximus the Confessor's Commentary on Psalm 59." In *The Harp of Prophecy: Early Christian Interpretation of the Psalms*, edited by Brian E. Daley, S.J., and Paul R. Kolbet, 257–83. Notre Dame, IN: University of Notre Dame Press, 2015.

———. "Realized Eschatology in Maximus the Confessor, *Ad Thalassium* 22." *Studia Patristica* 33 (1997): 258–63.

———. "The Transfiguration of Jesus Christ as 'Saturated Phenomenon' and as Key to the Dynamics of Biblical Revelation in St. Maximus the Confessor." In *What Is the Bible? The Patristic Doctrine of Scripture*, edited by Matthew Baker and Mark Mourachian, 83–101. Minneapolis, MN: Fortress Press, 2016.

Brown, Robert F. "On the Necessary Imperfection of Creation: Irenaeus' *Adversus Haereses* IV, 38." *Scottish Journal of Theology* 28.1 (1975): 17–25.

Brune, François. *Pour que l'homme devienne Dieu.* 2nd ed. Saint-Jean-de-Braye: Dangles, 1992.

Brunner, Fernand. "Création et émanation: Fragment de philosophie comparée." *Studia Philosophica* 33 (1973): 33–63.

Bulgakov, Sergius. *The Lamb of God.* Translated by Boris Jakim. 1933. Grand Rapids, MI: Eerdmans, 2008.

Casiday, Augustine M. C. "Deification in Origen, Evagrius, and Cassian." In *Origeniana Octava: Origen and the Alexandrian Tradition / Origene e la tradizione alessandrina: Papers of the 8th International Origen Congress, Pisa,*

27–31 August 2001, edited by Lorenzo Perrone, P. Bernardino, and D. Marchini, 995–1001. Leuven: Leuven University Press, 2003.

———. *Reconstructing the Theology of Evagrius Ponticus: Beyond Heresy.* Cambridge: Cambridge University Press, 2013.

Clark, Elizabeth A. *History, Theory, Text: Historians and the Linguistic Turn.* Cambridge, MA: Harvard University Press, 2004.

Clarke, Stephen. "'Christ Plays in Ten Thousand Places': The Relationship of *Logoi* and *Logos* in Plotinus, Maximus, and Beyond." 1–18. Unpublished paper, n.d.

Cooper, Adam G. *The Body in St. Maximus the Confessor: Holy Flesh, Wholly Deified.* Oxford: Oxford University Press, 2005.

———. "Saint Maximus on the Mystery of Marriage and the Body: A Reconsideration." In *Knowing the Purpose of Creation through the Resurrection: Proceedings of the Symposium on St Maximus the Confessor, Belgrade, October 18–21*, edited by Bishop Maxim Vaslijevic, 195–221. Belgrade: Sebastian Press, 2013.

Costache, Doru. "Living above Gender: Insights from Saint Maximus the Confessor." *Journal of Early Christian Studies* 21.2 (2013): 261–90.

Cross, Richard. "*Homo Assumptus* in the Christology of Hugh of St Victor: Some Historical and Theological Revisions." *Journal of Theological Studies* 65.1 (2014): 62–77.

———. "Individual Natures in the Christology of Leontius of Byzantium." *Journal of Early Christian Studies* 10.2 (2002): 245–65.

Daley, Brian, S.J. "The Origenism of Leontius of Byzantium." *Journal of Theological Studies* 27.2 (1976): 333–69.

———. "'A Richer Union': Leontius of Byzantium and the Relationship of Human and Divine in Christ." *Studia Patristica* 24 (1993): 239–65.

———. "Translator's Foreword." In *Cosmic Liturgy: The Universe According to Maximus the Confessor*, by Hans Urs von Balthasar, 3rd ed., translated by Brian Daley, S.J. 1941. Reprint, San Francisco: Ignatius Press, 2003.

Dalmais, I.-H. "Saint Maxime le Confesseur: Une synthèse théologique." *Vie Spirituelle* 107 (1962): 316–18.

———. "La théorie des *logoi* des créatures chez s. Maxime le Confesseur." *Revue des Sciences Philosophiques et Théologiques* 36 (1952): 244–49.

D'Ancona, Cristina. "Plotinus and Later Platonic Philosophers on the Causality of the First Principle." In *The Cambridge Companion to Plotinus*, edited by Lloyd P. Gerson, 356–85. Cambridge: Cambridge University Press, 1996.

Davidson, Thos. "The Grammar of Dionysios Thrax." *Journal of Speculative Philosophy* 8.4 (1874): 326–39.

Deneffe, August. "Perichoresis, circumincessio, circuminsessio: Eine terminologisches Untersuchung." *Zeitschrift für katholische Theologie* 47.4 (1923): 497–532.

Dienstbeck, Stefan. *Die Theologie der Stoa.* Berlin: De Gruyter, 2015.

Doucet, Marcel. "Vues récentes sur les 'métamorphoses' de la pensée de saint Maxime le Confesseur." *Science et Esprit* 31.3 (1979): 269–302.

Dysinger, Luke, O.S.B. "The *Logoi* of Providence and Judgment in the Exegetical Writings of Evagrius Ponticus." *Studia Patristica* 37 (2001): 462–71.

Edwards, Mark Julian. *Origen against Plato*. Aldershot: Ashgate, 2002.

Emilsson, Eyjólfur Kjalar. "Remarks on the Relation between the One and Intellect in Plotinus." In *Traditions of Platonism: Essays in Honour of John Dillon*, edited by John J. Cleary, chap. 8. Aldershot: Ashgate, 1999.

Erismann, Christophe. "L'individualité expliquée par les accidents: Remarques sur la destinée 'chrétienne' de Porphyre." In *Compléments de substance: Etudes sur les propriétés accidentelles offertes à Alain de Libera*, edited by C. Erismann and A. Schniewind, 51–66. Paris: Vrin, 2008.

Florovsky, Georges. *Collected Works*. Vol. 9, *The Byzantine Fathers of the Sixth to the Eighth Century*. Edited by Richard S. Haugh. Translated by Raymond Miller, Anne-Marie Döllinger-Labriolle, and Helmut Wilhelm Schmiedel. Vaduz: Büchervertriebsanstalt, 1987.

———. "Creation and Creaturehood." In *Collected Works*, vol. 3, *Creation and Redemption*. 43–78. Belmont, MA: Nordland, 1976.

Gadamer, Hans-Georg. *Truth and Method*. 2nd rev. ed. Translation revised by Joel Weinsheimer and Donald G. Marshall. London: Continuum, 2004.

Garrigues, Juan-Miguel. "Le dessein d'adoption du Créateur dans son rapport au Fils d'après s. Maxime le Confesseur." In *Maximus Confessor: Actes du symposium sur Maxime le Confesseur: Fribourg, 2–5 septembre 1980*, edited by Felix Heinzer and Christoph Schönborn, 173–92. Fribourg: Editions Universitaires, 1982.

———. *Maxime le Confesseur: La charité, avenir divin de l'homme*. Paris: Beauchesne, 1976.

Gersh, Stephen. *From Iamblichus to Eriugena: An Investigation into the Prehistory and Evolution of the Pseudo-Dionysian Tradition*. Leiden: Brill, 1978.

Gleede, Benjamin. *The Development of the Term* ἐνυπόστατος *from Origen to John of Damascus*. Leiden: Brill, 2012.

Graeser, Andreas. *Plotinus and the Stoics: A Preliminary Study*. Leiden: Brill, 1972.

Greig, Jonathan. "Proclus' Doctrine of Participation in Maximus the Confessor's *Centuries of Theology* I.48–50." *Studia Patristica* 75 (2017): 137–48.

Grillmeier, Alois, S.J. *Christ in Christian Tradition*. Vol. 2, pt. 2, *The Church of Constantinople in the Sixth Century*. Translated by John Bowden. 1989. Reprint, Louisville, KY: John Knox Press, 1995.

———. "Der Neu-Chalkedonismus: Um die Berechtigung eines neuen Kapitels in der Dogmengeschichte." In *Mit ihm und in ihm: Christologische Forschungen und Perspektiven*, 371–85. Freiburg: Herder, 1975.

Guérard, Christian. "La théorie des hénades et la mystique de Proclus." *Dionysius* 6 (1982): 73–82.

Guillaumont, Antoine. *Les "Kephalaia Gnostica" d'Évagre le Pontique et l'histoire de l'origénisme chez les Grecs et chez les Syriens.* Paris: Éditions du Seuil, 1962.

Gurtler, Gary M. "Plotinus and the Platonic *Parmenides.*" *International Philosophical Quarterly* 32.4 (1992): 443–57.

———. "Plotinus on the Limitation of Act by Potency." *Saint Anselm Journal* 7 (2009): 1–15.

Harl, Marguérite. "La préexistence des âmes dans l'oeuvre d'Origène." In *Origeniana Quarta: Die Referate des 4. Internationalen Origenskongresses (Innsbruck, 2.–6. September 1985)*, edited by Lothar Lies, 238–58. Innsbruck: Tyrolia-Verlag, 1987.

Harrison, Verna. "Perichoresis in the Greek Fathers." *St. Vladimir's Theological Quarterly* 35 (1991): 53–65.

Hausherr, Irénée. *Philautie: De la tendresse pour soi à la charité selon Saint Maxime le Confesseur.* Orientalia Christiana Analecta 137. Rome: Pont. Institutum Orientalium Studiorum, 1952.

Hedley, Douglas. "Pantheism, Trinitarian Theism and the Idea of Unity: Reflections on the Christian Concept of God." *Religious Studies* 32.1 (1996): 61–77.

Hegel, G. W. F. *Lectures on the Philosophy of Religion.* Vol. 1, *Introduction and the Concept of Religion.* Edited by Peter C. Hodgson. 1827. Reprint, Oxford: Clarendon Press, 2007.

Heinzer, Felix. *Gottes Sohn als Mensch: Die Struktur des Menschseins Christi bei Maximus Confessor.* Freiburg: Universitätsverlag Freiburg/Schweiz, 1980.

Heinzer, Felix, and Christoph Schönborn, eds. *Maximus Confessor: Actes du symposium sur Maxime le Confesseur: Fribourg, 2–5 septembre 1980.* Fribourg: Editions Universitaires, 1982.

Helmer, Siegried. "Der Neuchalkedonismus: Geschichte, Berechtigung, und Bedeutung eines dogmengeschichtlichen Begriffes." PhD diss., University of Bonn, 1962.

Hirschberger, Johannes. "Ähnlichkeit und Seinsanalogie vom platonischen Parmenides bis Proklos." In *Philomates: Studies in the Humanities in Memory of Philip Merlan*, edited by Robert B. Palmer and Robert G. Hamerton-Kelly, 57–74. The Hague: Nijhoff, 1971.

Hovorun, Cyril. "Maximus, a Cautious Neo-Chalcedonian." In *The Oxford Handbook of Maximus the Confessor*, edited by Pauline Allen and Bronwen Neil, 106–24. Oxford: Oxford University Press, 2015.

Jankowiak, Marek, and Phil Booth. "A New Date-List of the Works of Maximus the Confessor." In *The Oxford Handbook of Maximus the Confessor*, edited by Pauline Allen and Bronwen Neil, 20–83. Oxford: Oxford University Press, 2015.

Jenson, Robert W. "Jesus in the Trinity." *Pro Ecclesia* 8.3 (1999): 308–18.

Kant, Immanuel. *Religion within the Boundaries of Mere Reason: And Other Writings*. Rev. ed. Edited by Allen Wood and George di Giovanni. 1793. Reprint, Cambridge: Cambridge University Press, 2018.

Karayiannis, Vasilios. *Maxime le Confesseur: Essence et énergies de Dieu*. Paris: Beauchesne, 1993.

Koch, Hal. *Pronoia und Paideusis: Studien über Origenes und sein Verhältnis zum Platonismus*. Berlin: De Gruyter, 1932.

Köckert, Charlotte. *Christliche Kosmologie und kaiserzeitliche Philosophie: Die Auslegung des Schöpfungsberichtes bei Origenes, Basilius und Gregor von Nyssa vor dem Hintergrund kaiserzeitlicher Timaeus-Interpretationen*. Tübingen: Mohr-Siebeck, 2009.

———. "The Concept of Seed in Christian Cosmology: Gregory of Nyssa, *Apologia in Hexaemeron*." *Studia Patristica* 47 (2010): 27–32.

Krausmüller, Dirk. "Human Souls as Consubstantial Sons of God: The Heterodox Anthropology of Leontius of Jerusalem." *Journal for Late Antique Religion and Culture* 4 (2010): 43–67.

Kuhn, Thomas. *The Structure of Scientific Revolutions*. 3rd ed. 1962. Reprint, Chicago: University of Chicago Press, 1996.

Lang, U. M. "Anhypostatos-Enhypostatos: Church Fathers, Protestant Orthodoxy and Karl Barth." *Journal of Theological Studies* 49.2 (1998): 630–57.

Larchet, Jean-Claude. "Le baptême selon saint Maxime le Confesseur." *Revue des Sciences Religieuses* 65.1–2 (1991): 51–70.

———. "La conception maximienne des énergies divines et des *logoi* et la théorie platonicienne des Idées." *Philotheos* 4 (2004): 276–83.

———. *La divinisation de l'homme selon saint Maxime le Confesseur*. Paris: Cerf, 1996.

———. "Hypostase, personne, et individu selon saint Maxime le Confesseur." *Revue d'Histoire Ecclésiastique* 109 (2014): 35–63.

———. *Maxime le Confesseur: Médiateur entre l'Orient et l'Occident*. Paris: Cerf, 1998.

Lebon, Joseph. *Le monophysisme sévérien*. Louvain: J. Van Linthout, 1909.

Lévy, Antoine, O.P. *Le créé et l'incréé: Maxime le Confesseur et Thomas d'Aquin*. Paris: Vrin, 2006.

Lévy, Antoine, Pauli Annala, Olli Hallamaa, and Tuomo Lankila, eds. *The Architecture of the Cosmos: St Maximus the Confessor, New Perspectives*. Schriften der Luther-Agricola-Gesellschaft 69. Helsinki: Luther-Agricola, 2015.

Litwa, David I. "'I Will Become Him': Homology and Deification in the Gospel of Thomas." *Journal of Biblical Literature* 133.2 (2015): 311–41.

Lloyd, A. C. *The Anatomy of Neoplatonism*. Oxford: Oxford University Press, 1998.

Lochbrunner, Manfred. *Hans Urs von Balthasar (1905–1988): Die Biographie eines Jahrhunderttheologen*. Würzburg: Echter, 2020.

Lollar, Joshua. "Reception of Maximian Thought in the Modern Era." In *The Ox-ford Handbook of Maximus the Confessor*, edited by Pauline Allen and Bron-wen Neil, 564–80. Oxford: Oxford University Press, 2015.

Lonergan, Bernard. *Method in Theology.* 1971. Reprint, Toronto: University of Toronto Press, 1990.

Loofs, Friedrich. *Leontius von Byzanz und die gleichnamigen Schriftsteller der griechischen Kirche.* Leipzig: Hinrichts, 1887.

Loosen, Josef. *Logos und Pneuma im begnadeten Menschen bei Maximus Confes-sor.* Munster: Aschendorff, 1941.

Loudovikos, Nicholaos. "Being and Essence Revisited: Reciprocal Logoi and En-ergies in Maximus the Confessor and Thomas Aquinas, and the Genesis of the Self-Referring Subject." *Revista Portuguesa de Filosofia* 72.1 (2016): 117–46.

———. *A Eucharistic Ontology: Maximus the Confessor's Eschatological On-tology of Being as Dialogical Reciprocity.* Translated by Elizabeth Theokri-toff. 1992. Reprint, Brookline, MA: Holy Cross Orthodox Press, 2010.

Louth, Andrew. "Recent Research on St Maximus the Confessor: A Survey." *St Vladimir's Theological Quarterly* 42 (1998): 67–84.

———. "The Reception of Dionysius in the Byzantine World." In *Re-thinking Dionysius the Areopagite*, edited by Sarah Coakley and Charles M. Stang, 43–54. Hoboken, NJ: Wiley-Blackwell, 2009.

———. "St Maximos' Doctrine of the *logoi* of Creation." *Studia Patristica* 48 (2010): 77–84.

Lukacs, John. "History and Physics, or the End of the Modern Age." In *Historical Consciousness: The Remembered Past*, 273–315. 1994. Reprint, New York: Routledge, 2017.

MacDonald, George. *The Complete Fairy Tales.* 1893. Reprint, New York: Pen-guin Books, 1999.

MacIntosh, Mark A. *Christology from Within: Spirituality and the Incarnation in Hans Urs von Balthasar.* Notre Dame, IN: University of Notre Dame Press, 1996.

Madden, Nicholas, O.C.D. "Composite Hypostasis in Maximus Confessor." *Studia Patristica* 28 (1993): 175–97.

Martens, Peter W. "Embodiment, Heresy and the Hellenization of Christianity: The Descent of the Soul in Plato and Origen." *Harvard Theological Review* 108 (2015): 594–620.

———. "Origen's Doctrine of Pre-existence and the Opening Chapters of Gene-sis." *Zeitschrift für Antikes Christentum / Journal of Ancient Christianity* 16 (2012): 516–49.

———. "Response to Mark Edwards." *Zeitschrift für Antikes Christentum / Jour-nal of Ancient Christianity* 23.2 (2019): 186–200.

McFarland, Ian A. "'Always and Everywhere': Divine Presence and the Incarnation." In *The Gift of Theology*, edited by Rosemary P. Carbine and Hilda P. Koster, 59–79. Minneapolis, MN: Fortress, 2015.

———. *The Word Made Flesh: A Theology of the Incarnation*. Louisville, KY: Westminster John Knox Press, 2019.

McTaggart, J. M. *The Nature of Existence*. Vol. 2. Cambridge: Cambridge University Press, 1927.

Miquel, Pierre. "Πεῖρα: Contribution à l'étude du vocabulaire de l'expérience religieuse dans l'oeuvre de Maxime le Confesseur." *Studia Patristica* 7 (1966): 355–61.

Mitralexis, Sotiris. *Ever-Moving Repose: A Contemporary Reading of Maximus the Confessor's Theory of Time*. Eugene, OR: Cascade Books, 2017.

———. "Maximus' Theory of Motion: Motion κατὰ φύσιν, Returning Motion, Motion παρὰ φύσιν." In *Maximus the Confessor as a European Philosopher*, edited by Sotiris Mitralexis, Georgios Steiris, Marcin Podbielski, and Sebastian Lalla, 73–91. Eugene, OR: Cascade Books, 2017.

Moeller, Charles. "Le Chalcédonisme et le néo-chalcédonisme en Orient de 451 à la fin du VIe siècle." In *Das Konzil von Chalkedon: Geschichte und Gegenwart*, vol. 1, edited by Alois Grillmeier, S.J., and Heinrich Bacht, 637–720. Würzburg: Echter, 1951.

———. "Textes 'monophysites' de Léonce de Jérusalem." *Ephemerides Theologicae Lovanienses* 27 (1951): 467–82.

Mueller-Jourdan, Pascal. "The Foundation of Origenist Metaphysics." In *The Oxford Handbook of Maximus the Confessor*, edited by Pauline Allen and Bronwen Neil, 149–63. Oxford: Oxford University Press, 2015.

———. "Where and When as Metaphysical Prerequisites for Creation in Ambiguum 10." In *Knowing the Purpose of Creation through the Resurrection: Proceedings of the Symposium on St Maximus the Confessor, Belgrade, October 18–21*, edited by Bishop Maxim Vaslijevic, 287–96. Belgrade: Sebastian Press, 2013.

Nichols, Aidan, O.P. *Byzantine Gospel: Maximus the Confessor in Modern Scholarship*. Edinburgh: T. and T. Clark, 1993.

Norris, Richard A., Jr. "Two Trees in the Midst of the Garden (Genesis 2:9b): Gregory of Nyssa and the Puzzle of Human Evil." In *In Dominico Eloquio: In Lordly Eloquence: Essays on Patristic Exegesis in Honor of Robert Louis Wilken*, edited by Paul M. Blowers, Angela Russell Christman, David G. Hunter, and Robin Darling Young, 218–41. Grand Rapids, MI: Eerdmans, 2002.

Oakes, Kenneth. "The Question of Nature and Grace in Karl Barth: Humanity as Creature and as Covenant-Partner." *Modern Theology* 23.4 (2007): 595–616.

O'Regan, Cyril. "Von Balthasar and Thick Retrieval: Post-Chalcedonian Symphonic Theology." *Gregorianum* 77.2 (1996): 227–60.

Osborn, Eric. *Irenaeus of Lyons*. Cambridge: Cambridge University Press, 2001.

Ousager, Asger. "Sufficient Reason, Identities and Discernibles in Plotinus." *Dionysius* 21 (2003): 219–40.

Perczel, Istvan. "The Earliest Syriac Reception of Dionysius." *Modern Theology* 24.4 (2008): 557–71.

———. "St Maximus on the Lord's Prayer: An Inquiry into His Relationship to the Origenist Tradition." In *The Architecture of the Cosmos: St Maximus the Confessor, New Perspectives*, edited by Antoine Lévy, Pauli Annala, Olli Hallamaa, and Tuomo Lankila, Schriften der Luther-Agricola-Gesellschaft 69, 221–78. Helsinki: Luther-Agricola, 2015.

Perl, Eric D. "Hierarchy and Participation." *American Catholic Philosophical Quarterly* 68.1 (1994): 15–30.

———. "Metaphysics and Christology in Maximus Confessor and Eriugena." In *Eriugena: East and West—Papers of the Eighth International Colloquium of the Society for the Promotion of Eriugenian Studies*, edited by Bernard McGinn and Willemien Otten, 253–79. Notre Dame, IN: University of Notre Dame Press, 1994.

———. "Methexis: Creation, Incarnation, and Deification in Saint Maximus Confessor." PhD diss., Yale University, 1991.

———. *Theophany: The Neoplatonic Philosophy of Dionysius the Areopagite*. Albany, NY: State University of New York Press, 2007.

Piret, Pierre. *Le Christ et la Trinité selon Maxime le Confesseur*. Paris: Beauchesne, 1983.

———. "Christologie et théologie trinitaire chez Maxime le Confesseur, d'après sa formule des natures 'desquelles, en lesquelle et lesquelles est le Christ.'" In *Maximus Confessor: Actes du symposium sur Maxime le Confesseur: Fribourg, 2–5 septembre 1980*, edited by Felix Heinzer and Christoph Schönborn, 215–22. Fribourg: Editions Universitaires, 1982.

Plested, Marcus. *The Macarian Legacy: The Place of Macarius-Symeon in the Eastern Christian Tradition*. Oxford: Oxford University Press, 2004.

Portaru, Marius. "Gradual Participation According to St Maximus the Confessor." *Studia Patristica* 54 (2012): 281–94.

———. "The Vocabulary of Participation in the Works of Saint Maximus the Confessor." In *Naboth's Vineyard*, edited by Octavian Gordon and Alexandru Mihaila, 295–317. Cluj-Napoca: Presa Universitara Clujeana, 2012.

Prestige, G. L. *God in Patristic Thought*. London: Society for Promoting Christian Knowledge, 1952.

Przywara, Erich, S.J. "Between Metaphysics and Christianity" (1958). In *Analogia Entis: Metaphysics: Original Structure and Universal Rhythm*, translated by John R. Betz and David Bentley Hart, 520–36. Grand Rapids, MI: Eerdmans, 2014.

———. "The Scope of Analogy as a Fundamental Catholic Form" (1940). In *Analogia Entis: Metaphysics: Original Structure and Universal Rhythm*, translated by John R. Betz and David Bentley Hart, 348–99. Grand Rapids, MI: Eerdmans, 2014.

Radosavljevic, Artemije. "Le problème du 'présupposé' ou du 'non-présupposé' de l'incarnation de dieu le Verbe." In *Maximus Confessor: Actes du symposium sur Maxime le Confesseur: Fribourg, 2–5 septembre 1980*, edited by Felix Heinzer and Christoph Schönborn, 193–206. Fribourg: Editions Universitaires, 1982.

Rahner, Karl. "Jesus Christ—The Meaning of Life." In *Theological Investigations*, vol. 21, *Science and Christian Faith*, translated by Hugh M. Riley. New York: Crossroad, 1988.

Ramelli, Ilaria L. E. "The Stoic Doctrine of Oikeiosis and Its Transformation in Christian Platonism." *Apeiron* 47.1 (2014): 116–40.

Renczes, Philip Gabriel. *Agir de Dieu et liberté de l'homme: Recherches sur l'anthropologie théologique de saint Maxime le Confesseur*. Paris: Cerf, 2003.

Richard, Marcel. "Le néochalcédonisme." *Mélanges de Sciences Religieuses* 3 (1946): 156–61.

Riches, Aaron. *Ecce Homo: On the Divine Unity of Christ*. Grand Rapids, MI: Eerdmans, 2016.

Riou, Alain. *Le monde et l'Église selon Maxime le Confesseur*. Paris: Beauchesne, 1973.

Rorem, Paul, and John C. Lamoureaux. *John of Scythopolis and the Dionysian Corpus: Annotating the Areopagite*. Oxford: Clarendon Press, 1998.

Roueché, Mossman. "Byzantine Philosophical Texts of the Seventh Century." *Jahrbuch der österreichischen Byzantinistik* 23 (1974): 61–76.

———. "A Middle Byzantine Handbook of Logical Terminology." *Jahrbuch der österreichischen Byzantanistik* 29 (1980): 71–98.

Rowe, C. Kavin. *One True Life: The Stoics and Early Christians as Rival Traditions*. New Haven, CT: Yale University Press, 2016.

Russell, Norman. *The Doctrine of Deification in the Greek Patristic Tradition*. Oxford: Oxford University Press, 2004.

Rutten, Christian. "La doctrine des deux actes dans la philosophie de Plotin." *Revue Philosophique de la France et de l'Étranger* 146 (1956): 100–106.

Salés, Luis. Introduction to *Two Hundred Chapters on Theology: St. Maximus the Confessor*. Yonkers, NY: St. Vladimir's Seminary Press, 2015.

Schelling, F. W. J. *Philosophical Investigations into the Essence of Human Freedom*. Translated with an introduction by Jeff Love and Johannes Schmidt. 1809. Reprint, New York: State University of New York Press, 2006.

Schönborn, Christoph, O.P. "Plaisir et douleur dans l'analyse de S. Maxime, d'après les *Quaestiones ad Thalassium*." In *Maximus Confessor: Actes du Symposium sur Maxime le Confesseur, Fribourg (2–5 septembre 1980)*, edited by Felix Heinzer and Christoph Schönborn, 273–84. Fribourg: Éditions Universitaires Fribourg, 1982.

Sedley, David. "The Stoic Theory of Universals." *Southern Journal of Philosophy* 23.1 (1985): 87–92.

Sherwood, Polycarp, O.S.B. *The Earlier Ambigua of Saint Maximus the Confessor and His Refutation of Origenism*. Rome: Orbis Catholicus, Herder, 1955.

———."Maximus and Origenism: ΑΡΧΗ ΚΑΙ ΤΕΛΟΣ." In *Berichte zum XI: Internationalen Byzantinisten Kongreß*, 1–26. Munich: C. H. Beck, 1958.

———. "Survey of Recent Work on St. Maximus the Confessor." *Traditio* 20 (1964): 428–37.

Shults, F. LeRon. "A Dubious Christological Formula: From Leontius of Byzantium to Karl Barth." *Theological Studies* 57 (1996): 431–46.

Siovanes, Lucas. *Proclus: Neo-Platonic Philosophy and Science*. Edinburgh: Edinburgh University Press, 1996.

Skliris, Dionysios. "'Hypostasis,' 'Person,' 'Individual,' 'Mode': A Comparison between the Terms That Denote Concrete Being in St. Maximus's Theology." In *Knowing the Purpose of Everything through the Resurrection: Proceedings on the Symposium on St Maximus the Confessor, Belgrade, October, 18–21, 2012*, edited by M. Vasiljevic, 437–50. Belgrade: Sebastian Press, 2013.

Söhngen, Gottlieb. "Analogia idei: Die Einheit in der Glaubenswissenschaft." *Catholica* 4 (1934): 176–208.

———. "Analogia fidei: Gottähnlichkeit allein aus Glauben?" *Catholica* 3 (1934): 113–36.

Sokolowski, Robert. *The God of Faith and Reason: Foundations of Christian Theology*. Notre Dame, IN: University of Notre Dame Press, 1982.

Sorabji, Richard. *The Philosophy of the Commentators, 200–600 AD: A Sourcebook*. Vol. 3, *Logic and Metaphysics*. Ithaca, NY: Cornell University Press, 2005.

———. *Time, Creation, and the Continuum: Theories in Antiquity and the Early Middle Ages*. Chicago: University of Chicago Press, 1983.

Squire, A. K. "The Idea of the Soul as Virgin and Mother in Maximus the Confessor." *Studia Patristica* 8 (1966): 456–61.

Steel, Carlos. "Beyond the Principle of Contradiction? Proclus' 'Parmenides' and the Origin of Negative Theology." In *Die Logik des Transzendentalen: Festschrift für Jan A. Aertsen*, edited by Martin Pickavé, 581–99. Berlin: De Gruyter, 2003.

Steenberg, M. C. "Children in Paradise: Adam and Eve as 'Infants' in Irenaeus of Lyons." *Journal of Early Christian Studies* 12.1 (2004): 1–22.

———. *Irenaeus on Creation: The Cosmic Christ and the Saga of Redemption*. Leiden: Brill, 2008.

Stemmer, Peter. "PERICHORESE: Zur Geschichte eines Begriffs." *Archiv für Begriffsgeschichte* 27 (1983): 9–55.

Steven, Luke. "Deification and the Workings of the Body: The Logic of 'Proportion' in Maximus the Confessor." *Studia Patristica* 75 (2017): 237–50.

Straubinger, H. "Die Lehre des Patriarchen Sophronius von Jerusalem über die Trinität, die Inkarnation und die Person Christi: Mit besonderer Berücksichtigung in ihren Hauptpunkten zugleich verglichen mit den Sätzen des hl. Thomas." *Der Katholik*, 3rd ser., 35 (1907): 81–109, 175–98, and 251–65.

Studer, Basil, O.S.B. "Zur Soteriologie des Maximus Confessor." In *Maximus Confessor: Actes du symposium sur Maxime le Confesseur: Fribourg, 2–5 septembre 1980*, edited by Felix Heinzer and Christoph Schönborn, 239–46. Fribourg: Editions Universitaires, 1982.

Suchla, Beate Regina. "Das Scholienwerke des Johannes von Skythopolis zu den Areopagitischen Traktaten in seiner Philosophie—und theologiegeschichtlichen Bedeutung." In *Denys l'Aréopagite et sa postérité en Orient et en Occident: Actes du Colloque International Paris, 21–24 septembre 1994*, edited by Ysabel de Andia, 155–65. Paris: Institut d'Études Augustiniennes, 1997.

Tanner, Norman P. *Decrees of the Ecumenical Councils.* London: Sheed and Ward, 1990.

Thunberg, Lars. *Microcosm and Mediator: The Theological Anthropology of Maximus the Confessor.* 2nd ed. Chicago: Open Court, 1995.

———. "Spirit, Grace, and Human Receptivity." *Studia Patristica* 37 (2001): 605–17.

Tollefsen, Torstein Theodore. *Activity and Participation in Late Antique and Early Christian Thought.* Oxford: Oxford University Press, 2012.

———. "Christocentric Cosmology." In *The Oxford Handbook of Maximus the Confessor*, edited by Pauline Allen and Bronwen Neil, 307–21. Oxford: Oxford University Press, 2015.

———. *The Christocentric Cosmology of St Maximus the Confessor.* Oxford: Oxford University Press, 2008.

———. "The Concept of the Universal in the Philosophy of St Maximus." In *The Architecture of the Cosmos: St Maximus the Confessor, New Perspectives*, edited by Antoine Lévy, Pauli Annala, Olli Hallamaa, and Tuomo Lankila, Schriften der Luther-Agricola-Gesellschaft 69, 70–92. Helsinki: Luther-Agricola, 2015.

———. "Did St Maximus the Confessor Have a Concept of Participation?" *Studia Patristica* 37 (2001): 618–25.

———. "Proclus, Philoponus, and Maximus: The Paradigm of the World and Temporal Beginning." In *Platonism and Christian Thought in Late Antiquity*, edited by Panagiotis G. Pavlos, Lars Fredrik Janby, Eyjolfur Kjalar Emilsson, and Torstein Theodor Tollefsen, 100–114. New York: Routledge, 2019.

Törönen, Melchisedec. *Union and Distinction in the Thought of St Maximus the Confessor.* Oxford: Oxford University Press, 2007.

Trouillard, Jean. "Procession néoplatonicienne et création judéo-chrétienne." In *Néoplatonisme: Mélanges offerts à Jean Trouillard*, Cahiers de Fontenay, nos. 19–22, 79–108. Fontenay-aux-Roses: École Normale Supérieure, 1981.

Uthemann, Karl-Heinz. "Das anthropologische Modell der hypostatischen Union: Ein Beitrag zu den philosophischen Voraussetzungen und zur innerchalkedonischen Transformation eines Paradigmas." *Kleronomia* 14.2 (1982): 215–312.

———. "Das anthropologische Modell der hypostatischen Union bei Maximus Confessor." In *Maximus Confessor: Actes du symposium sur Maxime le Confesseur: Fribourg, 2–5 septembre 1980*, edited by Felix Heinzer and Christoph Schönborn, 223–33. Fribourg: Editions Universitaires, 1982.

———. "Der Neuchalkedonismus als Vorbereitung des Monotheletismus: Ein Beitrag zum eigentlichen Anliegen des Neuchalkedonismus." *Studia Patristica* 29 (1997): 373–413.

Van Deun, Peter. "Développements récents des recherches sur Maxime le Confesseur (1998–2009)." *Sacris Erudiri* 48 (2009): 97–167.

———. "Maxime le Confesseur: État de la question et bibliographie exhaustive." *Sacris Erudiri* 38 (1999): 485–573.

———. "Maximus the Confessor's Use of Literary Genres." In *The Oxford Handbook of Maximus the Confessor*, edited by Pauline Allen and Bronwen Neil, 274–86. Oxford: Oxford University Press, 2015.

Viller, Marcel. "Aux sources de la spiritualité de S. Maxime: Les oeuvres d'Évagre le Pontique." *Revue des Études Byzantines* 162 (1931): 156–84, 239–68.

Völker, Walther. "Der Einfluss des Pseudo-Dionysius Areopagita auf Maximus Confessor." In *Studien zum Neuen Testament und zur Patristik*, edited by Friedrich Zucker, 331–50. Berlin: Klostermann, 1961.

———. *Maximus Confessor als Meister des geistlichen Lebens*. Wiesbaden: Fisteiner, 1965.

Wen, Clement Yung. "Maximus the Confessor and the Problem of Participation." *Heythrop Journal* 58 (2017): 3–16.

Williams, Anna N. *The Ground of Union: Deification in Aquinas and Palamas*. Oxford: Oxford University Press, 1999.

Wolfson, Harry. "The Identification of *Ex Nihilo* with Emanation in Gregory of Nyssa." *Harvard Theological Review* 63 (1970): 53–60.

Wood, Jordan Daniel. "Both Mere Man and Naked God: The Incarnational Logic of Apophasis in St Maximus the Confessor." In *Maximus the Confessor as a European Philosopher*, edited by Sotiris Mitralexis, Georgios Steiris, Marci Podbielski, and Sebastian Lalla, 110–30. Eugene, OR: Cascade Books, 2017.

———. "Creation Is Incarnation: The Metaphysical Peculiarity of the *Logoi* in Maximus Confessor." *Modern Theology* 34.1 (2018): 82–102.

———. "A Novel Use of the Body-Soul Comparison Emerges in Neochalcedonian Christology." *Review of Ecumenical Studies* 11.3 (2019): 263–90.

———. "Stoic Motifs in the Cosmology of Maximus Confessor." *Dionysius* 37 (2019): 47–61.

———. "That and How *Perichoresis* Differs from Participation: The Case of Maximus Confessor." In *Platonism and Christian Thought in Late Antiquity*, edited by Panagiotis G. Pavlos, Lars Fredrik Hanby, Eyjolfur Kjalar Emilsson, and Torstein Theodor Tollefsen, 220–36. London: Routledge, 2019.

Yeago, David S. "Jesus of Nazareth and Cosmic Redemption: The Relevance of St. Maximus the Confessor." *Modern Theology* 12.2 (1996): 163–93.

Zachhuber, Johannes. "Christology after Chalcedon and the Transformation of the Philosophical Tradition: Reflections on a Neglected Topic." In *The Ways of Byzantine Theology*, edited by Mikonja Knezevic, 89–110. Alhambra: Sebastian Press, 2015.

———. *Human Nature in Gregory of Nyssa: Philosophical Background and Theological Significance*. Leiden: Brill, 1999.

———. "Once Again: Gregory of Nyssa on Universals." *Journal of Theological Studies* 56.1 (2005): 75–98.

———. *The Rise of Christian Theology and the End of Ancient Metaphysics: Patristic Philosophy from the Cappadocian Fathers to John of Damascus*. Oxford: Oxford University Press, 2020.

INDEX

JORDAN DANIEL WOOD

is an adjunct professor of theology at Saint Louis University.